Contents

List of Tables and Maps   ix

Acknowledgments   xi

1.   INTRODUCTION   1

     Statement of the Problem   1
     Thesis and Propositions   2
     Definitions   3
     Framework for Analysis: Planning General Purpose Forces   6
     Purpose, Methodology, Research Design and Organization   11
     Notes   13

2.   FORCE PLANNING FOR A LIMITED CONTINGENCY:
     CONSTANCY AND CHANGE IN THE U.S. STRATEGIC
     CONCEPT, 1960 - 1980   17

     Framework for Analysis   17
     Post-war Strategic Concepts   18
     The Limited War Critique of Massive Retaliation   23
     Planning Forces for "2-1/2 Wars," 1961-1968   25
     Planning Forces for "1-1/2 Wars," 1969-1976   38
     Planning Forces for "1-1/2 Wars," 1977-1979   50
     From "1-War-Plus" to "One and Two-Half Wars," 1979-1980   60
     Notes   67

3.   ORGANIZING FOR THE LIMITED CONTINGENCY:
     INSTITUTIONALIZING STRATEGIES OF RAPID
     DEPLOYMENT, 1960 - 1980   81

     Framework for Analysis   82
     The Strategic Setting, 1960   90
     STRIKE Command, 1961   93
     The Strategic Setting, 1972   106
     Readiness Command, 1972   107
     The Strategic Setting, 1977   113
     The Rapid Deployment Joint Task Force, 1980   117
     Notes   131

4. SUPPORTING THE LIMITED CONTINGENCY: MOBILITY
    SYSTEMS FOR RAPID DEPLOYMENT, 1960 - 1980   145

    Framework for Analysis   146
    SEALIFT: Mobility Systems for "2-1/2 Wars," 1961-1968   155
    AIRLIFT: Mobility Systems for "1-1/2 Wars," 1968-1976   166
    Mobility Systems for Rapid Deployment Forces, 1977-1980   178
    Notes   191

5. FORCE PLANNING FOR THE HALF WAR:
    THE RDJTF AS A LIMITED CONTINGENCY FORCE   205

    Introduction   205
    The "Half War" Strategic Concept   206
    "Half War" Organizations   208
    "Half War" Support   210
    Requirements for a Limited Contingency Force:
        Contingency Specific   212
    Requirements for a Limited Contingency Force:
        Multi-Service   215
    Requirements for a Limited Contingency Force:
        Adequate Logistics   218
    Requirements for a Limited Contingency Force:
        Deterrence and Defense   219
    Requirements for a Limited Contingency Force:
        Summary   220
    Notes   222

6. PLANNING FOR RAPIDLY DEPLOYABLE
    FORCES IN THE 1980s   227

    Introduction   227
    Planning for Rapid Deployment in the 1980s   228
    Organizing for Rapid Deployment in the 1980s   234
    Supporting Rapid Deployment in the 1980s   241
    Conclusion   247
    Notes   251

BIBLIOGRAPHY   259

INDEX   273

Tables and Maps

Tables

1.1   A Range of Force Planning Contingencies Imbedded In The "Half War," 1960-1980   8

2.1   The Allocation And Deployment Of Major General Purpose Forces Under The "2-1/2 War" Strategic Concept, 1965   34

2.2   The Allocation And Deployment Of Major General Purpose Forces Under The "2-1/2 War" Strategic Concept, 1968   37

2.3   The Allocation And Deployment Of Major General Purpose Forces Under The "2-1/2 War" Strategic Concept, 1973   51

3.1   Organizing For The "Half War": 1960-1980   130

4.1   Mobility Systems For Rapid Deployment   190

5.1   A Strategic Concept Envisioning Multiple Contingencies, 1981   221

6.1   Combat Forces Available To The RDJTF, 1982   233

6.2   U.S. Force Commitments To Rapidly Deployable Forces, By Service, August 1982   237

Maps

1.   U.S. Unified And Specified Commands   86

2.   Area Of Concern For U.S. Rapid Deployment Forces In Southwest Asia   239

Acknowledgments

During the course of this study, I benefitted from the advice and support of a number of individuals and organizations. I would like to thank them here for aiding in the accomplishment of this work. I would especially like to thank Professor William W. Kaufmann of the Massachusetts Institute of Technology for his guidance and assistance during my graduate program at MIT, where most of the research in support of this book was accomplished. His aid and advice throughout the writing of this study were invaluable. Additionally, I owe a large intellectual debt to Ted Greenwood for his advice on the analytical structure of the book, and for his help in translating my general thoughts into specific sentences. Stephen M. Meyer's instructive comments and criticisms also helped. If this study demonstrates a coherent research design, he deserves a healthy share of the credit.

From October 1980 until August 1983, I interviewed over fifty senior military officers and civilians active in the State and Defense Departments knowledgeable of the force planning process as it relates to "half war" strategy, organization and support. Although all of their names and positions are not listed here, the book could not have been written without their individual and collective help. I would particularly like to thank Commander Tim Travis at the Rapid Deployment Joint Task Force Headquarters for opening many doors that otherwise might have remained closed. I am grateful to Lt. Colonel Drue DeBerry for making available to me the resources of the Office of Air Force History, as well as for sharing with me his own research efforts. Thanks also go to Lt. Colonel Walt Causer at USCENTCOM for his help during my visit to that organization, as well as for his aid in the clearance process.

The bulk of the research and writing of this book was accomplished while I was a student at MIT under the auspices of the Air Force Institute of Technology, and after my return to the Department of Political Science at the Air Force Academy. Lt. Colonel Jack Kitch at AFIT and Ms. Anne Grazewski at MIT deserve thanks for their careful administration of my academic program, while my appreciation is also extended to Brigadier General Erv Rokke and Lt. Colonel Curt Cook at the Academy for their enduring support. The manuscript was typed and corrected by Janice Clayton. Captain Nancy Linzy was a patient and persistent proofreader. Quite simply, the book could not have been published without their efforts. Also essential in bringing the book to print were Fred Praeger at Westview, who spotted a book wrapped within a dissertation, and Dean Birkenkamp, who demonstrated patience and understanding as my editor.

Final words of gratitude go to my colleagues at the Center for International Studies in Cambridge and within the Department of Political Science at the Air Force Academy for their encouragement during the writing of this book. I should also note that, although the text has been cleared through the Defense Department's security review process, the views presented here do not necessarily represent those of the United States Air Force or the Department of Defense. Although many have contributed, I alone accept the responsibility for the content and conclusions of this work.

Robert P. Haffa, Jr.

1
Introduction

Statement of the Problem

The Duke of Wellington once remarked that "a great nation cannot fight in a small war." That aphorism could well be applied to the United States since its emergence as a great power after World War II. Certainly, the United States encountered serious political and military difficulties in attempting to constrain its involvement in the conflicts in Korea and Vietnam.[1] This is not to suggest, however, that the United States failed to accomplish force planning for a war limited in terms of scope, tactics, region and objectives. The need for general purpose forces to implement the policy of containment had been foreseen before Korea, and, by 1955, it was accepted that the principal components of U.S. defense policy included "American forces and allied forces strong enough to deter or to suppress small-scale aggressions of disorders inimical to American interests in the 'grey areas' of the world."[2] By 1979, after Vietnam but before the perceived need to plan general purpose forces to meet a limited contingency in Southwest Asia,[3] American policymakers had concluded that the following objectives should guide force planning:[4]

- the U.S. should be able to protect critical alliance interests that are endangered by a non-nuclear attack on the periphery by meeting such an attack at its own level;
- the U.S. response should be rapid enough to frustrate a quick takeover;
- the U.S. should have this capability steadily without sacrificing its ability to fight or deter a large war happening at the same time or sequentially;
- the U.S. should have a reliable capability that will meet a high level of confidence.

The Soviet invasion of Afghanistan in November 1979, coupled with the fall of the Shah of Iran only a few months earlier, set in motion a series of U.S. foreign and defense policy initiatives to support these declared objectives and to increase U.S. capabilities to conduct limited military operations against a major adversary in the "third world."

As the events in Afghanistan and Iran unfolded and as U.S. military responses and options were reevaluated, it became clear that U.S. conventional forces were not adequately designed, organized or supported to counter a modern army on a third world battlefield. This study focuses on past and present U.S. efforts to develop a defense strategy, construct an organization and procure deployment systems in order to create a coherent limited contingency force capable of meeting threats to American and allied interests in a less than major conflict.[5]

Owing to a variety of limiting factors to be developed within this study, forces allocated to cope with a limited contingency have historically lacked a coherent strategy, a capable organization and the strategic mobility required to accomplish the assigned mission. The Iranian revolution and the Afghanistan invasion, coupled with Western dependence on Persian Gulf oil, suggest that the neglect of U.S. forces to meet a lesser contingency is no longer benign. The possibility of U.S. armed forces facing a Soviet or proxy force on a third world battlefield in a conflict limited in scope, but conceivably linked to a major contingency in Europe argues for a strategy, force, organization and support dedicated to such a lesser contingency, alone.[6] Moreover, although these recent events in Southwest Asia have once again triggered a concern for the adequacy of force planning for a limited contingency, there is an attendant danger of focusing concern solely on that region. Historical trends developed in this study, when overlayed with a projection of the threat, imply the need to plan for the simultaneous occurrence of other lesser contingencies as well.

Thesis and Propositions

The principal thesis here is that previous strategic assumptions regarding the planning of forces to fight a lesser contingency no longer remain valid. In the past, because a limited war was, by definition, of less importance than a major military effort and might not occur simultaneously with a major contingency, it was tempting for the force planner to think that the military capability to handle one or two greater contingencies implied the ability to deal with a lesser one. This notion that the limited contingency is simply a "lesser included case" of the larger conflicts now appears to have outlived its usefulness. The fundamental conceptual premise of this study is that the United States must now consider the lesser contingency--or a set of lesser conflicts--as excluded cases. The requirement for a credible military force to support U.S. foreign policy objectives in areas of vital interest, apart from those regions associated with the major contingency, demands the capabilities of an independent force.

Such a thesis relies on a number of propositions, to be developed and supported within this study:

- the lesser contingency, although it has varied in size, scope, geographical region and adversary, has been an element contained within the U.S. strategic concept for the last two decades;
- despite that recognition, preparation has proved inadequate. Forces to meet a limited contingency were never adequately planned for, funded, constructed or supported;
- the strategy that depended on the flexibility of a central strategic reserve was unrealistic in terms of available resources and implementation;
- the organizations structured in support of that strategy confronted problems of unified command and faced interservice

conflict over assigned missions. Forces assigned to these organizations were not dedicated to the command and were based upon a false assumption of ground unit versatility;
- the mobility systems in support of a strategy of rapid deployment were not procured in numbers adequate to support that effort simultaneously with a major contingency.

These propositions suggest that force planning based on similar strategic concepts will not be adequate to meet successfully a simultaneous sophisticated attack in a remote, yet vital area. Given the Soviet threat, the definition of vital U.S. interests in Western Europe, Southwest Asia, Northeast Asia and the Caribbean basin as well as the requirements for U.S. military capability in these regions, a credible limited contingency force requires a strategy that disaggregates these contingencies, encourages organizational autonomy for command structures assigned regional responsibilities and supports the acquisition of rapid mobility systems to deploy forces to these separate regions against a range of potential adversaries.

In examining these propositions, this book develops a number of themes that run throughout the study. First, from a strategic perspective, there is the continuing gap that exists between policy guidance and force planning. Military men have consistently complained of the lack of precise strategic guidance that prohibits effective force planning. This has resulted in a continuing, albeit unsuccessful, effort to secure an agreed-upon statement of national policy which could lend itself to a well-defined force posture.

Secondly, the theme of flexible organizations and versatile ground forces will be developed. The lack of specific strategic objectives, when coupled with omnipresent budgetary constraints, has led to a philosophy of force versatility which has pervaded force planning for a limited contingency force. Rather than plan a limited contingency force specifically to meet a certain threat in a specified region, the pattern over the last twenty-three years has been to structure a force capable of rapid deployment to and operation in any contingency. This presumption of the capability of such a force to "go anywhere and do anything" will be questioned throughout the study, particularly with regard to the concept's application in a region of acknowledged vital interest and potential escalatory conflict.

Third, there is the strategy-force mismatch that continues to plague the force planner. Budgetary constraints necessarily result in a gap between those forces required to support the declared strategy and those that can actually be procured. These realities of the weapons acquisition cycle have had particular impact on the procurement of strategic mobility systems planned in support of a rapid deployment capability. In many cases, as will be evidenced below, systems could be allocated to a lesser contingency operation only if they were originally supported based on their contribution to missions of greater consequence.

Definitions

The limited contingency--It is important to understand first what is meant by the limited contingency, a concept that has undergone considerable change both in location and threat since 1960. Initially, the limited contingency was seen as a conflict that would need significantly fewer forces than would be required to combat a major Communist power, that is, the Soviet Union or the People's Republic of China. The limited contingency was first referred to as a "brushfire war,"[7] implying a police action against a lesser state in the third world. The principal scenario envisioned the application of a small U.S. force, perhaps in a counterinsurgent rather than a conventional role, to control or terminate quickly an uprising against a friendly government. Thus, the "brushfire" version of the limited contingency involved low-intensity warfare, just above the use of "force without war" along the spectrum of violence[8] and well below the commonly envisioned scenario of the major contingency--a NATO-Warsaw Pact conflict in central Europe. More recently, the limited contingency has come to connote the possibility of a limited conventional war, requiring the dedication of a significant force and existing in the mid-range between the "brushfire" and major contingency.

The "half war"--A spinoff from the term "limited contingency" was the term "half war."[9] Although this phrase was apparently not used publicly until 1968 (the more common term within the Kennedy/Johnson administrations was "two-plus" contingency planning), it is a term that has recently enjoyed some popularity, particularly when tied to formulations of the "2-1/2 war" or "1-1/2 war" strategic concepts. As both an analytical concept and as a guide to force planning, the "half war" has proved faulty, for it suggested both the singularity and the separateness of a limited war. The "half war" strategic concept implied that there might be only one lesser contingency or that others would not occur simultaneously with it or with a major conflict. Therefore, the "half war" was frequently portrayed as an inclusive war, one which could be met with forces and systems sized, organized and supported to meet a major contingency.

This study draws a major definitional difference between the "half war" as envisioned and planned for during the majority of the period under examination and the "limited contingency" now facing U.S. defense planners. As originally conceived, the "half war":

- required the application of minimal military force against a less than sophisticated enemy;
- required the rapid deployment of a central force, primarily ground units, to unknown and distant areas, with likely assistance from the nation being supported;
- offered prospects for a quick settlement, with little potential for escalation or linkage to a major contingency;
- involved areas of less than vital interest.

In contrast, the "limited contingency" of today:

- requires the application of a significant force against a sophisticated enemy--Soviet, proxy or, at least, Soviet armed and trained;
- requires the rapid deployment of a multi-service force, to include a wide range of combat capabilities, and with uncertain allied support;
- offers unclear prospects for a quick settlement, with a potential for escalation to other limited contingencies or to a major contingency;
- involves areas of vital interest to the United States.

Implications for force planning for the "half war" included:

- the need for conventional forces, primarily versatile ground units, capable of operating in a wide variety of climates, topographical conditions and against a range of possible, but primitive adversaries;
- a willingness to dedicate forces committed to other major contingencies under the assumption that the "half war" was unrelated to other international events or that the hostilities could be quickly terminated or put on "hold" in order to meet contingencies of greater priority.

Implications for force planning for a "limited contingency" included:

- the need for conventional forces, to include air, ground and naval units, dedicated to a specific geographical region;
- the need to dedicate forces to a specific contingency under the assumption that this lesser contingency may occur sequentially or simultaneously with a major conflict and that those forces dedicated cannot be easily redeployed to other theaters without jeopardizing the outcome in all regions.

Rapid Deployment--Throughout the period under study, the term "rapid deployment" has normally referred to the quick movement of forces based in the United States (CONUS) to areas where U.S. military presence is minimal or nonexistent. In contrast, terms such as "rapid reinforcement" or "rapid reaction forces" normally imply the movement of units earmarked to reinforce or support U.S. forces already stationed abroad, particularly with regard to the conduct of major combat operations in NATO Europe. Although this distinction between the missions of rapid deployment and rapid reinforcement does exist, "projection forces" and air and sealift mobility systems have been shared historically between the two. Thus, U.S. Marine and airborne units traditionally have been assigned to combat roles in both major and minor contingencies, while strategic mobility programs, such as the Fast Deployment Logistics Ship (FDL) and the C-5A air transport, were justified more on their capability to reinforce U.S. troops abroad rather than on their ability to deploy rapidly U.S. forces to limited contingencies.

Although this dichotomy between the "limited contingency" and the "half war" does exist, both in a definitional respect and as a guide to force planning, the thesis being developed here requires a more precise typology of lesser contingencies in order to describe adequately and differentiate completely among the range of military scenarios that lie imbedded within these concepts. During the period under study the "lesser contingency"--a more generic term to describe that part of the strategic concept under scrutiny here--underwent considerable definitional change in terms of level of intensity, geographic locale, potential adversary and assigned forces. For the purposes of this study, this range of potential conflict will be telescoped into three basic paradigms, or hypothetical scenarios, which attempt to describe the lesser contingency in terms of these variables.

a. Non-Soviet "brushfire"--This contingency envisioned a low-intensity conflict against lightly armed insurgents in a region providing considerable indigenous support, modest logistic requirements and relatively short supply lines. Although a combat role for U.S. troops was not ruled out in this scenario, the number of ground troops committed would be limited, and their mission would be confined to counter-insurgent type operations. Forces required and planned for such a contingency included rapid deployment or "projection" forces, lightly armed Marine or airborne units and limited tactical air forces. There was a low probability of escalation or additional external intervention. Examples of this model of the lesser contingency included the U.S. intervention in the Dominican Republic in 1965 and the early stages of U.S. involvement in Vietnam.

b. Soviet-proxy "field of fire"--This contingency envisioned a medium-intensity conflict against well-armed conventional forces in a region limited in scope and providing some indigenous or allied support, but which would require a significant U.S. presence. Forces required would probably be multi-service, with considerable organizational and logistic support necessary, possibly air or sea intensive. Although only a modest probability of escalation was present, continued Soviet/proxy support for the adversary could be anticipated. The model for this type of lesser contingency could be the Korean War and the locale designated normally Northeast Asia. This "half war" scenario was given the most credence under the Nixon Doctrine.

c. Soviet-U.S. "firefight"--This contingency envisions high intensity conventional warfare pitting U.S. forces against Soviet troops in an "out-of-area," non-NATO scenario. U.S. forces required would be the most sophisticated multi-service forces, with the model for the anticipated conflict being the high attrition warfare of the 1973 Middle East War. With U.S. and Soviet forces face to face in modern combat, this scenario poses the greatest danger for both horizontal and vertical escalation. Conceived generally as resulting from a Soviet thrust into the Persian Gulf region, this scenario ultimately formed the conceptual basis, if not the foundation for force planning of the Carter Doctrine.

This typology can then be formed into a matrix structure that suggests the range of military scenarios imbedded in the strategic concept of the "half war" and which have served as implicit force planning contingencies during the period 1960-1983. (See Table 1.1.)

Framework for Analysis: Planning General Purpose Forces

An emphasis on nuclear strategy, the defense of Central Europe and, momentarily, the counter-insurgency in Vietnam have dominated the interests and energies of the defense intellectual community over two decades.[10] Planning U.S. general purpose forces has, therefore, been concentrated at the extreme ends of a continuum of contingencies arrayed by level of violence rather than on concerns with a limited contingency. Complicating attempts at this type of force planning was the lack of an empirical referent for a limited contingency. The Korean conflict was waged as a limited war, but against a major Communist adversary in a region within the bounds of the envisioned major Asian contingency. Initially, Vietnam appeared as the limited contingency that had been postulated, but it soon engulfed U.S. forces equal in magnitude to those required and forecast for a major contingency. Even following the 1973 Middle East war and subsequent oil embargo, U.S. conventional force planning in the Persian Gulf region lagged considerably behind U.S. vital interests in other areas, primarily owing to the concurrent Vietnam force drawdowns and a refocusing on the major contingency in Europe.[11]

Lacking the stimulus of external events, conventional deterrence and defense in the middle range of combat intensity have received comparatively little theoretical or operational attention.[12] Studies of force planning that are publicly available are generally confined to strategic nuclear systems. Alexander George and Richard Smoke have suggested that the reasons for this concentration on strategic deterrence at the expense of the balance of conventional forces are both historical and intellectual.[13] The historical concern has been with the "locus of the most salient threat" and the analysts' "image of the relevant conflict." This concern resulted naturally in a focus on the U.S.-Soviet strategic nuclear exchange, and how best such an exchange could be deterred. Intellectually, the elegance of strategic theory allowed the force planner to operationalize the nuclear threat in a straightforward logic that was both intuitively appealing and easily calculable. While early theories of nuclear deterrence "could offer relatively precise criteria for contingency planning of operations and for decisions on force and procurement," the conventional emphasis implicit in the strategies of "flexible response," inaugurated in the 1960s, offered a much less complete guide to force planning:[14]

> While it could recommend that a complete range of forces and types of forces be procured and the intelligence, command and control and operational doctrine be developed to employ them feasibly to meet limited attack, it could not make recommendations concerning the amount of any one kind of force to procure, what to declare publicly about the force, where the force should be deployed or--most importantly--under what circumstances it should be used.

In other words, general forces do not lend themselves easily to the more "precise" analysis of force alternatives and mixes that can be calculated at the strategic level.[15] The U.S. must first identify an area of vital interest and then structure its military forces to deter conventional conflict (or defend if deterrence fails) while maintaining an appropriate relationship with allied and non-aligned states in the region. It is not surprising that NATO has received the most attention with regard to conventional force planning. But the task in this most obvious case also remains a difficult one, owing to the uncertainties inherent in conventional deterrence, traditional concerns of other states regarding the projection of American power and force presence and more general political restrictions on plans for military intervention.[16]

As former Secretary of Defense Robert McNamara was fond of pointing out, the size and character of general purpose forces are more difficult to determine than those of the strategic forces because of[17]

TABLE 1.1
A Range Of Force Planning Contingencies Imbedded In The "Half War," 1960–1980

SCENARIO/TYPE	ADVERSARY/SUPPORT	INTENSITY OF CONFLICT/ ESCALATORY POTENTIAL	U.S. FORCES	LOCALE/ U.S. COMMITMENT
NON-SOVIET "Brushfire"	Localized insurgency Minimal external support Primary combat role for indigenous forces	Low intensity Counter-insurgency Low probability of escalation	Limited projection force Possibly one service	Caribbean Kennedy counter- insurgency emphasis
SOVIET-PROXY "Field of fire"	Soviet armed and supported Some indigenous and allied aid Limited U.S. combat role	Medium intensity Conventional warfare Escalation possible	Significant multi-service commitment Air-sea intensive	Northeast Asia Nixon Doctrine
SOVIET-U.S. "Firefight"	US–USSR armed conflict Little in-theater allied support	High intensity Conventional war Horizontal escalation probable, vertical (nuclear) possible	Major commit- ment of multi- service forces Ground inten- sive	Southwest Asia Carter Doctrine

- the wide variety of possible contingencies they must be prepared to meet,
- the uncertainties regarding opposing forces,
- the uncertain allied contributions,
- the relatively important role of the Reserve forces,
- the interrelationship between the size of the force, its readiness and the ability to deploy it rapidly to wherever it may be needed and
- the sheer number and diversity of the units involved.

In approaching these complex issues, this study will utilize a force planning perspective. However, it is important to note here and consider, as the study develops, other elements of the defense policy planning process. Lawrence Korb has suggested that military policy is composed of four parts--planning, budgeting, procurement and training and operation-- of which the defense budget, he argues, is the most significant determinant of the resulting posture.[18] It is in the budget that eventual claims of a mismatch between strategy and force posture will have their roots. Although the overall strategic concept may be formulated outside the budgetary process, the complexion and composition of defense policy will change with the amount of defense spending or, more precisely, on the amounts allocated, authorized, appropriated and expended on specific program elements within the defense budget. Thus, in this examination of force planning for a limited contingency, we must not be too quick to condemn the strategic concept without inquiring into the collective national will to budget for and procure the forces in that strategy's support.[19]

The first justification for the maintenance of large, in-being, general purpose forces is normally stated in terms of requirements to meet U.S. foreign policy commitments abroad. From the Rio Pact in 1947 to the current attempts to construct a collective security regime in Southwest Asia, the United States in the post-war era has constructed treaty and other agreements pledging military assistance and aid with nearly 50 countries.

This logical relationship between foreign policy objectives and force planning requirements was given special emphasis by President Kennedy's original planning guidance to Secretary McNamara to "develop the force structure necessary to our military requirements."[20] Kennedy's intention, and McNamara's charter, was not to size forces based on the possibility that all commitments would have to be dealt with simultaneously.[21] Nevertheless, the interface between foreign commitments and general purpose force structure and deployment began a process of force planning based on "what types of conflicts we anticipate, what countries we choose to assist and to what degree these countries can defend themselves, in short, on what contingencies we prepare for."[22]

Because of the interaction between perceived international requirements and domestic policy constraints, force planning has become a complex process. Moreover, dealing with these important, but often emotional issues tends to obscure the rational approach to making force posture choices.[23] Nevertheless, a logical structure for force selection is essential and does exist. The following suggests a framework for rational choice in conventional force planning.[24]

A description of the threat is an essential element of force design. Although these perceptions of the threat are normally couched in terms of enemy capabilities and intentions, two sub-aspects of the threat seem relevant here. The first of these is the context, or circumstances. It is necessary to decide in a specific manner precisely what will be defended by the forces--a scenario-specific causus foederis. Early concepts of the limited contingency, as will be developed, failed to make this choice. Consequently, forces were allocated to a limited contingency based on the properties of versatility and flexibility rather than the achievement of a certain objective against a specified adversary in a designated region.

Another important factor in the threat equation is mobilization lead time--how fast the enemy can threaten and how much time the U.S. has to respond. In Europe, the U.S. has continued to lower its "worst-case" estimate of lead time available to counter a Warsaw Pact attack. Similarly, the argument has been made historically that forces planned for a limited contingency must be capable of rapid deployment worldwide. This assumption has affected the sizing and composition of any proposed limited contingency force in terms of the active duty/Reserve mix, the equipment possessed by the individual units and the capacity of air and sealift required.[25]

An assessment of the threat must also be accomplished and related to the forces being generated. This requires both the close cooperation of the force planning and the threat assessment functions as well as an accepted method of force comparison. There are two principal means of comparing forces against an adversary, thereby generating and supporting a certain force level requirement.[26] The first directly compares number of forces by type (such as tank to tank in central Europe) and is generally regarded as the easiest to do, the most widely used and the least satisfactory. Owing to technological differences in weapons types, national strategic and tactical divergences and other qualitative factors, such as training and leadership, little can usefully be derived from this sort of static comparison of forces.

The alternative method relies on various hypothetical and simulated force exchanges to describe and assess the opponents' capabilities. This approach relies on force effectiveness criteria (such as the fire power potential of an Army division) rather than simple numerical indices (such as the number of Army divisions) and evaluates the projected force postures under conditions of combat. While the static method is primarily concerned with inputs and is likely to encourage force planning based on a concept of mirror-imagery, the dynamic method involves the analysis of performance by focusing on the outcome of a specific scenario. This latter approach has emerged over the years as the principal guide to U.S. force planning and weapons acquisition. In the words of former Secretary of Defense Harold Brown, "this approach specifies that the way to measure the adequacy of our capabilities and to determine our programmatic needs is by analyzing hypothetical conflicts and their outcomes."[27]

This approach to sizing general purpose forces for contingencies has not been without its critics. The most common of the complaints has been that this approach, focused on outcomes, does not allow sufficiently for the uncertainties in the future.[28] A second assault on current force planning methodology applies a bureaucratic perspective. The contention of this school of thought emphasizes the complex array of factors that affects force planning and turns it into a dependent variable rather than the prevailing "oversimplification" of rational choice.[29]

Both of these critiques accurately reflect obstacles which face the general purpose force planner, but it is important to distinguish the conceptual framework utilized by the post-facto analyst from the variables and demands of the present. The force planner is not presented with a statement of national policy which clearly dictates a desirable force posture, and his ability to see into and plan for the future is limited.[30] Strategic concepts appear unclear (as well as underfunded); allied burden sharing uncertain; and qualitative factors, by definition, non-quantifiable. The force planner is aware, before the fact, that competing organizational interests will prove difficult to reconcile and that the lengthy and complex weapons acquisition process may postpone or ultimately terminate systems designed to support certain contingencies. Force posture, from its inception, cannot be based on supposition, perception or projection.

The approach that has survived over the years is simply that military requirements must be determined by "reasoned choice with the open participation of the responsible government officials, military and civilian."[31] The question "How much is enough?" will continue to be answered with a blend of judgment and analysis. It is, therefore, with an understanding of the virtues of this process as well as its shortcomings that this study will attempt to describe and explain the force planning efforts that have centered on a conventional capability to meet a limited contingency.

Purpose, Methodology, Research Design and Organization

This study explores the limited contingency as a strategic concept, questions the relationship between the strategic concept and forces planned in support of that declared strategy and, through an examination of U.S. force planning programs structured to support a limited contingency force, offers guidance to present and future force planners.

A major purpose is to make this work policy-relevant. A focus solely on decision making too often slights the more objective lessons that can be drawn from the case. An account of the technological dimensions of strategy frequently overlooks the operational requirements of the strategy.[32] This study will be macro-strategic rather than micro-tactical in its approach; the concentration here is on force planning, not on force employment. Therefore, the primary focus of this work will be on the strategic concept formulated, the organizations created and the mobility systems designed in support of a limited contingency force. The overall purpose is to develop the force planners' knowledge of the cyclical patterns and processes inherent in the system and to extend the planners' ability to choose the right method and course of action. Or, in the words of T. R. Fox, "the ultimate goal of political scientists is to give guidance to policy makers."[33]

This purpose will be pursued, propositions tested, and theses supported with data obtained from the following sources: (1) Congressional hearings and testimony, especially Department of Defense (DoD) appropriation and authorizations, (2) DoD "Posture Statements" and other public documents relating to defense policy and force planning, (3) military studies and official organizational histories obtained through the Air Force Office of History, the Naval War College and the Army Library in the Pentagon, (4) formal and informal interviews with participants in the force planning process in the Office of the

Secretary of Defense (OSD), the Service Staffs, the State Department, the Rapid Deployment Joint Task Force, the U.S. Readiness Command and the Central Command, (5) newspaper articles, particularly excerpts from Current News and the New York Times, 1960-1983, (6) publications by primary military, political and academic participants and (7) selected secondary sources for relevant background information.

The research design utilized in this study is an extension of the controlled comparison case study model developed and used by Alexander George, among others.[34] In this application the class of events under study is force planning for a limited contingency under differing strategic concepts, with a focus on three aspects within each class: the force designed, the organization constructed and the support systems procured.

Within each of these three aspects, appropriate cases will be selected for a controlled comparison of the force planning process. With regard to force planning under the strategic concept, the "2-1/2 war" and "1-1/2 war" strategic concepts will be compared and contrasted. Organizationally, the study will examine the Strike Command, the Readiness Command, the Rapid Deployment Joint Task Force and Central Command. With regard to strategic mobility systems, the study will compare past efforts to achieve adequate support for a limited contingency force with similar, ongoing programs.

In each of these areas a separate framework for analysis will be developed. The problem here, as George notes, is to design a theoretical framework "comprehensive enough to capture the major elements of the historical explanation."[35] The arbitrary choice of a decision-making, organizational or weapons acquisition model is unlikely to meet this requirement. Therefore, the approach adopted here is to let the gathered data determine what appears to be important and relevant and to formulate a model for each aspect based on those data. To lend coherence to this research design, similar general questions are phrased and asked of each case in the controlled comparison.

The final phase of the research design is to draw theoretical implications from the case studies examined in order to reveal the underlying strategic, organizational and political dynamics which appear to be persistent throughout the study. The use of this controlled comparison method, therefore, reinforces the purpose of the study by enabling the development of policy-relevant theory. Therefore, this book contributes not only to an enriched understanding of each of the individual cases considered, but also to a holistic perspective of planning general purposes forces for a limited contingency.

The organization of this work is based on this research design. In the chapter which follows, we will initially examine the philosophical underpinnings and nature of post-war U.S. defense policy that formed the backdrop for the emerging strategic concept of the lesser contingency. Of particular interest was the establishment of the fundamental paradigm of a two-theater war and a limited "brushfire" contingency. As the chapter progresses, we will develop themes of constancy and change in the strategic concept from the first days of the Kennedy administration through the end of the Carter years and to the formative concepts of Ronald Reagan. Under each variation on the strategic concept guiding force planning, the lesser contingency will be examined in terms of a framework of the perceived threat and how forces were raised and deployed to meet that threat.

The third chapter focuses on attempts to institutionalize concepts of force planning for the limited contingency through the creation of three major joint-service organizational entities: Strike Command, Readiness Command and the Rapid Deployment Joint Task Force. The analysis of the missions, forces and regions assigned to these commands will be preceded by a discussion of the broader issues that have attended the organizational debate. Some of these factors include the role of the limited contingency within the organizational structure of the Joint Chiefs of Staff and the manner in which the limited contingency has been envisioned in terms of organizational responsibility, scenario and service specificity and unit flexibility and versatility.

Chapter Four describes and explains efforts to support a limited contingency force in terms of strategic mobility by analyzing proposed and procured air and sealift systems. Although the forces assigned to a limited contingency as well as the organizations have been discussed previously, an equally important part of the rapid deployment equation is the ability to move that force to the battlefield. The shortfall in strategic air and sealift has been perhaps the most serious limiting factor on the capabilities of limited contingency forces throughout the period.

The penultimate chapter will draw together the evolution of the strategic concept, the organizational structure and the support systems in order to suggest an effective combination of these elements in meeting the requirements of a coherent limited contingency force. Key areas will be noted in which the force planning process appears to be undergoing a transformation and, based on these changes, how force planning for a limited contingency is most likely to prove effective in the near term.

Chapter Six evaluates how well the United States has learned these lessons of force planning for limited contingencies by examining the Central Command and speculating on the planning of rapid deployment forces in the 1980s.

NOTES

1. Robert Osgood had described some of these difficulties encountered by the United States in Korea in Limited War (Chicago: University of Chicago Press, 1957) and in Vietnam in Limited War Revisited (Boulder: Westview, 1979).

2. Quoted in Samuel Huntington, The Common Defense (New York: Columbia University Press, 1961), p. 27.

3. The region termed Southwest Asia is commonly thought to include all states on the Arabian peninsula, plus Iran, Iraq, Afghanistan, Pakistan, Ethiopia, Djibouti, Kenya and the Red Sea and the Persian (Arabian) Gulf.

4. These goals are extracted from the Department of Defense Annual Reports, also referred to here as "Posture Statements" for Fiscal Years (FY) 1979 and 1980. See Albert Wohlstetter, "Meeting the Threat in the Persian Gulf," Survey (Spring 1980), pp. 128-188.

5. Although there is an abundant and rich literature on the theory of limited war, beginning with Osgood above and listed elsewhere in these notes, little has been accomplished on force planning for that limited contingency from a strategic, organizational or logistical perspective. Only the recent focus on the Persian Gulf region has propelled the

importance of the lesser contingency into a sort of strategic parity with the major contingency. Contributions to this new strategy include Albert Wohlstetter, "Half Wars and Half Policies in the Persian Gulf," in Scott Thompson, ed., National Security in the 1980s (San Francisco: Institute for Contemporary Studies, 1980), pp. 123-172 and James Digby, "The Emerging American Strategy: Application to Southwest Asia" (Santa Monica: RAND, May 1981).

6. This concept is further developed in an unpublished paper entitled "Strategic Mobility Enhancement and Responsiveness of Marine Forces" by W. H. Westhoff and T. D. Stouffer (Newport: Naval War College, 1980).

7. The term "brushfire war" has served over the years in a number of meanings and interpretations. It originally was used to denote any conventional engagement of U.S. forces with non-Soviet troops. In a memo from General Maxwell Taylor, Army Chief of Staff, to Admiral Radford, Chairman of the Joint Chiefs, on October 11, 1956, Taylor outlined two types of war: the large atomic war and the small "brushfire war." Taylor argued that the Army especially needed to be prepared to meet the latter.

8. These diplomatic uses of force are comprehensively cataloged by Barry Blechman and Steven Kaplan in Force Without War (Washington: Brookings, 1979).

9. The term "half war" was apparently coined publicly by Charles Schlutze during Congressional testimony in which he attempted to characterize and rationalize, in terms of fraction equivalents, the strategic concept that guided general purpose force planning under the Kennedy and Johnson administrations. See p. 38 of this study. For differentiation between the "half war" and the limited contingency also see David W. Tarr, "The Strategic Environment, U.S. National Security, and the Nature of Low Intensity Conflicts" in Sam C. Sarkesian, ed., Non-nuclear Conflicts in the Nuclear Age (New York: Praeger, 1980), pp. 41-58.

10. This unintentional, but nevertheless significant ignoring of both planning for a conventional conflict and the implications of instability in the Middle East and the Persian Gulf is pointed out by Bard O'Neil in "Petroleum and Security" (Washington: National Defense University, 1977).

11. See William P. Snyder, "Military Intervention Forces," in Sarkesian, op. cit., pp. 185-206.

12. Conventional planning was being accomplished to both deter and defend during the post-war years. With a limited atomic capability, the U.S. planned to use a combination of both conventional and atomic responses to meet a major contingency. See George Quester, Nuclear Diplomacy (New York: Dunellen, 1970) for a review of early post-war U.S. military strategy. In the strategic reassessment of 1950, conventional planning, in the form of NSC-68, momentarily superseded atomic strategy. See Warner R. Schilling, Paul Y. Hammond and Glenn H. Snyder, Strategy, Politics and Defense Budgets (New York: Columbia University Press, 1962) and Thomas Etzold and John Lewis Gaddis, Containment: Documents on American Policy and Strategy, 1945-1950 (New York: Columbia University Press, 1978), p. 385.

13. Alexander George and Richard Smoke, Deterrence in American Foreign Policy (New York: Columbia University Press, 1974), particularly Chapter Two, "Contemporary Deterrence Theory."

14. Ibid. p. 42.

15. The point of view is found in Roswell C. Gilpatric, "Our Defense Needs: The Long View," Foreign Affairs, Vol. 42, No. 3 (April 1964), pp. 366-378. The term "precise" is used advisedly.

16. Thomas Fabyanic, "Changing Strategic Issues" in Sarkesian, op. cit. p. 38. There is abundant literature on intervention that enjoyed an academic popularity during the U.S. involvement in Vietnam, but now appears to have waned. For early conceptual approaches, see the issue devoted to intervention in the Journal of International Affairs, Vol. 22, (Summer 1968). More recently, see Ellen P. Stern, ed., The Limits of Military Intervention (Beverly Hills: Sage, 1977).

17. Robert S. McNamara, Department of Defense Annual Report FY 1965, p. 56.

18. Lawrence W. Korb. The Joint Chiefs of Staff (Bloomington: University of Indiana Press, 1976), p. 94.

19. A point emphasized to the author by Robert W. Komer, former Under Secretary of Defense of Policy, in a private interview, March 9, 1981.

20. Quoted in Alain Enthoven and K. Wayne Smith, How Much is Enough? (New York: Harper, 1971), p. 325. The remainder of the phrase, ". . . without regard to arbitrary budget ceilings," tended to fall in the realm of campaign rhetoric rather than in the area of realistic force planning.

21. It was suggested by defense officials during the early 1960s that it would take 53 divisions and a budgetary increment of $20 billion in order to prepare for all of the commitments/contingencies simultaneously.

22. Enthoven and Smith, op. cit., p. 211.

23. In an assault on current force planning methodology, Graham Allison has attempted to answer the question "What Determines Military Force Posture?" (with Frederic A. Morris, Cambridge, MA: Kennedy School of Government, 1975) by applying a bureaucratic perspective. Allison opposes the "prevailing oversimplification" of rational choice and notes that an array of factors has a significant effect on force posture. Force posture is, therefore, a dependent variable. Allison further notes that the time involved in the weapons acquisition process is so lengthy that the force posture at any single time is unlikely to be the product of any single doctrine or administration, thereby further invalidating rational choice as a method of analysis. Diluted by service organizational interests, roles and missions, the rational process appears to Allison to have been overcome by bureaucratic events.

24. These factors deemed most relevant to this study of force planning have been drawn from a more comprehensive treatment by Richard M. Lloyd and Dino Lorenzini in "A Framework for Choosing Defense Forces," Naval War College Review, Vol. XXXIII, No. 1 (January/February 1981), pp. 47-51.

25. Leslie Gelb and Arnold Kuzmack, "General Purpose Forces" in Henry Owen, ed., The Next Phase in Foreign Policy (Washington: Brookings, 1973), p. 214.

26. These approaches are more completely outlined in The Military Balance, 1978-1979 (London: International Institute for Strategic Studies, 1979), p. 114. That study also develops a third method of comparing opposing forces that looks at systems but which remains essentially a static, numerical comparison.

27.   Harold Brown, <u>Department of Defense Annual Report, FY 1980</u> p. 63.

28.   One of the most outspoken critics of the role of analysis in conventional force planning has been R. James Woolsey. He argues for flexibility in force generation based on the premise that forces built to match scenarios envisioned in the present will not be able to meet those of the future. Woolsey objects primarily to the "rigidities" which have been introduced into the planning process by the design of specific scenarios and the use of campaign analysis. His argument, which represents the traditional view of the Navy, sees forces as so flexible they should not be compressed or confined by certain scenarios. In failing to recognize the force multiplier inherent in that flexibility, Woolsey argues that systems analysis, as a framework for planning general purpose forces, has overstayed its welcome. See R. James Woolsey, "Planning a Navy: The Risks of Conventional Wisdom," <u>International Security</u> (Summer 1978), pp. 17-29.

29.   Allison, <u>op. cit.</u>

30.   Lloyd and Lorenzini, <u>op. cit.</u>

31.   Enthoven and Smith, <u>op. cit.</u>, p. 206.

32.   Michael Howard makes this argument in "The Forgotten Dimensions of Strategy," <u>Foreign Affairs</u>, Vol. 57, No. 5 (Summer 1979), pp. 975-986.

33.   T. R. Fox, as quoted by James N. Rosenau, "The Concept of Intervention," <u>The Journal of International Affairs</u>, Vol. 22 (Summer 1968), pp. 165-176.

34.   This approach is most completely spelled out in Alexander L. George, "Case Studies and Theory Development: The Method of Structured, Focused Compairson," in Paul Gordon Lauren, ed., <u>Diplomacy</u> (New York: The Free Press, 1979), pp. 43-68.

35.   <u>Ibid.</u>, p. 57.

2
Force Planning for a Limited Contingency: Constancy and Change in the U.S. Strategic Concept, 1960-1980

The constancy and change that characterize the development of U.S. strategic concepts during the post-war years can be interpreted in terms of shifting theoretical emphasis on the utility and probability of conventional warfare, limited nuclear war and central strategic war. Thus, the strategic concept--a statement of how many and what kinds of war the United States should be prepared to fight--reflects the national objectives it is intended to support and justifies the force planning process. The history of the limited contingency and forces planned in its behalf cannot be divorced from the more general development of U.S. defense policy since 1945. An examination of the limited contingency force and the planning attending it must, therefore, be accomplished with an awareness of the concept's inception, ascendance, elaboration and reassessment within the post-war evolution of U.S. military strategy.[1]

Framework for Analysis

To facilitate this examination of the U.S. strategic concept through eight presidential administrations, it is necessary first to establish a framework for analysis. Any typology used here will be somewhat artificial. Strategic concepts do not precisely coincide with new administrations, but rather reflect a gradual evolution of American military thought. The variables selected for analysis through time must allow for this flexibility. At the same time, however, they must be precise enough to describe and explain both the obvious and the more subtle changes in U.S. strategy for a lesser contingency and to operationalize these concepts as a basis for force planning.

The framework for analysis which will be used throughout this chapter attempts to relate the themes of the perception of the threat, the force planning response to the threat and the budgetary and public opinion constraints on that force planning process. This framework, relying on a method of controlled comparison, will ask the following questions of each major time period that resulted in an altered strategic concept. First, what was the perception of the threat? How did this perception affect the formulation of the strategic concept? Secondly, how were forces designed and deployed in support of the strategic concept? What priority was allocated to forces to meet a lesser contingency? Finally, what was the impact of budgetary or other constraints on the force planning process? These standardized questions have been developed to reflect adequately the key areas of analysis within this chapter.

Post-war Strategic Concepts

World War II revealed an American lack of preparedness in terms of military strategy designed in support of foreign policy objectives. The "Rainbow Plans"--U.S. war plans developed in the years between the world wars--had little operational significance because of a lack of logistic preparation and a failure to perceive the need to integrate military goals with political considerations.[2] The need for planning and policy guidance post-World War II was more evident given this failure, but the attitude of top-level military planners was that they could not conduct adequate force planning without precise foreign policy objectives stated clearly by elected politicians. In November 1947, Hoyt S. Vandenberg, the newly-created Air Force Vice Chief of Staff,[3]

> ... impatiently articulated his understanding of the point that defining national objectives was the function of the State Department, that the National Security Council would have to relate such objectives to military requirements and that only then could the Joint Chiefs of Staff prepare the many plans urgently necessary for effective national security programs.

Despite the General's concern, the Joint Chiefs had not failed to digest the strategic lessons learned from the war and were, in fact, outlining military objectives in order to facilitate contingency planning. Most relevant to this study, the concepts of rapid deployment, strategic mobility and overseas basing were established early on. A "Basis for the Formulation of U.S. Military Policy," dated September 19, 1945, listed the following objectives under the subheading, "Principal Supporting Military Policies:"[4]

- to maintain mobile striking forces in strength, composition and state of readiness for prompt and adequate action and to provide necessary fixed and mobile logistic support for such forces;
- to develop and maintain a system of outlying bases, adequately equipped and defended for the support of our mobile forces, and capable of rapid expansion.

What was the perception of the threat? How did the threat perception affect the formulation of the strategic concept?

The "Short Range Emergency War Plan" of July 21, 1948, assumed that war with the Soviet Union was a distinct possibility and that in the first phase of the war the Russians would be capable of "wide-ranging, concurrent and effective offensives in virtually every major region of the globe."[5] When the North Atlantic Treaty was signed in 1949 in response to this perceived threat, it became apparent that the newly-united Allies did not choose to match in-being Soviet conventional armies. Although the United States probably could have maintained a post-war standing army equal to that of the Soviet Union (which had conducted a clandestine mobilization), such a step would have violated an historical strategic premise. The United States had traditionally fought an overseas war with a citizen army and then rapidly demobilized when the war was terminated.[6] Moreover, the U.S. monopoly of atomic weapons made such an effort appear unnecessary. Thus, military strategy for a major contingency in Europe was, from its infancy, nuclear dependent.

Of greater significance to this analysis of general purpose force planning, is that a strategy for a lesser contingency or a localized conflict was not seen as a requirement at this time. In a post-war world of rebuilding Europe and colonial disengagement, there were relatively few powerful actors within the international political system. While Latin America remained essentially within the U.S. sphere of influence, events in the areas of the globe more remote from the U.S.--Africa, the Middle East or Southeast Asia--would be largely determined by the policies of European nations.

By the later 1940s, however, the perception of the probabiity of a future war and the nature of that war had begun to change. The U.S. foreign policy of containment appeared to demand not only a nuclear emphasis, but also general purpose forces to meet lesser contingencies. This emphasis on local-war capabilities, emerging primarily from the State Department,[7] initially received little enthusiasm from an Army unable to support such a manpower-intensive mission and an Air Force dedicated to the strategic nuclear mission role. As Samuel Huntington described the post-war planning environment, "the two great constraints on effective military planning, the doctrinal heritage from the past and the pressure of domestic needs, combined to produce a serious gap between military policy and foreign policy."[8]

The Soviet explosion of an atomic device and the victory of the Communists in China spurred an examination of American defense policy by a combined State/Defense Department Committee. Their final report, delivered to President Truman in April 1950, called for a substantial increase in the U.S. defense budget and added credence to earlier State Department warnings regarding the imminent danger of local wars.[9] By the time NSC 68/2 was finally approved by the President in September of that year, the events in Korea had already served to validate many of the paper's predictions. NSC-68's projection of Soviet-backed aggression, its anticipation of limited war and the rationale for increased defense expenditures added a strong motivation for the build-up of U.S. conventional forces to support U.S. interests in peripheral as well as central regions of concern.[10] Thus, the limited contingency visualized in NSC-68 departed from the original formulation implied in the strategy of "containment." NSC-68 adopted a Soviet-intensive model of the limited contingency--the "firefight"--based on the contention that the USSR nuclear force would match U.S. strategic capabilities by the mid-1950s.[11]

As a planning document, however, NSC-68 was ahead of its time and soon was cast aside as a guideline for the prevailing U.S. strategic concept.[12] The Eisenhower administration took a "New Look" at U.S. military posture in 1953 and rejected the tenets of NSC-68 along with the ambitious NATO goals for a conventional force build-up previously adopted in Lisbon.[13] NSC 162/2, dated October 30, 1953, established the strategic concepts of the New Look. Under this guidance, the Joint Chiefs of Staff (JCS) and the component military services could plan for the use of nuclear weapons in a tactical as well as a strategic context, "whenever they would be desirable from a military standpoint."[14]

The effect of this policy was to deny any of the services the justification for the generation of large manpower requirements to meet a full-scale conventional war. Henceforth, any wars larger than small "brushfires" were to be considered, for planning purposes, as nuclear conflicts. Thus, NSC 162/2 gave official sanction to what was known by 1954 as the strategy of "massive retaliation." This policy was interpreted to mean, in its most famous and widely cited formulation, that a U.S. nuclear strike on the Soviet Union could be triggered in response to any Soviet transgression of U.S. interests anywhere.[15] However, a local or lesser contingency was not yet conceived. For U.S. force planners responding to declared policy, the world was perceived in its bipolar, post-war nuclear image.

U.S. defense planners perceived a threat composed of a 175 division Soviet force, plus millions of Chinese foot soldiers that had demonstrated their manpower-intensive tactics in Korea. These conventional forces conceivably could not be matched in the West; therefore, continual reliance would have to be placed on nuclear weapons. The U.S. feared that it would be faced with a series of Koreas that would sap American economic and military strength and adversely affect the long-term American guarantee of European security. Because conventional force levels could not be raised to counter or contain this threat, nuclear deterrence appeared to be the most prudent and, although the term had not yet been adopted in the Pentagon, "cost-effective" choice.

How were forces designed and deployed in support of the strategic concept? What priority was allocated to forces designed to meet a lesser contingency?

Massive retaliation implied the United States would not involve itself in future limited wars and would deter the USSR through its strategic nuclear superiority. There was, therefore, no need for large general purpose forces. The United States did not have the resources to intervene in every conceivable trouble spot and "would not try to maintain the conventional power to police the whole world."[16]

Nevertheless, there was a role for the general purpose forces within this strategic concept. Although Eisenhower was concerned with the balance of payments deficit being accrued by the stationing of U.S. troops and their dependents in Europe, that military presence abroad remained. However, the conventional firepower of this force was regarded as too weak to resist aggression successfully. Rather, its deployment was intended to act as a "tripwire" which would trigger U.S. intervention in the event of a Warsaw Pact attack on NATO Europe.

Within the strategy of massive retaliation also lay the original U.S. formulation of a central strategic reserve of forces—which would later form the conceptual basis for a limited contingency force. In a New Look paper forwarded to the Secretary of Defense in December 1953, the JCS advocated the redeployment of several overseas divisions to the United States "in order to achieve greater flexibility, reduce support costs and minimize manpower requirements."[17] The JCS argued for the maintenance of a strategic reserve force within the continental U.S. with sufficient readiness and mobility to move quickly to trouble spots.

Thus, the New Look did not rule out the possibility of a lesser contingency nor the forces necessary to deter or fight such a conflict. Admiral Radford declared that the military mission consisted of "two principal requirements: to be prepared for lesser military actions short of all out war as well as global war."[18] This concept of a central strategic reserve to facilitate deployment to a lesser contingency was also prominent in the statements of other military leaders. As Glenn Snyder has previously explained, this relatively unknown aspect of the strategic concept as formulated under Eisenhower appeared to have been derived from three motivations:[19]

- first was the desire to get United States forces deployed in the best possible positions for the contingency of general war (seen as Europe);
- second came the desire to obtain more flexibility in the United States military posture . . . troops in a central strategic reserve could more easily respond to aggression anywhere in the world;
- the third reason was economic: having ground forces centralized within the U.S. would reduce support costs.

Although this original formulation of the concept of a "central strategic reserve" would ultimately lead to a force planned for and dedicated to a lesser contingency, such a force under the New Look was constrained in both mobility and flexibility. Because the phrase "mobility and mobile readiness" appeared often in administration elaborations of the New Look, the implication was that, "besides being centrally located, United States ground forces were going to be able to move faster to 'hot spots' anywhere in the world."[20] But these references to mobility relied more on the redeployment of forces to a central location rather than the acquisition of support systems to move troops rapidly. Nor was the intention to place more reliance on mobile air and naval forces substantiated in the FY 1955 budget.[21]

A second major constraint on this early formulation of a rapid deployment strategy was the principle of "balanced collective forces." According to this concept, aggression in less vital areas would have to be met by indigenous ground forces. Because the U.S. possessed only a "limited supply of manpower," it would concentrate on helping with "highly mobile offensive combat forces"--meaning air and sea power:[22]

The local ground forces of the allies would take the initial shock of the attack and, assisted by the efforts of the U.S. air and naval forces, would hold off the enemy until a contingent of 'hard-hitting, mobile ground forces' from the central strategic reserve of the United States arrived on the scene.

In addition to these early formulations of a rapid deployment strategy, the Eisenhower administration also maintained a means of global power projection through a network of overseas air bases. However, these bases were seen as requirements to enhance the credibility of the strategic deterrent, not for their support of a strategy of rapid deployment of conventional forces. Nevertheless, the bases created a rationale for their existence, later to be applied to the global deployment of conventional forces: "They allow the U.S. to maintain tactical forces close to potential trouble spots; they promote U.S. political interests by giving our allies tangible evidence of our solidarity and give reason to the policy of containment."[23]

What was the impact of budgetary or public opinion constraints on planning forces to meet a lesser contingency?

The emerging strategic concept was also affected by domestic reactions to the limited war in Korea. The enormous budgetary expenditures required for the conduct of the Korean War brought fears of an economic collapse to President Eisenhower. He believed that the foundation of future U.S. military strength lay in a sound economy that could mobilize to meet a future, global threat (as it had done in World War II) but that the economy could not safely expand and simultaneously keep a large in-being military force. The evolving strategic concept was thus based on a belief that the U.S. could not afford both to deter and to contain the USSR. The search was for a concept that would provide, in Eisenhower's words, for "security and solvency."[24] The conservative defense economics of the Eisenhower administration, therefore, demanded a balanced budget and a cut in defense spending.

The public reaction to the limited war in Asia was encapsulated in the popular phrase, "No more Koreas." By 1954, American public opinion had come to regard any war fought only with conventional weapons as irrational, for such a war would fail to capitalize on U.S. nuclear supremacy. In this regard, the affinity for strategic air power that characterized and operationalized the strategy of massive retaliation can be better understood. U.S. technology was a source of public and political pride--the visible evidence of the superiority of the American system and age of global competition. The belief that strategic air power and nuclear weapons could provide the complete answer to the nation's military needs stemmed from the notion that technology could substitute for manpower. By relying on its qualitative edge, the United States could compensate for its quantitative shortfall in conventional force levels and simultaneously reap economic advantages.[25]

In the course of questioning a series of general purpose force items being proposed in the FY 1961 defense budget, Eisenhower again made clear the philosophy that underlay his guidance of U.S. military strategy during the 1950s. He was concerned primarily, he confided, "with keeping the economy sound for another ten years" and stated the only way the U.S. would win the struggle with the USSR was to "maintain its strategic deterrent." Mobile forces, he foresaw, would continue to have little utility, for the President could not envision any "little wars."[26]

Thus, Eisenhower remained faithful to a strategic concept that worked successfully in the Second World War and one that seemed to him to offer the only rational solution to the avoidance of future Korea-like conflicts. The Korean War and the Truman-MacArthur controversy had left a popular and political legacy of disenchantment toward the involvement of the United States in future limited contingencies. From 1953 to 1960, it was widely believed--and force levels were tailored to this threat--that although there might be "brushfire" wars of the kind that occurred in Malaya and Indo-China, there would not be another "field of fire" like Korea. Thus, the prevailing strategic concept during this period centered on the threat from the Soviet Union and argued that strategic forces would deter limited aggression and general war. Even if deterrence failed, nuclear forces could be used to limit violence in small wars by threatening nuclear escalation. General purpose forces were useful only to meet conflicts of low-level intensity against a non-Soviet adversary, but such lesser contingencies, post-Korea, were highly unlikely.

In the event of a contingency above the "brushfire" level, indigenous ground forces would be required to do the bulk of the fighting, while U.S. involvement would be ordinarily restricted to air and sea support as well as large measures of foreign aid.

The Limited War Critique of Massive Retaliation

This prevailing strategic concept of the 1950s that essentially obviated the planning and deployment of forces to meet a lesser contingency faced serious and substantial critiques. The theory of limited war began to garner attention with the conflict in Korea, grew more intense in the debate surrounding massive retaliation after 1954, and grew to full flowering after the Soviet launch of Sputnik in 1957. Throughout this period were developed the intellectual underpinnings for a revised strategic concept stressing the importance of military preparedness for a lesser contingency at a higher level of intensity.[27]

Serious academic thought on limited war--in addition to that of the defense planners who had conceived NSC 68--began about the time of the U.S. involvement in the Korean War. In 1950, the Bulletin of Atomic Scientists published an editorial adumbrating the fundamental concept that for the next decade would guide those opposed to a sole reliance on nuclear deterrence. The Bulletin essay warned, much like NSC-68, that the near future was likely to be marked by a series of "small wars waged by satellite armies"--the Soviet-proxy model--in which the atomic bomb would be of little value. Therefore, it was incumbent on the United States to develop "large, adequately equipped mobile land forces."[28]

Despite the validation of this prophecy by the Korean conflict, additional arguments in support of maintaining adequate and versatile general purpose forces were stymied by the official formulation of the strategy of massive retaliation. The first, and most widely circulated, critique of this strategy was William W. Kaufmann's "The Requirements of Deterrence," in which he argued that the threat of massive retaliation would not be credible in local conflict. Bernard Brodie added to this argument in November 1954 in a summary of a previously classified document. Brodie argued for the need to find some way to use the military instrument effectively in support of foreign policy objectives without relying exclusively on the threat of mass destruction with atomic weapons.[29]

In 1956, Kaufmann published one of the first general treatments of limited war. His primary focus, in an essay entitled "Limited Warfare," was on the political and military prerequisites for a successful U.S. foreign policy. Although Kaufmann and others were arguing for an adequate conventional capability, strategic thought at the time was also being devoted to the scenario of a limited nuclear war against the USSR. Henry Kissinger and Robert Osgood stated that the major problem facing the U.S. military was the prospect of a "local limited war" that could go nuclear. Both of these strategies advocated, initially, a limited nuclear response.[30]

These critiques received widespread attention in the growing U.S. defense intellectual community but did not reach their peak of public influence until 1957 when the Russians launched their Sputnik. With the orbiting of man's first earth satellite, the strategy of massive retaliation, for the first time, appeared to have a bipolar application. This event not only carried with it a nuclear missile threat to the American mainland, but also created the impression of Russian technological and military superiority.

In the fall of 1957, the Preparedness Subcommittee of the Senate Armed Services Committee, under Senator Lyndon Johnson, began a "serious inquiry" into U.S. defense posture. These hearings provided a forum for the forces opposing the prevailing strategic concept.[31] Simultaneously, one of the earliest government-sanctioned critiques of massive retaliation appeared in a "top secret" report entitled "Deterrence and Survival in the Nuclear Age." Known more popularly as the Gaither Report, this inquiry into the state of the nation's defense was presented to the National Security Council one month after the launch of the Soviet satellite. In the report, the Presidential Commission concluded that the United States needed to improve all aspects of its military forces, not only its strategic deterrent now threatened by an unanticipated Soviet capability. Given the new Soviet strategic threat—and the beginnings of rumors of a "missile gap"—conventional forces would probably be required to deter and defend against limited war.[32]

However, the Eisenhower administration was unwilling to accept such a sweeping indictment of its military strategy, even when couched in terms of "greater than expected threat." An admission of military weakness, or failure in military strategy, would be costly both politically and economically. The launch of Sputnik clearly encouraged an accelerated effort in the strategic sector but, given the economic constraints basic to the fundamental concept, the administration reemphasized its belief that no major increase in general purpose forces spending was necessary or desirable.

Nevertheless, the criticism continued to mount. In January 1958, the Rockefeller Brothers Fund published a report on the military aspects of national security. The study group, under the direction of Henry Kissinger, revised its previous thesis regarding the use of nuclear weapons in support of foreign policy post-Sputnik and stressed the importance of standing and capable conventional forces:[33]

> It is, therefore, imperative that in addition to our retaliatory force we develop units which can intervene rapidly and are able to make their power felt with discrimination and versatility. For this task we require modern sealift and airlift capacity we do not now possess. Our mobile forces must be tailored to the gamut of possible limited wars which may range from conflicts involving several countries to minor actions.

These public complaints regarding the adequacy of U.S. force levels again brought to the fore the impact of public opinion on defense spending, an issue that had remained relatively quiescent in the post-Korea years. Close Congressional scrutiny on defense policy issues now heightened public concern and anxiety. During the immediate post-Sputnik period, despite a broad fluctuation in the public perception of the Russian threat, "the administration's critics had lodged with at least a small attentive public the suspicion that arbitrary budget ceilings prevented the government from considering foreign and defense policies on their own merits."[34]

Thus, according to the influential critiques of the time, Eisenhower's attempt to buy military flexibility on the cheap had failed. As Paul Hammond has described the consensus:[35]

The New Look began as a serious effort to take advantage of technological developments in order to cope with the problem of having only limited resources that could ultimately be deployed for military capabilities. But this strategy went astray in two respects: in the inadequacy of our defense budget and planning and in the facile and imprecise spinning out of strategic concepts.

With increasing and influential criticism of U.S. policy by Kissinger, Army Chief of Staff Maxwell Taylor and others, the question of national defense quickly escalated as an election, not an esoteric, issue.[36] Taylor, who retired from the Army in 1959 to publicize his disagreement with the Eisenhower administration, testified that military experts had been permitted to judge defense issues "only within the confines of rigid budgetary ceilings imposed in advance." According to Taylor, "the American capacity for low-level conventional military response had been eliminated in favor of sole reliance on strategic airpower on the basis of budgetary constraints."[37] Conventional force capability was, therefore, lacking in both U.S. and allied active forces.

Maxwell Taylor wanted increased defense expenditures in order to buy conventional force capability and flexibility. But it remained the responsibility of the new administration, of which Taylor would soon become a member, to judge the accuracy of these critiques and fashion a revised strategic concept in their support. In the following pages we will examine how that administration and those succeeding spun new concepts, attempted to weave them into a coherent whole and wrapped within them the rationale for a limited contingency force.

Planning Forces for "2-1/2 Wars," 1961-1968

In the years following World War II, the United States elected a strategy that combined containment of Soviet expansion with an atomic deterrent to aggression. Yet, the initial military concentration, just briefly described, was on deterrence at the strategic, as opposed to the conventional, level. Moreover, the prevailing strategic concept developed during the 1950s considered nuclear weapons not only as the primary military instrument of deterrence, but also as the most effective means of defense.[38]

Critiques of this policy, bolstered by a heightened perception of the Soviet threat and a resulting public demand for increased defense spending, became issues in the presidential election of 1960. In partial response to these stimuli, the Democratic Party platform of 1960 called for a new administration to[39]

- provide forces and weapons of a diversity, balance and mobility in quantity and quality to deter both limited and general aggressions;
- insure continuous modernization of these forces through intensified research and development, including essential programs now slowed down, terminated, suspended or neglected for lack of budgetary support.

The Democratic standard-bearer did not shrink from these explicit party policies. Shortly after declaring his candidacy for the presidential nomination, John F. Kennedy called for "increased defense spending to allocate the resources necessary to give the next Commander-in-Chief the ability to intervene effectively and swiftly in any limited war anywhere in the world." Not surprisingly, the newly-elected President's inaugural address focused solely on foreign policy and called for a strong defense in its support.[40]

The posture of the United States' general purpose forces inherited by the new administration did not match these enhanced foreign policy objectives. Although outgoing Defense Secretary Gates, in his final report to President Eisenhower, informed the President that the "largest part of our armed forces were trained and equipped for countering local aggression," their capability to meet commitments was questioned by the new team in Defense. Secretary McNamara found that of a total of fourteen Army divisions in active service, three were training divisions without combat-ready manpower, seven were committed or deployed to Europe or Korea, with only one division on Hawaii and three in the United States to form the central strategic reserve. Moreover, "their equipment was aging, they lacked the supplies that would give them significant staying power, and the available air and sealift was sufficient to move only a fraction of them into a combat theater within a month."[41]

This neglected state of U.S. conventional forces indicated their inability to deploy rapidly to an overseas contingency and wage successfully a limited war without recourse to nuclear weapons. The concept of a central strategic reserve had not been adequately supported. General Taylor substantiated this allegation in his testimony to Congress in 1960, stating that he[42]

> ... based the limited war requirement of the Army on being able to close a corps of three divisions in an overseas theater in two months and to have the necessary logistics backup to fight these divisions until a supply line was established ... something more than we could do.

Kennedy's first foreign policy crisis in Laos brought home to him the accuracy of Taylor's description, the relevance of the pre-election critiques of massive retaliation and the lack of a U.S. capability to respond rapidly with conventional forces to a lesser contingency. When proposals were advanced by his advisers for the dispatch of a force of ground troops to Laos to demonstrate U.S. concern and resolve, it became clear that such an undertaking would require more men than were available and uncommitted. In the words of Roger Hilsman, an adviser who was present during many of the "long and agonizing meetings,"[43]

> ... the Eisenhower 'New Look' had reduced the ground forces in favor of air power, and it would have been impossible to put that many troops in Laos without taking troops from Europe--right at the time when the Berlin crisis was daily becoming more acute.

Arthur Schlesinger asserts that Kennedy was "appalled" to discover that to send ten thousand troops to Laos theoretically would have depleted the strategic reserve and prohibited reinforcements to other theaters or deployments to simultaneous contingencies.[44] These perceived limits placed on an ambitious foreign policy were unacceptable. President Kennedy directed Secretary McNamara to begin the work of building a versatile military establishment that would "liberate diplomacy

from the constraints imposed by a rigid military strategy."[45]   This
directive led to a policy review within the Pentagon and to a number of
studies that recommended various ways in which U.S. general purpose
forces could be improved.

In 1954, Secretary of Defense Charles Wilson had remarked that "we
won't have any small wars--we can't afford them."   In 1961, with
budgetary constraints relaxed, force planning for small wars began in
earnest. In February 1961, a "Limited War Study Committee," under the
direction of Assistant Secretary of Defense Paul Nitze, reached two broad
conclusions: 1) U.S. general purpose forces must be of the highest caliber
to meet the missions that were likely to be assigned them under a new
strategy of conventional emphasis, and 2) the increased spending required
for these force improvements would help the sluggish economy--an assist
to the Kennedy campaign promise to "get this country moving again."
This study was granted additional credibility by an informal memorandum
from Secretary of State Rusk to McNamara that echoed and enumerated a
diplomatic   rationale   for   strengthening   conventional   forces   and
emphasized the need to move from a reliance on strategic weapons in
order to strengthen U.S. negotiating positions.[46]

A second study, conducted through the channels of the military
services and under the direction of Secretary of the Navy John Connally,
was forwarded to Secretary McNamara in May of 1961. However, this
proposal mirrored the past practices of the separate services in planning
conventional forces rather than adopting a new strategic concept. The
Defense Secretary complained to the President in a memo attached to the
forwarded report that the services had merely used the opportunity to
generate a "Shopping List" rather than to structure joint forces in a
coherent conventional strategy.[47]   This divergence in the OSD and JCS
approach to force planning, accompanied by the expressed desire of the
services for specific policy guidance on which to base their force
projections, suggested the bureaucratic battle that lay ahead. This style
of conventional force planning by the separate services--lacking unity and
coherence--led Secretary McNamara to approach general purpose force
planning through a systematic, cost-effective process and with a goal of
obtaining truly joint service capabilities in the conventional arena.

A third study group established to make recommendations on U.S.
limited war capability was headed by Dr. Luis W. Alvarez of the Lawrence
Radiation Laboratory. This report, issued in 1961 to Harold Brown as the
Director of Defense Design, Research and Engineering, echoed the
criticism of a defense policy relying totally on atomic weapons and
brought to the fore the lack of a coherent doctrine accepted by the
services. The Alvarez panel warned that the Army, Navy and Air Force
were basing force requirements on differing concepts of the war the
United States was preparing to fight. Because no one knew precisely the
kinds of contingencies in which the U.S. was likely to become involved,
there was little guidance for force planning. The conclusion of the report
was that a new concept of American defense policy would have to be
enunciated in order to provide this force planning guidance.[48]

**What was the perception of the threat? How did the threat affect
the formulation of the strategic concept?**

As President Kennedy received the varying reports of evidence of a
force planning process in disarray, he was also particularly concerned with

Premier Khrushchev's speech in early 1961. In that address, the Soviet leader indicated his determination to support and encourage "wars of national liberation." According to Arthur Schlesinger's account, the "bellicose confidence" of the speech and the "declared faith in victory through rebellion, subversion and guerrilla warfare" led the President to believe that the Russians were pursuing new tactics of universal expansion and aggression. Kennedy believed that the world's southern hemisphere-- the "third world"--would now become a battlefield, albeit a low-intensity one, in the East-West struggle for the allegiance of the emerging nations. Thus, Kennedy warned in his 1961 State of the Union message that "we must never be lulled into believing that either power (the USSR or PRC) has yielded its ambition for world domination."[49]

The events in Laos and, to a greater extent, the fiasco in the Bay of Pigs in April 1961 reinforced the President's perception of the threat in lesser-developed countries. To assist in an ongoing appraisal and reorganization of the general purpose forces to meet this threat at an appropriate level, Kennedy invited Maxwell Taylor back into the government, first as Chairman of the Cuban Study Group following the Bay of Pigs, next as the Military Representative to the President and ultimately (in October 1962) as Chairman of the Joint Chiefs of Staff. These positions allowed Taylor to exercise a strong influence on the strategy and planning of conventional forces.[50]

Although Taylor's concerns with the Soviet-directed threat to the "third world" matched those of Kennedy and, therefore, focused on a lesser contingency, the possibility of a major contingency in Europe could not be ignored. In that same January speech, Khrushchev had declared the allied position in Berlin "especially vulnerable" and, with a threat of signing a separate peace treaty with East Germany, gave warning of an impending European crisis as well.

West Berlin was viewed from inside the U.S. government as an immediate, but not an isolated problem. The construction of a strategic concept within the Kennedy administration allowed for the allocation of priorities among possible contingencies, but it would not compromise, in theory at least, the capabilities to meet one contingency with those of another:[51]

> The threat is worldwide. Our effort must be equally wide and strong and not obsessed by any single manufactured crisis. We face a challenge in Berlin, but there is also a challenge in Southeast Asia. We need the capability of placing in any critical area at the appropriate time a force which . . . is large enough to defend our rights at all costs--and to meet all levels of aggressive pressure with whatever levels of force are required.

The basis for the change in the U.S. strategic concept was then not so much a change in the perception of the threat from that of the early 1950s, but of force planning in reaction to that threat. The major cold war issue between the two powers, as set forth by Kennedy in his 1961 meeting with Khrushchev in Vienna, was the apparent Soviet desire to disrupt the existing equilibrium by means of local communist insurrections. That Moscow was the global center of this unrest was not an issue of contention between the strategies of massive retaliation and "flexible response." What was different was the locale and the level of conflict at which to meet this Soviet challenge. General purpose forces structured under a nuclear-intensive strategic concept were not adequate to meet the contingencies now being envisioned.

How were forces designed in support of the strategic concept? What priority was allocated to forces planned to meet a lesser contingency?

In his first defense budget message to Congress in March 1961, President Kennedy emphasized the need to bolster the general purpose forces, particularly in terms of flexibility and mobility. He believed that a U.S. capacity to move sizeable forces on short notice and to be able to support those forces in one or more crisis areas could avoid the need for a much larger commitment later. Although this early enunciation of a rapid deployment doctrine was included as a necessary guideline for the build-up of the general purpose forces, Kennedy's interest in the lesser contingency was derived from a concern with a guerrilla-type war rather than a limited war on a conventional battlefield:[52]

> Given the great likelihood and seriousness of this (guerrila warfare) threat, we must be prepared to make a substantial contribution in the form of strong, highly mobile forces trained in this type of warfare, some of which may be deployed in forward areas, with a substantial airlift and sealift capacity and prestocked overseas bases.

President Kennedy's May address to Congress furthered his commitment to rapid deployment strategies and continued his advocacy of enhanced forces for a limited war:[53]

> The Army is developing plans to make possible a much more rapid deployment of a major portion of its highly trained Reserve forces. When these plans are completed and the Reserve is strengthened, two combat-equipped divisions, plus their supporting forces, a total of 89,000 men, could be ready in an emergency for operation with but three weeks' notice.

This statement evidenced the fact that the Reserve forces as well as active units were to become important instruments in the implementation of the new strategic concept and the emphasis on a conventional military response to crises. However, although this initiative was generally applauded, it also met with skepticism regarding the readiness of the Reserve and the relatively token increase of 5,000 men requested above the previously authorized ceiling for the regular forces. Looming crises and the continued influence of Maxwell Taylor within the administration resulted in a series of proposals to expand the general purpose forces.[54]

The administration's program presented to Congress in July of 1961 called for expanding the Army to over one million men, considerably above the previous authorized limit of 875,000. This proposal included raising the Seventh Army in Europe to full strength and developing a genuine combat-ready force within the active forces to perform the role of a central strategic reserve. Secretary McNamara had testified that, on assuming office, the Kennedy administration "had available for use only eleven Army divisions, plus three Marine Corps and three Army divisions in training."[55]   This, he concluded, was inadequate to meet U.S. obligations in Europe and in possible lesser contingencies.

Instead of three Strategic Army Command (STRAC) divisions in the continental United States, the Kennedy proposal called for six fully ready regular Army divisions in the CONUS, plus supporting forces and additional air and sealift.   In support of the program, Secretary McNamara made it clear that the proposed increases in defense spending were not simply to handle a Berlin crisis but to achieve ". . . a peak readiness of our military establishment to respond promptly and with appropriate forces and in adequate strength to any kind of armed Communist aggression anywhere in the world."[56]

The proposal was well received and quickly approved in Congress. Along with authorization for the increase in regular Army force levels, the Congress also passed a resolution authorizing the President to call up 250,000 men of the Ready Reserve during the next fiscal year (for twelve months' service until July 1962).   The administration's concept in calling up the Reserves was not necessarily to use these forces in combat or even to deploy them to Europe but to use them to fill out understrength forces in the United States and to bolster airlift and submarine forces.[57]

However, the Reserve call-up during the Berlin crisis "revealed flaws in mobilization procedures, provoked ciriticism on the part of a vocal minority of citizen soldiers and created political costs in the form of anti-administration attacks by the media and in Congress."[58] The troops were generally unprepared militarily, but the situation was made worse by inadequate amounts of supplies and equipment.   There were a number of administrative errors surrounding the call-up of certain units as well, which, when combined with the disruption of individual careers, led to severe morale problems among the men activated.   Although the reverberating complaints from the soldiers called to duty prompted President Kennedy's famous "life is unfair" remark at a press conference, Deputy Secretary of Defense Roswell Gilpatric offered a more honest appraisal:[59] "We made a mistake. The Reservists are not oriented to the thought that they are called up to prevent a war rather than to fight."

Thus, the unsuccessful attempt to utilize Reserve forces in a lesser contingency role during the Berlin crisis appeared to decouple these forces, politically, from such a scenario.   In the judgment of top-level administration officials, the future mobilization of the Reserve could be justified only in a major contingency when the cries of unfairness would not be heard and the units would be utilized in a combat role.   Further, the military shortfalls demonstrated by the units that were activated had revealed that the training time required to bring the forces to a state of combat readiness precluded their immediate use in a lesser contingency if the scenario demanded rapid deployment.

Force planners within the Department of Defense similarly concluded that the active forces required additional combat-ready, rapidly deployable forces. The concept of a central strategic reserve composed of active forces was thus given greater emphasis, while the role of the Reserves in a lesser contingency was seen as negligible. However, conventional force planning remained based on the assumption that a major contingency, requiring a commitment of a major portion of the Strategic Army Force in the CONUS, would result in a Reserve mobilization and that forces required in sustained combat operations would be supplemented and supported by the Reserves. This dichotomy in force planning would affect both the reluctance to mobilize the Reserves during the Vietnam war and the resulting modification of the strategic concept by the Nixon administration.[60]

By January of 1962, in the first defense budget prepared wholly by the Kennedy administration, the conventional force build-up began to take on a recognizable form. In his prepared statement before the Senate Armed Services Committee, Secretary McNamara noted that although problems still existed with planning the general purpose forces-- characterized as a joint rather than a unified process--the tailoring of conventional forces to meet specific contingencies would continue. Key to this conventional force posture was a requirement of six Army divisions needed for the reinforcement of NATO, with an additional "reserve of ready divisions available to other parts of the world." The Kennedy plan in 1962 was to increase the number of regular Army divisions from the eleven inherited to sixteen, with the following breakdown of ground forces and their deployment:[61]

- 5 Divisions deployed to Europe,

- 2 Divisions deployed to Korea,

- 1 Division stationed in Hawaii and

- 8 Divisions stationed in the CONUS as a strategic reserve.

The divisions in the standing Reserve meant that the Strategic Army Command would grow from three to eight divisions in order to provide a force big and flexible enough "to cope with possible simultaneous troubles in widely separated areas of the world."[62] With six of the eight divisions committed to the reinforcement of a major contingency in Europe, two Army and two Marine divisions remained to reinforce U.S. troops already deployed to Asia or to form a mobile "fire brigade" capable of rapid deployment to a lesser contingency.

The sizing of the "fire brigade" and its ability to deploy to a lesser contingency continued to depend to a large extent on the capability of the Reserves to reinforce U.S. troops in Europe or Asia. Although Secretary McNamara had also learned from the mistakes of the Berlin mobilization, he remained convinced of the need to call up the Reserves if the U.S. were faced with troop level requirements that equated to those projected for a major contingency. Only with the Reserves called to service could U.S. general purpose forces meet major contingencies in Europe and Asia while maintaining a capability to deploy to a limited contingency as well:[63]

The requirement for active duty general purpose forces is also influenced by the size and character of our Reserve forces. To the extent that our Reserve units can be brought to bear in a timely manner, the requirement for active forces is reduced. But to be fully effective, certain portions of our Reserve forces must be maintained at a high level of readiness since, as we have seen, a quick response on our part to a Communist aggression can do much to forestall a much greater military effort. Thus, there is a great premium on highly ready Reserve forces which can be used to augment quickly our active forces.

These premises for the planning of the general purpose forces-- sizing ground troops and their support to meet specific contingencies, a reliance on the Reserves for major contingencies and the creation of a central strategic reserve of mobile, ready, active forces to meet a lesser contingency--continued to gain respect as well as advocates during the Kennedy years. By January 1963, these elements of general purpose force planning appeared to be narrowing to a well-defined strategic concept. In his "Posture Statement" for that year, Mr. McNamara referred to the "General Purpose Force Studies," conducted under the direction of the Chairman of the Joint Chiefs of Staff, that had examined "the general purpose force requirements to meet various kinds of attacks in four broad geographic regions--Europe, the Middle East, Southeast Asia and Northeast Asia." These studies, McNamara contended, "constitute a very useful approach to the problem of determining the force requirements for a limited war."[64]

Summarizing the general purpose force situation by quoting the conclusion of the Weapons System Evaluation Group (WSEG), Secretary McNamara stated:[65]

Readiness and mobility can greatly reduce requirements for general purpose forces. This is simply the principle of getting there first with the most, before the situation deteriorates and greater forces are required to recover lost ground.

Modern equipment, weapons and munitions in sufficient quantity to support the existing forces in combat until production can catch up with consumption are far more important at this particular point in time than additional U.S. forces.

Proper support of indigenous forces on the scene would give a greater return to collective defense than additional U.S. forces.

The presently programmed forces, in general, could by non-nuclear means alone counter a wide spectrum of Sino-Soviet bloc aggressions in regions other than Europe.

Thus, McNamara had concluded, after two years in office, that U.S. conventional forces were capable of containing Soviet aggression in a non-NATO contingency. Only in Europe were deployed U.S. conventional forces inadequate, thereby requiring a recourse to the use of nuclear weapons in the event of a Soviet/Warsaw Pact attack. But that estimate, too, was subject to revision. Mr. McNamara noted that previous estimates of Soviet Block strength in Europe had led to "an unduly pessimistic view of our prospects in a non-nuclear war." The problem in Europe, like those facing units earmarked for a lesser contingency, were related more to "readiness, deployment capability and certain shortages in equipment and stocks than they are to overall manpower levels or defense budgets."[66]

Prior to the beginning of the U.S. troop deployment to Vietnam, a strategic concept had been formulated that was based on fighting a conventional war in Europe, facing the possibility of another major contingency in Asia while maintaining the capability to deploy rapidly forces from a central strategic reserve to a lesser contingency elsewhere:[67]

We must build into our general purpose forces a capability to deal with both the kinds of contingencies we judge to be most likely and the kind we judge to be most vital to the security of the United States . . . .

We must continue to provide in our general purpose forces a capability to participate with our allies in a large-scale war in Europe . . . .

The capability to deal with the largest contingency does not necessarily give us the capability to deal effectively with the more likely ones at the lower end of the scale . . . .

A mobile 'fire brigade' reserve, centrally located in the U.S. and ready for quick deployment to any threatened area of the world, is a more economical and flexible use of our military forces . . . .

Falling between these extremes is the wide range of contingencies which stem from overt armed aggression by a Communist state against a neighbor. Forces to deal with such contingencies must also be available.

Our analysis of the various kinds of limited war situations we are likely to face over the balance of this decade indicates a requirement for an Army of about 22 divisions, plus two special purpose divisions, with six of these divisions in the Reserves . . . .

By 1965, the force structure fashioned in support of this strategic concept actually formed a 28-1/3 division force, with an active force of 19-1/3 divisions, including three Marine divisions and nine divisions in the Reserves. Table 2.1 suggests a contingency-based allocation of these ground forces based on the "2-1/2 war" strategic concept as it had evolved by 1965.[68]

This table depicts, and the foregoing discussion underlines, the relationships between the major and the lesser contingencies as envisioned under the "2-1/2 war" strategic concept--normally thought of geographically as Europe, Korea and Cuba. The planned build-up of conventional forces under Secretary McNamara was directed toward meeting these contingencies on a conventional level and based on the assumption that no more than the two major and one minor contingencies would occur simultaneously. However, although general purpose forces would be planned to meet these contingencies, the resulting forces were not to be committed to a specific anticipated theater or contingency, but would be versatile, flexible and capable of rapid deployment to any trouble spot. Given the relative lack of mobility of the presumed adversary, the lesser contingency, in a legacy of the Eisenhower defense policy, remained as a "brushfire" war, while the Soviet-proxy or Soviet-intensive versions of the "half war" planning contingency remained imbedded in the major conflicts foreseen under this strategic concept. Thus, there was no attempt to disaggregate a range of lesser contingencies according to levels of intensity or adversary under the "2-1/2 war" concept.

What was the impact of budgetary or public opinion constraints on the process of force planning for a lesser contingency?

The major factor that served to limit the effectiveness of the general purpose force planning done under the Kennedy/Johnson administrations and that negated the precise allocation of conventional

TABLE 2.1
The Allocation And Deployment Of Major General Purpose
Forces Under The "2-1/2 War" Strategic Concept, 1965

CONTINGENCIES

1 War and	2 War +	1/2 War
Warsaw Pact attack in Europe	Chinese attack in Asia	"Brushfire" in Western Hemisphere
Allied Support	Limited Allied Support	Some Allied Support
Vital to U.S.	Vital to U.S.	Not Vital to U.S.

FORCES
(Army and Marine Divisions)

	1 War	2 War	1/2 War
CONUS	4	3	--
DEPLOYED	5	4	--
STRATEGIC RESERVE	--	--	3 1/3
RESERVE	8	--	1

STRATEGIC CONCEPT

Duration of conventional war in Europe limited to three months	Did not allow for simultaneous attack in Korea and Vietnam	Rapid deployment to come from strategic reserves
Forces in-place adequate to meet intermediate attack	Holding action required while Reserves mobilized	Forces allocated based on simultaneous contingencies
Reserve mobilization required	Reserve reinforcement required	Strategic reserves could also be used for major contingency reinforcement

Sources: Enthoven and Smith, How Much is Enough?, p. 215.
Gelb and Kuzmack, op. cit., p. 207.
Charles Schultze, ed., Setting National Priorities: 1973
Budget (Washington: Brookings, 1972).

forces by major and minor contingencies was the war in Vietnam. At some point in time during the long U.S. involvement in Vietnam, that conflict's characteristics matched each of those along the "2-1/2 war" spectrum. Although Vietnam started in the early 1960s as a "brushfire" or counter-insurgency operation, it soon escalated to being characterized as the Asian example of "overt aggression by a Communist state" and ultimately absorbed forces equivalent in number to those planned to be committed to a major contingency in Europe. Vietnam, in this regard, was an aberration that defies accurate description within the confines of the strategic concept. In the end, it certainly was not representative of a limited contingency that demanded a strategy of rapid deployment; in many ways, and for many years, Vietnam required the long lines of communication and continual reinforcement of men and material that characterize a major contingency. The purpose here is to view the Vietnam war only in terms of its impact on the prevailing strategic concept and to ascertain how budgetary constraints and the limits of public opinion constrained force planning for a limited contingency as a result of the war.[69]

A brief chronological accounting of U.S. troop deployment to Vietnam suggests a deliberate, but almost imperceptible slide from a limited contingency to a major commitment. When Lyndon Johnson became President in 1963, there were 16,000 U.S. troops in Vietnam, serving primarily as "advisers." By the end of 1964, the number totalled 23,000. The key period of ground force expansion was between the end of March and the beginning of July 1965, when "we moved from the mission of base security to the mission of actual combat."[70]

These troop deployments, both prior to this point and subsequent to it, were made gradually, partially owing to a strategy of incremental escalation, but frequently because of constraints existing within Vietnam itself. Although in 1966 Secretary McNamara was urging the services to accelerate their deployments to Southeast Asia, he also noted that the logistical base in South Vietnam was "inadequate . . . to absorb troop units at a rapid rate." Moreover, because the President refused to mobilize the Reserves as the JCS recommended, "the troops were simply not available --raising them through the draft and training them took time."[71]

By early 1967, it was clear that, without a Reserve call-up, forces in the U.S. earmarked for the major contingency in Europe and those composing part of the strategic reserve would have to be deployed to Southeast Asia. On August 7, it was announced that the latest 45,000 man increment (raising the total deployment to over 500,00) would consist of units previously classified as the strategic reserve. In ordering this deployment, Secretary McNamara argued that the use of these forces was necessary to hold down the cost of raising additional forces and that the strategic reserve was intended for the reinforcement of what had come to be a major contingency in Vietnam.[72]

By this time it was also clear that Vietnam had taken on all the earmarks of a major contingency and that the central strategic reserve in the U.S. was no longer available for deployment to lesser contingencies. This fact was detailed in a dialogue between Secretary McNamara and Senator Jackson.[73] (author's italics)

> Sen. Jackson: It seems to me that what is really involved here is a question of whether the central reserves here are adequate to meet future contingencies.

Sec. McNamara: I think the answer, and I want to make this very clear, is we would call the Reserves. We do not maintain in the Active Force today forces sufficient to meet another major contingency without calling the Reserves.

Sen. Jackson: In other words, what you are saying is that the 9 divisions (in the U.S.) plus the 3 (Marine Corps divisions), 12 divisions that you had available prior to the build-up were part of the contingency reserve?

Sec. McNamara: Yes.

Sen. Jackson: You have used part of that contingency?

Sec. McNamara: Yes.

Sen. Jackson: You intend to make up the difference by calling Reserves?

Sec. McNamara: Absolutely. I want to make it very clear to the committee that we never contemplated meeting one major contingency without calling up the Reserves. We are doing that today in Southeast Asia. I think that shows a tremendous capacity. We would not contemplate trying to meet a second contingency without calling the Reserves.

Despite McNamara's assurances to Congress that the depletion of the strategic reserve did not limit U.S. troop deployment to other, lesser contingencies, the Tet offensive at the end of January 1968 exacerbated the issue and raised again the question of mobilizing the Reserve forces.[74] Given the unexpected breadth and unity of the Viet Cong attacks in the South, however, this debate was now cast under increased doubt regarding the extent and worth of the U.S. commitment to Vietnam.

General Westmoreland, the commander of the U.S. Military Assistance Command in Vietnam, had requested a moderate reinforcement of 10,500 men soon after the Tet attacks. This request was initially turned down by the Joint Chiefs. Their position, a portent of the more vociferous debate to come, was that it was irresponsible to deplete further the strategic reserve in the absence of Reserve force mobilization. According to several accounts, the JCS saw the Tet offensive as the opportunity to convince the President to call on his Reserve forces, "believing that Johnson was now ready to move in the direction of decisive escalation that they had been pushing for years."[75]

In March 1968, Westmoreland was pressured by the JCS to make a request for an additional 206,000 men. The intent may have been to make this figure so large that the Reserves would have to be mobilized. Half of that number would allow replacement and redeployment to Vietnam, while the remainder would be used to reconstitute the central strategic reserve. This attempt to make available additional forces in the event of the occurrence of additional contingencies failed because this request for a significant rise in the level of U.S. troop deployment sparked a reassessment of the U.S. commitment rather than a rededication of effort.

Although a limited number of Reserve units were called to active duty,[76] the need for a much larger mobilization now pointed the way for a deescalation of the conflict. A reappraisal of the war by the advisers closest to the President, coupled with demands by the military leaders for a full-scale Reserve mobilization, moved Johnson to retrench in Vietnam and ultimately to withdraw from the presidential campaign. Gelb and Betts report that Johnson had decided as early as 1965 that he

TABLE 2.2
The Allocation And Deployment Of Major General Purpose Forces Under The "2-1/2 War" Strategic Concept, 1968

CONTINGENCIES		
<u>1 War</u> <u>and</u>	<u>2 War</u> +	<u>1/2 War</u>
Warsaw Pact attack in Europe	US support of South in Vietnam	"Brushfire" in Western Hemisphere
Allied Support	Limited Allied Support	Some Allied Support
Vital to U.S.	Declared vital to U.S.	Not Vital to U.S.

FORCES (Army and Marine Divisions)			
CONUS	6	--	--
DEPLOYED	5	12	--
STRATEGIC RESERVE	--	--	2/3
RESERVE	8	--	1

STRATEGIC CONCEPT		
Duration of conventional war in Europe limited to three months	Forces equating to a major contingency deployed to Southeast Asia	Strategic reserves deployed to Southeast Asia
Reserve mobilization required	Reserves would not be mobilized for this contingency	No limited contingency capability remains in CONUS active forces

Sources: <u>DoD Annual Reports, FY 1966-1969</u>

would not put the country on a "real wartime footing" by calling up the Reserves. Throughout the early years of the American commitment in Vietnam, as stressed by Herbert Schlander, "when the President began to search for the elusive point at which the costs of Vietnam would become unacceptable to the American people, he always settled upon mobilization."[77]

Without the mobilization of the Reserves, the war would eventually wind down. But, without this call-up, the war would also be prolonged, continuing the depletion of the strategic reserve and limiting a possible U.S. response to an additive contingency. Moreover, the projection forces generally earmarked for rapid deployment, such as the three Marine divisions and the 101st Airmobile and 82nd Army divisions, had been affected significantly by Vietnam deployment. Senator Russell pointed this out to the Secretary of the Army in May 1968.[78]

> Senator Russell: How many people do you now have in the standing reserve? I opposed very vigorously sending the one brigade of the 82nd to Vietnam because I didn't feel we had enough reserves in this country to take care of situations that might arise in the Caribbean and Central America.
> Secretary Resor: When these two Reserve brigades come on active duty on May 13 (1968), we will have 5-1/3 divisions in the CONUS, including Hawaii.

The highest total of U.S. troops in Vietnam, recorded in early 1962,[79] was 543,000. The enormity of this force, greater than the number of forces projected to meet a major Asian contingency prior to Vietnam, severely limited the capability of active U.S. forces to meet a NATO contingency and effectively eliminated projection forces planned for a rapid deployment to a lesser contingency. The "half war" envisioned in the early strategic concept of the Kennedy administration--the war that Vietnam might have been, but certainly was not--had escalated to the force level equal to a major contingency. The demand for troop strength in Vietnam, plus the political unwillingness to mobilize the Reserves, deprived forces committed to a major European contingency of their planned reinforcement and depleted the strategic reserve dedicated to a lesser contingency.

Thus, while the United States was preparing to fight two major conflicts--originally conceived of as Europe and Northeast Asia--the Vietnam war reduced the American capability to deploy forces to a lesser contingency elsewhere and questioned the U.S. capability to wage simultaneous major conflicts. Even greater constraints on this capability were to be imposed by a new administration that, in the wake of Vietnam and in response to limits being imposed by public opinion, sought to reduce defense expenditures and retreat from U.S. military commitments in Asia.

Planning Forces for "1-1/2 Wars," 1969-1976

Many members of the U.S. Senate expressed surprise when, in early 1969, former Budget Director Charles Schultze explained the force planning guidance of the previous eight years by testifying that the U.S. had "developed its military attitude toward simultaneously countering a possible Soviet attack in Europe, a possible Red Chinese move in Asia and a smaller "brushfire" skirmish elsewhere, most likely in the Western Hemisphere."[80] At a time when the single war in Southeast Asia was beginning to seem excessive to many of the Senators and their constituents, planning for another one and a half seemed extreme.

Schultze, a senior fellow at the Brookings Institution at the time of his testimony, had a larger purpose in mind than merely the education of the Senate in the underlying assumption of past U.S. strategic policy. He pointed out that, although the end of the Vietnam war should legitimately result in substantial defense budget savings approximating $20 billion each year, that "peace dividend" was in danger of being eroded by the continual procurement of new and expensive weapons systems already planned and programmed.[81] Further, although it was important to scrutinize carefully budget requests for weapons acquisition, it was perhaps of greater consequence to review the basic assumptions and military commitments that generated these forces and systems. If the U.S. were to reduce the commitments and plan for a fewer number of contingencies, then the 60% of the U.S. defense budget currently allocated to the general purpose forces could be reduced significantly.[82]

Carl Kaysen, former aid to McGeorge Bundy in the Kennedy administration, went a step further in the establishment of a new force planning rationale. Writing in Agenda for the Nation, Kaysen argued for a scaling down of U.S. force levels post-Vietnam, not to the level preceding the involvement, but to a considerably smaller force. If the defense budget rested ultimately on U.S. commitments, as Mr. McNamara had so frequently stated, then the means to a long term budget and force level reduction was to reduce the number of American commitments abroad:[83]

> Prior to the large troop commitments to Vietnam, the United States maintained about ten divisions in the continental United States ... the size of this force was rationalized in terms of the need to meet, on short notice, the contingency of three military involvements at once; one in Europe, one in South or East Asia, both on a substantial scale, and a small third one elsewhere in the world. The foregoing discussion suggests that we should determine our force needs on the basis of more modest plans. These plans would include the capability of meeting simultaneously on short notice a large troop requirement in Europe and a small one elsewhere in the world.

Kaysen's article appears as the first concrete call for a retreat to a "1-1/2 war" strategic concept. The way to achieve this goal was to drop the Asian contingency, a process seen as already in progress through the phased American withdrawal in Vietnam. Kaysen also called for a reduction of U.S. troops in Korea and Europe and greater reliance on air and naval forces in the Pacific.

What was the perception of the threat? How did the threat affect the formulation of the strategic concept?

These arguments for a revised strategic concept depended for their coherence on a changed perception of the threat. The elimination of a major contingency in Asia stemmed from the conclusion that the Sino-Soviet split had lessened the probability of a simultaneous contingency in Europe and Asia. But other critics of the "2-1/2 war" strategic concept used this period of disenchantment with the military instrument of foreign policy to argue that a conventional conflict was both unlikely to occur and difficult to deter:[84]

It is not clear that (conventional) forces contribute to deterring major non-nuclear conflicts or that such conflicts are sufficiently likely to justify their standing by in readiness. Only military planners, professionaly committed to belief in the worst contingencies, today assign significant probability to a sudden Soviet march across the north German plain ... or even an unheralded descent by Communist China on Burma or Thailand. Equally, it is unclear what role American non-nuclear forces can play in the kinds of minor wars that do appear probable.

As Henry Kissinger noted, this argument did not question "whether the probability of Soviet conventional attack might be affected to some extent by the size of the opposing forces." Nevertheless, these critics had drawn the "amazing" conclusion from the impending American withdrawal in Vietnam and the approaching numerical parity in strategic forces with the USSR that "we should cut our conventional forces, in which we were already vastly inferior."[85] Whatever the logical merit of this critique, a public atmosphere characterized by calls for U.S. military force reduction and retreat resulted in a reappraisal of the "2-1/2 war" strategic concept by the new administration.

At Kissinger's initiative, a National Security Study Memorandum (NSSM-3, January 21, 1969) "launched a reexamination of the assumptions of the 'two and one-half war' concept." The resulting study under the direction of Deputy Secretary of Defense Packard was called "the most comprehensive study of this type since World War II."[86] As first reported, the study offered ten general purpose force options, ranging from a minimum $14 billion a year defense budget with only seven active Army divisions (a pre-Korea force) to an $85 billion budget with 40 divisions. As the extremes were pared away, an Interdepartmental Group fashioned five options from the ten in an attempt to match contingencies with projected force posture. In addition to the ultimately selected "1-1/2 war" strategy, this formulation also included:[87]

-   a so-called 'Europe only' strategy, with only a tiny, token American military force retained in Asia, and no preparation of U.S. units to fight in Asia, and an estimated cost of $50-60 billion;
-   a continuation of the '2-1/2 war' strategy, maintaining an equivalent force of 2.6 million men in the armed forces after Vietnam, with an estimated cost of $90-100 billion;
-   a '3-1/2 war' strategy, having the capability to fight simultaneously not only a big war in Europe, but also both a Northeast and Southeast Asia conflict, and an estimated cost over $120 billion;
-   a 'conventional emphasis' strategy to bolster general purpose forces in Europe and reduce the reliance on theater nuclear weapons, plus a simultaneous, limited conventional capability in Asia, and an estimated cost of $80-90 billion.

As Kissinger recalls, his staff then narrowed these choices to three options for a Presidential decision:[88]

- Strategy 1 would maintain conventional forces for an initial (ninety-day) defense of Western Europe against a major Soviet attack and for simultaneous assistance (logistical support, plus limited U.S. combat forces) to an Asian ally against threats short of a full-scale Chinese invasion.
- Strategy 2 would maintain forces capable of either a NATO initial defense or a defense against a full-scale Chinese attack in Korea or Southeast Asia. That is, we would not maintain forces to fight on a large scale in Europe and Asia simultaneously.
- Strategy 3 (essentially the U.S. strategy before the Vietnam War) would maintain U.S. forces for a NATO initial defense and a defense of Korea or Southeast Asia against a full-scale Chinese attack. The forces would be capable of meeting the major Warsaw Pact and Chinese attacks simultaneously.

On October 2, 1969, Kissinger recommended "Strategy 2," a "1-1/2 war" strategic concept based on the belief that ". . . a simultaneous Warsaw Pact attack in central Europe and a Chinese conventional attack in Asia is unlikely. In any event, I do not believe such a simultaneous attack could or should be met with ground forces."[89]

Under this new strategic concept the lesser contingency could take many forms short of a U.S. confrontation with a major Communist state. In describing the joint formulation process of what was to become the Nixon Doctrine, Henry Kissinger notes that he and the President agreed that the U.S. would eschew getting the U.S. involved in foreign civil wars. The Nixon Doctrine was, therefore, needed to provide policy guidance for U.S. military action in the "gray area in between" local conflict and superpower confrontation, that area seen then as the range of a lesser or limited contingency.

The doctrine and its implications for force planning were first outlined in President Nixon's Guam press conference on November 3, 1969, and elaborated in his Foreign Policy Report of February 18, 1970:[90]

- the United States will keep all its treaty commitments;
- we shall provide a shield if a nuclear power threatens the freedom of a nation allied with us . . . ;
- in cases involving other types of aggression we shall furnish military and economic assistance when requested and as appropriate. But we shall look to the nation directly threatened to assume the primary responsibility of providing the manpower for its defense.

How were forces designed and deployed in support of the strategic concept? What priority was allocated to forces planned to meet a lesser contingency?

From a force planning viewpoint the important issue within the Nixon Doctrine was the extent of U.S. military involvement abroad. In maintaining U.S. overseas commitments the Nixon Doctrine countered the proposals of Kaysen and others and sought to achieve what Robert Osgood has termed "military retrenchment without political disengagement."[91] Moreover, although the original Guam doctrine was aimed primarily at U.S. Asian policy and served as a rationalization for the "Vietnamization" of the war, Nixon soon indicated that the strategy would have wider application:[92]

> We cannot expect U.S. military forces to cope with the entire spectrum of threats facing allies or potential allies throughout the world. This is particularly true of subversion and guerrilla warfare of wars of national liberation. Experience has shown that the best means of dealing with insurgencies is to preempt them through economic development and social reform.

It was unclear, however, exactly how the Nixon Doctrine would result in a reduced conventional force posture. Because forces to meet fully the "2-1/2 war" strategy allegedly had not been generated, the magnitude of the cuts was uncertain. Although the Doctrine implied that the U.S. would not intervene with ground troops in the event of "other types of aggression" in Asia, there was still a need for strong naval and air units as well as sufficient ground forces to maintain all U.S. treaty commitments. In addition, a capability for rapid response with active forces as well as quick mobilization for follow-on forces seemed a necessary component of the strategy. Thus, as the force planners sat down to operate under the Nixon Doctrine and the strategic concept of "1-1/2 wars," their guidance was far from explicit.

In his 1970 Posture Statement, Defense Secretary Laird suggested the meaning of the "1-1/2 war" strategic concept for general purpose force planning:[93]

> The stated basis of our conventional posture in the 1960s was the so-called '2-1/2 war' principle. According to it, U.S. forces would be maintained for a three-month conventional forward defense of NATO, a defense of Korea or Southeast Asia against a full-scale Chinese attack and a minor contingency simultaneously. These force levels were never reached.
>
> In the effort to harmonize doctrine and capability, we chose what is best described as the '1-1/2 war' strategy. Under it we will maintain in peacetime general purpose forces adequate for simultaneously meeting a major Communist attack in either Europe or Asia, assisting allies against non-Chinese threats in Asia and contending with a contingency elsewhere.
>
> An important objective of the new strategy is smaller, more mobile and more efficient general forces . . . .

These three principles underlying general purpose force planning in the Nixon administration are significant in several respects. The first statement alleges that forces for the "2-1/2 war" strategy were never generated. But this argument depends critically on whether the Reserves were counted as part of the forces dedicated to a major contingency. If, as Mr. McNamara had insisted, a major contingency was planned for and required a Reserve mobilization, the countering argument can be made that forces were available to meet dual, major contingencies, but there was a political decision not to utilize them.[94] If the revised strategic concept was merely an acknowledgement of the decoupling of the Reserves from a major, non-European contingency, such an action would not lead immediately to force reductions.

There appeared to be a number of ways in which the new strategy could be rationalized. In one conception, the strategic shift was allowing force posture to dictate policy. In order to "harmonize" strategy and force posture in this regard, all that was necessary was to reduce the number of contingencies while keeping the active force posture intact. But this did not appear in keeping with either the pledge to reduce defense spending or to maintain all U.S. treaty commitments. From another viewpoint, the change in the strategic concept could be seen as a rationale for the eventual withdrawal of U.S. troops from Vietnam. If the other contingencies remained covered adequately through a combination of active and Reserve forces, then the nation's ground forces could be reduced, conceivably by the ten divisions in Southeast Asia, thereby accruing a considerable "peace dividend."[95]

None of these interpretations completely or accurately describes either the motivation or the resulting force posture. The Nixon administration was faced with the need to proffer the appearance of a reduction of the U.S. effort in Southeast Asia, to cut defense spending, to end conscription and lower the total force while simultaneously giving the assurances of maintaining U.S. commitments abroad. In this regard, the Nixon Doctrine, and the blending of these conflicting goals within a coherent strategic concept, was an artful design.[96]

Key to the planned force reductions under the Nixon Doctrine was a concept of "local area defense" that had emerged from the original NSC analysis of general purpose force planning for the administration. The espoused aim was to withdraw U.S. troops stationed abroad and concentrate them in the continental U.S.--a quasi-renewal of the concept of the strategic reserve that had been depleted in spirit and in strength during the Vietnam deployments. However, these forces constituting a central reserve were not tasked with a mission of global intervention. The reasoning behind the redeployment was explained by G. Warren Nutter, Assistant Secretary of Defense for International Security Affairs:[97]

This concept is not so much one of bottling up and containing the Soviet Union and China solely with our own forces, as relying more heavily on the idea of local defense. We want these countries to defend themselves in all but cases of massive attack. We are committed to maintaining our combat forces in Europe for the time being, but not elsewhere.

Secretary Laird elaborated further on the concept in his 1972 Posture Statement when he explained that the deterrent to localized conflict--apart from a large-scale Soviet or Chinese attack--"will be provided by Allies and friends who themselves have a capability and national will to defend themselves."[98]

The Nixon Doctrine, the concept of local area defense, and the clamor from Congress for NATO nations to assume a greater role in Alliance burden-sharing made a strong case for the reduction of U.S. general purpose forces. The question now became, in a semantic reversal of previous yardsticks of force sufficiency, "How little would suffice?"

Several models of conventional force posture, offered publicly to match the revised strategic concept, suggest the classified options being prepared in the Pentagon. Carl Kaysen posited that the U.S. withdrawal from Vietnam and a reduction of U.S. commitments in Asia "might permit a total reduction of between five and six divisions" in the active ground forces. However, to allow for the maintenance of an appropriate strategic reserve, even though the new strategy would rule out "emergency interventions in substantial force on short notice on a world-wide basis," Kaysen advocated a total reduction of between "four and five divisions, with corresponding . . . (although proportionately smaller) reductions in naval and tactical air forces." This reduction in force would discourage U.S. unilateral intervention in sub-Saharan Africa and Latin America, and would limit severely a U.S. conventional response in the Middle East.[99] By taking the pre-Vietnam FY 1964 defense budget, adjusting it to FY 1969 prices and then applying his proposed reductions, Kaysen arrived at a total obligational authority for some future year "197x" of approximately $50 billion, equating to a $12.6 billion reduction of the 1964 budget cost in 1969 dollars.[100]

In attempting to forecast and allocate the "fiscal dividend" derived from ending the war in Southeast Asia, Charles L. Schultze was less optimistic regarding such an abrupt reduction in the defense budget. Assuming a reduction in defense spending in FY 1971 of some $21 billion, Schultze, nevertheless, projected a Total Obligational Authority (TOA) of $70 billion. He further warned that unless a "very vigorous screening of currently approved and proposed weapons systems developments" was combined with a reduction of U.S. commitments abroad and attendant general purpose force reductions, the action-reaction dynamic of the arms race would result in defense budgets "well beyond that level in subsequent years."[101]

For another group of analysts attempting to match force posture with strategy, the Nixon administration needed to adopt as an aim the general purpose force levels that existed under the Eisenhower administration--a total of 14 Army and Marine divisions with accompanying air support. These forces, they projected,[102]

> . . . would entail no significant reduction in the American capability to meet a major European contingency and would leave a small force for dealing with a minor contingency. If actually established, such force levels would cost approximately $30 billion per year less than the present general purpose forces, $17 billion annually less than those advocated within the military establishment for a baseline posture and $10 billion less than those projected as a result of President Nixon's decision to prepare for one major and one minor contingency.

Attracted by these projected savings, the Nixon administration initiated significant reductions in U.S. ground forces. First proposals called for a total reduction of three active divisions, and Secretary Laird noted that future redeployments from Southeast Asia "would probably result in greater troop reductions."[103]

Aiding these additional force reductions was the concept of "total force planning" which called for the use of all conventional forces--regular, Reserve and allied--to meet possible major or minor contingencies. To assist in the force planning for a range of contingencies, a new lexicon of force planning categories was created "to provide a more definitive explanation . . . on how the total force concept will be applied to specific regional situations:"[104]

Combined force planning will allow the integration of U.S. forces with local forces (NATO and Korean).

Complementary force planning anticipated a U.S. military obligation, but no predeployed U.S. force (i.e., Thailand). In this case the U.S. would provide specialized support or assistance designed to augment the local forces.

Supplementary force planning called for the U.S. to supplement local forces through the provision of security assistance (Iran in the mid-seventies).

Unilateral force planning outlined U.S. requirements for responding to contingencies where U.S. interests were at stake but in situations where the U.S. would not expect active support from other states.

Further, under this concept of total force planning, National Guard and Reserve forces were to play a key role. "Reserve components will be the initial and primary source of augmentation of the active forces during a contingency. The increased reliance on the Reserves requires much higher readiness than they have had in the past."[105]

This combination of total force planning,"Vietnamization" and the Nixon Doctrine resulted in a force of 13-2/3 Army divisions, plus three Marine divisions by the end of 1972. The rationale for the reductions included the allies' capability for "realistic deterrence," the capacity of local forces to deter or defend against a small conventional threat and the growing cost of U.S. forces, given the end of the draft and the increasing expense of an all-volunteer force.

The total force for a "1-1/2 war" strategy under the Nixon Doctrine at the end of the major U.S. involvement in Vietnam was described in the following manner:[106]

About one third of our general purpose forces are necessarily deployed abroad to provide a capability for responding rapidly to threats to American and allied interests. . . . The forces remaining in the United States serve as a ready reserve for reinforcing our forward deployments and for protecting our interests in other parts of the world.

Our NATO force in Europe consists of 4-1/3 divisions . . . .

United States forces in Asia consist of those still supporting operations in Indochina and normal forward deployments not directly related to Vietnam needs. The basic forces include one Army division stationed in Korea and 2/3 of a Marine division located in Okinawa.

What was the impact of budgetary or public opinion constraints on the process of planning for a lesser contingency?

At first glance, a comparison of the allocation of forces to the lesser contingency under the "1-1/2 war" strategy does not appear markedly different from that portrayed for the "2-1/2 war" strategy (See Table 2.3 on page 51). Although the total forces had been reduced, the strategic reserves and the projection forces dedicated to rapid deployment appear to remain intact. But as often is the case, this static comparison of the forces does not provide a complete accounting of the capability of the forces, nor do the forces procured in support of the strategy completely explain the rationale behind that force posture. This qualitative shortfall of conventional forces capable of rapid deployment to a lesser contingency during this period can be more completely explained in terms of budgetary and public opinion constraints.

The force posture in support of this revised strategic concept resulted from imposed external constraints of manpower, money and the public opposition to the Vietnam war. In the first case, the adjustment to a "1-1/2 war" capability could be seen merely as a reaction to the realities of matching strategy to forces available and as an acquiescence to manpower constraints rather than as a conceptual breakthrough. As Secretary McNamara knew, a major contingency required a Reserve call-up. With the President's reluctance to take this action, it appeared that one of the (simultaneous) major contingencies would have to be eliminated from the strategic concept.

This debate regarding the capability and utility of the Reserve forces in a lesser contingency was not new. Prior to the Vietnam deployments, the Joint Chiefs had differed sharply with the Secretary of Defense on whether the force in being represented a "2-1/2 war" capability because they disputed the ability of the Reserve units to be deployed rapidly. General Earle Wheeler testified: "You can't put Reserve forces into combat in ninety days as was planned. They aren't ready. You need four months to call them, train, equip and ship them to a combat zone."[107]

After Vietnam, the political reluctance to call up the Reserves seemed to have made permanent the break between the use of the Reserves and a limited contingency. Maxwell Taylor had concluded by 1970 that the single most important lesson of the Vietnam war was that "limited war in the present climate is not a realistic option of U.S. foreign policy." The only option left to the President was a "declared war of clearly defined objectives, rapidly conducted without conscripts or Reservists."[108]

If the Reserves were excluded from fighting in a limited contingency, then the forces to meet such a conflict would have to be drawn from the strategic reserve of conventional forces stationed in the United States. But the readiness of these forces during the Vietnam drawdown was less than adequate to meet the demands of rapid deployment. General Wheeler's testimony as to the effect of U.S. rotation policies on the effectiveness of CONUS forces is illuminating:[109]

> We drew down very heavily on the strategic reserve forces here in the U.S. In effect, the divisions here were replacement units for the divisions in Vietnam. They were not 'ready' divisions. In effect, we directed most of the resources of the Army and the Air Force to fighting the war in Vietnam.

In substantiation of this thesis, a report issued by Senate Preparedness Investigating Sub-committee dealing with Army and Marine units assigned to the strategic reserve in 1969 concluded that manpower constraints and rotation policies had resulted in "shortages of qualified officers, noncommissioned officers and enlisted men" that generally hampered the "ability to attain reasonable combat effectiveness."[110] In most cases it was judged that the units would require further advanced training after overcoming personnel and equipment shortages in the event of a subsequent contingency requiring deployment.

A second major theme in the explanation of the revision of the strategic concept was the need to reduce the defense budget. This strategic reappraisal, conducted with the goal of reducing defense spending, made no attempt to break away from the concept of matching forces to anticipated contingencies, such as reverting to an Eisenhower-like "cap" on the defense budget or assigning a certain percent of the budget or of the GNP to defense. The way to reduce defense expenditures, it was posited, was to reduce U.S. defense commitments abroad.

Thus, in responding to limits imposed on U.S. defense spending as reflected through public opinion and the Congress, the Nixon Doctrine altered the perception of the threat, emphasized the technologically-intensive air and sea arms over the manpower-intensive ground forces and, in the process, adopted many of the anti-intervention critiques of American foreign and defense policy. Although the United States still intended to meet its commitments, the assumption was that this objective could be met through a diminished military presence abroad and attendant lower defense spending.

In the third case the U.S. had to extricate itself from the quagmire of Vietnam. Even if the Nixon administration had wanted to demonstrate an "exuberant confidence" in the capability of the U.S. to intervene in lesser, third-world contingencies, public opinion acted to prevent such a stance. Reducing the American presence in Vietnam would lessen U.S. defense spending while simultaneously lowering the profile of a war rapidly rising in unpopularity. There was no room in the U.S. strategic concept for a second simultaneous major contingency. Vietnam, through the process of Vietnamization and in response to manpower and budgetary constraints, became compressed into an image of a lesser contingency--at least as visualized through the lens of a "1-1/2 war" strategy.

Despite this strategic readjustment to external constraints, there was still a need for CONUS-based divisions flexible enough to respond to an unanticipated contingency. Those who advocated a minimum general purpose force structure argued also for an "increasing mobility" of conventional forces to make "the same units available for a wide range of secondary contingencies." This approach to a rapid deployment capability remained economically attractive; for given the desirable assumptions of mobility and flexibility of the strategic reserve, it was assumed that "the requirements for these contingencies are not additive."[111]

Secretary Laird confessed in his 1972 Posture Statement that such a capability was not at hand, owing to the fact that the U.S. faced serious strategic mobility problems in executing this rapid deployment concept required in the early stages of a contingency. However, he favored such a concept for its ability to provide an element of conventional deterrence at a relatively inexpensive price even as he expressed displeasure with the concept of force planning for a "half war":[112]

I don't like those terms (2-1/2 war or 1-1/2 war). What I think is important is to develop that kind of strategy which is necessary to deter war and to prevent war. I don't believe that our strategy should be based, as Secretary McNamara and President Kennedy had

> used those terms, on the basis of fighting wars. I think we should base our strategy on the best kind of capability that will prevent war . . . .

Given this line of reasoning, it is conceivable that, barring external events that perturbed the steady decline of conventional forces under the Nixon administration, the "1-1/2 war" strategy might have devolved into some more general terminology to describe the construction of general purpose forces with a deterrence rather than a war-fighting mission. However, two events in the Middle East--the Jordan crisis in 1970 and the October war in 1973--served to document the poor state of U.S. general purpose forces in terms of a rapid deployment capability.

In assessing its military options in the Jordanian crisis that threatened to involve Syria, Iraq, Israel and, perhaps, the superpowers, the Nixon administration, like Kennedy's administration in Laos, found its conventional force choices severely constrained:[113]

> An analysis of our capabilities indicated that we had only four brigades capable of reaching Jordan quickly, and such an operation would enlist our entire strategic reserve. It would take . . . 72 hours to commit the 82nd Airborne Division from the United States.

The 82nd Airborne apparently was the only unit capable of rapid deployment to Jordan, but the division was so understrength that only two of the three brigades could have been deployed in combat-ready status. The situation resulted in a high-level Army investigation into the status of the division, and a subsequent increase in its manpower and materiel priority.[114] Congressional inquiries attendant to the inability of the U.S. to respond effectively added further urgency to the matter and appeared to be an important factor in arresting the continuing decline of the number of active divisions in the strategic reserve, if not in turning around the defense budget.

The reforms were not widespread. Two years later the 82nd remained the only combat-ready unit in the strategic reserves. In testimony before the Senate Defense Appropriations Subcommittee, Army Chief of Staff Westmoreland told of his concern regarding the "inadequate level of readiness" of forces stationed within the United States. "Today I must tell you that this condition continues, caused primarily by a shortage of trained personnel and the severe reduction in strength we are undergoing this year."[115] Westmoreland testified that, as of March 1972, the Army had only one of its seven divisions assigned to the strategic reserve ready for immediate use in the event of an emergency.[116]

The inability of the United States to respond with conventional forces to this type of emergency was brought home during the brief Soviet-U.S. confrontation in the Middle East during the October War in 1973. In this instance, and for reasons still not totally clear, the United States raised the military bidding above the conventional table stakes in a nuclear bluff.[117] Although provocation was present in the form of a "brutal" Soviet note threatening unilateral intervention, the U.S. response appeared as an overreaction in its inclusion of the alerting of strategic nuclear forces in a situation which apparently required only the application of conventional force--if it had been available.

As a result of these two crises, questions regarding the sizing of U.S. general purpose forces began to surface again, and the constraints of public opinion and defense spending appeared to relax somewhat. A broad reassessment of the Nixon Doctrine was occurring as well. The Doctrine had argued that U.S. commitments should determine the force posture, but under these constraints the forces had been reduced while the political pledges--most pointedly in Jordan and Israel--remained intact.[118] Without a strong strategic reserve and some method of rapidly augmenting allied forces in a crisis, it appeared that the United States had surrendered the military component of this deterrence doctrine.

Warning that deterrence of war "does not simply derive from a pile of nuclear weapons," Secretary of Defense Schlesinger called in October 1974 for an increase in the strength of the Army from 13 to 16 divisions.[119] Schlesinger claimed that at its current level "the Army is hard pressed to fulfill even the nominal requirements" of the post-Vietnam "1-1/2 war" strategy. The Defense Secretary also spelled out a new conventional force posture in support of this strategy:[120]

> When the present administration changed the strategic concept and set an objective of 13 Army divisions, it did so on the assumption that the National Guard and Reserves would be rapidly deployable and effective. We have now concluded that such key reliance on guard and Reserve forces for initial defense missions would be imprudent.

This increase in force structure was further dictated by the balance of force ratios in the current strategic concept, the maintenance of two major strong points in conjunction with our allies and the need to provide for a "highly combat-ready force for initial defense."[121]

By 1976, the last of the Nixon-Ford years, the strategic concept as the basis for planning general purpose forces had been turned upside-down, and the lesser contingency was restored again to a matter of high priority. In 1977, Secretary of Defense Rumsfeld referred to the primary contingencies that generated the conventional forces as the standard scenarios in NATO and Korea, plus[122]

> ... what has in the past been described as the lesser contingency, such as might arise in the Caribbean or the Middle East, and initially involve U.S., but not Soviet forces. ... Because the variety of non-nuclear contingencies is so great, it is particularly important to test our posture in a number of 'off-design' cases. A conflict in the Persian Gulf is an example of a case which could make demands on the U.S. posture not brought out by any of the base cases.

Despite the somewhat circular logic that characterized the general purpose force planning of the Nixon-Ford years, a number of assumptions had been put to rest, while other force planning factors had been raised. The "1-1/2 war" policy appeared to have replaced the "2-1/2 war," although forces dedicated to the lesser contingency were uncertain, at best. The Reserves appeared, once again, to be solely dedicated to respond to a major contingency, while the requirement to improve the flexibility and mobility of the strategic reserves was again being overemphasized, if underfunded. The dominant contingencies remained in Europe and Northeast Asia, but consideration was being given to other areas of U.S. interest that posed different and difficult force planning conditions.

Whether or not the adjustment in the U.S. strategic concept from "2-1/2 wars" to "1-1/2" was more apparent than real, it was clear that a change in the manner in which the "half war" was envisioned would have a significant impact on force planning for a limited contingency. Post-Vietnam, the Nixon Doctrine rejected the Kennedy administration's image of the "half war" as a non-Soviet "brushfire" and posited that local forces would now assume any U.S. ground force's role in a lesser contingency. The lesser contingency as seen under the Nixon Doctrine, therefore, appeared to emphasize the Soviet-proxy "field of fire" model to ensure U.S. involvement, at the expense (or actually with the savings) of planning for lesser scenarios and with the Middle East evidently assuming increasing importance. Similarly, the far end of the spectrum of conflict of the "half war" was ignored. In a period of detente, US-USSR conflict beyond the borders of Europe was unthinkable.

However, there were signs also that this strategic concept was unlikely to remain constant through the next four years.[123] The Soviets in 1973 hinted at a conventional capability that could reach beyond the confines of Eastern Europe to the Middle East. The aftermath of those events focused global attention on a new arc of crisis and the political power and potential of oil and its control. In that regard, Secretary Rumfeld's remark regarding the problems posed by a Persian Gulf contingency would prove prescient. However, it would be some time before the new administration, in an iterative process of reappraisal, retrenchment and rededication and, in response to its own perceptions of budgetary and public opinion constraints, would perceive that this new Soviet threat in a vital region demanded a restructuring of U.S. forces to meet a limited contingency.

Planning Forces for "1-1/2 Wars," 1977-1979

U.S. presidents do not assume office and then quickly renounce the foreign and defense policies of their predecessors. On the contrary, there is a marked strain of policy consistency and an honoring of past commitments that runs consecutively through the post-war administrations. Thus, although the strategy shifted, U.S. alliances, military treaties and foreign obligations through previous executive agreement have remained notably intact and have served as a justification for the planning of general purpose forces since 1945.[124]

Despite this continuity in policy content and commitment, there is a considerable discontinuity in policy process and style. Michael Nacht has noted a major constraint on the policy process which he has termed the "clean slate phenomenon."[125] Each newly-elected administration "seeks to make its mark by evaluating the major policies and programs it has inherited, by dismantling . . . ineffective practices and by introducing as many distinctively new initiatives as the system will tolerate." So it was with the Carter administration. Before the commitments and concepts of the outgoing President could be claimed as his own, Jimmy Carter first directed a reexamination of U.S. strategy and force posture.

TABLE 2.3
The Allocation And Deployment Of Major General Purpose Forces Under The "1-1/2 War" Strategic Concept, 1973

CONTINGENCIES

1 War and	1 War +	1/2 War
Warsaw Pact attack in Europe	Chinese conventional attack in Asia	Lesser contingency elsewhere, possibly the Middle East
Allied support	Limited allied support	Allied support questionable
Vital to U.S.	Vital to U.S.	Not Vital to U.S.

FORCES
(Army and Marine Divisions)

CONUS	4-2/3	2-1/3	--
DEPLOYED	4-1/3	1-2/3	--
STRATEGIC RESERVE	--	--	3
RESERVE	8	--	1

STRATEGIC CONCEPT

Nuclear capability of U.S. strategic/theater forces serves as a deterrent to full-scale Soviet attack in Asia

Prospects for a coordinated 2-front attack on U.S. allies are low because of the risks of nuclear war and the improbability of Sino-Soviet cooperation

Reserves may not have to mobilize

Non-Chinese threat in Asia, Middle East or Latin America, force planning dependent on allied contribution

In case of subversion, guerilla war, wars of national liberation, U.S. will not be involved, will preempt through economic development, social reform

Sources: Kissinger, White House Years, p. 220 ff.
Gelb and Kuzmack, op. cit., p. 208.

What was the perception of the threat? How did this threat perception affect the formation of the strategic concept?

Nacht might also have noted that many of the changes from old to new administrations are those of style rather than substance. Thus, Carter changed the name of the former NSSM/NSDM system to that of a series of Presidential Directives (PD). On February 18, the President signed a Review Memorandum (PRM-10, Military Strategy and Force Posture Review), thereby directing a reassessment of the U.S. strategic concept.

The original terms of reference of this study called for a "thorough investigation of alternative national strategies for the United States."[126] This broad charter raised old questions of departmental claims to national security turf: the State Department feared an invasion of its diplomatic domain, while the Defense Department was concerned with the impact of an externally-developed "national strategy" on its internally-developed force posture. Thus, a bureaucratic battle of policy participants ensued.

The result, predictably, was a compromise. The study was divided into two parts. A "net assessment," which was to include possible national strategies in a general sense, particularly with regard to the Soviet threat, was managed under a Specal Coordination Committee and chaired by Presidential Security Assistant Zbigniew Brzezinski. A "force posture statement," dealing with the specifics of the military balance and alternative military strategies, was managed by a Policy Review Committee under the Assistant Secretary of Defense for International Security Affairs (ISA) and chaired by Secretary of Defense Harold Brown.[127]

The two sections of the memorandum, being the product of different joint authors, quite naturally constructed different models of the threat existing within the structure of the contemporary international political system. These varying perspectives added to the confusion surrounding PRM-10 and resulted in conflicting interpretations of it. The author of the first draft of the "net assessment" portion of the document was reported to be Harvard professor Samuel Huntington. His original work expressed pessimism regarding the ability of the United States to defend against a Soviet attack in Western Europe. This view--particularly the alleged charge that the U.S. would be forced to abandon the NATO doctrine of "forward defense" as well as a significant amount of territory within the Federal Republic of Germany (attributed to co-author Lynn Davis)--met with predictable opposition within the policy process and was subsequently modified. Nevertheless, in treating the US-USSR relationship as the "overriding issue of American diplomacy and strategy," the "net assessment" draft made few concessions to the visions of an international order based on detente evoked by the President in his recent campaign speeches.[128] Perhaps more important for this study, the document's focus on the Soviet threat in central Europe continued to ignore the need to plan general purpose forces for a range of lesser contingencies that might occur simultaneously.

The official version of the document was not released to the public, but its central themes can be surmised by referring to Huntington's published work. Although President Carter had assumed office claiming that the cold war had ended, Professor Huntington, writing in Foreign Policy, offered a differing interpretation of international events. According to Huntington, Soviet-American relations had entered a new phase--"Era II"--of the cold war that would be characterized by a complex relationship of both competition and cooperation and an "incongruence of power resources." This asymmetry in national power was particularly acute in the area of military capabilities. Although Huntington's first, hard-line contentions of Soviet military superiority in central Europe were eventually softened to describe a rough equivalence, it was evident that he saw a weakened U.S. military as the least effective instrument of U.S. foreign policy. Because of this relative weakness vis-a-vis the USSR, the U.S. should take advantage of its economic strength and technological superiority "in resolving regional conflicts, reducing tensions and achieving adequately verifiable arms control agreements."[129]

While the "net assessment" portion of PRM-10 was obviously not ignored, the majority of the implementing actors within national security sectors of the government saw the "force posture" part of the study as more significant. Certainly it would prove to have the most direct and immediate impact in terms of budgetary allocation, regardless of the ultimately approved image of the US/USSR relationship. The force posture statement in PRM-10 was also an ambitious undertaking. Its purpose was to define a wide range of alternative military strategies and construct appropriate military force postures and programs in support of these strategies. In keeping with the olympic-like competition in comprehensive military reappraisals, waged in this country when the presidential election results in a party change as well, this policy review claimed to be the "most important review of U.S. national security policy since NSC-68."[130]

Within the "force posture" section of PRM-10, interagency task forces studied five broad areas:[131]

- a possible conflict in central Europe against the Warsaw Pact,

- an East-West war outside Europe,

- possible conflicts in East Asia,

- national wars of liberation on the Vietnam scale and

- central strategic (nuclear) war with the Soviet Union.

Assessments of the military needs to meet contingencies, derived from these broad categories, reportedly led to over 200 "strategic packages" that could dictate required force levels. These options were then narrowed to a few strategic concepts to simplify presidential choice.

Presidential Directive 18 (PD-18) was signed in response to PRM-10 on August 24, 1977. This directive established a national strategic concept and provided initial guidance for military programs and policies. As reported by the press, the directive contained five major elements:[132] 1) A greater emphasis on the non-military aspects of American foreign policy (the Huntington 'Era II' thesis); 2) a stress on the use of conventional arms in an age of nuclear parity; 3) an emphasis on NATO and Europe (in Huntington's words, "this is a Europe-oriented administration"); 4) an emphasis on mobility (including the ability to deploy forces to the Third World); and 5) a stress on the importance of the Middle East and the Persian Gulf (but primarily as they related to NATO interests).

From the viewpoint of this study, the Presidential Directive is particularly notable for the added weight given to the power and influence of conventional military force as well as for its emphasis on the major contingency in Europe rather than on a lesser contingency elsewhere.[133] The Directive called for American forces in Europe to achieve an enhanced ability to respond to a conventional attack. Another instruction called for the construction of a so-called "light" divisions to be readied for possible use in the Middle East, the Persian Gulf or East Asia. These forces should be capable of operating without requiring fixed bases, such as the Army's XVIII Airborne Corps, and would be supported by selected naval and tactical air units.

This European and Middle East focus was spelled out in greater detail in the Consolidated Guidance issued by Defense Secretary Brown to the Joint Chiefs in early 1978. According to this strategic concept, U.S. armed forces were to prepare to counter a Soviet "blitzkrieg" in central Europe while simultaneously coping with a non-Soviet "brushfire" in the Persian Gulf. The Secretary's guidance included the following:[135]

> Our near term objective is to assure that NATO could not be overwhelmed in the first few weeks of a blitzkrieg war, and we will invest and spend our resources preferentially to that end.
>
> When that assurance is reasonably in hand, we will turn our attention to what additional capability, if any, NATO might need
>
> . . . .
> Events in the Persian Gulf could soften the glue that binds the alliance as surely as could an imbalance of military force across the inter-German border. But we are as yet unsure of the utility of U.S. military power in the Persian Gulf contingencies.

This Consolidated Guidance implied that the strategic concept of "1-1/2 wars" in the Carter administration had undergone a transformation in both the anticipated geographic location of the lesser conflict and its sequence and relationship to the major contingency in Europe. Secretary Brown was directing the services to prepare to fight one and one half wars in which the whole was the Warsaw Pact invasion and the half could be a flare-up in the Persian Gulf that might precede the war in Central Europe.

This somewhat revised "1-1/2 war" strategic concept, as formulated by the Carter administration, was further clarified by Secretary Brown in his FY 1980 Posture Statement:[136]

> It has become difficult to imagine another separate large war with another major power breaking out, simultaneously with one in Europe, that would require a large U.S. intervention. A simultaneous lesser contingency, on the other hand, not only seems plausible, it could also be the triggering event for a much larger conflict.

The administration's strategic concept was further delineated in Secretary Brown's response to Senator McClellan's question: "Does the new administration intend to retain 1-1/2 wars as policy guidance?"[137]

> Yes. It is unlikely that we would increase the force planning criteria beyond 1-1/2 wars. It is possible to consider expanding the one war concept to include more specific consideration of forces

required for a world-wide war. . . . The development of such a concept would require the U.S. to consider more explicitly its goals and objectives around the world.

How were forces designed and deployed in support of the strategic concept? What priority was allocated to forces planned to meet a lesser contingency?

Although the Carter administration intended to continue the strategic concept of its predecessors, the strategy and force posture for the lesser contingency appeared to be undergoing some modification. However, the frequent and ambivalent references to the Soviet-proxy model of the lesser contingency in Northeast Asia or a "brushfire" war in the Caribbean made it apparent that the Carter administration had not decided which of the conflicts within a range of "half war" scenarios the U.S. should plan its forces to deter or fight. By 1977, however, the Persian Gulf and the Eastern Mediterranean were frequently noted in official statements as "particularly volatile areas that could well be the scene of possible 'half war' contingencies."[138]

In focusing on a specific locale for the "half war," Secretary Brown was adding credence to the Rumsfeld scenario of a lesser contingency in Southwest Asia for which U.S. general purpose forces were unprepared. In explaining that an attack on Western Europe by the Warsaw Pact remained "the most plausible major contingency" and, therefore, was the prime drive for U.S. conventional force levels, he also noted:[139]

> The basis for determining whether we also have the capability for a simultaneous lesser contingency is less easy to identify. A conflict in Korea ... should not impose a requirement for U.S. ground forces on anything like the scale needed in a European war. A conflict in the area of the Persian Gulf, on the other hand, and occurring either prior to or simultaneously with a war in Europe, would obviously subject our posture to a most rigorous test.

This admission implied that under the defense policies of the Carter administration, the "off-design" case in that Persian Gulf was being recognized as a limited contingency capable of generating its own dedicated forces. The fact that a conflict in the Persian Gulf could be linked to a NATO scenario seemed to require forces capable for dealing with each contingency separately.[140] Further, the notion that the minor contingency could occur almost concurrently with the major conflict, coupled with the assumption that it would prove difficult to shift forces between the theaters, appeared to argue for the construction of additive and separate limited contingency forces in the Persian Gulf. But prior to 1979, the threat in Southwest Asia was still regarded officially as non-Soviet at the highest levels in the administration. This limited contingency, as defined, would "initially involve U.S., but not Soviet forces."[141] Given this formulation of the threat--as a "brushfire" or "field of fire" model--the case of a Soviet-intensive contingency in the Persian Gulf and force planning in its behalf were neglected for all practical purposes until 1979.

Therefore, this geo-strategic modification of the lesser contingency under the Carter administration did not significantly affect general purpose force levels. Most of the programs proposed under President Ford to expand U.S. ground forces were accepted.[142]   These force level adjustments, in keeping with the present interpretation of the strategic concept, were aimed primarily at increasing U.S. capabilities in Central Europe. Increases in U.S. troop strength authorized in 1974-1975 resulted in a 9,500-man rise in U.S. forces stationed in Western Europe, increasing to six the number of U.S. division equivalents deployed to NATO.[143] Additional force posture improvements were evidenced by an increase in the prepositioning of division sets of supplies in Germany. Reserve forces continued to remain at the same strength, with selected Reserve component units now designated to round out and augment active Army divisions upon mobilization.

With the strategic reserves in the United States increasingly allocated or earmarked to the major contingency in Europe, lesser contingency forces were narrowed to the projection forces--those "configured primarily to respond rapidly to Presidential Directives for long-distance entry into enemy territory against armed opposition."[144] These forces included the two divisions of the U.S. Army XVIII Corps, the 82nd Airborne and the 101st Airmobile stationed in the CONUS, plus the three Marine divisions (one division was deployed to the Pacific) as well as the naval and tactical air forces not already committed to rapidly reinforce NATO.

But these projection forces, planned and sized to project U.S. power in a show of force, were not sized or designed to carry the complete burden in a limited contingency. For the most part, they were "light" forces without a sustainable combat capability over the long term.[145] The 101st, for example, was not really designed for forcible long-range insertion into enemy territory, but rather to follow up an intervention force, operating its helicopters from secure bases at short range.[146] Thus, despite a strategic concept that appeared to recognize the presence of a range of scenarios within the "half war" planning contingency, force planning remained restricted to the need for the rapid deployment of a "brushfire" force, while the Soviet-proxy or Soviet intensive models were generally ignored.

However, the strategic shift of the limited contingency to the Eastern Mediterranean or the Persian Gulf demanded light forces that could be deployed rapidly. The strategic reserves in the United States were dedicated to NATO, too heavy for rapid deployment and without adequate air or sealift. Unlike the contingency envisioned in Northeast Asia, there were no active U.S. forces deployed in Southwest Asia. Therefore, forces that could operate without secure bases or with only limited external support were required.

Thus, by 1979, a strategy-force mismatch was evolving in the Persian Gulf region. Forces designed for rapid deployment appeared inadequate for a sustained combat in the distant region against a sophisticated adversary, while forces capable of such a military mission were dedicated to the major contingency and essentially immobile. The Persian Gulf began to look increasingly like a plausible lesser contingency without a coherent limited contingency force.

What was the impact of budgetary or public opinion constraints on the process of force planning for a lesser contingency?

It is clear that both budgetary and public opinion constraints played a major role in limiting the defense policies of the Carter administration, particularly in these early years. In their FY 1977 issue of "Arms, Men and Military Budgets,"[147] the National Strategy Information Center advocated increasing the general purpose forces growth rate to ten percent per annum for a five year period. This program, among others advocated within the study, was based on the belief that the current and projected U.S. defense posture and budget was inadequate to meet the threat posed to it by the military power of the Soviet Union.

In contrast to these advocates of increased defense spending, the "Setting National Priorities" series issued by the Brookings Institution offered a different estimate of the situation, especially in their assessment of the Soviet threat.[148] Although the authors of this study were also concerned with the real increase in Soviet defense spending, they noted "that not all aspects of the Soviet military build-up threaten significant U.S. interests." Although U.S. defense spending would have to be increased to improve capabilities in Europe and the Middle East, proposed force reductions in Northeast Asia could lessen that additional burden.

The Carter administration appeared to lean towards the Brookings' interpretation, particularly with regard to the themes of a concentration on Europe and a withdrawal from Asia. However, these policies, too, were continuations of established trends rather than new innovations. As the United States began to withdraw its forces from Southeast Asia in the late 1960s, also in response to budgetary and public opinion limits, the Department of Defense had attempted to remedy the deterioration of U.S. forces both in the continental strategic reserves and in Europe caused by the diversion of men and material to Vietnam.

In a slightly different twist on a old theme, President Carter embarked on a carefully and politically-hedged gradual withdrawal of U.S. forces from South Korea, a view considerably softened from his pre-election promise to remove all forces in a more rapid manner.[149] This planned retreat from Asia was seen as a Carter extension of the Nixon Doctrine--reducing U.S. ground forces while continuing to provide aid, naval and tactical air support. Thus, the tendency to substitute technology for manpower, to continue to respond to the public mood of reducing U.S. military presence abroad and to hedge on significant increases in defense spending remained important aspects of U.S. defense policy in 1977--especially with regard to planning general purpose forces for limited contingencies.[150]

This accent on the major contingency in Europe and the proposed withdrawal from Korea led to a perceived departure from the strategic concept fashioned during the Nixon-Ford years and began to stir some public criticism. Although the defense policies constructed under the Nixon Doctrine had been concerned with Europe, they had not allocated such a singular dedication to the short war scenario on the central front. The policies prevailing until 1976 had envisioned the conduct of a longer European war, including U.S. operations on the northern and southern flanks of NATO.[151]

This implied and apparent reduction from the "1-1/2 war" strategic concept resulted in a significant American defense policy debate in early 1978. The major issue was whether the new emphasis on strengthening Western defense in Europe would be at the expense of a capacity to respond to lesser contingencies in other regions. The administration refuted such charges. Secretary Brown in a February speech declared "that the United States was enlarging its military capabilities in Europe, but not at the expense of U.S. strength elsewhere." President Carter in a major foreign policy address at Wake Forest University denied that the U.S. was retreating from its global interests and allies and asserted that the United States stood ready "to counter any threats to our allies and our vital interests in Asia, the Middle East and other regions of the world."[152]

Notwithstanding the administration's denials, the charges of a neglect of the concept and the forces for a lesser contingency continued to mount. One group of analysts saw particular danger in that the U.S. build-up in Europe suggested a loss of interest in maintaining the balance of power in Northeast Asia and the Pacific. Many old Asian hands and "Asia-firsters" argued that the proposed U.S. withdrawal from Korea disturbed a precarious political and military equilibrium.[153] Concerns were voiced from the military side as well, the most vocal of those belonging to the soon-to-be-relieved Army Major General in Korea, John K. Singlaub.

A second criticism saw the European emphasis as ignoring the new set of security problems brought on by a growing U.S. and allied dependence on Persian Gulf oil. Although these strategists were somewhat mollified by the priority apparently granted the region within the strategic concept, it was their contention that minor conflicts in the Persian Gulf and southern Africa posed a much more likely threat in the next decade than a major war in Europe and, therefore, should be accorded the force planning priority due that probability.[154]

The armed service particularly aggrieved was the Navy, whose members and outside supporters saw the revised strategic concept as favoring ground over naval forces. Analysts sharing these views contended that the focus on the central region amounted to a "continental" strategy that ignored the threat on the flanks. In testimony before the Senate Budget Committee in February 1978, Eugene V. Rostow said that he viewed the risks of a Soviet "envelopment" strategy on the flanks of NATO as greater than an attack on West Germany.[155] In analyzing the early defense policies of the Carter administration, Lawrence J. Korb argued that NATO had been emphasized at the expense of weakening U.S. capability at the flanks, decreasing the capability and flexibility of forces to be used outside Europe and failing to maximize U.S. power projection advantages over the USSR.[156]

Finally, the concentration on Europe appeared to be eroding the analytical concept of the "half war" as well as the forces to support it. At a National Defense University conference in July 1977, Geoffrey Kemp and Harlan Ullman pointed out that the "half war" still retained value both as a method of sizing forces for a lesser contingency and as an analytical concept that linked together a "series of related policy issues including unanticipated crises which may require a military response." The authors feared that the lesser contingency as an element in the force planning process was eroding for a number of reasons: the emphasis on NATO Europe, the Vietnam experience and the increasing cost of weapons and manpower. Unfortunately, they concluded, it appeared that the perceived importance of the "half war" contingency was declining precisely at the moment when its implications were of growing importance--specifically, the need for a limited contingency force to counter-intervene in the Persian Gulf or elsewhere.[157]

Adding a final note of criticism to the European-oriented doctrine was the revelation of the so-called "swing strategy"--a plan to shift forces from Asia and the Pacific to Western Europe in the event of a Warsaw

Pact attack against NATO. The war plan, secret for years despite the fact that it accurately reflected stated U.S. interests and priorities since the Second World War, was questioned in a staff study prepared for the Secretary of Defense. This study of U.S. defense policy in Asia noted that the concept of swinging U.S. force from Asia to Europe "had a positive effect on NATO," but also warned that "public disclosure or official notification of our Asian allies of our interest to swing forces could further undermine the credibility of our commitments in Asia and become an issue in our defense relations with Japan."[158] The study went on to note that "in the eyes of some Asians, the American withdrawal from Vietnam and the decision to withdraw ground forces from South Korea has been viewed as the beginning of a general American withdrawal from the region." Therefore, the swing strategy, a de facto representation of the priority granted to Europe in time of a major contingency, could reinforce perceptions of a declining American security commitment to the Asian allies.[159]

In an attempt to soothe strained U.S.-Japanese relations, Secretary Brown, in Tokyo, emphasized that forces could be moved either way--into the Pacific (as evidenced by the U.S. deployments to Vietnam) or away from it. But there was little doubt, reading between the lines of his reassuring words, that U.S. defense efforts were currently focused elsewhere. The Secretary stressed that the "1-1/2 war" concept "does not say anything in the way of a total commitment as to how operations would take place in a given conflict." Moreover, Mr. Brown concluded that Japan, like Europe, depended for its supply of oil on the Persian Gulf states. "Therefore, deployments in case of a conflict to that region might be the best way of improving the security of Western Europe and Japan as well as the United States."[160]

During the first years of his administration, President Carter, basing his actions on his perception of the threat and in response to constraints imposed by public opinion, made the defense budget a key element in his approach to national security policy. Because the allocation of defense dollars in one important regard makes defense policy, critics complained that the accent on the major contingency in Europe and the low priority given non-NATO contingencies resulted in a "one war-plus" strategy from 1977 to 1979.[161] Whether or not this criticism was justified, the Carter administration had failed to delineate clearly among a range of conceivable "half war" scenarios and had, therefore, resisted having to plan general purpose forces in their support. In fact, it appeared that the administration had retreated successfully from each of the models of the limited contingency suggested in this study: an extension of the Nixon Doctrine that acted to limit any U.S. role in a "brushfire" war, a proposed U.S. troop withdrawal from Korea that suggested a reluctance to engage Soviet-proxy forces in Northeast Asia and an unwillingness to accept the likelihood of a direct Soviet challenge to U.S. interests in the Persian Gulf. However, international events in 1979 were to foment a change in the public mood, encourage a real increase in the defense budget and breathe life back into the flagging strategic concept of "1-1/2 wars." But these events would stress only one paradigm of the lesser contingency, at the expense of a continuing lack of preparation and force planning for the other, more likely, contingencies.

From "1-War-Plus" to "One and Two-Half Wars," 1979-1980

The international events that occurred from the fall of 1979 until the U.S. presidential election in 1980 have been widely regarded, as close as we are to them, as a major turning point in American foreign and defense policy. The attempt here is not to describe or explain these complex occurrences but to assess their impact on the U.S. strategic concept and, more precisely, on U.S. force planning for a lesser contingency.

What was the perception of the threat? How did this threat perception affect the formulation of the strategic concept?

In September 1979, the Carter administration revealed the existence of a Soviet "combat brigade" in Cuba. Despite statements by the President and the Secretary of State that this was "unacceptable," the Soviets refused to admit even the presence of the troops, let alone alter the status quo.[162] The creation of a U.S. Caribbean Task Force Headquarters in response to this Russian recalcitrance possessed a greater political significance than represented by that command's military might. This approach of adopting a military solution to the most recent Cuban problem suggested the possibility of a U.S.-Soviet-proxy confrontation away from the standard NATO scenario. This vision of an American-Russian conflict in the third world would soon be transferred to more strategic locales.

On November 4, 1979, the mercurial Iranian revolution boiled over when a group of militant students seized the American Embassy in Teheran, taking its U.S. diplomatic and military occupants hostage. The inability of the United States to respond militarily at that moment as well as the aborted rescue attempt in April of the following year added to the growing dissastisfaction, both in and outside the government, with U.S. conventional, rapid-response capability.[163]

In allegedly the most serious threat to identified American interests, the Soviet Union sent some 85,000 troops into Afghanistan beginning on December 29, 1979, in spite of warnings from President Carter that a Russian intervention would have a deleterious effect on U.S.-Soviet relations.[164] The exercising of this Soviet capability, their first post-war incursion into an area apart from their recognized sphere of interest in Eastern Europe, indicated to some a Soviet intention to continue their southward march to the oil fields of the Persian Gulf. Additionally, the Soviet thrust gave added credence to the arguments of those within the U.S. government warning of a lesser contingency characterized by a U.S.-Soviet confrontation separate from the major contingency in Europe.

The cumulative effect of this series of unpleasant events caused the President to revise his estimate of Soviet intentions, prompted the formulation of the "Carter Doctrine" in January 1980 and resulted eventually in the formation of the Rapid Deployment Joint Task Force. Although the Soviet invasion precipitated these actions, similar initiatives had been underway quietly since the administration had issued its first defense policy guidance.

PD-18, in August 1977, directed that ground forces with naval and air support be prepared for possible use in the Persian Gulf. In response to that directive, a Joint Chiefs of Staff strategy review was completed in the summer of 1978, implicitly recognizing the need and establishing the conceptual basis for the joint-service Rapid Deployment Force. This study also questioned the reliance on the "1-1/2 war" strategy that had obscured the reality that a "half war" could also become a counter-Soviet conflict of great intensity. Although this image of a limited war in the third world against a Soviet-supported adversary was also being advocated in the Program Analysis and Evaluation Branch of the Office of the Secretary of Defense, it had difficulty gaining attention--and, therefore, the impetus for action--at high decision-making levels.[165] Thus, there was a growing realization within the Department of Defense of certain Soviet-intensive scenarios imbedded within the "half war" planning contingency and that the United States could continue to ignore them only at its own peril.

If the Soviet threat was not yet considered an officially accepted model of the lesser contingency, events in Iran motivated key officials to presage the "Carter Doctrine" and suggest a concern with both Soviet capabilities and intentions. In February 1979, both the Secretary of Defense and the Secretary of Energy said that the U.S. would defend its vital interests in the Middle East and the Persian Gulf with military force if necessary. However, each hedged his statement. Secretary Brown declared that "we'll take any action that's appropriate," but noted that military force was not necessarily called for in every circumstance. "The only thing I would say is that less intrusive and less obvious forms of U.S. presence or possibly military influence, such as ship visits and so on, are clearly the right way to begin such activities, and I think that may be as far as we want to go."[166]

James Schlesinger, the Secretary of Energy, said the Carter administration was considering a plan to establish American military presence in the Persian Gulf region:[167]

> The United States has vital interests in the Persian Gulf. The United States must move in such a way that it protects those interests, even if that involves the use of military strength or of military presence.

However, although Mr. Schlesinger acknowledged that military presence would involve military personnel as well as military equipment, he said that sending ground combat troops to the region was "another question."

By April 1979, contingency plans for the rapid deployment of a joint service force to the Mideast were underway, motivated by the collapse of Iran's stabilizing military influence and increasing interest on the part of the U.S. armed services. The Navy was buoyed by the consideration of the formation of a new United States fleet, the fifth, rumored as being one of several options under study for the establishment of an American military presence in the region.[168] The Army also began to make plans. No longer content with limiting its planned deployment force to light projection forces, Army planners envisioned a heavy "unilateral corps" composed of units capable of meeting Middle East armies manned with heavy Soviet equipment. These forces, drawing on CONUS-based divisions not earmarked or committed to NATO, would form the reservoir for an organization that would be capable of rapid and worldwide deployment.[169]

In an elaboration of these early strategies as well as a description of some of the problems inherent in them, an insightful article published in the May 1979 <u>Fortune</u> sketched the forces that conceivably could be deployed and the spectrum of contingencies they might be required to face. Whatever the likelihood of each individual scenario's occurrence, ranging from a domestic coup in Saudi Arabia to a Soviet invasion of Iran, the dominant picture that emerged from the analysis was a lack of "high confidence" that the U.S. possessed the right forces in adequate numbers to meet the emerging threats to its vital interest. Although the projection forces to fight a lesser contingency had been designated, they could form a potent deterrent and fighting force only if they were kept in readiness and properly exercised--and could be assured success only if the threat remained non-Soviet.[170]

The vulnerabilities implied in this survey of meeting a lesser contingency in the Persian Gulf with forces allocated under the existing strategic concept were laid bare in an influential study published by the Congressional Reference Service only a month later.[171] This report cited high, possibly unacceptable, military risks coupled with severe political and economic consequences in the event of the operations' failure as arguments against plans for U.S. military intervention in the Persian Gulf. Moreover, there was a "distinct possibility" of Soviet intervention, raising the risk calculus even higher. Although the study was devoted primarily to the thesis that the oil fields were indefensible, it also raised a number of issues suggesting the quantitative and qualitative weaknesses of any intervening U.S. force as structured under the "1 war+" strategic concept:[172]

> Contingency planners who contemplate possible employment of U.S. forces in the Persian Gulf find a fairly small proportion of our active military forces presently unfettered. In a best case of facing opponents something less than second rate, between one-fourth and one-third of military forces would be available. But in the worst case of facing the Soviets in a limited contingency in the Gulf, availability would be from 0 to 22% because of the need to cover other dangers arising from a Soviet confrontation.

By mid-June of 1979, aware of the deteriorating situation in Iran and advised of the limitations on the use of military force in the Persian Gulf region, the President's Policy Review Committee met to consider the following options:[173]

- establishing a new military command for the Middle East, able to draw on earmarked units from other commands;
- forming a quick-response combat force, either a 100,000 man 'strike force' or a trimmed-down 'surge deployment';
- maintaining continuous upgraded naval presence in the Arabian Sea and Northeast Indian Ocean;
- expanding port facilities and barracks at Diego Garcia and
- considering more formal and regular joint military consultations and planning exercises in the region.

The rapidly unfolding events in the fall of 1979 elevated the options that advocated a military capability to deal with the increasing threat. In his 1980 State of the Union address, President Carter warned that "the implications of the invasion of Afghanistan could pose the most serious threat to world peace since the Second World War."[174] In this speech, the President went on to develop what has been referred to as the "Carter Doctrine"--a broad outline of future U.S. policy in the Persian Gulf region and the basis for a revised strategic concept under his administration:[175]

> Let our position be absolutely clear: Any attempt by an outside force to gain control of the Persian Gulf region will be regarded as an assault on the vital interests of the United States. It will be repelled by use of any means necessary, including military force.

With this Presidential declaration of policy, the administration appeared to recognize officially the possibility of a US-USSR confrontation in the Persian Gulf. Such an official recognition required the administration to reinvigorate the "1-1/2 war" strategic concept and begin force planning in earnest for the capability of rapid deployment to a Soviet-U.S. "firefight" model of the limited contingency in Southwest Asia.

How were forces designed and deployed in support of the strategic concept? What priority was allocated to forces planned to meet a lesser contingency?

In his presentation of the FY 1981 defense budget to Congress in January 1980, Defense Secretary Brown, somewhat uncharacteristically but very much in tune with the just-delivered State of the Union, questioned the capability of the U.S. to meet its military commitments in light of the growing Soviet threat. The Secretary reminded the Senate and House Armed Services Committees that the "1-1/2 war" strategy had provided the basic measure of the adequacy of U.S. general purpose forces since 1969. Although he was willing to admit that the U.S. lacked the capability to wage those conceptualized conflicts simultaneously, the constraints on Soviet power that had acted to limit Soviet adventurism during that period were no longer present:[176]

> ... But now times are changing. Without reducing the large forces stationed in Eastern Europe, the Soviets have tripled the size of their forces in the Far East, and they are developing naval and other capabilities that will permit them to operate beyond the periphery of the USSR. We no longer can preclude their being able to operate simultaneously in several parts of the world.

The Defense Secretary's remarks were significant in two respects. First, he recognized the ability of the USSR to act counter to U.S. vital interests in a non-NATO contingency, thereby underscoring the President's concern and giving a new priority to a lesser contingency. But in referring to the Soviet's ability to "operate simultaneously in several parts of the world" the Secretary was also suggesting that the Russian threat was not limited to Europe or to the Persian Gulf.

Elsewhere in the Posture Statement, Brown noted the threat of Soviet expansion could be coupled with the proliferation of uncontrolled "turbulence" in the third world:[177]

The number of unresolved international disputes increased and old ones continue to fester. Because such turbulence threatens vital American interests--especially oil--we must be prepared to use force in defense of these resources. In a world of disputes and violence, we cannot afford to go abroad unarmed.

It was evident that the administration was considering the use of the U.S. military against Soviet forces in a non-NATO scenario. What was less clear was the composition of this force and its geographic area of responsibility. Secretary Brown, speaking at the Commonwealth Club in San Francisco on July 30, 1979, said:[178]

Mobile and capable conventional forces are essential not only to support our allies in Europe, but also to execute contingency plans to assist friends outside the NATO area. . . . For this latter purpose we continue to maintain ready general purposes forces--we have called these "Rapid Deployment Forces"--distinct from those forces earmarked for or assigned to NATO. Naturally, as their name suggests, these forces are available for use wherever required, even in the NATO area.

The concerns addressed by the Secretary of Defense and the President in late 1979 and early 1980 resulted in the official establishment of the Rapid Deployment Joint Task Force (RDJTF) on March 1, 1980. This organization will be discussed more completely in the following chapter. The key factor to be emphasized here is that the RDJTF was not a separate category of fixed, sized forces. Rather, at inception, it was a command structure and planning group with vague drawing rights on a reservoir of combat units based in the United States. Thus, although new scenarios for the "half war" were now being recognized within that planning contingency, the initial force planning reaction was not to structure new and separate units to meet these additive contingencies, but rather to design a military headquarters which could direct existing forces in combatting the most serious threat that might arise within a range of options.

Without the addition of new units to meet a lesser contingency, the shift in the strategic concept in 1980 could be accused of being one of style rather than substance. But at least, and at last, a framework had been established under which forces for a lesser contingency could be justified, organized and supported. Moreover, although the RDJTF was charged with the Gulf as the first of its tasks, Secretary Brown's version of the Carter Doctrine implied that the U.S. would continue to be concerned with other limited contingencies as well.[179]

In support of this revised strategic concept that now appeared to be adding rather than subtracting conventional contingencies, Under Secretary of Defense Robert Komer informed NATO officials in April 1980 that the old "swing strategy" had also been revised. President Carter had agreed to a new strategic plan that no longer committed the U.S. to send Pacific-based forces to Europe in the event of a Soviet attack there. Cited in the rationale for the strategy shift were the new U.S. military comitments in Southwest Asia, the dedication of naval forces in the Pacific to a Persian Gulf contingency and the Soviet build-up of forces in the Far East. But Komer made it clear in later testimony that these moves were considered necessary precisely because

U.S. general purpose forces had not been planned or structured to fight multiple or simultaneous lesser contingencies:[180]

> Senator Nunn: Do you believe that we really have had in the last three to four years the capability to carry out the '1-1/2 war' strategy prior to the (expansion of our definition of our interest to include the) Persian Gulf?
> Secretary Komer: I think that in the last several years our ability to respond simultaneously to the two scenarios (NATO, plus a lesser contingency) was less than adequate.... if we were confronted simultaneously with a major contingency in NATO with a major all out Korean attack and with, let us say, a Soviet offensive in the Persian Gulf and Indian Ocean area, we would really be stretched. That is not a '1-1/2 war.' I think that is a one and two halves war scenario.

Mr. Komer's acknowledgment that U.S. general purpose forces would be stretched to failure in attempting to meet simultaneous events such as those described helped to set in motion a number of initiatives. In June, President Carter asked Congress for the authority to call up as many as 100,000 Reservists on his own in an emergency, twice the amount then authorized. The Department of Defense said in an official statement that the President needed the "flexibility to deal with crises requiring a measured response but for which declaration of a national emergency might be premature or have undesirable international or domestic consequences."[181] In a related manpower move, the Supreme Court ruled in July that the program for registration for the draft, called for by President Carter in his "State of the Union," could continue.[182]

But an emergency authorization to call up the Reserves and a nascent conscription registration program, although demonstrating national resolve, could do little to bolster the capability of the standing forces to meet the new commitments. The planned military build-up in the Persian Gulf caused a significant redeployment of U.S. naval forces, including the temporary shifting of carriers and a Marine Amphibious Brigade from the Mediterranean to the Indian Ocean. Additionally, plans were under consideration to obtain B-52 basing rights in Australia, to relocate or deploy land-based tactical air to southern Europe in order to compensate for the loss of carrier-based air power in the Mediterranean and a search for "facilities" to allow better access for U.S. forces in Kenya, Oman and Somalia.[183]

By the end of 1980, U.S. forces for a non-NATO contingency had earned their own chapter in the DoD annual report, evidence of a strategic realization, if not a force planning dedication, of the need to meet contingencies beyond the limits of previous strategic concepts:[184]

> When this administration came into office four years after the 1973 oil embargo, we found that the United States had little or no capability for quickly deploying military forces to that critical area of the world. We have begun a careful effort to design and implement a security strategy for that region and a capability to execute that strategy.... While the potential missions of Rapid Deployment Forces are global, in practice most of our planning and programming has focused on Southwest Asia.

Thus, the lesser contingency that had been repressed in the Carter administration's strategic concept suddenly emerged--not as previous versions of a "brushfire" or Soviet-proxy model, but rather as a US-USSR "firefight" in the Persian Gulf region. It was initially unclear whether forces planned to meet this contingency, as institutionalized by the Rapid Deployment Force, would be structured as flexible and versatile units capable of meeting a range of lesser contingencies or if the focus of the RDF on Southwest Asia would restrict its force planning and operation to the implied counter-Soviet scenario. In either case, specific force planning against lesser adversaries in other regions in non-Soviet versions of a lesser contingency was left unattended.

What was the impact of budgetary or public opinion constraints on the process of planning for a lesser contngency?

The events of 1979 that prompted a strategic reappraisal and motivated general purpose force restructuring also loosened the constraints imposed by public opinion and called for an increase in defense spending. Although such constraints are never completely removed, it is clear that public attitudes, particularly with regard to the American hostages held in Iran, but also with an appreciation of growing Soviet hostility in the region, became more permissive regarding the possible use of American military force. The proportion of the public favoring an increase in defense spending rose from 24% in early 1979 to over 63% by the end of that year. The majority of movement within the index of popular opinion occurred between September and December.[185]

Commitment to a larger defense budget within the administration essentially mirrored the altered mood of public opinion. Throughout most of 1979, President Carter remained adamant about staying with his proposed 3% rise in defense spending, but by September Secretary Brown told the Senate Foreign Relations Committee that amounts equating to greater than 3% real growth in the defense budget were being considered.

In addition to the change in public attitude just mentioned, Lawrence Korb has noted three additional pressures on the Carter administration to increase defense spending.[186] In September, a Senate vote on the FY 1981 and FY 1982 defense budget resolutions suggested that the SALT II treaty would not be ratified without at least a 5% real increase in the defense budget. Secondly, the events in Cuba and Iran added greater urgency to cries both within and without the government for elevated defense priority. Finally, in 1979, the CIA revealed that the Soviet Union was outspending the U.S. on defense by approximately 50% and projected the widening of that gap into the 1980s.[187] Thus, the Afghanistan invasion merely became a capstone lending coherence to a series of influential forces that encouraged a rise in defense spending and had already gained considerable momentum.

This chapter has traced the rise and fall of the strategic concept and the lesser contingency imbedded within it by examining the declaratory policy, the forces deployed and the budgetary and popular support granted the concept. In reflecting on the story told, one could conclude that general purpose forces designed to meet a limited contingency have suffered from both a concentration on force planning for the major contingency and a lack of appreciation for a range of scenarios--in terms of geographic locale, intensity of warfare, potential adversary and required forces--imbedded in the strategic concept of the "half war." Under the "2-1/2 war" strategic concept, the "half war" could remain as a "brushfire" with the "field of fire" and the "firefight" models being subsumed under the category of major contingencies. But the reduction of the planned-for major contingencies from two to one and a concomitant and disproportionate emphasis on the European case within that planning contingency required that the "half war" be disaggregated in order to allow adequate force planning for a range of lesser contingencies that appeared more probable. Over time, the conceptual failure to realize the need for U.S. forces to be capable of meeting a spectrum of limited and possibly simultaneous contingencies resulted instead in a concentration on a high intensity US-USSR conflict in a non-NATO scenario, while lower level conflicts in other regions and against lesser adversaries continued to be ignored.

Despite the difficulty in bringing together the disparate elements of defense policy--declaratory policy, deployed forces, budgetary and public opinion constraints--to meet successfully only one of these force planning contingencies, there were a number of organizational attempts to structure a limited contingency force to meet a range of lesser contingencies during the period examined. The following chapter traces the rise and fall of those organizations.

NOTES

1. Again, Robert Osgood has developed these contextual differences as a backdrop for his development of limited war theory. See his works cited earlier.

2. See Dana Mead, "U.S. Peacetime Strategic Planning, 1920-1941: The Color Plans to the Victory Program." Cambridge: MIT (unpublished PhD dissertation), 1967.

3. Etzold and Gaddis, op. cit., p. 17.

4. Ibid., p. 43.

5. Ibid., p. 315.

6. For an expansion of this contention, see Henry Nash, American Foreign Policy (Homewood, IL: Dorsey Press, 1973), Chapters 1 and 2. For a more complete comparison of U.S. and USSR post-war demobilization policies and practices, see Cristann Lea Gibson, "Patterns of Demobilization: The USA and USSR after World War II." Denver: University of Denver Graduate School of International Studies (PhD dissertation), 1982.

7. Glenn Snyder has pointed out that it was the Policy Planning Staff of the State Department that first recognized the need for adequate conventional forces to fight limited wars, well ahead of the development of a similar doctrine by the U.S. Army. See Schilling, Hammond and Snyder, op. cit., pp. 435-436.

8. Huntington, op. cit., p. 47.

9. For recent observations on the drafting of NSC-68, see Samuel F. Wells, Jr. "Sounding the Tocsin: NSC-68 and the Soviet Threat," International Security (Fall 1979), pp. 116-158, and John Lewis Gaddis and Paul Nitze, "NSC-68 and the Soviet Threat Reconsidered," International Security (Spring 1980), pp. 164-176.

10. Morton H. Halperin, Contemporary Military Strategy (New York: Little Brown, 1967), p. 45. See also Etzold and Gaddis, p. 384. The

"Report by the Secretaries of State and Defense on U.S. Objectives and Programs for National Security," April 7, 1950 (NSC-68) was declassified on February 25, 1975. It is reprinted in its entirety in the Naval War College Review (May-June 1975).

11. John Lewis Gaddis has contrasted the images of conventional conflict as enunciated by NSC-68 with the then-prevailing paradigm of the "brushfire." While NSC-68 envisioned "piecemeal aggression" by Soviet or Soviet-proxy forces which could ultimately result in the sacrifice of U.S. areas of vital interests, George Kennan's recommendations were confined to the "development of elite, highly mobile, compact units, capable of responding quickly to counter Soviet capabilities." See Gaddis, Strategies of Containment (New York: Oxford, 1982), pp. 97-98.

12. See William W. Kaufmann, The McNamara Strategy (New York: Harper and Row, 1964), p. 18.

13. J. T. Trotman, "NATO in Theory and Practice," Survival, Vol. XIII, No. 6 (November/December 1971). For an analysis of the demise of NSC-68, see Huntington, op. cit., pp. 47-53.

14. Schilling, Hammond and Snyder, p. 436.

15. The most famous formulation of the doctrine was by Secretary of State John Foster Dulles, "A Policy for Boldness," Life (May 19, 1952), p. 146. For an analysis and a development of the strategic concept within the Eisenhower administration, see Townsend Hoopes, The Devil and John Foster Dulles (Boston: Little Brown, 1973), p. 126 ff. See also Dulles, "The Evolution of Foreign Policy," U.S. Department of State Bulletin, 30 (January 25, 1954), pp. 107-110, and "Challenge and Response in United States Policy," Foreign Affairs (October 1957), pp. 25-43.

16. Eisenhower, Dwight D., Waging Peace (Garden City N.Y.: Doubleday, 1965), p. 454. Eisenhower opposed the possibility of a long inconclusive limited war along the lines of Korea and the political and social upheaval that would attend the mobilization needed to fight such a war. The United States, Eisenhower commented, "cannot be strong enough to go to every part of the world where our enemies may use force or the threat of force and defend these nations." See Gaddis, op. cit., p. 133.

17. Schilling, Hammond and Snyder, p. 452. It is interesting to note that this paper also recommended the complete withdrawal of combat forces from Korea.

18. Ibid., pp. 466-467. However, the "New Look," from Eisenhower's perspective, did not include a conventional capability beyond a "brushfire" that would require "a few Marine battalions or Army units." If the conflict grew to Korea-like proportions, Eisenhower wrote that "the action would become one for the use of atomic weapons. Participation in small wars . . . is primarily a matter for Navy and Air." See Gaddis, op. cit., pp. 147-149.

19. Ibid., p. 480 ff.

20. Schilling, Hammond and Snyder, pp. 482-483.

21. Ibid., p. 483. Snyder notes that the budget actually reduced the Army's capacity for rapid deployment by cutting the air transport strength from 16 to 13 wings, with a further reduction to 11 wings planned in 1957.

22. Ibid., p. 485. The parallels between the defense policies of the Eisenhower administration after Korea and those of his Vice-President, Nixon, after Vietnam some twenty years later are striking, both in

strategic and general purpose force planning. Both doctrines, of course, were based on similar perceptions regarding economic and public opinion limits on the defense budget and on the projection of American power abroad. For another perspective on the manner in which massive retaliation supported American foreign policy, see Samuel F. Wells, "The Origins of Massive Retaliation," Political Science Quarterly, Vol. 96, No. 1 (Spring 1981), pp. 31-52.

23. Letter from Thomas Gates, Acting Secretary of Defense, to President Eisenhower on October 29, 1959, subject "Overseas bases." The letter cited these conclusions as excerpts from the Nash Report on the overseas basing system.

24. Schilling, Hammond and Snyder, p. 388.

25. Halperin, op. cit., p. 46.

26. "Memorandum on Presidential Conference on Defense." December 8, 1960. The Limited War Panel of the President's Science Advisory Committee was instructed in September 1959 to approach its study with the assumption that nuclear weapons, including "tactical" nuclear weapons, would not be used. But Eisenhower later dismissed the report as "unreliable." The reason that the U.S. could intervene quickly in many areas with small forces was that the force would be armed with atomic weapons. "We were unfortunately so committed to nuclear weapons that the only practical move would be to start using them from the beginning without any distinction between them and conventional weapons." Gaddis, op. cit., pp. 174-175.

27. See H. A. Deweerd, "Historian's Perspective," Army (January 1963). The intent here is not to construct a bibliographical essay on the literature of limited war. For an excellent pre-Vietnam effort in this regard, see Morton Halperin, Limited War (Cambridge, MA: Harvard Center for International Affairs, May 1962). See also his annotated bibliography in Limited War in the Nuclear Age (New York: John Wiley, 1963), pp. 133-184.

28. "Atomic Weapons and the Korean War," Bulletin of Atomic Scientists, Vol VI (July 1950), p. 194.

29. William W. Kaufmann, "The Requirements of Deterrence" in Kaufmann, ed., Military Policy and National Security (Princeton: Princeton University Press, 1956), pp. 12-38. Bernard Brodie, "Unlimited Weapons and Limited War," The Reporter, XI (November 18, 1954), pp. 16-21.

30. William W. Kaufmann, "Limited Warfare" in Kaufmann, op. cit., pp. 102-136. Henry Kissinger, Nuclear Weapons and Foreign Policy (New York: Harper and Bros., 1957), Osgood; Limited War, op. cit.

31. Desmond Ball, Politics and Force Levels (Berkeley: University of California Press, 1980), p. 67.

32. Jerome H. Kahan, Security in the Nuclear Age (Washington, D.C.: Brookings, 1975), pp. 40-42. See also Morton Halperin, "The Gaither Committee and the Policy Process," World Politics, Vol. XIII, No. 2 (April 1961), pp. 360-384. The "missile gap" did not really become a public issue until the publication of an article in the New York Times in mid-January 1959. See Arnold L. Horelick and Myron Rush, Strategic Power and Soviet Foreign Policy (Chicago: University of Chicago Press, 1966), p. 78.

33. "International Security: The Military Aspect," Special Studies Report II of the Rockefellers Brothers Fund (New York: Doubleday, 1958), p. 23.

34. Paul Y. Hammond, The Cold War Years: American Foreign Policy Since 1945 (New York: Harcourt Brace and World, 1969), p. 103.
35. Ibid., p. 134.
36. The classic works are by Kissinger, Nuclear Weapons and Foreign Policy; by Wohlstetter, "The Delicate Balance of Terror," Foreign Affairs, 37 (January 1959); by Taylor, The Uncertain Trumpet (New York: Harper and Bros., 1959).
37. Hearings, Senate Armed Services Committee, "Major Defense Matters," Part I (1959), pp. 44-45.
38. Schilling, Hammond and Snyder, p. 468.
39. Congressional Quarterly Almanac, 1960 (Washington, D.C.: USGPO, 1961), p. 776.
40. John F. Kennedy, A Compilation of Statements and Speeches (Washington, D.C.: USGPO, 1964), pp. 926-935. For the inaugural address, see Public Papers of the Presidents of the United States: John F. Kennedy (Washington, D.C.: USGPO, 1962-1964) Vol. I.
41. Kaufmann, The McNamara Strategy, p. 34. See also Schlesinger, A Thousand Days, p. 295.
42. Testimony of General Maxwell Taylor before the House Committee on Government Operations, 86th Congress, 1st session (Washington, D.C.: USGPO, 1961), p. 794.
43. Roger Hilsman, To Move A Nation (Garden City: Doubleday and Co., 1967), p. 127.
44. Schlesinger, op. cit., p. 295.
45. Ibid.
46. "Limited War Study Sees Use for Billions," Washington Evening Star, February 14, 1961. "Rusk's Ideas," St. Louis Post-Dispatch, March 5, 1961.
47. Memo from Secretary McNamara to President Kennedy attached to the Connally Report, "Reappraisal of Conventional Forces," May 19, 1961.
48. One reason for this lack of coordination was the lack of a central plan. "Neither service had recourse to any authoritative statement of the approved force structure plan of any of the other services." See Enthoven and Smith, op. cit., p. 11. McNamara had similarly reported to the President that there were too few "Pentagon-wide plans for each kind of contingency. The Army was relying on airlift the Air Force could not supply. The Air Force was stocking supplies for a war lasting a few days while the Army stockpiles assumed a war of two years." See Theodore Sorensen, Kennedy (New York: Harper and Row, 1965), p. 603.
49. John F. Kennedy, "Annual Message to the Congress on the State of the Union, January 30, 1961," Public Papers (Washington, D.C.: USGPO, 1962-1964), Vol. I, pp. 19-28.
50. Sorensen, op. cit., p. 631.
51. John F. Kennedy, "Radio and Television Report to the American People on the Crisis in Berlin, July 25, 1961," Public Papers (Washington, D.C.: USGPO, 1962-1964), Vol. I, pp. 441-446. See also "Kennedy Girds for Small Wars," Baltimore Sun, July 26, 1961.
52. John F. Kennedy, "Recommendations Relating to our Defense Budget" (Washington, D.C.: USGPO, 1961), pp. 3-4.
53. John F. Kennedy, "Special Message to Congress, May 25, 1961," Public Papers (Washington, D.C.: USGPO, 1962-1964), Vol. I, p. 401.

54. John G. Norris, "Pentagon Patrol," The Officer (September 1961). According to Norris, published accounts that Taylor was primarily responsible for the new defense proposals were disputed in the Pentagon, even though the plan contained many of Taylor's previously rejected views. If the scheme was his, Taylor, nevertheless, remained unsatisfied. In a memo to President Kennedy in November 1961, Taylor called for a raise in the total manning of the army to 1,055,700, a one billion dollar increase in Army procurement, an increase in funds for strategic airlift, the deployment of an Army division to the Western Pacific and the need to prepare a division in Korea for rapid deployment elsewhere in Asia.

55. Robert S. McNamara, Department of Defense Annual Report FY 1963 (January 19, 1962), p. 34. To simplify the discussion of the process of force planning and force deployment throughout this chapter, the unit of analysis will be restricted to the Army division. Force planning for the size of ground units has been most effectively accomplished by using the concept of the "division force," projecting the anticipated threat and constructing dynamic campaign analyses using firepower ratios against that threat. Tactical air forces can then be sized to the emerging divisional structure required to maintain stability at the front. The Air Force has generally considered approximately five tactical fighter squadrons to each division an adequate force, although it disagrees with the Army as to the primary mission of these aircraft. The Navy, on the other hand, has generally resisted force planning by contingency, preferring to plan Naval forces based on a global mission. See John A. Williams, "U.S. Navy Missions and Force Structure," Armed Forces and Society (Summer 1981), pp. 499-527. Nevertheless, the lesser contingency under study here is basically a land engagement and, therefore, will rely on the Army division to describe the changes in force structure allocated to the "half war" planning contingency.

56. Quoted in Norris, op. cit.

57. See U.S. Congress, Senate Committee on Armed Services, "Authorizing the President to order units and members of the Ready Reserve to Active Duty for not more than 12 months." Senate Joint Resolution 224, 87th Congress, 2nd session (Washington, D.C.: USGPO, 1962), p. 15.

58. "New Army Divisions Recast Defense Plans," Washington Star, June 7, 1962.

59. Roswell Gilpatric, quoted in the New York Herald Tribune, December 18, 1961. McNamara, a strong believer in a capable and ready Reserve force later echoed similar sentiments: "I think it is a mistake to have the facade of a combat-ready force, but only the facade. The fact of the matter is that when we called personnel to active duty in the fall of 1961 for training purposes during the Berlin crisis and when we prepared to call personnel to active duty in the fall of 1962 during the Cuban crisis, we lacked training equipment to even keep these men busy." U.S. Congress, House of Representative, DoD Appropriations for 1964, 88th Congress, 1st session (Washington, D.C.: USGPO, 1964), p. 137.

60. See John D. Bruen, "Repercussions from the Vietnam Mobilization Decision," Parameters, Vol. II, No. 1 (Spring/Summer 1972), pp. 30-39.

61. McNamara, DoD Appropriations for 1964, p. 138.

62. "U.S. Triples Alert Force," New York Herald Tribune, February 24, 1962. For clarity in this paper, the "standby reserve" or "strategic reserve"--regular forces stationed in the CONUS on active duty and

assigned a mission of rapid deployment or reinforcement--will be left in lower case, while the augmentation forces, those that are non-active and require mobilization, will be capitalized, e.g., the Army Reserve, Ready Reserve and the National Guard.

63. U.S. Congress, House of Representatives, DoD Appropriations for 1963, 87th Congress, 2nd session, Part 2 (Washington, D.C.: USGPO, 1962), p. 48.

64. Robert S. McNamara, Department of Defense Annual Report, FY 1964, p. 52. Actually, the eleven theaters in which it was anticipated the U.S. would be required to commit military forces resulted in a projected force structure of 55 divisions. But this was far above a force likely to be supported by Congress. Although these studies are still classified, a good description of the planning factors underlying this force can be found in William W. Kaufmann, Planning Conventional Forces 1950-1980 (Washington, D.C.: Brookings, 1982), pp. 5-9.

65. U.S. Congress, House of Representatives, Committee on Appropriations, DoD Appropriations for 1964, 88th Congress, 1st session, Part 1 (Washington, D.C.: USGPO, 1963), p. 130. The Weapons System Evaluation Group was a staff composed of over 300 military and civilian personnel charged with the review and study of defense systems for the Joint Chiefs and the Office of the Secretary of Defense (OSD). Their studies of strategic mobility were especially noteworthy and will be further mentioned in Chapter IV. By the beginning of 1963, the group appeared to be fully under the administrative control of Dr. Harold Brown in DDR&E.

66. Robert S. McNamara, DoD Annual Report, FY 1965, p. 89.

67. The following statements are compiled from the "posture statements" given by Secretary McNamara in both 1964 and 1965. The statements are slightly rearranged in an attempt to portray best the "2-1/2 war" strategic concept as it had evolved prior to Vietnam. There are arguments that the creation of this force and these concepts "encouraged, allowed or permitted"--some say "determined" the U.S. involvement in Vietnam. For this type of reasoning, which we will encounter again in the FDL case study in Chapter IV, see Adam Yarmolinsky, The Military Establishment (New York: Harper and Row, 1971), p. 233.

68. This table is adapted from a similar presentation in Leslie Gelb and Arnold Kuzmack, "General Purpose Forces" in Henry Owen, ed., The Next Phase in Foreign Policy (Washington, D.C.: Brookings, 1973), p. 207. As those authors confess, the allocations are somewhat arbitrary because DoD does not choose to make public such allocations. The numbers here differ slightly from Gelb and Kuzmack's based on the information previously presented and derived from public sources. Obviously, the forces could be realigned to meet a "greater than expected threat," while the strategic reserve also hedged against an underestimation of the forces required to meet a single contingency. The "half war" units were likely to be the 82nd or 101st Airborne, Army special forces, or a CONUS-based Marine division, depending on the scenario. The "2-1/2 war" strategic concept was never clearly or publicly articulated in terms of policy guidance or force planning direction. For the best available explications of the implemented strategy--rather than the Nixon-Laird interpretations of it--see Robert S. McNamara, Report of the Secretary of Defense FY 1969, pp. 78-79, and Kaufmann, Planning Conventional Forces, pp. 7-10.

69. The best primary source that develops the U.S. involvement in Vietnam remains the Pentagon Papers (New York: Bantam, 1971). For an

analysis of the operation of the foreign policy decision making system during the war and additional primary sources made available since the publication of the Pentagon Papers, see Leslie Gelb and Richard K. Betts, The Irony of Vietnam (Washington, D.C.: Brookings, 1979).

70.   Memorandum from McGeorge Bundy to President Lyndon B. Johnson, July 24, 1965, published in Gelb and Betts, pp. 372-374. Those authors speculate that the willingness with which LBJ set out to dispatch troops to Vietnam during this period may have been prompted by the ease of operation in the Dominican Republic.   For a listing of the forces deployed in that episode, see Herbert K. Tillema, Appeal to Force (New York: Thomas Y. Crowell, 1973), p. 64.

71.   Gelb and Betts, p. 132.

72.   "Pentagon Plans to Trim U.S. Strategic Reserve," New York Times, August 7, 1967. The strategic reserve was now being thought of as all remaining ground forces in the United States, whether or not they were originally committed to NATO. At this time, that reserve force consisted of six divisions (82nd Airborne, 1st and 2nd Armored Divisions, 5th Infantry Division, 6th Armored Cavalry Regiment, plus the 11th and 198th Infantry Brigades and two brigades of the 101st (Airmobile)).

73.   U.S. Congress, Senate, DoD Appropriations for FY 1967, 89th Congress, 2nd session (Washington, D.C.: USGPO, 1966).

74.   In January 1967, with over 500,000 men in Vietnam, Secretary McNamara attempted to reassure the Congress that the Department of Defense had not overcommitted its forces. McNamara noted that the U.S. had not been forced to reduce other deployments, call up the Reserves or declare a limited industrial mobilization. There were still 7 divisions (including the Marine Corps) in the CONUS and 9 divisions in the Reserves. See DoD Annual Report FY 1968, p. 67.

75.   Gelb and Betts, p. 173.

76.   General Harold K. Johnson, U.S. Army Chief of Staff, testified that about 3% of the Reserves--76 selected Army National Guard and Reserve Forces--were ordered to 24 months active duty on April 11, 1968. As planned, these forces were used primarily to strengthen the strategic reserve, thereby allowing further deployment of the active forces to Vietnam.   See U.S. Congress, House, Committee on Armed Services, Hearings on Military Posture for FY 1969, 20th Congress, 2nd session (Washington, D.C.: USGPO, 1969), p. 8954.

77.   Gelb and Betts, op. cit., p. 177.

78.   U.S. Congress, Senate Committee on Armed Services, Hearings on H.R. 1870, 20th Congress, 2nd session (Washington, D.C.: USGPO, 1969).

79.   Clark P. Clifford, Department of Defense Annual Report FY 1969.

80.   Charles L. Schultze, quoted in Joseph Albright and Martin Schram, "U.S. Defense Based on 2-1/2 Wars," Long Island Newsday, May 28, 1969.

81.   See Charles L. Schultze, "Budget Alternatives after Vietnam" in Kermit Gordon, ed., Agenda for the Nation (Washington, D.C.: Brookings, 1968), pp. 13-48.

82.   General purpose forces expenditures were then projected to be about $58 billion of a $80 billion defense budget. Vietnam costs were variously estimated between $20 and $30 billion. See Albright and Schram, op. cit.

83. Carl Kaysen, "Military Strategy, Military Forces and Arms Control" in Gordon, ed., op. cit., pp. 577-578.

84. Graham Allison, Ernest May and Adam Yarmolinsky, "Limits to Intervention," Foreign Affairs, Vol. 48, No. 2 (January 1970), p. 246.

85. Henry Kissinger, White House Years (Boston: Little Brown, 1979), p. 200.

86. "U.S. Study offers 10 options on Conventional Forces," New York Times, May 2, 1969.

87. William Beecher, "Mr. Nixon's Strategy," The National Guardsman, April 1970.

88. Kissinger, White House Years, p. 221.

89. Ibid.

90. Richard M. Nixon, U.S. Foreign Policy for the 70s: A New Strategy For Peace. A Report to the Congress, February 18, 1970.

91. "The Nixon Doctrine and Strategy" in Robert Osgood, ed., Retreat From Empire (Baltimore: Johns Hopkins Press, 1973), p. 9.

92. Richard Nixon, A New Strategy for Peace, p. 127.

93. Melvin R. Laird, DoD Annual Report FY 1971, pp. 10-11.

94. Throughout the late 1960s, the military chiefs argued that to fight two and one-half wars would require thirty regular Army and Marine divisions, not twenty-one, an attendant 36 air wings, not 26; and a correspondingly larger air and sealift capability. The Joint Chiefs testified that if the other major contingency were to be fully funded it would cost approximately $20 billion more each year in the projected defense budget. See Juan Cameron, "The Armed Forces' Reluctant Retrenchment," Fortune (November 1970) and U.S. Congress, Senate, DoD Appropriations for FY 1971, 91st Congress, 2nd session (Washington, D.C.: USGPO, 1970), p. 150.

95. A number of approaches to the obtaining of that peace dividend were outlined in testimony before the Joint Economic Committee in 1969. See "The Military Budget and National Economic Priorities," Hearings before the Subcommittee on Economy in Government of the Joint Economic Committee, 91st Congress, 1st session, Part 1, 1969.

96. This point was stressed by Robert Komer in a personal interview. See also Leslie Gelb and Arnold Kuzmack's discussion of force allocation, op. cit., p. 206.

97. Warren Nutter, quoted in Cameron, op. cit.

98. Melvin R. Laird, DoD Annual Report FY 1972, p. 107.

99. Kaysen, op. cit., p. 577-578. Kaysen posited that the likelihood of renewed major conflict in the Middle East depended on US/USSR relations, which he saw to be improving.

110. Kaysen also realized that this projection was optimistic and depended upon a mutual Soviet-American acceptance of the need to increase international stability through the reduction and control of both nuclear and conventional arms. See pp. 582-584.

101. Charles L. Schultze, "Budget Alternatives after Vietnam," pp. 40-41.

102. Allison, May and Yarmolinsky, op. cit., pp. 260-261.

103. Quoted in Grover Hieman, "Restructuring for the Nixon Doctrine," Armed Forces Management, April 1970. Composition of the Army force of 17-1/3 divisions included 1 airborne, 2 airmobile, 4-1/3 infantry, 4 mechanized, 4 armored and 5 independent brigades.

104. Melvin R. Laird, DoD Annual Report FY 1972.

105. Melvin R. Laird, DoD Annual Report FY 1973.

106.   Richard M. Nixon, U.S. Foreign Policy for the 1970s: Shaping a Durable Peace. A Report to the Congress, May 3, 1973, pp. 188-189.

107.   Quoted in Cameron, op. cit.   See also Lynn D. Smith, "Is Pentagon Reserve Planning Realistic?" Army (February 1972).

108.   Maxwell Taylor, Address to the National War College, September 1970, quoted in Cameron, op. cit.

109.   Testimony of General Earle D. Wheeler, U.S. Congress, Senate, DoD Appropriations for FY 1971, 91st Congress, 2nd session (Washington, D.C.: USGPO, 1970), p. 150.

110.   Typical of the units examined was the 6th Armored Cavalry Regiment at Fort Meade, Virginia. Although the unit was technically capable of deployment to anywhere in the world, Vietnam personnel policies and materiel demands had sapped its strength. Units were maintained at between 75 and 80% of optimum strength, in a constant state of flux due to the one-year combat assignment and chronically short of training items. See George W. Ashworth, "Pentagon Studies Rebuilding of Forces for Long-term Needs," Christian Science Monitor, February 17, 1969. On the matter of fluctuation in personnel, the subcommittee found in the 2nd Marine Division that during the calendar year 1967, the division received a total of 15,106 Marines who were Vietnam returnees while losing 10,441 Marines by direct transfer to the Western Pacific. Authorized strength of the Division was 18,457.

111.   Allison, May and Yarmolinsky, op. cit., p. 260.

112.   Quoted in Lloyd Norman, "Mr. Laird and the No-War Strategy for the 1970s," Army (February 1971).

113.   Henry Kissinger, White House Years, p. 605.

114.   George Ashworth, "U.S. Army's Worldwide Profile Shrinks under Budget Axe," Christian Science Monitor, December 7, 1970.

115.   Testimony of General William C. Westmoreland, quoted in "Rapid Manpower cuts leave Army with 1 Combat Division in U.S.," Baltimore Sun, March 20, 1972, p. 8.

116.   The poor state of the strategic reserves was further detailed in a report by the General Accounting Office in May of 1972 that concluded, "many units in the Strategic Army Forces in the United States are not combat ready." The deficiencies alleged in this review related to both manpower and materiel failures, with a large amount of equipment in either poor or unusable condition and across-the-board shortages in qualified personnel. In a comment on the report, the Army rejected a suggestion to reduce further the size of the strategic reserve (holding at six divisions in 1972) to equal the dwindling manpower resources. Thus, it appeared that a certain floor in the number of active divisions had been reached, even though the quality of the force remained highly suspect. See "U.S. Report Calls Many Units of Strategic Forces Unready," New York Times, May 18, 1972, p. 1.

117.   See Barry Blechman, "The Nuclear Alert: Too Big a Stick?" Washington Star News, December 2, 1973. Also see Henry Kissinger, Years of Upheaval (Boston: Little Brown, 1982), pp. 587-589.

118.   See Drew Middleton, "U.S. Global Role: Are Forces Big Enough?" New York Times, March 17, 1974.

119.   Schlesinger Seeks more Army Divisions," Washington Post, October 17, 1974, p. 6.

120.   James R. Schlesinger, DoD Annual Report, FY 1976, p. III-14.

121.   Ibid.

122.   Donald Rumsfeld, Department of Defense Annual Report FY 1978, p. 53.

123.   See Francis J. West's interpretation of the principles underlying the "1-1/2 war" strategy in "Conventional Forces Beyond NATO" in Thompson, ed., National Security in the 1980s, pp. 319-336.

124.   For a graphic display of this continuity of presidential commitments, see Henry Nash, op. cit., pp. 26-27.

125.   Michael Nacht, "Toward an American Concept of Regional Security," Daedelus, Vol. 110, No. 1 (March 1981), p. 13.

126.   Robert G. Kaiser, "Memo sets stage in Assessing US-Soviet Strength," Washington Post, July 6, 1977, p. 1.

127.   Thus, the split between net assessment and force planning, introduced first by Secretary Laird and considered by many force planners to have an adverse effect on contingency analysis, was established early in the Carter administration.

128.   Kaiser, op. cit.

129.   Samuel P. Huntington, "Trade, Technology and Leverage," Foreign Policy, No. 32 (Fall 1978), pp. 63-80.

130.   Quoted in Alan Wolfe, "Carter's New Defense Budget," The Nation, February 18, 1978, p. 166.

131.   Kaiser, op. cit.

132.   PD-18 also indicated the need for more studies, specifically in the areas of intervention (conducted by OSD/PA&E), and an assessment of the vulnerability of the U.S. to a cutoff of its oil supply (conducted jointly by State and JCS).

133.   Wolfe, op. cit.

134.   "Carter Orders Steps to Increase Ability to Meet War Threats," New York Times, August 26, 1977, p. 1.

135.   George C. Wilson, "New U.S. Military Plan: European, Persian Focus," Washington Post, July 27, 1978, p. 1.

136.   Harold Brown, DoD Annual Report FY 1980, p. 98.

137.   U.S. Congress, Senate Committee on Appropriations, DoD Appropriations for FY 1978. 95th Congress, 1st session (Washington, D.C.: USGPO, 1977), p. 223.

138.   Remarks of Secretary of Defense Harold Brown before the National Security Industrial Association, DoD News Release, September 15, 1977.

139.   Harold Brown, DoD Annual Report FY 1980, p. 99. It was assumed that a Northeast Asia contingency could demand a higher U.S. force level than a non-Soviet conflict in the Persian Gulf. However, the Korean contingency was seen as a less likely major contingency. If North Korea invaded the South, it would presumedly do so with the aid of the USSR or PRC. Therefore, the conflict would have exceeded the prevailing conceptual limits imposed on the "half war." See U.S. Congress, Congressional Budget Office, U.S. Projection Forces: Requirements, Scenarios Options (Washington, D.C.: USGPO, 1978), p. 5.

140.   Harold Brown, DoD Annual Report FY 1980, p. 98.

141.   Harold Brown, DoD Annual Report FY 1978, pp. 53-54.

142.   Congress had already approved the division expansion recommended by Secretary Schlesinger. Additionally, in 1976 the Army presented to Congress a second force expansion plan that called for the conversion of two infantry divisions to mechanized infantry--although one of these was the 2nd Infantry Division to be converted rather than

deactivated upon its redeployment from South Korea. See "U.S. Ground Forces," The Defense Monitor, Vol. VII, No. 9 (November 1978), p. 1.
143. Harold Brown, DoD Annual Report FY 1980, p. 47.
144. U.S. Projection Forces, p. xiii.
145. For a good distinction between "light" and "heavy" units and their application to the RDF, see Raymond E. Bell, Jr., "The RDF--How Much, How Soon," Army (July 1980), pp. 18-24.
146. U.S. Projection Forces. The forces were also becoming NATO-mission oriented. See note 157.
147. William Schneider and Francis Hoeber, eds., Arms, Men and Military Budgets FY 1977 (New York: Crane Russak, 1976).
148. Joseph A. Pechman, ed., Setting National Priorities: The 1978 Budget (Washington, D.C.: Brookings, 1977), p. 8.
149. "Carter's decision on Korea traced to Early 1975," Washington Post, June 12, 1977, p. 15. PRM-13 was issued in mid-March 1977 to guide U.S. force posture in Asia. The review did not ask whether U.S. troops should be withdrawn, but rather sought options as to how this reduction in U.S. presence could best be accomplished.
150. See "Inscrutable Americans in Major Asian Strategy Shift," New York Times, July 31, 1977, p. E-3.
151. Korb, op. cit., p. 25. This concentration on the short war in the central region did not leap from the brow of the Carter administration. A considerable body of defense literature had been critical of the US/NATO force posture in Europe for its inability to counter a short war, a scenario that had grown more plausible with increased Soviet conventional capabilities. See, for example, John Erikson, "Soviet Military Capabilities in Europe," in RUSI Journal, Vol. 20, No. 1 (March 1975). See also Richard Lawrence and Jeffrey Record, U.S. Force Structure in NATO: An Alternative (Washington, D.C.: Brookings, 1974) and U.S. Congress, Senate Committee on Armed Services, "NATO and the New Soviet Threat," Report of Senators Sam Nunn and Dewey Bartlett, 95th Congress, 1st session (Washington, D.C.: USGPO, 1977).
152. Quoted by Richard Burt, "U.S. Defense Debate Arises on Whether Focus on Europe Neglects Other Areas," New York Times, March 24, 1978, p. 3.
153. See Frank Gibney, "The Ripple Effect in Korea," Foreign Affairs, Vol. 56, No. 1 (October 1977), pp. 160-174.
154. See Geoffrey Kemp, "Contingency Planning and Persian Gulf Options" and Clark A. Murdock, "Political and Military Dimensions of the African Problem, 1980-2000" in 1979 Proceedings of the National Security Affairs Conference (Washington, D.C.: National Defense University, 1979), pp. 61-95.
155. Quoted in Burt, "U.S. Defense Debate." For Navy concerns, see U.S. Congress, Congressional Budget Office, U.S. Naval Forces: The Peacetime Presence Mission (Washington, D.C.: USGPO, 1978) and Larry Levy, "Sea Plan Worries Navy," Tulsa Tribune, April 25, 1978, p. 1.
156. Lawrence J. Korb, "The Policy and Impacts of the Carter Defense Program," in Sarkesian, ed., Defense Policy and the Presidency (Boulder: Westview, 1979), p. 190.
157. However, the authors made no attempt to distinguish among differing geographic locales, adversaries or general purpose force requirements in order to meet a range of scenarios within "half war" contingency planning. Practical as well as theoretical problems were encountered in this shift in defense priorities. Preparing forces for

combat in Europe necessarily reduced their effectiveness and flexibility for use elsewhere. For example, the program to "heavy up" certain divisions with tanks and artillery to perform in a NATO scenario made these forces less able and effective to meet a rapid deployment mission to a lesser contingency. Lawrence Korb noted that by the early 1980s, Army heavy divisions would outnumber the light divisions by 11 to 5, compared to an 8-8 split in the pre-Vietnam force of 16 divisions. A similar difficulty arose with the plans to increase the prepositioning of stocks and equipment in Europe: prepositioning supplies in Europe made them less deployable to other regions. Finally, the rapid reaction concept proposed in PD-18 received little initial support from State or Defense. This added to criticism of the administration's sole concentration on Europe. See Korb, FY 1979-1983 Defense Program, p. 42. Also see Burt, "U.S. Defense Debate." Further undermining this concept of rapid deployment forces having a world-wide capability was the growing application of these forces to the NATO scenario. See, for example, "101st Airborne undergoes critical test in Europe," Washington Post, October 7, 1976, p. G-7, and "Marines to 'Invade' Turkey to Stress Value in European War," Washington Post, August 10, 1977, p. 5.

158. Richard Burt, "War Plan, Secret 25 Years, Creates Dilemma for U.S.," New York Times, October 9, 1979, p. 1.

159. Ibid.

160. Quoted by Bradley Martin, "Brown Tries to Molify Opponents of 'Flexible Capability' Forces," Baltimore Sun, October 21, 1979, p. 1.

161. Lawrence Korb, The FY 1978-1983 Defense Program (Washington, D.C.: American Enterprise Institute, 1978), p. 25. John Collins has also described the strategy in this fashion and records that the term "one plus" had gained some parlance within the JCS. See his note on page 158 in American and Soviet Military Trends since the Cuban Missile Crisis (Georgetown University: The Center for International and Strategic Studies, 1978).

162. Hedrick Smith, "Carter Feels Certain Soviets will Alter Brigade in Cuba," New York Times, October 3, 1979.

163. "The World is Not on Your Side," Washington Post, November 22, 1979, p. 21.

164. Terrence Smith, "Carter Tells Soviets to Pull its Troops from Afghanistan," New York Times, December 30, 1979, p. 1.

165. Personal Interviews, OSD/PA&E, January 1981. See also Paul K. Davis, "Observations on the Rapid Deployment Joint Task Force: Origins, Direction, and Mission" (Santa Monica: RAND P-6751, June 1982).

166. Richard Halloran, "Two Aides Say U.S. Will Defend Oil Interests in the Mideast," New York Times, February 26, 1979, p. 12.

167. Ibid.

168. Charles W. Corddry, "U.S. Considers Indian Ocean Fleet," Baltimore Sun, March 8, 1979, p. 5.

169. Drew Middleton, "U.S. Earmarks Force for Fast Deployment in Mideast," New York Times, April 20, 1979, p. 12.

170. Juan Cameron, "Our What-If Strategy for Mideast Trouble Spots," Fortune, May 7, 1979, pp. 154-158.

171. John M. Collins and Clyde R. Mark, "Petroleum Imports from the Persian Gulf," Library of Congress, Congressional Reference Service (Washington, D.C.: USGPO, 1979).

172.	Quoted in Henry S. Bradsher, "U.S. Called Unprepared to Fight for its Persian Gulf Oil Interests," Washington Star, May 2, 1979, p. 8.

173.	Jim Hoagland, "A Carter Doctrine for Mideast Oil?" Washington Post, June 3, 1979, p. D-1.

174.	Terrence Smith, "President Says U.S. Would Use Military," New York Times, January 24, 1980, p. 1.

175.	"Text of the President's Address on the State of the Union." New York Times, January 24, 1980, p. 1-F. Robert W. Tucker has noted the declaration is clearly aimed at the Soviet Union, "since it is only the Soviet Union that represents 'any outside force' capable of gaining control of the Persian Gulf." See "American Power and the Persian Gulf," Commentary, Vol. 70, No. 5 (November 1980), pp. 25-41.

176.	Quoted in Richard Burt, "One and a Half War Strategy Now Means Just What It Says," New York Times, February 3, 1980, p. E-1.

177.	Quoted in Michael T. Klare, "The Brown Doctrine," The Nation, March 8, 1980, p. 257.

178.	Secretary of Defense speech, July 30, 1979 (DoD news release).

179.	Most significant, there was the reversal, based on a revised estimate of North Korean capabilities as well as political pressures, of the policy to withdraw the U.S. 2nd Infantry Division from Korea.

180.	U.S. Congress, Senate Committee on Armed Services, Hearings on S2294. 96th Congress, 2nd session (Washington, D.C.: USGPO, 1980), pp. 1243-1244. See also Richard Burt, "U.S. Strategy Shifting From Europe to the Pacific," New York Times, May 24, 1980, p. 3.

181.	George C. Wilson, "More Troops Sought for Crisis Force," Washington Post, June 19, 1980, p. 1.

182.	Richard Halloran, "Draft Registration of Men May Begin, Brennan Declares," Washington Post, July 20, 1980, p. 1.

183.	Michael Getler, "U.S. Forces Around the World Are Stretched by Gulf Buildup," Washington Post, July 19, 1980, p. 1.

184.	DoD Annual Report FY 1982, p. 81.

185.	Korb, op. cit., p. 27.

186.	Ibid.

187.	For a note on the index number problem of comparing U.S. and Soviet defense expenditures, see Paul Cockle, "Analyzing Soviet Defense Spending: The Debate in Perspective," Survival, Vol. XX, No. 5 (September/October 1978), pp. 209-219.

3
Organizing for the Limited Contingency: Institutionalizing Strategies of Rapid Deployment, 1960-1980

The previous chapter focused on the relationship between the declared strategic concept and the forces planned to meet a limited contingency. The principal questions now to be addressed are: why has the United States failed to construct a coherent limited contingency force in support of these strategic concepts, and what lessons can be drawn from the experience to assist in the formulation of an effective and adequately supported organization? The answers to these questions lie in the following two chapters of this study. This chapter examines the organizations formed to command limited contingency forces, while Chapter 4 questions the adequacy of resources and mobility systems acquired in support of those forces and organizations.

This chapter describes and explains the proposal, establishment and disestablishment of organizations designed to command forces dedicated to a limited contingency. These organizations parallel and, to an extent, mirror the history of the lesser contingency already related in terms of the declared strategic concept. The most ambitious strategy, the "2-1/2 war" concept, permitted the most aspiring organization, STRIKE Command, to develop. At the end of the 1960s as the strategic concept withered from "2-1/2 wars" to "1-1/2," the command headquarters also declined. Readiness Command (REDCOM) assumed operational control over all CONUS-based ground and air forces previously assigned to STRIKE. But REDCOM was not a combatant command and was not assigned a geographic area of responsibility. Most recently, the reemergence of the strategic importance of the lesser contingency has also brought with it an organizational component--the Rapid Deployment Joint Task Force.

Although these curves that scribe the sinuous status of limited contingency commands drawn over a score of years closely approximate those that define the rise and fall of the lesser contingency within the strategic concept, they tell a different story and require a separate framework for analysis. The organizational history cataloged in this chapter is a second cut at the "half war," and attempts to examine force planning to meet a range of lesser contingencies from an organizational perspective.

There is ample methodological reference and empirical evidence to substantiate an organizational approach to the study of a limited contingency force. But the attempt here is not to embark upon an exercise in decision-making analysis from an organizational or bureaucratic perspective.[1] Rather, the primary purpose of this chapter is to say something about the conditions under which the United States can maintain an effective military organization to deal with lesser and possibly simultaneous contingencies. In this case, an organizational frame of reference provides a powerful functional and analytical model to enhance that process of description and explanation. This organizational "cut" is not meant to provide a complete or alternative means of explanation. It is offered to examine the constancy of certain organizational features that appear to be inherent in commands designed to meet a lesser contingency and to question the value of those features in past and present "half-war" organizations.

Framework for Analysis

The purpose of this introduction is to point out the organizational issues that appear critical in the successful functioning of a limited contingency force. In particular, a study of the organizations fashioned in support of limited contingency operations during the period under study suggests that the following factors are most important in a consideration of the structure of a coherent limited contingency force and, therefore, serve as a model for this organizational development of past and current efforts:

-   the degree to which the command is unified;
-   the degree to which units from each armed service component are dedicated to the organization;
-   if a specific scenario, contingency or adversary was assigned to the organization for force planning purposes;
-   if forces assigned to the organization were either trained or exercised for combat operations in a specific theater.

A unified command structure

The U.S. strategic concept and the unified command structure have followed patterns established during World War II. Just as the two-front war led to a "2-1/2 war" strategic concept, the command relationships created in Europe and Asia during the war were carried over into peacetime force planning. A World War II theater commander controlled and coordinated land, sea and air forces engaged in a common mission in the same geographical area of operations.[2] This concept of a joint or unified command with specific regional responsibility and operational control over all component forces was incorporated into the National Security Act of 1947. This act provided the legal basis for the unified command concept and established a principle of federation that called for the central control of combatant commands by the Joint Chiefs of Staff. The organizational rationale for the unified command structure was formally established in the Report of the Secretary of Defense in 1948:[3]

It was the policy to set up unified commands in selected areas containing elements of two or more services where possible hostile action might require such a single commander to react tactically to a threat without awaiting guidance or decision from Washington.

According to this concept, the President, through the Secretary of Defense and with the advice and assistance of the Joint Chiefs of Staff, may establish joint (Unified) and single service (Specified) combatant commands. The basic guidance for the structure and geographical areas of responsibility of these commands is contained in the Unified Command Plan.[4]

The design of the unified command structure is influenced to a large extent by various mutual security arrangements and U.S. treaty agreements. These commitments condition the command plan just as they affect force planning for specific contingencies. However, in many cases the extent of control of the unified commander over the forces and regions purported to be assigned to him were unclear. The Defense Reorganization Act of 1958 attempted to clarify this issue by giving the unified commander "full operational control" over these forces, thereby establishing a legislative equality between the Commanders and the Service Chiefs and diminishing the possibility that a component commander might be ordered by the chief of his service to withdraw his forces from the unified command. But, since the individual services retained the authority to organize, train and equip forces for the unified commands and to administer and support the forces assigned to those commands, considerable authority was left to the separate services, and the joint commands were weakened accordingly.[5]

Thus, the original goal of a decentralized unified command system operating separately from the Service Chiefs directly under the Secretary of Defense was not met. The commanders of the separate services desired to keep the unified commanders well below that level of independence envisioned by the earlier objective of acting "without guidance or decision from Washington." In the opinion of a 1970 Defense study group, the net result was "an organizational structure in which 'unification' of either the command or of the forces is more cosmetic than substantive" owing to the service orientations of the Joint Chiefs and the lack of constituency for the CINCs (Commanders of the unified commands).[6]

Given the difficulty in negotiating a command compromise to please the organizational interests of both the service chiefs and the unified commanders, the JCS have been reluctant historically to "open up" the Unified Command Plan for reassignment. Therefore, the control over specific geographical regions by particular commands, as new areas of interest have arisen, has increasingly been dealt with by a series of ad hoc organizations to meet new missions rather than by assigning these duties to the established unified commands.[7] The creation of limited contingency commands has suffered particularly with regard to this trend. These organizations created outside the unified command structure have served to weaken the organizational structure designed to cope with lesser as well as major contingencies, while the forces assigned the unified commands when coupled with their regional responsibilities have essentially rendered the ad hoc commands inoperative.

Units dedicated from each armed service component

The establishment of ad hoc organizations to meet new threats or areas of responsibility were often service intensive rather than commands composed of joint or unified services. This tendency to assign lesser contingency missions to only one or two services has been pronounced during the evolution of a limited contingency force. Although it is extremely difficult in a significant tactical operation of greater than three divisions for a single service to "go it alone," the general lack of an accepted doctrine for joint operations in a limited contingency has led to service-specific efforts and organizations to meet these objectives.[8] One of the factors that leads to this conception of independent action on the part of the separate services is the assignment and allocation of specific "roles and missions" to each of the armed services.

There is no official definition of assignment of "roles and missions" as they pertain to the separate services. The existing laws and directives that are normally cited in this regard are Title 10, United States Code, which confirms fundamental functions for each military service. The Department of Defense, with Presidential approval, prescribes primary and collateral functions in greater detail.[9] Thus, "duty and function," as James Donovan has noted, are probably more appropriate terms than "roles and missions."[10]

Yet, despite the lack of a DoD imprimatur, these terms have stuck--probably because they are less precise and, therefore, connote uncertainty about where the responsibilities of one service end and those of another begin. There have been a few attempts to define roles and missions, beginning with the National Security Act in 1947. Following that Act, the Department of Defense published the "Key West Agreement" that further clarified separate service functions. Subsequent revisions and specifications agreed to at the Joint Chiefs level were first published as doctrine in the document Joint Action Armed Forces and, following the Defense Reorganization Act of 1958, United Action Armed Forces. This current guidance for service roles and missions defines how forces are to interact in joint operations and stresses the principle of unity of effort.[11] This unity is to be achieved by the exercise of operational command and control by the Unified Commander (CINC), adherence by the separate component forces to common strategic plans and by sound operational and administrative command relations and organization.[12]

The fact that these relations do not work as smoothly as advertised is not surprising or new. But an appreciation of these organizational struggles for interests, "command relations" and doctrinal disputes is important to include in this analytical framework.

These difficulties pertaining to inter-service rivalries, Unified Command Plan ineffectiveness and joint command inefficiencies suggest that proposals to give a limited contingency mission to a single service would be the rule rather than the exception, and there is some tradition to support this suggestion. Until World War II the only genuine "rapid deployment force" was the Marine Corps.[13] As U.S. post-war interests and commitments expanded, the other services contributed concepts and forces to the rapid deployment strategy. First, land and carrier-based air were added to the already in place amphibious capability. In the 1950s, the Air Force developed the Composite Air Strike Force (CASF), a deployment package concept, and also procured a modest strategic airlift capacity that facilitated the establishment of the Strategic Army Corps--designated units of the strategic reserve to be capable of rapid deployment. Both of these concepts would be eventually absorbed under STRIKE Command. The U.S. Navy, with the Marine Corps separate from STRIKE, stressed its mission of military presence and its capability for power projection.

The willingness of the separate services to commit themselves to a lesser contingency mission has obviously fluctuated with the importance assigned that mission within the strategic concept. The outline of these arguments, both in favor and opposed to a single-service limited contingency force, must necessarily remain brief in this introduction. In addition to the evident organizational and budgetary interests attached to the desire as a single service to become the sole repository for U.S. rapid deployment capability, proponents of a service-intensive limited contingency force point to the tactical advantages of a single doctrine, well coordinated command, control and communication and accepted and practiced operational procedures. The failure of joint forces to operate effectively together in limited operations (such as was experienced in certain Vietnam battles or in the aborted rescue operation in Iran) are frequently cited in support of this position.[14]

The rebuttal of these views--again apart from the organizational or bureaucratic arguments--is essentially that modern warfare is likely to demand the individual capabilities of each of the services. Although a solely amphibious operation could probably be limited to the inherent capabilities of a Navy/Marine Corps team, the likelihood of such a limited operation has been declining with the geographical expansion of U.S. interests and the military capabilities of potential adversaries. Once the requirements of the operation extend beyond that of a Marine division, the other services are likely to play a vital function in its success.[15] An effective operation against a sophisticated adversary on a major land mass, argue proponents of a unified limited contingency force, cannot be mounted without the capabilities and contributions of each of the armed services. These types of arguments will resurface as this element of the framework for analysis is applied to the organizational development of the limited contingency force.

However, the key to understanding a good deal of this organizational debate relates back to the development of the strategic concept of the "half war" in the previous chapter. The services tended to plan their projection forces separately to meet service-specific combat scenarios inbedded in the "half war." Thus, the Marine Corps and elite Army airborne units concentrated on the "brushfire" war, while the more conventional Army and Air Force units geared their force planning to a more sophisticated enemy that might be encountered in a "field of fire" or "firefight" version of the lesser contingency. Therefore, what was missing from the development of the strategic concept of the "half war," we also will find absent in the organizational development of the "half war" commands that follows: the failure to plan forces to meet a range of multiple or sequential scenarios that were likely to occur. Growing from this conceptual failure was a tendency to believe that a single all-purpose force could meet any lesser contingency most effectively and economically.

A specific scenario or contingency for planning purposes

In addition to inter-service rivalries regarding roles and missions, the unified command structure has also been characterized by uncertainty pertaining to the most effective way to allocate joint service responsibilities--functionally or geographically. The present division of labor represents a mix; but, significantly, it is the joint (unified) commands that are assigned particular regions (Atlantic Command,

Map 1
U.S. UNIFIED AND SPECIFIED COMMANDS

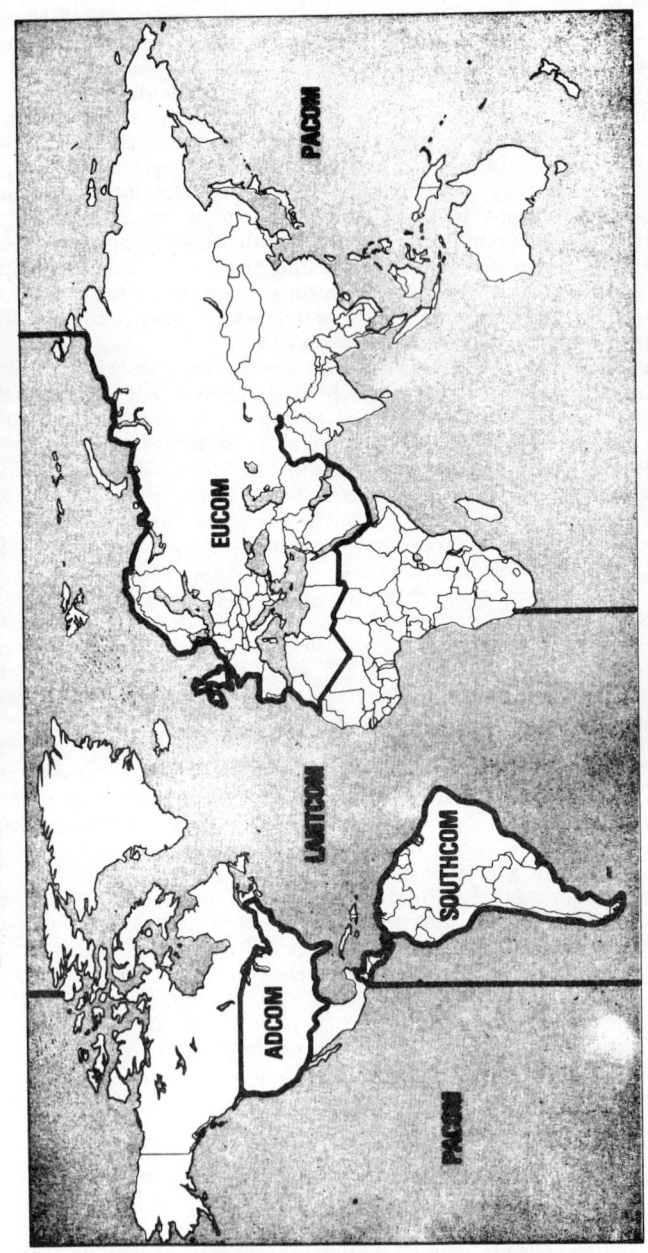

NOTES: Whether or not there is a boundary between EUCOM and PACOM through the Soviet Union is classified information. Readers can presume that if such a line could be identified, it would in some way join the two water boundaries between those commands.

Canada and Mexico, being contiguous to the United States, enjoy special security relationships. No unified or specified command has responsibility for Africa South of the Sahara.

Source: John M. Collins, U.S.-Soviet Military Balance: Concepts and Capabilities 1960-1980, New York: McGraw-Hill, 1980.

European Command, Pacific Command and Southern Command, while the single service (specified) commands are delegated singular functions (Aerospace Defense Command, Military Airlift Command and Strategic Air Command). Readiness Command, the current organization structured to direct forces deployed to a lesser contingency, is somewhat of an anomaly: it is a unified command without a geographic area of responsibility; it is not a combatant command, yet, prior to 1983, held the Rapid Deployment Joint Task Force under its administrative control.[16] As such, it represents many of the shortcomings that exist in the evolution of organization for a limited contingency force.

The geographic rationale for the joint command structure evolved from the need for unity of effort in the execution of common military missions. Unified commanders are said to have "full operational control" of forces assigned to them. However, this is not always the case. Although the unified commander has responsibility for joint training of assigned forces, the component services maintain control over the organization, training and supply of the separate forces assigned and keep close watch over the integrity of service doctrine and the machinations of personnel administration and assignment.[17] Thus, the geographic rationale is often overtaken by an organizational one.

However attractive the approach of meeting U.S. global commitments through the establishment in each geographic region of a unified command responsible for force and contingency planning and execution within that region, this system has not been allowed to operate effectively. Service perceptions of roles and missions and, consequently, a reluctance to accept a change of operational command (chop) of component forces to a unified commander of a different service have prevented an effective unification of the combatant commands. This problem proves particularly acute in an unforeseen contingency requiring the forging of new command relations. Thus, the Army will generally accept a change in operational command only if the sub-unified command controlling Army ground forces has direct access to the JCS; the Navy normally is not willing to have its surface combatants under the command of any other service; and the Air Force similarly maintains a tight control over its strategic forces.[18]

An attempt to solve partially this dilemma of the unified commands and separate services has been to suggest the organization of joint commands on a functional basis of the mission to be performed rather than the geographic foundation for existing commands.[19] While some halting steps have been taken in this direction since 1970--MAC, for example, became a specified command--the geographic basis for the joint (unified) command structure has remained relatively unaltered. As long as this remains the case, a command oriented toward a lesser contingency, but without a specific area of responsibility in which to meet that contingency, will always be faced with the difficulties inherent in deploying a force (belonging to another command) to a region (the responsibility of a second unified command) and in probable opposition to the organizational interests and doctrine represented by the component services of each of the interacting commands. These difficulties have not proven easy to overcome.

Forces trained and exercised for combat in a specific region

In developing an analytic framework, these first paragraphs have suggested that the assignment of a specific geographical area of responsibility to a limited contingency force and the dedication of multi-service units to that force without the intervening control of the separate services may avoid past organizational struggles surrounding the structuring of a coherent and effective limited contingency force. But, as the previous chapter implied, there has been considerable difficulty and disagreement in establishing a particular geographic location as well as the proper place in the strategic concept for the lesser contingency. Although certain locales and scenarios have enjoyed a general popularity through the years as likely limited contingencies--the Caribbean, the Korean peninsula, the Persian Gulf--the lesser contingency, during the period under study, was never accorded a single specific scenario for contingency planning or force sizing. More precisely, as will be stressed throughout this study, a strategic concept envisioning a range of lesser contingencies that required force planning for differing locales and varying adversaries was never formally adopted or consistently applied.

As we shall trace in this chapter, prevailing concepts of force flexibility and versatility were instrumental in this decision not to allocate a limited contingency force to a specific region, but rather to hold to the belief that a limited contingency force could and should be capable of deploying anywhere in the globe and then be capable of conducting effective limited military operations.

Thus, probably the most important, yet frequently overlooked factor weighing against the appointment of a specific region and scenario to the lesser contingency was the belief that U.S. general purpose forces were flexible and versatile enough to meet any contingency. Moreover, tailoring these forces to a specific threat would limit their deployment and employment in other theaters. Writing in 1967, even while the strategic reserves in the United States ostensibly dedicated to the lesser contingency were being deployed increasingly to a very specific contingency in Southeast Asia, Secretary of the Air Force Harold Brown made his position clear:[20]

> If continued military strength is still necessary to achieve a more peaceful world, the single most important characteristic of future forces will probably be flexibility. . . . The variety of contingencies which our military systems must be prepared to meet is very great, and the most efficient composition of tactical forces employed in future limited conflict can never be fully known. . . . It is sometimes forgotten that the first necessity is for a highly qualified professional force in-being capable of quick reaction and rapid doctrine change.

Although Secretary Brown was writing from the perspective of acquiring highly flexible weapons and support systems--such as the C5-A and the FDL to be discussed in the following chapter--he was willing to extend his argument for technological and doctrinal flexibility to a position advocating force versatility as well. If we did not know, he posited, where our general purpose forces would be required to operate (although by 1967 that was becoming increasingly evident), then our forces should be capable of deploying and operating anywhere.

Again in this introduction, the presentation of the arguments for and against the versatility of forces assigned to a lesser contingency must be necessarily truncated. In brief compass, those who oppose a specific scenario for a limited contingency force argue that the United States, as a global power in world-wide interests, cannot predict where the application of force will be required. Moreover, a force that is assigned a world-wide mission documents U.S. resolve to defend those interests. On the other hand, those who favor a force dedicated to a specific contingency point out the force planning advantages and the deterrence and defense effectiveness of matching the strategy and forces in a specific region in which the United States has declared its vital interests. Both in their singular arguments miss the point that the United States may require specific and versatile forces in order to accomplish military requirements occurring simultaneously within a range of lesser contingency scenarios.

Similar to the organization of the unified command structure and the issues attending service roles and missions already developed, the concept of force versatility also emerged from the U.S. combat experience in World War II. In 1962, a survey of major Army commanders was taken on the future need for "forces trained, equipped and manned to perform their missions under a specific set of circumstances of terrain or climate."[21] The general tone of the replies received was that the infantry division that had emerged from World War II and Korea had demonstrated its adaptability to fight in any environment or in any kind of specialized operation simply through an "on-the-job" training approach. Further, most commanders argued that such a training concept would prove both expensive and wasteful of manpower if certain units were trained to fight only in a single environment.[22]

Nevertheless, the Army did move toward an organizational concept that would facilitate the tailoring of divisions to suit their geographic area of combat employment. The "ROAD" reorganization of the early 1960s grew out of the new emphasis on the general purpose forces and moved away from the "pentomic" divisional structure designed originally for ground combat in a nuclear weapons environment. The Reorganization Objective Army Divisions allowed a division mix of infantry, mechanized, armor or airborne components that could be tailored to the mission and the area of operations.[23]

Of course, what has happened over time is that the enormous task of training and planning forces for operation in a major contingency has resulted in the generation of two very specific and unique forces, oriented at the present towards the major contingencies in NATO Europe or Northeast Asia. Historically, however, owing to the geographical uncertainty of the lesser contingency, such precise force planning for that limited case could not be accomplished. Force versatility, therefore, became a premium added to units designated for lesser contingency operations. These units, principally the Marines and Army airborne divisions, were assigned to the central strategic reserves with the mission of preparing for rapid deployment to trouble spots anywhere.[24] Until a "lesser" contingency assumed a strategic parity with the major contingencies or until there was a general realization that such a versatile force was incapable of meeting specific objectives varying over a spectrum of conflict, the economic and military attractiveness of military versatility would continue to dominate the planning for a limited contingency force.

This introduction has suggested a framework for analysis with which to examine the rise and fall of organizations designed to command and control forces allocated to a lesser contingency. The relevance of each of the elements of the model developed herein will be reemphasized through the remainder of the chapter as we develop the manner in which U.S. general purpose force planning for the "half war" was influenced by the organizational structures of the STRIKE Command, the Readiness Command and the Rapid Deployment Joint Task Force. As before, focused, iterative questions will be asked in each of the following sections in order to reach a more general and cumulative conclusion.

The Strategic Setting, 1960

With the limited war critiques of massive retaliation in the late 1950s, came new concepts of limited war and arguments for readily deployable conventional forces to meet low-intensity conflicts according to the non-Soviet "brushfire" model of a lesser contingency. These original considerations were, however, generally single-service efforts and displayed an ambivalence regarding the proper roles and missions for such forces. Moreover, these limited missions were generally derived from the basic characteristics of the forces already in-being. Thus, the emphasis was on a "show of force" by naval, marine or air forces, while the Army argued that intervention by ground forces would be required in a limited war as well as a major conflict. In 1955, Admiral Radford acknowledged this split by suggesting that all of the services had a role to play in the construction of a limited war force:[25]

> Sometimes the presence of a ship or a squadron of airplanes in a given situation might have a very salutary effect. In other situations it might not. In many cases, if you really want to control a situation on the ground, you've got to have the military personnel there on the ground. They may not have to be in great numbers, but the visible presence of a military force, whatever its service, is very often a stabilizing effect.

As themes of conventional deterrence and defense began to be developed in a more systematic fashion, arguments also began to be made that mobile, rapid-response conventional forces could not only display U.S. concern in a limited war, but also possessed a deterrent effect on possible low-level conflict. In 1957, a study conducted by the Stanford Research Institute declared:[26]

> Instantly ready, mobile task forces appear to be the necessary means of meeting the requirements for a policy of limited warfare. The effectiveness of a mobile force depends in great part on its ability to accomplish an extremely rapid commitment to combat in the theater of operations. This is of fundamental importance to avoid being confronted with a fait accompli. The problem of dislodging an agressor after he has obtained his objective is vastly greater than that of containing the aggressor at the outset.

Although rapid deployment capabilities gradually came to be seen as a necessary mission for the U.S. armed forces, there was little agreement on how that force might best be designed or organized.[27] The Navy, based on its traditional missions of sea control and power projection, was generally content with show-of-force operations while leaving the limited war ground mission to the Marine Corps. Moreover, the Navy implied in its official statements that it could accomplish the limited contingency mission without the assistance of the other services and that the Navy amphibious task force was the only truly integrated force capable of meeting the varied requirements of limited war.

On the other hand, the Marines were forced to fight an organizational battle to retain their autonomy and their mission. Although World War II had been regarded as the "golden age of amphibious warfare," Binkin and Record have noted that the War Department, dominated by the Army and Air Corps after the war, viewed the Marine Corps as an "unwanted competitor" and favored its "drastic reduction."[28] A 1953 amendment to the National Security Act finally preserved the Corps' amphibious mission as well as its autonomy and guaranteed the USMC a minimum force of three divisions.[29]

The Army, overshadowed after Korea by the defense policies of massive retaliation, did not have the capability or the support to assume a limited war mission. In the 1958 Defense Reorganization Act, the Army's combat forces had been placed under the unified commanders abroad, thereby limiting the newly-formed Strategic Army Corps (STRAC) to three divisions.[30] But these divisions lacked the dedicated strategic airlift to meet genuinely a rapid deployment requirement and needed either organic tactical air support or closely-coordinated Air Force support to be protected adequately in a limited war. In addition, the other U.S. divisions in the strategic reserves were relegated to a training function. Thus, the Army strategic reserves stationed in the United States, prior to 1961, had little rapid deployment capability.[31]

One of the main reasons the Army was not capable of forming a viable limited war command in the late 1950s was the Air Force dedication of its resources to the primary strategic mission of massive retaliation. Air Force doctrine supported the view that the forces available to deter or win a general war could also deter and win a limited war. Moreover, the Air Force felt that forces required to meet lesser contingencies (both its tactical fighters and airlift) were in insufficient supply to meet and support an unanticipated limited war while maintaining U.S. strategic commitments elsewhere. Thus, U.S. Air Force resources were dedicated to the major contingency, with little close air support or airlift allocated to the support of Army quick-reaction forces.[32]

However, the Air Force did take steps to meet the limited war mission on its own by establishing the Composite Air Strike Force (CASF) concept. The CASF grew from the recognition of a need for a tailored force of tactical aircraft to operate in situations of less than total war. The number of aircraft in the strike force was not specified, but varied according to the contingency to be "capable of rapid deployment and sustained operations in any area of the world."[33] The Air Force did not yet envision the lesser contingency as a support operation requiring airlift and close air support for ground forces. The CASF concept was more in tune with the tenets of massive retaliation than those of flexible response and emphasized theories of tactical nuclear weapons use in a limited war. If a force of nuclear-armed fighter bombers could be moved to the trouble spots of the world quickly enough, it could effectively counteract the "obvious Soviet policy of quick jabs at the soft spots."[34]

To implement this concept, the Tactical Air Command (TAC) activated the 19th Air Force. The mission of this organization was to be prepared to fight a limited war--to include nuclear operations --anywhere in the world. According to the 19th Commander,[35]

> . . . we have a plan for every conceivable trouble spot. Operations plans provide for a CASF to operate as an independent force for at least 30 days. Our belief is that if we get to a point of trouble rapidly with a small effective force, we can maintain peace.

With the Navy belief in a single-service limited war mission and the Air Force concentration on the tactical or strategic nuclear mission, it was left to the Army to generate initiatives for a joint organization oriented towards the lesser contingency. In 1957, a volunteer group of eight officers at the Command and General Staff College undertook a study of how to develop effective national military power flexible enough to engage in the various types of conflict short of general war.[36] Their purpose was to develop an "integrated strategy" to deter and fight a limited war based on the growing belief--in the Army at least--that such a conflict, in view of the apparent US/USSR nuclear stalemate, was most likely.

The study concluded that the command should be composed jointly of all the services, should be a force in-being and should not affect the mobilization status of NATO or other major contingency forces:[37]

> What is urgently needed now to cope with the demonstrated Communist proclivity for expansion in the peripheral area is a ready force in being--mobile, deployed, trained and tailored to the capability of the application of a measured degree of force in any threatened area. This force must not be tied down on other priority tasks.

The concepts envisioned in this seminal study--including a permanent unified command with principal subordinate commands assigned regional responsibility in the Far East and the Middle East--were considerably ahead of their time. However, several other reports of the same vintage were arriving at similar conclusions regarding the need for an increased emphasis on general purpose force planning to meet a limited war. In 1957, the Gaither Report indicated that the Middle East and Asia were the most likely regions for limited conflict.[38] The report emphasized the importance of keeping such a war limited and recommended that the U.S. train and equip its forces for conventional land warfare. Although the Gaither report was not accepted by the Eisenhower administration as an official guide to force planning, it is apparent that the Gaither study, along with the Rockefeller report the following year, formed a conceptual basis for the change in the strategic concept under Kennedy.

STRIKE Command, 1961

Was the organization a unified command with direct control over its assigned forces?

The impetus for the establishment of a unified command to meet a lesser contingency was provided by President Kennedy in 1961 after completion of a reevaluation of U.S. military strategy. In March 1961, the Secretary of Defense requested the Joint Chiefs develop a plan for the integration of the Army's three-division Strategic Army Corps (STRAC) with TAC's 19th Air Force and CASF capabilities. The ensuing deliberations of the JCS considered many of the issues presented previously as an analytical framework: Should it be a unified command or a joint task force? Were the Navy and Marines to be included? How would the command conduct contingency operations? With what forces?[39]

This JCS decision-making process was characterized by Army-Air Force agreement, stemming from previous coordination at the major command level, but also by a lack of Navy and Marine Corps enthusiasm. In July 1961, both the Commanders of TAC and CONARC (Continental Army Command, including STRAC) recommended the establishment of a United Tactical Command as a joint headquarters, with Army, Navy and Air Force component commands. They visualized that this command would be organized around a relatively small unified headquarters, would possess great mobility and would be capable of rapidly deploying fully effective combat units to areas of crisis.[40]

The JCS study, with Navy and Marine demurrals, was forwarded to the Secretary of Defense in mid-August. One month later Mr. McNamara announced that a new unified command would be formed by combining forces of the Strategic Army Command and the Tactical Air Command. Its purpose was to "develop doctrine for the integrated deployment and to be responsible for the land and tactical air forces assigned."[41] However, the Secretary's decision left unclear many things about the new command --including the mission and forces assigned. The announcement did serve to appoint the new commander of the as yet unnamed force, General Paul D. Adams, U.S. Army. It also provided for the "Joint Terms of Reference," the official guidance allocated to each unified command by the JCS. This document included the direction to "maintain a general reserve of combat-ready forces to reinforce other unified commands" and to "plan and direct contingency operations as directed."[42]

By December 1963, STRIKE Command had been charged with a multi-faceted mission that required it to support other commands while still maintaining the capability for autonomous operations:[43]

- to conduct operations in the Middle East, Southern Asia and Africa South of the Sahara;
- to augment other unified commands;
- to execute contingency missions (or other operations such as mercy or evacuation) as the Joint Chiefs might direct;[44]
- to provide a strategic reserve of combat ready forces;
- to develop doctrine for the employment of forces assigned;
- to be responsible for the joint training of the forces assigned;

- to conduct joint training exercises to insure maintenance of a high state of combat effectiveness and a rapid reaction capability.

The forces available to STRIKE Command to accomplish these missions were not assigned to STRIKE on a day-to-day basis. Rather, these forces were to come under the Commander's control only during joint training exercises, when the JCS directed the reinforcement of other commands or for the conduct of limited contingency operations by STRIKE Command. This meant that the commanders of the component forces were "dual-hatted." In fulfilling a JCS-directed STRIKE mission, the Commander, CONARC would become "Commander in Chief, U.S. Army Strike." His Air Force colleague in TAC would also switch hats as appropriate. For all other missions and military purposes, however, the Army and Air Force tactical commanders remained responsible to their separate services and in control over the component forces.[45]

As originally conceived in 1961, the majority of STRAC and TAC forces stationed in the CONUS as the strategic reserve was to be placed under the operational control of STRIKE Command: that meant the 82nd Airborne, the 101st and the Fourth Infantry Division, plus TAC's fighter, reconnaissance and troop carrier wings. Also to be included were the three Army "training" divisions, then being upgraded to combat-ready status under the new conventional emphasis of the Kennedy administration.[46]

U.S. STRIKE Command assets were specifically organized, trained and equipped to be entirely air mobile and capable of commanding and controlling joint Army and Air Force units (as well as Navy and Marines if the JCS so provided) in various sizes and mixes ranging from a show of force to sustained combat.[47] The principle of "usable power" as advocated by Secretary McNamara served to guide the selection of forces assigned to STRIKE and to be deployed under its command. This "package force concept" established standardized prepackaged forces flexible enough to permit rapid tailoring to meet any contingency in a variety of environments.[48]

Owing to the limits imposed on STRIKE by the failure to include naval forces and STRIKE's lack of control over the forces, the original mission was redesigned.[49] Soon the analogy of a "packaging and delivery service" was used to describe the way that STRIKE should operate rather than the missions and responsibilities normally assigned to an autonomous unified command. Under this revised concept, the JCS would call for a balanced military force to meet certain requirements in a contingency. STRIKE force planners then determined the necessary forces, drew them from their component commands, "packaged" them with a command element and "delivered" them to the theater.[50] The task force commander was selected based on the preponderance of force to be utilized and could be drawn from the STRIKE headquarters staff or from the component commands. CINCSTRIKE himself was also capable of moving to the contingency area and commanding STRIKE forces, but only if the contingency fell outside the bounds already assigned to other unified commands.[51]

Thus, STRIKE ostensibly was capable of directing combat operations as either a unified command or as a joint task force, depending on the location of the contingency.[52] At its inception and in response to the need to meet multiple contingencies as well as conduct joint training exercises, STRIKE Command formulated a "two joint task force headquarters" concept that allowed planning, operational and administrative flexibility. Thus, one JTF headquarters could participate in the training mission, while the second, in times of tension or impending deployment, could be occupied with real-world contingencies. This concept allowed STRIKE the command flexibility of meeting two limited contingencies simultaneously.[53] However, because STRIKE did not maintain control over its assigned forces, the conduct of such simultaneous operations under the direction of STRIKE Command was unlikely.

Observing the situation at the end of the 1960s, the Blue Ribbon Defense Panel did not see the value of assigning the limited war mission to a unified command that lacked authority and control over its assigned forces and was continually overtaken by external events. Rather than calling for a separate command with assigned forces and a specific region of responsibility however, the Blue Ribbon Panel called for putting the entire general purpose force under a single commander who would be responsible for conventional planning and employment worldwide:[54]

> It is not possible to plan precisely for limited war. Therefore, contingency plans must be rapidly adjusted to the developing situation. With the forces designed for limited war assigned to six separate commands, it is not possible to achieve the coordinated planning, flexibility in resource allocation and mission assignment and the training required to assure the capability to react rapidly and effectively to a crisis situation.

Without such organizational reform, the Panel expressed concern that in future limited contingencies the command and control of the dedicated force would continue to be exercised from the National Command Authorities through a series of ad hoc arrangements rather than through the forces designed and designated for the mission.[55]

General Momyer, the TAC commander, also concluded at approximately the same time that the attempt to form STRIKE as a unified command without assigning it control over its own forces had proved to be an unworkable concept.[56]

> One of the arguments advanced for STRIKE is the availability of a headquarters to deploy to a contingency without disturbing the theater command organization. This argument has proved to be erroneous. When we deployed to SEA, CINCPAC created his own organization and expanded it from CONUS resources. . . . We found the same attitude of the theater commanders to provide their own command structure during the Formosan, Lebanon and Berlin crises. Hence, we can't sustain the need for STRIKE for this function.

This point touched on the most telling reason for the decline of STRIKE Command as a limited contingency force and presents one of the strongest arguments for designing such a organization with autonomous forces. STRIKE ceased to have operational significance because the war it might have been designed to fight--or at least a transmutation of it in Vietnam--had absorbed its forces without requisitioning the command structure. As suggested in the preceding chapter, the depleted strategic force in the United States by 1970 had little capability for meeting a lesser contingency. In General Holloway's words, "STRIKE Command just sort of withered on the vine because most of the forces they had to work with went to Southeast Asia."[57]

STRIKE Command, as General Momyer correctly pointed out, had merely become an internal facilitator for the mobilization of combat troops destined for Vietnam. To manage this large deployment of U.S. forces, the JCS in April 1965 directed STRIKE to take responsibility for movement coordination of all Air Force and Army units. At the ports, for units moving by sea or at 140° West longitude (between San Francisco and Honolulu) for elements deploying by air, PACOM assumed responsibility for the forces once available to STRIKE.[58] General Adams' account of the decline of STRIKE's mission and men agrees with this assessment:[59]

> We deployed all of the forces--but it took quite a lot of forces from the U.S. It certainly was not the forces we had in the beginning. 1965-1966 was when the significant deployments were coming along. Strike Command was probably incapable of conducting many of the contingency operations which it had been instructed to get ready to do.

Were units dedicated to the command from each armed forces component?

Although designed as a limited war command, STRIKE was denied dedicated forces from all the services. This limitation continually prevented STRIKE from effectively planning and coordinating joint operations in any contingency. The reluctance of the JCS to assign naval forces to STRIKE Command resulted in the inability of the command to conduct limited operations.

One of the original reasons justifying the lack of Marine and Navy participation in STRIKE was that the new command was designed to resolve doctrinal differences between the Army and Air Force with regard to rapid deployment and close air support. With the close integration of Marine divisions and air wings, the Navy and Marine position was that their own units already provided a proper mix of air, sea and ground power--a doctrinal issue that the Army and Air Force were only beginning to grapple with. Thus, the insertion of the Marines into this important issue could only complicate it and, possibly, result in the loss of the cohesiveness already existing between Marine ground and air forces.[60]

Although the initial plan for the combining of STRAC and TAC supported by both the Army and the Air Force had contemplated the inclusion of Marine and Navy forces, this joint initiative was not successful. The official explanation was that Navy and Marine units were already formed as components of unified commands in the Atlantic and the Pacific.[61] Secretary McNamara responded to questions regarding the services missing from the STRIKE Command by saying that they had been considered but were left out because of their "special" mission.[62] But, retiring TAC Commander General Frank Everest noted that "such a force will not be fully effective unless it included a Navy contingent." Sea lines of communication, in addition to airlift, were required if the force were to accomplish its mission effectively.[63]

This focus on service doctrine tended to obscure a much larger issue of service autonomy. One of the major concerns of each service at this time was that the new emphasis on general purpose forces might be captured by a single service. The Defense Secretary had promised that STRIKE would be assigned certain contingencies but had temporarily left them undefined. If the STRAC-TAC command were to fall heir to most of the limited war missions, it could conceivably gain a "monopoly on crises." Thus, the Navy-Marine position in 1961, fearing the loss of the limited war mission to the Army, was considerably different from that adopted twenty years later when they would attempt to claim the rapid deployment mission for themselves:[64]

> No force, however versatile, can be all things to all men. The STRAC-TAC command cannot possibly extinguish every brushfire in every part of the globe on a unilateral basis. In conjunction with other forces and in a complementary role this unit can make a significant contribution. . . . If the resulting product is a complementary image of the Navy-Marine amphibious force in readiness, we have achieved a notable success. If it is not, we simply have one more competitor for service roles and missions.

It was not only roles and missions that were being threatened as organizational interests, but service autonomy and essence as well. There was a perception, particularly in the Navy, that the merger of the Air Force and Army forces in STRIKE Command was a harbinger of the new administration's desire to centralize and ultimately unite the separate services.[65]

On the other hand, the Commander of STRIKE, General Adams, related that the lack of cooperation on the part of the Navy made certain that any such unification efforts would not succeed, even at the lowest levels of a unified command such as STRIKE:[66]

> General LeMay (the new Air Force Chief of Staff) supported it (STRIKE) one hundred per cent, but the Navy was very reluctant. They did not want any unified command unless it was commanded by the Navy--a very unfortunate attitude. . . . There has always been a schism between the Navy and the Army/Air Force regarding STRIKE. One CNO told me, 'We don't need any Army or an Air Force . . .' Now that is pretty narrow minded.

Finally, STRIKE proved incapable of solving the doctrinal dispute that continued to plague Army-Air Force joint operation within the command. The Commander of TAC at the time of STRIKE's organizational dissolution, General Momyer, noted that the STRIKE Command had been unable to resolve these doctrinal differences that existed only between the two services:[67]

> The main thrust for establishing STRIKE came from former Secretary of Defense McNamara. At the time, we were having major doctrinal arguments with the Army as a result of the Howze board. . . . McNamara and some members of his staff held the view that STRIKE would be the agency for the resolution of the doctrinal differences. We had the GOLDFIRE tests and the Army continued field tests of the Howze Board concept. STRIKE soon admitted it couldn't resolve doctrinal issues and, to date, has never been involved.

It is true that, under STRIKE as well as other areas, these doctrinal problems were not completely resolved. Fundamental doctrinal divergences--and organizational interests--surrounded the new Army concept of air mobility that threatened traditional Air Force control of the air space over the battlefield. Secretary McNamara and the JCS had envisioned testing the airmobile concept under the supervision of STRIKE Command but ran into an organizational dispute. The development of joint doctrine was assigned to the Air Force (specifically to TAC) by the United Action Armed Forces document, but STRIKE Command also had a charter from the JCS to develop joint doctrine for its forces assigned: STRAC and TAC. Moreover, tests of the air mobile concept conducted by the separate services tended to support their own doctrine.[68] The Army desired an enhanced air mobility capability through the acquisition of its own resources, while the Air Force contended that the missions of air mobility, reconnaissance and close air support must remain within their domain. The failure to resolve these differences offered little hope of integrating naval and marine forces into joint operations and appeared to lock STRIKE Command into a dual-service limited contingency force.

Was a specific or geographic region assigned the command for contingency planning?

A major issue attending the organization of STRIKE Command was its designated geographic area of responsibility. At the time of STRIKE's establishment, almost the entire globe was allocated to the jurisdiction of one of the existing unified commands. The only exception to this policy was Africa, south of the Sahara. But, earlier in 1961, Joint Task Force Four had been created in Norfolk to prepare contingency plans for operations in that area. Although it remained unclear how STRIKE and that new joint task force would interface, it soon became evident that STRIKE's planning would also focus on that region. In his 1962 Posture Statement Mr. McNamara remarked:[69]

> The recently created STRIKE Command--comprised of units from the Strategic Army Corps and TAC--is intended to provide an integrated, mobile, highly combat ready force which has trained as a unit and is instantly available for use as an augmentation to existing theater forces under the unified commanders or as the primary force for use in remote areas such as Central Africa or the Middle East.

Although STRIKE Command had no clearly assigned area of responsibility in which to conduct autonomous operations, there was a gradual focus on the organizational vacuum existing in the Middle East and Africa. This proposed transfer of Middle East responsibilities to a unified command located within the United States ran counter to Naval doctrine that stressed the flexibility of forces within an assigned geographic region. Therefore, it was over the dissenting opinions of the Navy and the Marine Corps that the JCS recommended that the Naval Forces Eastern Atlantic and Mediterranean (CINCNELM) should be phased out of existence and that CINCSTRIKE should be made responsible for all U.S. defense activities in the Middle East and Africa, south of the Sahara. Under this new responsibility, accorded in December 1963, CINCSTRIKE also became CINCMEAFSA.

The assignment of an area of responsibility to a command that was ostensibly functional rather than geographic in nature met with both military and political opposition. Members of the U.S. Congress expressed doubt regarding the assignment of a certain geographic region to a command that was supposedly capable of responding to any lesser contingency, anywhere:[70]

> Mr. Hardy: There was some considerable doubt in the minds of some of us as to why it was done because I know that hardly any of us had any notion that STRIKE was to become a unified command.
> Mr. McNamara: The real reason why it was done was that we had a very ineffective administration over several functions of the Department. Military assistance in Africa was still being handled by the Department of the Navy, CINCNELM, an atrophied organization was responsible for contingency planning, but had no units assigned to it.

Allies of the Navy in Congress were particularly concerned that, as a result of the change in the Unified Command Plan, the Navy lost command of the Military Assistance Advisory Groups (MAAGs) in the Middle East and operational control over the U.S. Middle East Force (USMIDEASTFOR) in Bahrain:[71]

> Mr. Flood: I speak now on the question of the revision of the commands. The idea of a functional concept as distinguished from what we have always known as the geographical concept and that you have upset a lot of people, particularly in the Marines and the Navy.
> Mr. McNamara: I asked the Chiefs whether they felt that the assignment for the preparation of contingency plans of that area should remain with CINCNELM, located in London, or whether it should be transferred to some other part of the Department. . . . The Navy in particular and I believe the Marine Corps as well dissented from the view of the majority of the Chiefs that it should be transferred to CINCSTRIKE. . . . STRIKE had the capability, it was felt, to do this.
> Mr. Flood: Even in Florida?
> Mr. McNamara: Yes.

STRIKE Command evolved rapidly into the organizational structure deemed necessary by the Kennedy administration to guide its general purpose forces and, despite its geographical focus, was frequently characterized as a command noted for its global mission and its rapid deployment capability. "Never before," said General Adams in a 1962 interview, "has a command with the scope and responsibility of STRIKE been organized and started functioning in so short a period."[72] In testifying to Congress on the need for rapid deployment forces, Secretary McNamara more clearly spelled out the rationale for a limited war command:[73]

> Our limited war forces should be properly deployed, trained and
> equipped to deal with the entire spectrum. . . . The ability to
> respond promptly to limited aggressions, possibly in more than one
> place at the same time, can serve both to deter them and to prevent
> them from spreading out into larger conflicts.

The phrase "entire spectrum" was an operative one, for STRIKE was
touted as a force that could provide "swift tactical reaction in every
known environment." Toward that end, STRIKE had absorbed many of the
functions formerly performed separately by the XVIII Army Corps and the
19th Air Division.[74]
This global mission called for a great number of contingency plans
and a wide variety of exercises. Over 22 separate contingency plans were
drawn up in the first five years of STRIKE's operation. In a
representative period during STRIKE's halcyon days, from January 1962 to
June 1963, STRIKE Command engaged in 27 joint operations, including
exercises in Alaska, the Philippines, the Caribbean and Europe.[75] Despite
the difficulties inherent in operating in these various locales, early
evaluations of the command portrayed STRIKE as being capable of
satisfactorily meeting the limited mission:[76]

> During the last year, the STRIKE Command has improved its
> organizational structure and has gained operational experience
> through day-to-day operations and the conduct of joint training
> exercises. The number of combat-ready Army divisions available to
> STRIKE Command has increased from three to eight. Recent events
> have confirmed that STRIKE Command has greatly improved the
> responsiveness of the Defense establishment to a variety of military
> contingencies and has added considerable flexibility to the
> employment of combat forces.

However, the performance of STRIKE under conditions actually
approaching a limited contingency left a great deal to be desired,
primarily owing to the command's inability to perform as a unified
organization in the contingency area. These shortfalls can be adumbrated
in a brief accounting of STRIKE operations during the Cuban Missile
Crisis, the intervention in the Dominican Republic and the Six-day war in
the Middle East.
STRIKE Command was not tasked and did not play a major role
during the Cuban Missile Crisis in the fall of 1962.[77] The official
rationale was that there had not been time for STRIKE to take over the
contingency planning for Cuba.[78] That was not the case. A more
complete explanation would take into account the fact that naval and
marine forces were required, but could not be placed under the
operational control of STRIKE Command. Moreover, the Caribbean was
within the geographical boundaries assigned to the Atlantic Command;and
CINCLANT, a Navy admiral, had been one of the main points of
resistance in the Navy's opposition to the STRIKE concept.[79]
Although STRIKE Command continued to draw up contingency plans
for the possible rapid deployment of U.S.-based forces to many areas of
possible conflict, the Cuban Missile Crisis evidences that these plans were
likely to be superseded by standing unified command arrangements and ad
hoc decision making. General Paul Adams recently recalled that the plans
prepared in advance for a Cuban contingency (evidence that STRIKE was

involved in the planning) were, nevertheless, ignored once the crisis developed:[80]

> We drew up a plan to react if someone in Washington said, 'Do something about Cuba.' I took it up to present it to the Joint Chiefs and the Navy wouldn't even look at it. The Chiefs of the Army and the Air Force thought it was a good plan. . . . LeMay was ready to take off on it. The plan just lay there. It called for air strikes followed by airborne troops. . . . I expected the Navy would react when they were ordered to. . . .
> CINCLANT was responsible for Guantanamo. . . .The JCS passed the mission to him to get ready for it. We got the troops alerted. General Sweeney (the TAC Commander) was in close contact with Admiral Moorer (CINCLANT), trying to work out a joint aerial operation down there. Sweeney asked if I objected to him using the STRIKE air operations plan in Cuba. He showed me a Northeast-Southwest line drawn on a map of Cuba--one section had been designated 'Air Force Air'--he was working from scratch. I told him to use ours--we'd back him up.
> Oddly enough they passed the Army elements to CONARC to operate under CINCLANT. CINCLANT came along with the decision that the Marines had to land first. Then it took the Marines a week to get their boats together and another three days to get there. So it delayed everything ten days. We had our operation pulled together in 24-48 hours and had to wait a week or more for the Marines.

In the Dominican Republic in 1965, another organizational conflict between the unified commands limited a coordinated use of U.S. military force in what was not, but may have been perceived to be, the beginnings of a limited contingency in the Caribbean. With an apparent revolution in progress in the capital city of Santo Domingo, President Johnson ordered the Atlantic fleet toward the island on April 25, 1965. "The ships were to remain out of sight of land but to stand by in case of need."[81] Four hundred marines landed on April 28. On the following day, advance elements of the 82nd Airborne Division enroute from Fort Bragg, North Carolina, to Ramey Air Force Base in Puerto Rico were diverted directly to Santa Domingo. Again, General Adams explains the operational and planning problems encountered in attempting to place STRIKE-earmarked units under CINCLANT control:[82]

> The Joint Chiefs put that operation under CINCLANT. They ordered the dispatch of the 82nd under our plan to move the division. The Navy commander was on a ship at sea--away over the horizon and was in communication with the forces only about half the time. I told CINCLANT that we would handle the deployment for them. The key to it was communications. We put that outfit into business and immediately the communication problem was solved. We finished the deployment for them.

Admiral Moorer acknowledged the capabilities of STRIKE Command in later Congressional testimony but pointed to the fact that, despite STRIKE's alleged rapid deployment capability, it rarely commanded these mobile forces:[83]

STRIKE had the commitments, the staff, and the men and the plans, for that matter, by which they could deploy divisions overseas. This capability was never used in the various crises. The forces were assembled by the STRIKE Command and then moved out and immediately turned over to the unified commander in whose area they were going to operate. The Dominican Republic is an example.

In 1967, this time in STRIKE's area of responsibility in the Middle East, the Marines and the Sixth Fleet were once again assigned the mission to provide protection and/or evacuation of U.S. citizens rather than forces under STRIKE organization or command. In analyzing this operation, the Blue Ribbon Defense Panel noted the problems that develop when the Service Chiefs do not allow the Unified Command Plan to work and, in this case, replaced the geographical responsibilities of STRIKE Command with assets of the European Command:[84]

> An example of the confusion that can be created in the present Command structure occurred in the Arab-Israeli War of 1967 when the U.S. military was directed to evacuate U.S. nationals. The crisis was in the area of responsibility of STRICOM; however, a decision was made to perform the evacuation with airlift assets assigned to EUCOM.

After a good deal of confusion and delay stemming from this decision, a STRIKE command and control aircraft was eventually assigned to EUCOM, and the European Command was directed to execute the STRIKE evacuation plans. Thus, it was demonstrated that STRIKE, without the command and control of naval forces, would not be allowed by the JCS to direct such forces in limited military operations, even in STRIKE's own region of responsibility.[85]

The Blue Ribbon Panel was arguing that merely assigning a unified command an area of responsibility was not sufficient and that command also needed assigned forces within the region or the command lines would continue to remain unworkable. General Momyer pointed out that the assignment of the Middle East to STRIKE, therefore, made little sense. A more prudent choice would have been the Caribbean, but that region, as previously noted, was already assigned to a unified command with forces outside the jurisdiction of STRIKE:[86]

> McNamara also thought that STRIKE would assume responsibility for all the contingencies in the Caribbean. This meant CINCLANT would be divested of his responsibilities in that area. . . . Today we are no closer to getting these responsibilities for STRIKE than the day the command was formed some nine years ago. Without these responsibilities STRIKE has no significant operational function.

The co-commanders of STRIKE, General Adams and General Holloway, shared this view that STRIKE should be awarded an area of responsibility in the Caribbean, but the lack of naval forces under STRIKE's control made such an event highly unlikely. Contingency operations in the Caribbean were sure to involve naval and marine forces, thereby effectively eliminating STRIKE Command from the scenario. The experiences in the Cuban Missile Crisis and the Dominican intervention seemed to support that contention.

Thus, STRIKE's geographic dilemma was both apparent and real. STRIKE could not direct forces in the area contiguous to its headquarters because those forces would be predominantly sea-going and were, therefore, not included in the JCS Terms of Reference for STRIKE Command. On the other hand, the region assigned to STRIKE was unrealistic in terms of the amount and types of forces that STRIKE could bring to bear under its own command and control:[87]

> The argument most advanced for the need for STRIKE is the planning and employment of forces south of the Sahara. In my judgment, we pay an awfully high price in resources for this task when we would be dependent on CINCEUR for major support in the event of operations in the area. Due to the very tenuous probability of any significant U.S. operation in the area, it seems to me we would be prudent to give the task to CINCEUR. He is closer to the problem and will have resources committed regardless.

Were forces assigned to the command trained and exercised for combat in a specific region or contingency?

The STRIKE Command concepts of rapid mobility and force versatility emerged from the post-World War II belief in the proven adaptability of the infantry division to a variety of combat environments. Of equal attractiveness was the economic benefit that could be derived from a central strategic reserve force within the United States that could be deployed rapidly to an area of limited conflict. The view of Army and Air Force commanders assigned to STRIKE reflected an unbounded enthusiasm for the capability of the organization to deploy and employ its forces rapidly and effectively:[88]

> STRIKE Command is the answer to a long-term requirement. . . . It forms the apex of a triangle that brings together the highly specialized forces of TAC and the Army to provide a flexible and selective strike force. . .that can move swiftly and with unbelivable power and flexibility to meet any threatening situation.

Such claims were not completely out of place if the original mission of STRIKE, the "brushfire" or "show of force," was emphasized to the exclusion of more wide-ranging military operations. If these low-intensity operations required only a military presence, then the versatility and adaptability of the units deployed to a combat environment was of little consequence. However, if forces were deployed to engage in a combat role, the advantages of training the units for operation in that environment became more apparent. Such was the case for ground forces deployed to Vietnam under the aegis of STRIKE Command in the mid-60s.[89]

The lessons of Vietnam in terms of force versatility can perhaps best be discussed under the headings of the strategy applied, the doctrine transferred and the bureaucratic imperatives that acted to prevent organizational adaptation to the environment. There is a general consensus, among those who have attempted to draw military and political "lessons learned" from the Vietnam conflict, that the strategy of attrition adopted by the United States in the war was ill-suited to the region and the capabilities of the adversary.[90] The point here is not whether that strategy was misapplied, but that the selection of that strategy stemmed from the process of force planning and guidance based on the major contingency in Europe or Asia--seen as conventional warfare--not on a guerrilla type of war in the jungles of Southeast Asia. By the end of 1968, the futility of the strategy of attrition was described in a summary of responses to an NSSM entitled, "The Situation in Vietnam":[91]

> There is general agreement with the JCS statement, 'The enemy, by the type of action he adopts, has the predominant share in determining enemy attrition rates.' Three-fourths of the battles are at the enemy's choice of time, place and duration. . . . With his safe havens in Laos and Cambodia and with carefully chosen tactics, the enemy during the last four years has been able to double his combat forces. . . .

The implication here is that the strategy of attrition, transferred from the image of the type of war U.S. forces would be required to fight, was inappropriate and that forces managed under this strategy proved ineffective against the enemy.

For with the strategy of attrition came service doctrine in support of that strategy. Despite the requirements in Vietnam for a mix of counterinsurgency and conventional warfare techniques, U.S. forces deployed to Southeast Asia generally employed the doctrine and techniques more suitable to a major conventional conflict.[92] U.S. forces had been sized, equipped and trained primarily to meet sophisticated Soviet forces on the plains of Europe. Elements of service doctrine, such as strategic bombing and interdiction in the case of the Air Force, were transferred to a theater in which those missions were often inappropriate. Not only did the doctrine employed tend to follow the overall strategy, but also the war in Vietnam, because it was not seen as a major contingency, tended to be used as a testing ground for what could be the "real" war in NATO Europe. Personnel rotation policies, the failure to mobilize the Reserves and the "guns and butter" syndrome--all served to support this contention. Thus, there was a tendency within the armed services not to abandon the doctrine under which they had been trained, but rather to perfect those combat skills to gain the experience that might prove worthy in the event of a major conflict in Europe.

Robert Komer has suggested that this lack of versatility on the part of U.S. armed forces as evidenced in Vietnam is more than a result of strategy and tactics learned and can be interpreted with a bureaucratic perspective. Komer claims that the U.S. combat performance cannot be fully understood "unless it is seen as a function of our playing out our military repertoire--doing what we were most capable and experienced at doing."[93] The higher priorities allocated to NATO and Korean contingencies naturally limited any special preparations made for a lesser contingency. Thus, the "general purpose forces" did not turn out to be very flexible at all, "nor did the prevailing concept that conventional forces designed to meet the worst-case contingency--high-intensity, non-nuclear conflict--would also be suitable for lesser contingencies prove to be as valid as expected."[94]

STRIKE Command, of course, was not a perpetrator of this American way of warfare, but an organizational victim of it. Neither strategist nor tactician had anticipated such a massive U.S. commitment to Vietnam, and no one had prepared for it. Forces were committed to Southeast Asia, not from just the strategic reserve over which STRIKE had been granted training and deployment responsibilities, but from all of the major ground units in the Army, as personnel policies conducted replacement on an individual and annual basis. The military expertise applied was then not precisely tailored to the environment but most often became those of the lowest common denominator of basic military training, strategy and doctrine. Moreover, these concepts of strategy, doctrine and organizational practice and interest were not only strong enough to defeat attempts at innovation and specialization, but they were also carried over into the Readiness Command and the Rapid Deployment Joint Task force.

This section has suggested that STRIKE Command suffered from a number of respects in terms of the variables that contribute to an effective limited contingency force. STRIKE existed as a unified command, but without naval capabilities; with a geographical area of responsibility, but without the means to exercise control over that region; a joint command, but without assigned forces; and as a versatile force that was overcome by traditional strategies, doctrines and practices. However, the final axe to fall on the STRIKE Command was budgetary rather than strategic.

U.S. STRIKE Command was surveyed by a joint defense manpower team in May of 1969 and again in June. As a result of these studies, the Director of the Joint Staff asked that a review be conducted of the tasks and organization of the STRIKE Command. During the review, after noting that STRIKE Command Headquarters had grown from 300 manpower spaces to approximately 1500 in the eight years of its existence, the JCS reached the general agreement that the size of the headquarters should be reduced.[95]

The result of this directive was a cutting in half of the number of permanent CONUS-based Joint Task Force Headquarters to be maintained by STRIKE, from two to one. This had the immediate effect of limiting the effectiveness of the organization and essentially halted the joint exercise program of the command. Although this action was taken based on new budgetary constraints being imposed on the Department of Defense, it proved an indicator that STRIKE no longer possessed an important mission and no longer enjoyed JCS support.[96]

Therefore, in a reexamination of the Unified Command Plan, the Joint Chiefs of Staff recommended the elimination of STRIKE Command's limited contingency mission. STRIKE Command was to be replaced by Readiness Command, an organization that would be charged only with a training function for the CONUS strategic reserves. On July 8, 1971, the Defense Department announced that the U.S. STRIKE Command, "organized ten years ago as a fire brigade organization to speed military forces to world trouble spots," would be dissolved and its duties assumed by "various American military headquarters throughout the world." Under the reorganization, to be effective January 1, 1972, all U.S. forces in the Middle East would be under the jurisdiction of the U.S. European Command.[97] The attempt to organize a limited contingency force had ended, temporarily, in failure.

The Strategic Setting, 1972

As just explained, the organizational capability of STRIKE Command to act as a coherent limited contingency force was severely constrained. Its organizational heir, Readiness Command, clearly was not designed to assume the mission of the rapid deployment of forces to a lesser contingency. Nevertheless, as a successor to STRIKE and a predecessor to the Rapid Deployment Joint Task Force, REDCOM forms an important institutional link in the historical attempt of the United States to create an effective limited contingency force.

An understanding of this organizational change requires an acknowledgement of the wider strategic setting. The prevailing moods of public opinion and budgetary constraints that affected the strategic concept formed during this period also acted upon the organization and functions of the Readiness Command. This atmosphere can be quickly re-created with reference to two themes evident and surrounding American foreign and defense policy in the early 1970s: a growing public mood of neo-isolationism and the legislative embodiment of this opinion in the War Powers Act of 1973.

Although critiques of expansionist U.S. foreign policy were fashionable during this period, few of the authors of such laments were willing to accept being labeled as isolationists. Even Senator Fulbright, one of the Vietnam war's most severe and persistent critics, denied that he was "counseling the President to withdraw from the world."[98] Rather than isolation, Fulbright called for global interdependence: "Instead of unilateral interventionism we should be for cooperative internationalism through international organizations."

One of those willing to champion overtly the isolationist school of thought was Professor Robert W. Tucker. In his 1972 work A New Isolationism,[99] he argued that the time had come to dismantle the system of military alliances and commitments that formed the base for general purpose force planning. Tucker's thesis was that U.S. national security needs could be met with a strong and secure strategic nuclear deterrent and with a powerful U.S. Navy to guarantee access to international waters. Rather than conducting U.S. defense policy to achieve a "paramount influence" or ideological "imperialist" goals, the U.S. should seek a more modest means to security. Tucker's main objection was that the price of supporting such an expansionist defense policy was far too high.

Adam Yarmolinsky, not claiming to be an isolationist, joined the debate with his book The Military Establishment.[100] Aware of the uncertainties inherent in the complex issues of conventional force levels, Yarmolinsky simply called for a retreat from the "automatic priority" given military spending that had "prevailed over the last decade." The ways to achieve this new balance were several: the pressure of public opinion, reforms within the military establishment and, most significant, presidential control over the defense budget. As to the key to establishing limits on expanding defense commitments, Yarmolinsky agreed with de Toqueville in positing that the attitudes of the general public were most influential. Within those attitudes in the early 1970s, Yarmolinsky detected a polarization between those who envisioned the United States as a global policeman and ". . . other groups--growing in numbers--willing to withdraw into a fortress America or hoping to substitute policies embodying a narrow interpretation of the national interest."[101]

The legislative embodiment of this isolationist momentum is represented in the War Powers Act, passed on November 7, 1973. Enacted over President Nixon's veto, the Act was a Congressional attempt to control the ability of the President[102]

> ... unilaterally to introduce American armed forces into situations of imminent or actual hostilities ... or in numbers which substantially enlarge American forces located in a foreign state and equipped for combat in the absence of a formal declaration of war or specific Congressional authorization.

Under this act, the President has been limited to a maximum of ninety-two days in which to commit U.S. military force abroad without Congressional approval. A concurrent resolution passed by the legislative branch any time during that period can also order that the forces be removed. Although Richard Haass has pointed out that the documented use of the act has been meager, he concluded that the War Powers Act will, to some extent, "inhibit the executive from contemplating the use of force in those situations where a rapid, low-cost and low-risk situation does not seem assured."[103] Such a description would appear to exclude all but "brushfire" versions of a lesser contingency and, therefore, suggests the War Powers Act constrains the formation and operation of a limited contingency force.

Readiness Command, 1972

Was the organization a unified command with direct control over its assigned forces?

The Readiness Command appears in this historical development of limited contingency forces as an organizational pause during a national transition from a period of foreign policy expansion to one of retrenchment, if not isolation. The change of command titles from "STRIKE" to "Readiness" actually suggests the change in the military mission in support of these foreign policy objectives. Like STRIKE, the primary role of Readiness Command was to provide for a central strategic reserve of land-based general purpose forces to augment any overseas unified or specified command. Unlike STRIKE, REDCOM was not assigned a specific geographic area of responsibility and was not charged with the mission of directing forces in the event of a lesser contingency. In the Readiness Command the accent was placed on training, as it had been before the Kennedy build-up, not on a capability for rapid deployment to a combat theater.

This emphasis on training robbed the Readiness Command of a sense of urgency and mission that generally characterizes a combatant command.[104] Moreover, because the separate services making their forces available to REDCOM had not abdicated their training function in favor of the joint command, Readiness Command was forced to delegate this principal role to the component commands. General John Hennessey, Commander-in-Chief, Readiness Command, described this relationship in 1976:[105]

Within the framework for the unified command system, USREDCOM is responsible for the readiness of the Army and Air Force general purpose forces assigned and must insure that they are trained and capable of performing most joint operations. The individual parent services are responsible for recruiting the personnel, acquiring the weapons systems and directing the individual and unit training to achieve desired levels of readiness. This unit training is the responsibility of the two USREDCOM components--the U.S. Army Forces Command (FORSCOM) and the Tactical Air Command.

In addition to providing the strategic reserve for Army and Air Force general purpose forces, USREDCOM was also originally charged with:[106]

- deployment planning for assigned and programmed forces to reinforce other unified commands;
- joint training of assigned forces, including exercises and recommendations to the Joint Chiefs on joint tactics, techniques and procedures;
- contingency planning for areas not assigned another command;
- relief/evacuation operations in areas not assigned to other unified commands.

These terms of reference assigned forces to REDCOM only with regard to its training and deployment responsibilities. Readiness Command, unlike STRIKE Command, was restricted from the direction of forces under combat conditions. In this regard, REDCOM was considerably less important than STRIKE in its ability to contribute to limited contingency operations. REDCOM's mission was to support and augment other unified commands--not to fight alongside them militarily or against them bureaucratically.

Were units dedicated to the command from each armed forces component?

Within REDCOM remained some of the elements that had given STRIKE the theoretical capability of autonomous operation in the event of a deployment. These included a standing joint task force headquarters and a Joint Communications Support Element capable of independent deployment and operation.[107] But within REDCOM also remained STRIKE's incompleteness as a joint command: no Navy or Marine Corps forces were assigned or likely to be made available. However, because REDCOM lacked an autonomous combat capability or mission, this lack of naval forces was seen as considerably less harmful to its organizational interests when compared with the experience of STRIKE Command.[108]

Although the Readiness Command was specifically tasked with the responsibility for the development of recommendations to the Joint Staff regarding doctrine and techniques of joint operation, these inputs have been limited to the employment of Army and Air Force units assigned. While one study portrays REDCOM as a "figure of near-heroic proportions in the doctrinal system," that study also notes the drawbacks inherent in confining such a command to these two forces:[109]

There is no effective provision for the full doctrinal integration of naval forces into REDCOM's joint team. REDCOM, the JCS doctrinal surrogate, has not been allocated naval forces, and their assignment to joint exercises is dependent on the cooperative spirit of CINCLANT. There is no agent for joint naval doctrine except within the Department of the Navy.

Although the JCS, through the Unified Command Plan, have delegated the responsibility for the development of joint doctrine for "forces assigned" to REDCOM, that command has not been given the authority needed to perform the mission in the absence of assigned naval forces. This has caused attempts at the formulation of joint doctrine to remain within a bilateral forum and produces, one study asserts, "less than fully joint doctrine." Moreover, this lack of all-service doctrine fails to test fully the systems developed: "Only through testing the total interaction of all available resources can optimal results be obtained-- doctrinally or in the actual application of force."[110]

The major organizational changes involved in the switch from STRIKE to Readiness Command were the assignment of the MAAGs and missions in the Middle East to the European Command and the corresponding loss of the Directorate of Military Assistance (J7) in the Readiness Command.[111] The size of REDCOM also equated with the manpower-reduced form of STRIKE, with a command staff of approximately 300 personnel. Forces available to REDCOM continued to include the rapidly deployable army units of the XVIII Airborne Corps and the tactical fighter and airlift resources of the Tactical Air Command.[112] But without an organizational vehicle to facilitate, direct and command the rapid deployment of independent forces to the scene of a lesser contingency, the separate services within REDCOM began to examine once again single-service means of rapid deployment.[113] Although the organizational fabric had been torn away from the rapid deployment mission, the services were convinced that the requirement remained. These efforts were reinforced and accelerated, even in a time of military retrenchment and disengagement, by an increasing focus on the likelihood of a lesser contingency in the Persian Gulf.

Was a specific scenario or geographic region assigned the command for contingency planning?

The moods of isolationism and anti-interventionism just described had a constraining effect on any initiative to increase U.S. rapid deployment capability, even after the events surrounding the October 1973 war and subsequent oil embargo. With the U.S. withdrawal from Vietnam, defense planners were reluctant to point to any specific region as one likely for the next U.S. limited military involvement. For these reasons, as well as others drawn from the STRIKE Command experience, the Readiness Command was not assigned a specific region of responsibility and could count on deploying its resources on humanitarian or mercy missions only to areas not already allocated to other unified commands in accordance with the Unified Command Plan. However, the brief 1973 US/USSR confrontation in the Middle East did serve to focus the gaze of U.S. defense planners on that region. Moreover, the concerns for U.S. national security resulting from instability in the Middle East led a number of actors to consider the possibility of limited U.S. military action in a Persian Gulf.

The chain of public events leading to a discussion of an application of military force to assure a steady supply of oil to the West was initiated by Secretary of State Kissinger in an interview in Business Week in January, 1975. The operative questions and responses were:[114]

Q: One of the things we also hear from businessmen is that in the long run the only answer to the oil cartel is some sort of military action. Have you considered military action on oil?

A: Military action on oil prices?

A: Yes.

A: A very dangerous course. We should have learned from Vietnam that it is easier to get into a war than to get out of it. I am not saying that there is no circumstance when we would not use force. But it is one thing to use it in the case of a dispute over price; it's another where there is some actual strangulation of the industrialized world.

A: Do you worry about what the Soviets would do in the Middle East if there were any military action against the cartel?

A: I don't think this is a good thing to speculate about. Any President who would resort to military action in the Middle East without worrying about what the Soviets would do would have to be reckless. The question is to what extent he would let himself be deterred by it. But you cannot say you would not consider what the Soviets would do. I want to make it clear, however, that the use of force would be considered only in the gravest emergency.

The public furor that followed these remarks--particularly the threatened use of force in the event of "strangulation"--may have been an overreaction. Nevertheless, the Secretary of State had suggested the utility of conventional military force, both as an exercise in coercive diplomacy and as a means of coping with a possible lesser contingency in the Persian Gulf.

In the first case, Kissinger's statements were only first in a series of remarks by high government officials that appeared to recognize the need for effective military force that could be deployed to the region. President Ford also refused to rule out the use of military force, while Defense Secretary Schlesinger made even stronger statements.[115] Perhaps more important from the view of an effective structure of coercive diplomacy, these statements were accompanied by tangible demonstrations of military might. In Novenber 1974, the aircraft carrier Constellation and its attendant escorts passed through the Straits of Hormuz, the first time in twenty-five years that a U.S. carrier had entered the Gulf. In early January, significantly timed with the release of Kissinger's remarks, a second carrier, the Enterprise, also deployed to the Indian Ocean. In addition, that month the United States requested landing rights and airspace access to the British air base on the island of Masira, off the east coast of Oman.[116]

These actions, significant in themselves, were also indicators of a U.S. willingness to use conventional force as a diplomatic signal, if not yet as a full-fledged counterintervention force. As Barry Blechman suggested, this sequence of force deployments implied:[117]

... that conventional military capabilities can provide important support for the nation's foreign policy.... When displayed subtly, tailored to specific objectives and orchestrated with diplomatic and verbal initiatives, the armed forces can be used short of actual violence to achieve important national interests.

The geographical focus for the mobile limited contingency force ultimately to be established under REDCOM came from an unlikely source. In a widely cited article in Commentary, Robert W. Tucker, seemingly now writing as an ex-isolationist, posited that owing to the serious threat the oil cartel presented to the industrialized Western world, military force was a legitimate option to control the cartel and secure the energy lifeline to the West.[118] Tucker expressed astonishment at the apparent absence of force as an instrument of foreign policy in the energy crisis that was now enveloping the nation:[119]

> There is no evidence that the alternative of military intervention or the credible threat of intervention has been given serious consideration by the American government. There probably are contingency plans for military intervention in the Persian Gulf ... but such plans exist for almost any conceivable contingency ... their existence indicates next to nothing about the seriousness with which governments consider the prospects of armed intervention.

While contending that the U.S. had dismissed the option of intervention--notwithstanding the remarks by the Secretary of State and other high officials in the government--Tucker was arguing that the Persian Gulf stood as a special case for U.S. military intervention and, implicitly, for the need to assign that mission to a specific force. Although he acknowledged that military intervention may be "militarily unfeasible, politically inexpedient and morally repugnant," he also suggested that there might be no other exit from the energy crisis. More broadly, Tucker was addressing the growing conviction that the use of armed force had lost most of its former utility and legitimacy. "The view that armed intervention is not technically feasible is persuasive," he wrote, "only if it can be shown that the military difficulties of seizing and holding the area for an indefinite period are beyond our capabilities."[120] Tucker was offering a strong argument, within the range of military feasibility, for a scenario-specific limited contingency force to defend what he perceived as the vital interests of the industrialized allies.

Were forces assigned to the command trained and exercised for combat in a specific region or contingency?

REDCOM fails this test on both counts. Because it was not a combatant command and because it was not assigned a geographical region of responsibility, the chances of a limited contingency force being developed under REDCOM to meet growing concerns began to revive concepts of a flexible force capable of rapid deployment that had been developed within STRIKE Command and implied that REDCOM's control over reserve forces in the United States should be expanded to include deployment and combat capability.

In an April 1974 article in Foreign Affairs, given added substance by Kissinger's interview, Maxwell Taylor resurrected his ideas for a flexible strategic reserve in order to enhance U.S. capability to meet a lesser contingency:[121]

> I share the common view that major limited war appears unlikely, at least during the next few years . . . On the other hand in the troubled world which I have postulated, minor wars are very probable, although unpredictable as to specifics. We shall need mobile, ready forces to deter or, in some cases, suppress such conflicts before they expand into something greater. This task is the primary justification for an uncommitted central reserve in the United States ready for presidential use as an instrument of national policy.

This force proposed by General Taylor, without a specific mission or area of responsibility, appeared as a return to the earlier concepts of a "go-anywhere, do-anything" force that had spawned the STRIKE Command.

Other voices were also heard in this new version of an old debate, voices that suggested even if a military force were assigned a specific military mission in the Persian Gulf, the results were uncertain and the costs could prove unacceptable. An article appearing in the March 1975 Harper's, entitled "Seizing Arab Oil," called for the invasion and occupation "for at least ten years" of the huge oil fields in Saudi Arabia operated by the Arabian-American oil company (ARAMCO).[122] But these military plans were questioned from the viewpoint of military feasibility as well as on the grounds of foreign policy prudence. In interviews conducted with senior American military officers, Drew Middleton of the New York Times elicited a consensus that such a military operation was feasible but that it ignored "the difficulties that would arise in the second phase."[123] These included the problem of operating in a desert environment, maintaining a flow of supplies by sea and air and considering the high probability of guerrilla activity or counterintervention by Soviet forces or proxies. Nevertheless, it was now becoming apparent that the limited contingency being envisioned--in popular and scholarly literature, if not within the Defense Department--was of considerably greater intensity than the pre-Vietnam "brushfire" or the Nixon Doctrine's air and sea-intensive model of the lesser contingency. The question now being asked was whether or not the United States possessed the armed forces, organized and equipped, to meet a "greater than expected" threat.

Perhaps the most pessimistic study of U.S. military capabilities in the Persian Gulf was a 1975 analysis, conducted by John Collins and Clyde Mark, entitled "Oil Fields as Military Objectives."[124] In the study, the authors ruled out the possibility that the United States could seize and hold the oil fields in order to provide the U.S. and its allies with adequate petroleum supplies in the event of a total OPEC embargo.

The study also critically evaluated the chances for military success. To accomplish the mission of restoring the flow of oil, the military option would have to[125]

> . . . seize required oil installations intact, secure them for weeks, months or years, restore wrecked assets rapidly, operate all installations without the owner's assistance and generate safe overseas passage for supplies and petroleum products.

The authors also noted the ease with which the oil fields could be sabotaged prior to the invasion and that the probability of a successful surprise attack would be "close to zero."

The magnitude of the force required for such an operation was also a consideration. The requirement to cover all 600 installations over a 10,000 square mile area "could easily swallow three divisions, plus a fourth in reserve."[126] In a less demanding scenario, the probability for success was greater. Yet, a small-scale invasion also possessed the possibility of escalation. In either event, there was the danger that the U.S. could be drawn into a conflict that would escalate beyond the American capability to match the level of conflict.

As Robert W. Tucker has suggested in a more recent appraisal of the scenario,[127] in the mid-seventies the U.S. response to the threatening of its interests in the Persian Gulf region was divided between those who argued that there was no need to consider the "reassertion of Western power in order to preserve vital interests" and those who argued that regardless of need, "adequate and effective means for such reassertion did not exist." This effort depended, to a large extent, on the presumed adversary and the assumed level of intensity of the conflict. The search for those "adequate and effective means" became an active one within the military services and inside the Department of Defense. Given a new requirement and a focused scenario, the task became to size the force, calculate the air and sealift required and to fashion an organization to direct the rapid deployment and operation of U.S. forces deployed to a lesser contingency in the Persian Gulf.

In this pursuit of a suitable force structure and organization, there were several barriers to be surmounted. REDCOM had kept intact many of the properties which had constrained STRIKE Command and kept it from acting as a coherent limited contingency force. As the need to structure such a force capable of responding to a new scenario was perceived, the baggage of STRIKE and REDCOM would continue to weigh down new organizational efforts. REDCOM continued with business as usual: a unified command without assigned forces, a joint command limited in its doctrinal formulation to the operation of two services, a limited contingency force without a specific region of responsibility, an organization of loosely-connected forces plagued with erroneous notions of force flexibility to match a vague, yet global mission.

Readiness Command had served as an institutional buffer--an organizational holding company for the strategies and tactics of the non-Soviet "brushfire" or Soviet-proxy model of the lesser contingency that was now being replaced with an altered perception of the threat. REDCOM stands between the demise of rapid deployment as a concept and STRIKE Command as an organization in the late sixties and the reemergence of these policies in the eighties. STRIKE Command would soon be characterized as an organizational concept, born twenty years too soon, whose time had come.[128] Its direct descendant, fathered by the limited contingency command in-waiting Readiness Command, was the Rapid Deployment Joint Task Force.

The Strategic Setting, 1977

Although the Rapid Deployment Joint Task Force was not officially established until March 1980, the concept of "rapid deployment forces" was evident in the early defense policies of the Carter administration.

However, the conceptual base, prior organizational experience and declared interest in such a force, were necessary, but not sufficient conditions to prompt its formation. Two external events in 1979--the Iranian Revolution and the Soviet invasion of Afghanistan--were required to regenerate interest in the force and to tailor the force to a specific threat and region.

As related earlier, the Persian Gulf region was receiving a good deal of attention in U.S. foreign and defense policies by the time of Jimmy Carter's election to the Presidency. In a review session on PRM-10 in July 1977, Secretary of Defense Brown cited the Soviet Union's proximity to Iran and to other oil-producing nations in the Persian Gulf as one of Russia's strategic advantages and reflected concerns of the U.S. Navy that warned of a Soviet ability to shut off NATO's oil supply by controlling the few strategic straits transited by the supertankers.[129]

The scenarios generated by PRM-10 were reflected in the guidance of PD-18 with language calling for "light, mobile and flexible forces to meet threats in such areas as the Middle East, the Persian Gulf and East Asia."[130] According to the deployment concept enshrined in this directive, these forces would be supported by selected naval and tactical air force units that could operate without dependence on fixed bases overseas. The document also suggested that the 2nd Infantry Division, planned to be withdrawn from Korea over a period of four to five years, might also be given special responsibility as a rapid reaction force in Asia. In neither case, however, did the Presidential Directive state how this rapid deployment force would be planned or organized.

According to PD-18 and the Consolidated Guidance issued in its wake, the general purpose forces in the 1979-1983 time frame were to be committed to operations not significantly different from those embodied in past strategic concepts.[131] The primary mission remained the major contingency in Europe, although that conflict now was described as a short, intense war.[132] Also, as in the past, the general purpose forces were expected to respond to a lesser contingency, more or less simultaneously with a major conflict; but an appreciation for the range of scenarios that could be involved remained absent, and force planning for those scenarios ignored.

Referring to the Administration's concerns for the lesser contingency--considered to be possible in South Korea or the Eastern Mediterranean as well as in Southwest Asia--Secretary Brown stated: "Conflict in one of these areas might require the dispatch of some appropriate U.S. forces to the scene in support of friends and allies; such contingencies could very well precede and even set off a crisis or conflagration in Europe."[133] Moreover, because of a possible connection between the lesser contingency and the greater one, a US/USSR confrontation in a non-NATO contingency began to receive some attention. Secretary Brown also pointed out that although hostile local forces "might undertake the initial attack," they could be supported by "light Soviet expeditionary forces delivered by air or sea from the USSR."[134]

The first assignment of a specific force size to these missions requiring rapid deployment came in early 1978. Reports were circulated that the United States was earmarking as a rapid reaction strike force three divisions, to include initially the Army's 82nd and 101st Airborne units and one Marine division.[135] These divisions were considered as being already in a high state of preparedness and specially trained for a rapid deployment role. According to this early strategy, these units could also be used to reinforce a major contingency in NATO if they were not already engaged elsewhere.

This force was referred to by President Carter in a speech at Wake Forest. The President stated that one of the ways U.S. conventional defense policy would be implemented was by[136]

> ... maintaining and developing forces to counter any threats to our allies and our vital interests in Asia, the Middle East and other regions of the world. ... The Secretary of Defense at my direction is improving and will maintain quickly deployable forces--air, land and sea--to defend our interests throughout the world.

In press briefings following the address, a "top White House National Security expert" explained that Carter was talking about a "deployable global force capability." In this interpretation of the concept, new military forces would not be required, but existing forces would be upgraded to assure quick and better strike capability. Although this new force had not yet been granted a title, it was being referred to in the National Security Council as the "rapid reaction strike force."[137]

Although this Presidential address, and subsequent elaboration of it established the intellectual premise for action on the Rapid Deployment Force within the administration, there was no program or budgetary support for such a force. Although Lawrence Korb has suggested that the "first defense budget lays the foundation for the defense policy of the entire administration,"[138] such was not the case for RDF funding, which belatedly occurred following a revised perception of the threat. Without adequate funding in the FY 1979 defense budget for the required "upgrading" of in-being units, the rapid deployment force remained on paper.[139]

The reluctance of the administration to request additional funding for such a force did not prevent the Congressional staffs from speculating on what those costs eventually might be. In April 1978, the Congressional Budget Office detailed estimates of the costs of a rapid-reaction force, constructed in varying sizes, over the next five years.[140] The CBO assumed that the Defense Department would focus on the Persian Gulf and Eastern Mediterranean as regions where "U.S. interests are so great that the United States may undertake military options to defend them." The contingencies considered to size forces evidence that the scenarios now being envisioned as a limited contingency approached the Soviet-proxy or Soviet-intensive models were:

- U.S. support of Iran against an attack, possibly Soviet-supported, from Iraq;
- U.S. intervention in an Arab-Israeli war;
- U.S. defense of the oil fields in Saudi Arabia or the Persian Gulf.[141]

In addition to a considerable expense such a force would accrue, with a total five-year cost ranging as high as $30 billion, the CBO study also suggested that the force would be unable to conduct a "quick hit in remote places" because it lacked the required strategic mobility.[142] But, according to National Security Adviser Brzezinski, the U.S. was placing a "premium on pre-emption because who gets there first has command of the situation."[143] Thus, in certain offices of the administration, the rapid deployment force was seen as a means to deter or counter possible Soviet intervention in the Persian Gulf.

Although the FY 1980 budget, like its predecessor, did not reflect additional programmatic support for rapid deployment forces, the events in Iran were soon to grant those forces an elevated priority. In April, the New York Times reported that the United States was forming contingency plans "to establish a force of 100,000 troops for use in defense of American interests in sensitive areas."[144] The article noted that the planning was initially being conducted by the separate services as opposed to joint planning and that the Defense Department was primarily concerned at this time with "defining the functions that each service might perform in an emergency." The pace of this planning had been increased noticeably by the recent and apparent collapse of Iran's military power and the possible need to insert U.S. forces into the region.

President Carter publicly mentioned a "rapid deployment force" for the first time on October 1, 1979, in a speech on the Russian brigade in Cuba. In his address to the nation, the President ranged well beyond the Caribbean in his call for greater military readiness:[145] "We must be able to move our ground, sea and air units to distant areas--rapidly and with adequate supplies." Stating that the United States had a "worldwide interest in peace and stability," President Carter announced that he had directed Secretary Brown to "further enhance the capability of our rapid deployment forces to protect our interests and to act in response to requests for help from our allies and friends."[146]

By December 1979, the crisis in Iran and the Soviet troop episode in Cuba had accelerated the administration's plan to create a special quick-strike military force for a lesser contingency. Although the rapid deployment forces had not yet been granted program autonomy, it was evident that funds would be set aside for strategic mobility programs designed to support the force in the FY 1981 budget. According to administration statements, the new defense budget would ask Congress to begin to procure the air and sealift needed to deliver a quick reaction force to "places like the Persian gulf."[147] Although Secretary Brown had stressed that the rapid deployment force could be used to respond to crises in Asia, Africa and Latin America, officials acknowledged privately that its principal role would be to defend against any military threat to oil supplies in the Persian Gulf.[148]

The decision to embark on this course of action appeared as a major departure from U.S. foreign and defense policy over the preceding ten years. Since the Nixon Doctrine in 1969 and following the U.S. withdrawal from Vietnam, successive American administrations had generally followed the dictum that local military forces, not U.S. ground troops, had the primary responsibility for providing that component of a combined effort in a limited contingency. The United States chose to place its reliance on strong regional actors to preserve U.S. interests in the areas deemed vital. But the collapse of the Shah forced a review of the foreign policy of non-intervention and a revival of the defense policy of rapid deployment. However, these vague and inchoate "rapid deployment forces" still lacked an organization, assigned forces and a specific mission. Moreover, it was now becoming clear that the substitution of U.S. forces for regional or indigenous troops would not necessarily insert U.S. units into a "brushfire" conflict but, instead, might face them with a Soviet or proxy force.

In addition, there were opponents of the rapid deployment concept that considered it both militarily unnecessary and politically provocative.[149] Some State Department officials argued that a large interventionary force would be of little use in countries and situations like Iran, in which instability emerged from internal revolt. Others, both within and outside the administration, argued that Soviet political penetration of the Middle East could not be blocked by military force and that a Soviet-U.S. military confrontation in the area remained unlikely owing to its escalatory probability. The arguments advanced against the effectiveness of military force in securing the oil fields were also reborn. Still other opponents of this major U.S. military demarche believed that the very existence of the rapid deployment force would create severe political problems abroad. In a letter to President Carter in August 1979, Senator Hatfield of Oregon and 26 members of the House of Representatives argued that an interventionary force would ". . . raise tensions in the area, jeopardize both the diplomacy of the region and the availability of its oil and, most importantly, critically undermine the credibility of the United States as a peacemaker."[150]

Thus, there were essentially four reasons why the rapid deployment force experienced slow and halting progress during the early years of the Carter administration.[151] First, the basic foreign and defense policies of the United States, stretching back to 1969, incorporated concepts of retrenchment rather than intervention. The fall of the Shah had not been foreseen, while the administration's view of Soviet intentions in the Middle East were not uniformly pessimistic. Second, the administration's general purpose force policy was oriented toward the improvement of U.S. conventional force improvements in Europe. These programs, principally carry-over initiatives from the Ford years, occupied much of the Defense Department's attention and the majority of the general purpose forces' budget. If the "half war" planning contingency had been ignored at the expense of the major anticipated conflict, that neglect had occurred with the implicit assumption that the "half war" would occur at a low level of conflict and not a high-intensity scenario which would require significantly higher defense costs in its support. The Carter administration was not prepared to commit itself to greater defense expenditures in this area. Third, the rapid deployment force lacked State Department support. These objections to a more overt, and possibly perceived as interventionary, U.S. policy in the Middle East were also echoed in Congress and the media. Fourth, the military services, as in the past, were not enthusiastic about a joint scheme to construct another limited war organization. Although the separate services had their own programs underway to ensure a role in the limited war mission, they had become increasingly concerned with Europe and were constrained by a lack of funding to pursue even these more traditional missions in support of the major contingency.

The Rapid Deployment Joint Task Force, 1980

Was the organization a unified command with direct control over its assigned forces?

By mid-December 1979, the Rapid Deployment Force was well on its way to becoming an organizational entity. In a press conference at the Pentagon on December 14, Secretary Brown announced that the force would be commanded by a three-star general and co-located with the U.S. Readiness Command. But the organizational structure of the force was not yet well defined. The force was to be tailored to meet a lesser contingency, with its size configured to meet the emergency at hand. It should be able to deliver a fighting force ranging in size from an Army battalion to an Army Corps, while Marine and naval forces, notably, should also be made available. However, this first official description of the organization seemed to describe the force as an all-purpose deterrent rather than as a specific force designed for conventional war-fighting in a particular region. Brown thus argued that it was not necessary to exercise the force as long as it "was visibly strong enough" and pointed to the fact that the ability to deliver and sustain substantial force at the early stages of a potential conflict could prove decisive to the outcome.[152] Once again, the "rapid deployment" side of the organization appeared to be stressed without concern for the composition of the force itself, and the force, by design, would be capable of meeting conflicts across the spectrum of "half war" scenarios from the "brushfire" to the "firefight."

The newly-formed Rapid Deployment Joint Task Force, in order to get firm commitments regarding number and types of forces made available to it by the separate services, faced traditional disputes about service roles and missions. Because it was structured originally as a joint task force, the RDJTF had to be placed under a unified command or made directly responsible to the JCS. This proposed recreation of a STRIKE-like command under the jurisdiction of Readiness Command, therefore, raised delicate questions of assigned vs. earmarked forces and the future of Readiness Command, still formed primarily of only Army and Air Force units.

Two studies dealing with the issue of assigned forces to the new organization supported the concept of a standing tactical headquarters to unite forces from all four services. PRM-10 had called for the construction of light forces to meet non-NATO contingencies, thereby implying a multi-service effort, if not a unified command.[153] In September 1977, although not in response to concerns regarding U.S. limited warfare capability, President Carter had commissioned a "searching organizational review" of the Defense Department to examine "alternative reforms in organization, management and decision processes."[154] One of the documents resulting from the effort, "Report on the National Military Command Structure" (the Steadman Report), addressed the inadequacies of the present unified command system to meet the strategic environment and noted that changes in the Unified Command Plan might be required. The report favored the enhancement of the role of Readiness Command in coordinating the day-to-day aspects of mobilization/deployment planning of the unified commands, including a more active role for the Navy, Air Force and Marines in the development of joint doctrine and their increased participation in joint REDCOM exercises.[155]

These two studies formed the organizational premise for a joint rapid deployment command, but were insufficient in themselves to promote joint service interest and to gain the required budgetary support from Congress. Although former Under Secretary of Defense Robert Komer stated "we made the Navy participate in the RDF," he also acknowledged that forces greater than bureaucratic ones within DoD had to coalesce to assure widespread interest from each of the services.

A growing Congressional willingness to fund conventional forces, a likely role for fast sealift in support of the rapid deployment strategy and the need for amphibious and power projection capability all appeared to promise a growing Naval and Marine interest in the RDF.[156]

However, even a Navy willingness to participate in the force would not guarantee the dedication of assigned forces. Naval combatants, like combat-ready forces from the other services already deployed overseas, were dedicated to other unified commands and had no organizational ties to Readiness Command. Therefore, the concept of "force packaging" was carried over from STRIKE Command, and the RDJTF, like STRIKE Command before it, was deprived of direct command and control over the forces designated for its use.[157] However, if a range of scenarios within the "half war" planning contingency was now being acknowledged, there was still a reluctance to visualize separate organizational units dedicated individually to each region, adversary and level of intensity. In the words of the RDJF's commander:[158]

> Rather, the concept is to have a central reservoir composed primarily of CONUS-based units from which forces can be drawn to deal with a specific contingency. The size of the force selected will depend on what is determined to be required. . . . The reservoir of forces I referred to has been identified as the RDJTF. It is comprised of CONUS-based Army divisions, a Marine amphibious Force and appropriate U.S. Air Force and Navy units.

In Congressional testimony on the establishment of the Rapid Deployment Joint Task Force, the Commander of REDCOM, General Warner, explained the decision to place the RDJTF under the operational control of the Readiness Command and suggested how that command and control system might operate during the deployment of the force:[159]

> What is new is the deploying of these forces together under a single command headquarters. . . . With regard to the relations between USREDCOM and HQRDJTF, during planning, joint training and exercising and preparing to deploy and employ designated forces of the RDJTF, the Commander of the RDJTF works for me. During actual deployment and employment, he could work for me, for another unified commander or for the National Command Authorities through the Joint Chiefs of Staff, depending on the circumstances, the area and the NCA guidance.

However, in a later interview, General Warner acknowledged that past efforts to form joint limited contingency forces such as the RDJTF had met failure at the hands of vested organizational interests:[160]

> But, instead of pulling together under a single headquarters, (the services) have been pulling apart. They've been driven by service interest as opposed to an operational commitment. And, a joint command can do a great service by converting the armed forces from a strategy-by-budget to a strategy based on operational demands. . . . So, the RDF will perform a long overdue, much needed mission if we can just overcome the services' biased interests and prejudices, yank it together, and make it an operational headquarters.

This attempt to "yank the services together" in a joint command met head-on issues inherent in a clash of organizational interests. One of the first squabbles over service roles and missions involved the control of the air element of the RDJTF. Marine air, closely tied to their own ground forces, traditionally gave first priority to the close air support (CAS) mission. The Air Force, to the Army's dismay, has generally allocated a lower percentage of sorties and a lower priority to the CAS mission in comparison with its other tactical missions of air superiority and interdiction. However, the Air Force proposed to the Joint Chiefs that, apart from the Marine speciality of purely amphibious operations, Marine air in any RDJTF action should come under the control of the local Air Force commander. Such a proposal, to the Marine Corps, was unacceptable.[161]

The Marine Corps also encountered a challenge from the Army regarding the command of the RDJTF's ground forces. Both the Army and the Marine Corps had found salvation for their light rapid reaction forces with the birth of the RDJTF. Accordingly, both Army and Marine leaders had concluded that gaining control of the rapid deployment mission was crucial to the future of their service. An organizational struggle for command and control of the ground element of the rapid deployment forces ensued, with the battle being fought on several fronts and levels, and the results remaining inconclusive.[162]

The assignment of forces under the proper command to the RDJTF was made more difficult by the narrowing of the geographic focus for the force to the region of Southwest Asia. Military responsibilities and command relationships in that region were already complex, and the addition of the RDJTF as an organizational player further complicated the force planning process. The Unified Command Plan directed that naval units in the area were under the command of CINPAC, a Navy admiral, while any ground forces entering the area would be controlled by CINCEUR, an Army general, or his Air Force deputy. It remained unclear how a rapid deployment force under the command of a Marine "three star" in Florida could command or control his assigned forces within that organizational milieu.

Although it appeared that the RDJTF would not have its own assigned forces, the organization under which these forces would be allocated and assigned to the RDJTF remained uncertain. A reopening of the Unified Command Plan, initially avoided by the ad hoc creation of the Rapid Deployment Joint Task Force, now began to receive increased attention as the only way to resolve these organizational disputes. According to one formulation of the dilemma, there were three basic ways that the command structure for the RDJTF could be modeled.[163]

The first and "best" option was to live within the constraints of the Unified Command Plan: to divide the world geographically, establish within each region a joint command composed of unified forces from all of the services and to assign to that command the responsibility for both peacetime planning and wartime operations.

The "second-best" solution would be the establishment of a unified command headquarters in the region without assigned forces, but with a designated area of responsibility, the authority to conduct contingency planning and the capability to accept forces deployed from the United States to support those contingency plans.

The "third-best" scheme was a resurrection of the STRIKE Command concept and the track which the RDJTF appeared to follow: a unified command <u>in the United States</u> assigned a specific region overseas and with the control of forces to be assigned to that command when the contingency in that region occurred.

This outline of proposals for the command organization of the RDJTF and a proposal for the reopening of the Unified Command Plan formed a conceptual framework for the continuing debate. That debate centered around those issues of a unified command structure, dedicated forces from all of the services, and a specific area of responsibility already developed within this chapter. The RDJTF, like the limited war commands before it, was facing the problems of how to control available, but not assigned forces.[164] Moreover, if the RDJTF was not to be granted the organizational strength to "yank the services together" by the JCS, there was added incentive for each of the services to seek their own and independent rapid deployment capabilities.

Were units dedicated to the command from each armed service component?

Although the need for a unified command to meet the lesser contingency was established, the organizational framework was lacking. One of the most important issues in this regard was the degree of service unification that the new command would achieve. It appeared, for the first time, that this limited contingency force called the RDJTF would actively incorporate elements of the Navy and Marines as well as the Army and Air Force. But these unification efforts were slowed by the attempts of the separate services to claim the rapid deployment mission for themselves.

Allusions to the need for rapid deployment forces in PD-18 had offered the services the motivation, if not the management, the mission or the money, to structure a limited contingency force, either separately or jointly. But, for reasons suggested previously, initial efforts were minimal. The Navy and the Air Force were not willing to divert a significant portion of their already constrained budgets to sea or airlift, missions seen traditionally as supporting roles for the ground forces. The Marine Corps and the Army, rather than tailoring their light projection forces for a lesser contingency, were more concerned with demonstrating that such forces had a role to play in the major contingency in Europe.

This European orientation of the projection forces can be described in terms of organizational interests--the need to reestablish, post-Vietnam, missions emphasizing service autonomy and budgetary priority-- as well as a response to the salient threat. Thus, by the mid-seventies, there appeared to be an emerging concept within the Marine Corps and the Defense Department that the three Marine divisions could be counted on as a reserve force for the major contingency rather than as an interventionary force.[165] In support of this new mission for the Corps, its newly-appointed Commandant, General Wilson, emphasized that all Marine divisions need not be "mirror images" of the others as previously required by Marine doctrine, training and equipment. Rather, it should now be possible and desirable to move away from traditional notions of the need for force versatility and structure the Marine divisions based on the regions--seen as the NATO flanks--in which they were likely to fight.

The problem in dedicating Marine divisions to combat in Europe was that they were "light" units, without the heavy armor or logistics support needed for conventional combat in that theater. Converting the Marine divisions into true "general purpose" forces required them to be "heavied up" with tanks, armored personnel carriers and artillery. Moreover, although some Army support could be provided, the intent was not to make the Marines just another branch of the ground forces, but to seek a way to maintain the elite nature of the Marine Corps mission.[166]

Three doctrinal dilemmas of the Marine Corps were further highlighted in a 1976 Brookings study of the future of the Corps.[167] Martin Binkin and Jeffrey Record argued that it was time for the Marine Corps to shift its principal focus from seaborne assault to a more appropriate mission, such as "garrisoning the remaining U.S outposts in Asia or defending central Europe."[168] The analysts, in arguing that the Marines should return to a mission emphasizing a forward strategy rather than one of rapid intervention and show of force, did not foresee that the post-Vietnam domestic political barriers to a rapid deployment mission would be overtaken by a reevaluation of U.S. vital interests in Southwest Asia. Nor did they appreciate that the traditional Marine Corps mission as a light interventionary force would still meet the important, if understated requirement for a force capable of counter-intervention at a lower range of conflict.

Thus, the rebirth of the rapid deployment concept was especially timely for the proud, but aging U.S. Marine Corps. By the end of 1979, Marine leaders disclosed that they had been ordered to organize a 50,000 man spearhead for the Rapid Deployment Force.[169] In explaining this new emphasis in the Marine mission, Major General P. X. Kelley, then Director of Marine Requirements and Programs, asserted that the traditional Marine mission had not been changed at all. Rather, that mission had merely been refocused on the third world. The rapid deployment concept that had always been an element of the Marine role now had a "tremendous utility" in the area of the Indian Ocean.[170]

As the rapid deployment mission gained more visibility and greater promised budgetary support, the Army also sought to gain a controlling interest in what now appeared to be a going concern. The Army projection forces, the 82nd and the 101st, were also characterized as "light" units. They had traditionally shared the rapid deployment mission with the Marines and, like the Corps, had also been forced to look to Europe as a primary mission upon their redeployment from Vietnam.[171] These Army forces were also given an additional lease on their service lives by the new emphasis on rapid deployment in 1979. By June of that year, the outgoing Army Chief of Staff, General Bernard Rogers, described the Administration-directed creation of what he termed the "Unilateral Corps." This force was to include approximately 100,000 Army troops as well as supporting air and naval units for "possible intervention outside the NATO alliance areas."[172]

There was some question as to whether the term "unilateral" referred to a single service as the principal component of the command or to a single-nation effort. General Rogers, in response to a question regarding the force mix, replied: "The Army intends to do this."[173] However, while it appeared that the Army had been granted the primary planning responsibility for the force-to-be, high-level civilian guidance was leaked to the media that called for a force size of two Army divisions and one Marine division. Thus, the "unilateral corps," to emerge ultimately as the Rapid Deployment Force, was apparently multi-service from its inception in the eyes of the Administration.[174]

Nevertheless, a series of studies questioning--or advocating--a service-specific rapid deployment force began to appear. In April 1978, a Congressional Budget Office paper postulated three options for U.S. projection forces to meet the lesser contingency as implied in the ruling strategic concept.[175] In addition to a "risk-averse" option that required all existing projection forces to be maintained at present levels, the study also proposed options that could reduce the projection force posture below the existing baseline. In one case in which optimistic assumptions were made regarding allied capabilities and which regarded Soviet intentions in the region as harmless, the force was postured to be Army-intensive. This option allowed the reduction of Marine forces by retiring the manpower equivalent of one Marine division and air wing. In a second option, also derived from optimistic assumptions, funds saved from retiring one of the Army's airborne brigades were used to "heavy up" the Marine division allocated to Central Europe. The Marine air wing was preserved in this choice in order to support the European division or be dedicated to a non-NATO contingency.[176]

A second CBO study focusing more directly on the Marine Corps mission was published in 1980.[177] Here, one of the four options considered for the future of the Corps called for the Marines to provide the bulk of those units committed to the Rapid Deployment Force. This choice was not only service-specific, but also scenario specific: equipping Marine forces solely for a Middle East contingency and dedicating Army forces to the major European contingency. In this formulation of the Marine Corps as the RDF, amphibious lift would be increased to permit the constant deployment of a Marine Amphibious Battalion in the Indian Ocean.[178]

This reliance on the Marine Corps in a lesser contingency in the Middle East would, according to the CBO, obviate major drawbacks in the current Department of Defense plan for a Rapid Deployment Force. Amphibious capabiity would replace the requirement for landing and docking facilities provided by friendly states and, thereby, remove the necessity of relying on these facilities in regions of political and military instability.[179]

The ultimate argument for a Marine Corps-specific Rapid Deployment Force is contained in Jeffrey Record's study for the Institute for Foreign Policy Analysis.[180] Record's primary argument against an RDF that contains multi-service units is that the commitment of these forces would be "critically dependent on pre-hostilities access to bases and airfields ashore and would require the creation ashore of a huge support infrastructure." Record contends that it was this kind of Vietnam-style, massive logistical presence on land that invariably excites the hostility of indigenous nationalism. He further argues an RDF composed of land-based forces would ultimately depend on the "momentary political calculations of potential host regimes in the Gulf." These deficiencies can be overcome through "the replacement of the present force by a small, agile tactically capable intervention force." Such a force could be created by "transferring responsibility of the rapid deployment mission to the United States Marine Corps, which by virtue of its traditions and capabilities is the only service suitable for the mission."[181]

These narrow arguments in favor of a single-service composition of the force encountered a more broadly-based emerging consensus regarding the need to make multi-service units available to the RDJTF. The basis of this force structure was that the perception of the threat in Southwest Asia became increasingly seen as Soviet, Soviet inspired or Soviet supported. This concern with Soviet intentions in the region stressed the strategic importance of the lesser contingency and a possible link to the major contingency in Europe. The Soviet ability to project power and to support proxies in the Southwest Asia region had increased to the point where, in one interpretation, "it had become increasingly difficult to separate the region's own internal conflicts from the broader question of U.S.-Soviet military rivalry."[182]

Thus, the issue of the number and types of units that should be earmarked for the Rapid Deployment Joint Task Force came to depend increasingly on the perception of the threat as world-wide or focused specifically on Southwest Asia. If focused on Southwest Asia, should the force be structured to meet only the more likely and less intense case of intervention against local forces in an internal revolt or must the force be capable of meeting sophisticated Soviet-like forces?[183]

In each case, the issue of a service-specific force--whether or not forces from all the services should be allocated to the RDJTF--depended on the scenario postulated: the adversary, the intensity of the conflict, and the geographical area of responsibility assigned.

Was a specific scenario or geographic area of responsibility assigned the command for contingency planning?

A narrowing U.S. focus on the Persian Gulf and an increasing U.S. concern with the possibility of Soviet intervention in that region are two themes that reinforce the perceived need to orient the rapid deployment force toward that region. At the beginning of the Carter administration, however, neither of these themes played a dominant role in early planning for a lesser contingency force. Thus, the story of force planning for the rapid deployment force as it ultimately emerged is to a large extent a description of the evolution of a general acceptance of the need to construct a force capable of countering possible Soviet intervention in the Persian Gulf and a concurrent ignoring of lesser threats in other regions, presumed at the time to be diminished in strategic importance and unworthy of additive defense expenditures.

There were early suggestions of this ultimate direction. Explicit in PD-18 was the need to protect the Persian Gulf states, particularly Iran, from external Soviet attack, including the need to develop contingency plans for the use of military forces in the region.[184] The Consolidated Guidance in support of this initiative called for a three division force, "structured, manned and equipped for contingencies that could precede a major war in Europe."[185] Particularly favoring this force was National Security Adviser Brzezinski, who argued that in time of nuclear standoff there was a greater likelihood of Soviet intervention in the Persian Gulf.[186]

A year later, however, the rapid deployment force was neither geographically focused nor scenario specific. In early 1978, the Presidential Directive was being interpreted as requesting rapid deployment forces capable of intervening in three areas: the Persian Gulf (to protect the oil fields), the Middle East (to protect Israel) and South Korea (to reinforce that country following the planned U.S. military drawdown).[187]

Following the Soviet move into Afghanistan, however, President Carter deliberately moved the U.S. security umbrella so that it shaded the Persian Gulf.[188] The President's statement in January 1980 appeared to elevate the Gulf to the status of Western Europe, Japan and South Korea as areas of primary and vital U.S. interest. The realignment of U.S. foreign and defense policy implied by this statement resulted primarily from a response to an external threat, not from an internal bureaucratic importance of the region and certainly not from a conventional force in-being (like STRIKE) that required the allocation of a geographical area of responsibility. Although Brzezinski, Brown and Schlesinger had played major advocate roles for the rapid deployment force and lesser lights had been instrumental in gaining the administration's acceptance of the likelihood of a non-NATO US-USSR confrontation, the external events in Iran and Afghanistan had proved ultimately persuasive. Congressional testimony supports this contention:[189]

> Mr. Rosenthal: Could you tell us with respect to this build-up of forces in the Persian Gulf and the Indian Ocean and the development of the use of bases in these areas . . . how did that policy evolve?
>
> Mr. Komer: There were looming emergencies. First, there was the chaos in Iran, the taking of our hostages. Second, there was the Soviet invasion of Afghanistan which gave a big push to what had previously been a long term policy of building up our capability in the area against what we had thought was a rather longer range threat. So, I would say that the great speeding up of our policy formulation . . . is primarily a response to the events in Iran and Afghanistan.

Although the resulting deterioration of United States relations with Iran and the Soviet Union argued for the acceleration of military planning in the region, a number of opponents of the rapid deployment strategy being proposed and the increased focus on the Persian Gulf questioned the link between those "looming emergencies" and the build-up of U.S. conventional forces. One position suggested that the Soviet Union would now be less likely to invade Iran than before. The political vacuum existing in Iran was more susceptible to Soviet political penetration than previously under the Shah, and the Soviet military adventure in Afghanistan was already resulting in great and unexpected expenditures of blood and treasure. Thus, it was likely that the U.S. forces should be prepared to deal with Soviet subversive activity rather than a blunt overt aggression.[190]

A second position expressed concern with attempting to define the terms of a limited US-USSR war apart from the traditional NATO guidelines. Because it was hard to imagine a conflict in the Gulf that did not rapidly spread and escalate, the force planning implications of these threatening Soviet actions were not to emphasize the general purpose forces, but to initiate improvements in across-the-board U.S. military capabilities, beginning with the strategic deterrent.[191] Others argued that the renewed U.S. emphasis on the use of force in the region would only prompt a Soviet counter-move, thereby in a process of action-reaction, heightening the tension in the area and increasing rather than decreasing the likelihood of conflict.[192]

Although these arguments arrived at differing conclusions and started from separate premises, they are indicative of the attention that a US-USSR non-NATO confrontation was receiving. If such a conflict had become more likely, the RDJTF should be a force that could tailor its response to meet a "worst-case" scenario--the "firefight" in the Persian Gulf region. Thus, the geographic focus and specific Soviet scenario being envisioned continued to strengthen contentions for a multi-service force with an assigned area of responsibility.

In an attempt to clarify the mission and composition of the RDJTF, the Joint Chiefs of Staff on July 25, 1980, approved a revised statement of the Terms of Reference for the Rapid Deployment Joint Task Force, superseding the guidance of February 4. Under this revised charter, the RDJTF was directed to focus primarily on the Persian Gulf.[193] The Commander of Readiness Command, General Warner, stated:[194]

> ... the focus for planning (for the RDJTF) has narrowed to Southwest Asia only. ... We did have a worldwide planning mission originally, but since then tension in the area has heightened. ... The RDF has been ordered to narrow its focus from the world to the Persian Gulf/Indian Ocean.

By the end of 1980, the Rapid Deployment Joint Task Force was devoting all of its time and effort exclusively to contingency planning for Southwest Asia. Yet, some confusion still remained, primarily owing to the command's original charter and to the general connotation assigned the term "rapid deployment." The FY 1982 Department of Defense Annual Report did little to clarify the issue. In discussing non-NATO contingencies, the report states: "While the potential missions of our Rapid Deployment Forces are global, in practice most of the planning and programming has focused on Southwest Asia."[195] A subsequent discussion of limited contingencies in East Asia does not reference the use of "rapid deployment forces." Under the heading "Rapid Deployment Force" the statement is made: "We created the Headquarters Rapid Deployment Joint Task Force to consolidate in one dedicated organization the responsibility for developing operational plans for likely contingencies, particularly in Southwest Asia."[196]

Thus, it appeared that the United States had not surrendered its espoused strategy of deploying forces to non-NATO contingencies apart from Southwest Asia. However, in the event of a lesser contingency occurring elsewhere, it appeared unlikely that any forces deployed would be placed under the command of the Rapid Deployment Joint Task Force. The RDJTF, by JCS direction, was concentrating solely on the Persian Gulf. Moreover, given this growing concentration of the RDJTF on the "firefight" model of the lesser contingency in the Gulf, it appeared that other lesser contingencies (in Northeast Asia and the Caribbean) and attendant force planning would continue to be ignored as long as NATO and Southwest Asia dominated the strategic stage.

Were forces assigned to the command trained and exercised for combat in a specific region or contingency?

The ambivalence regarding a specific geographic focus or a service-specific composition for the limited contingency force reflected conceptual hangovers from previous organizations designed to accomplish similar functions. One of these organizational remnants was the economic attractiveness of a force that could respond to any global contingency. A second was the theory of force versatility that posited that the projection forces designed for a lesser contingency could also be used effectively in Europe or in any other region with little regard for the combat environment or nature of the adversary. A third concept was the belief that a large flexible organization could be constructed with the capability to deploy forces to meet any limited contingency. All of these considerations were brought to bear in early force planning for the Rapid Deployment Force.

Two publications by General Maxwell Taylor presaged a good deal of this debate and served to revive the popular notions of the flexibility accorded by a combat-ready strategic reserve, that was [197]

> ... capable of reinforcing NATO or other overseas garrisons, of defending the primary security zone in the Western Hemisphere and its approaches and of providing a relatively small expeditionary force for intervention at a greater distance where our interests may come in conflict with those of the USSR or lesser adversaries.

In a 1979 article in Foreign Policy and Defense Review,[198] General Taylor called for the generation of a conventional force structure to be based "on their ability to contribute to coping with the economic threat arising from dependence on imports." This reference to what could have been construed as a specific Persian Gulf force was broadened in its formulation. Taylor argued that a force structured for this contingency should have the "size, range and versatility to be sufficient to meet other contingencies requiring limited conventional forces." This view appeared close to that originally espoused by the administration in its early formulation of "rapid deployment forces." The force was to be sized against a Persian Gulf contingency because it was so demanding, but should also be capable of meeting other, lesser contingencies elsewhere or of being deployed in support of the major contingency as well.

General Taylor's views, as well as those of others, were represented in a panel discussion on the topic "Politics and the Limited Contingency Force," conducted under the auspices of the National Defense University in July 1979.[199] Although there was some difference in opinion expressed regarding how versatile forces could be expected to be, given the varying conditions of battle,[200]

> Most panelists agreed that a U.S. limited contingency force should not be region or scenario-specific but should be planned and configured to meet as wide a range of contingencies as possible. Forces need to be interchangeable for many missions.

The reason the panel was able to reach this conclusion regarding force versatility may have been that the panel "faced, but never resolved, whether the United States would have to, or would want to, engage Soviet ground forces in that (Persian Gulf) theater." The concern most frequently expressed was that force planning for a lesser contingency against the USSR in the Persian Gulf might degrade the U.S. capability to wage a major war in Europe.[201]

These deliberations by the participants in the force planning debate appear to be representative of the positions vying for influence within the

Carter administration. Although much of the early work on the Rapid Deployment Force was done in OASD/PA&E, this preliminary force planning was in response to the development of a non-Soviet contingency, generally constructed as an Iraqi attack on Iran or Saudi Arabia.[202] The events in Iran in 1979 and the influence of several key players within this policy debate gradually adjusted the prevailing scenario requiring the rapid deployment of U.S. forces to the region to one envisioning a U.S.-Soviet confrontation.[203]

One of the key documents that established the basis for force planning and resulted in an official appreciation of the range of scenarios that could face a limited contingency force in that region, was the Wolfowitz report of July 1979. Properly titled "Capabilities for Limited Contingencies in the Persian Gulf," the report was published in response to PD-18 guidance. While the document was classified "secret," the central theses of the study, particularly with regard to force planning, were leaked to the media.

According to these reports,[204] the study emphasized the political and military instability of the Persian Gulf region and the wide spectrum of conflict that could affect planning for a deployment force. The limited contingency force designed for such a region needed to be composed of joint forces in order to be both diverse and flexible. But the key contribution of the report was the elevation of the Soviet threat. Soviet intervention could occur at any point along a line denoting military involvement, ranging from the mere establishment of a Soviet military presence, ostensibly at the invitation of a local government, to an overt Soviet invasion of Iran to include attacks on the oil fields and the sea lines of communication. Although the report was pessimistic regarding the U.S. capability to deal with all of these threats, the study was most significant for its willingness to point to the nature of the threat and the implications for the sizing of the Rapid Deployment Force. Given the Soviet threat in the region, a limited contingency force dedicated to the Persian Gulf could not afford the versatility of light infantry or projection forces that might prove easily deployable, but less survivable. Force planning for the limited contingency in Southwest Asia would have to consider primarily the possibility of armed conflict between U.S. and Soviet forces.

The RDJTF, created as a subordinate command of U.S. Readiness Command on March 1, 1980, was not assigned initially a specific area of responsibility, but was pledged to "deploy and employ forces in response to contingencies threatening U.S. interests anywhere in the world."[205] Such a mission tended to rekindle past theories of force versatility and the need to plan units for rapid deployment anywhere. But, as the focus of the force narrowed to the Persian Gulf and acknowledged the Soviet threat within that region, these theories of force versatility lost their attractiveness. At the end of 1980, the RDJTF, although still denied assigned and dedicated forces, was beginning to take on the earmarks of a limited contingency force that focused on a specific region, was sized with multi-service forces and would be trained and exercised against a specific Soviet threat in the region.

This dedication to a specific threat and region, coupled with the issues of force organization, command and control and service roles and missions, utlimately resulted in the removal of the Rapid Deployment Joint Task Force from the overlordship of the Readiness Command. But a proposal to establish a new theater command in the Mid-east and

Africa--a STRIKE Command II--generated little service support outside the HQRDJTF because it would lack a geographic base of operations in the area and appeared politically insensitive to local opposition to U.S. military presence. A compromise position recommended by the Joint Chiefs was to place the RDJTF under the European Command, thereby maintaining the current division of labor in the Persian Gulf between PACOM and EUCOM and avoiding the bureaucratic battles attendant to the reopening of the Unified Command Plan.[206]

By the time the organizational issue reached the desk of the Secretary of Defense,[207] the options for the command structure of the Rapid Deployment Joint Task Force had been narrowed to four:[208]

-   to give command of the RDJTF to the Commander-in-Chief, Pacific Command, who would be allocated additional tactical air squadrons and air and sealift resources to meet the additional mission;
-   to put the Army and Air Force units of the Readiness Command under the European Command, which would control operations in the Indian Ocean as far east as Diego Garcia;
-   to establish a separate command in the Indian Ocean, drawing on the resources now assigned to the Readiness Command, PACOM and EUCOM;
-   to not change the present structure because the Readiness Command and the RDJTF focused almost exclusively on Southwest Asia.

Early in 1981, the Secretary of Defense announced plans to create a separate unified command to facilitate the rapid deployment of U.S. forces to the Persian Gulf area. Although present command arrangements would be maintained in the interim, a "senior military planner" disclosed that the Joint Chiefs had a preference for placing the headquarters and a sizable proportion of the troops "on land in, or somewhere very close to, Southwest Asia."[209] The concept that was envisioned was initial basing in the CONUS, a temporary transfer to a floating headquarters in the Gulf, and ultimately a land-based command headquarters in the region.

The selection of this option of a separate unified command in a region to include, but not bounded by the Indian Ocean was significant as a step to reconcile the competing organizational interests that had characterized the debate over a limited contingency force for the past twenty years. Moreover, the establishment of a new command rejected the JCS approach of a separate administrative structure to enhance rapid deployment, but with little operational control or responsibility. In calling for a new unified command, the Defense Secretary had rejected an exclusive reliance on the concept of rapid deployment directed by a large and flexible organization with versatile forces and had proposed in its place a quasi-autonomous force planned and supported to meet a specific threat in a designated geographic area. In an important respect, this decision marked the end of force planning for the "half war" and substituted in its stead the declared need for a limited contingency force focused solely on the Gulf and the attendant Soviet threat. In an equally important respect, this decision represented an apparent or temporary abandonment of organized forces planned to meet lesser contingencies away from the Persian Gulf region and against other than Soviet threats.

TABLE 3.1
Organizing For The "Half War": 1960-1980

ORGANIZATION	PRIMARY MISSION	SCENARIO SPECIFIC	SERVICE SPECIFIC	ACTIVE GROUND FORCES AVAILABLE
STRIKE, 1963	To execute contingency missions and provide a strategic reserve of combat forces	GLOBAL	Army-Air Force	6-1/3 Divisions including 82nd Airborne and 101st
STRIKE, 1970	Movement coordination of all AF and Army units to SEA	GLOBAL w/focus on MEAFSA	Army-Air Force	4-1/3 Divisions including 2/3 of 82nd Airborne
REDCOM, 1975	Joint training of assigned forces, reinforcement of overseas commands	NONE	Army-Air Force	5-2/3 Divisions including 82nd and 101st
RDJTF, 1980	To be prepared to deploy and employ designated forces in response to contingencies threatening U.S. vital interests	FOCUS ON SOUTHWEST ASIA	All 4 Services	5 Divisions including 82nd and 101st + 1-1/3 Marine Division

In examining the organizational attempts to construct a coherent U.S. limited contingency force from 1960 to 1980, this chapter has focused on the issues of a unified command, the assignment to that command of multi-service forces and the designation of a specific geographic area to facilitate force planning and training. Until the very end of this period, no limited contingency force was successful in combining these characteristics and, consequently, failed to meet successfully the limited contingency mission. With the Rapid Deployment Joint Task Force, the limited contingency force, for the first time, was designated as an autonomous command, granted a specific region and promised assigned all-component forces. As important as that decision was in terms of structuring specifically organized forces to meet a limited contingency, it simultaneously limited U.S. capabilities to respond to a range of plausible scenarios imbedded in the "half war" planning contingency.

Such a force also implied an evolution in the theories of strategic mobility. Traditional approaches to rapid deployment to a lesser contingency visualized flexible light forces to meet global contingencies against less than sophisticated adversaries. The new strategy posited a more forward, prepositioned and fixed force both to deter and to defend against a limited contingency in a specific region. The evolution of that change in strategic mobility theories, methods and systems as well as the apparent failure to realize that both of these elements of a rapid deployment strategy were required will be traced in the following chapter.

NOTES

1. The formulation of an organizational paradigm stems from the work of Herbert Simon and from the behavioral models of business firms structured by Cyert and March. These models have been transferred to the study of political science, particularly foreign and defense policy making, in the works of Graham Allison and Morton Halperin. See Herbert Simon, "Theories of Decision Making in Economics and Behavioral Science," American Economic Review, 49, No. 3 (June 10, 1959), pp. 253-283, and Richard Cyert and James March, A Behavioral Theory of the Firm (Englewood Cliffs, N.J.: Prentice Hall, 1963). Allison's classic piece is "Conceptual Models and the Cuban Missile Crisis," The American Political Science Review 63, No. 3 (September 1969), pp. 689-718. Morton Halperin and Arnold Kanter have also presented the bureaucratic perspective in Readings in American Foreign Policy (Boston: Little Brown, 1973) and Bureaucratic Politics and Foreign Policy (Washington, D.C.: Brookings, 1974).

2. Theodore W. Bauer and Eston T. White, Defense Organization and Management (Washington, D.C.: National Defense University, 1975), p. 87.

3. Quoted by W. O. Staudenmaier in "Contemporary Problems of the Unified Command System," Parameters, Vol. IX (March 1979), pp. 84-94.

4. See a description of the operation of the Unified Command Plan in John L. Frisbee, "Command Lines for Combat Forces," Defense '81 (August, 1981), pp. 9-17.

5. Bauer and White, op. cit., p. 14.

6. This is the first of several excerpts from the Blue Ribbon Defense Panel, Report to the President and the Secretary of Defense on the Department of Defense, July 1, 1970. Also known as the Fitzhugh Report, the Blue Ribbon Panel was particularly critical of defense management and organization. The panel submitted 113 recommendations, of which about half were adopted and implemented. Approximately 20 of the more controversial recommendations, particularly those relating to the unified command structure and JCS decision making, were rejected. See Bauer and White, op. cit., pp. 15-16. Halperin noted that the Blue Ribbon Panel exists as a case study in decision making itself, representing the difficulty in progressing from recommendation and decision to implementation. See Halperin and Kanter, op. cit., pp. 363-364.

7. As posited by the retired Commander of Readiness Command, General Volney Warner. See "General Quits in Split Over Forces," New York Times, May 22, 1981, p. 16, and "Sound Strategy," Fayetteville Times, June 25, 1981.

8. See Fred H. Borneman, et al, "The Development, Promulgation, and Implementation of Doctrine for Joint Operations" (Carlisle Barracks, PA: U.S. Army War College, 1979). The tendency to view the limited contingency as a "brushfire" (which would probably demand less than three divisions) was an influential argument in favor of limiting the composition of any limited contingency force to a single or, at the most, a two-service organization.

9. These Title 10 functions are listed in Annex D of Collins' American and Soviet Trends, pp. 439-446.

10. James A. Donovan, Militarism, U.S.A. (New York: Charles Scribners' Sons, 1970), p. 140.

11. These documents can be found in The Department of Defense: Documents on Establishment and Organization, 1944-1978 (Washington, D.C.: OSD Historical Office, 1978).

12. Joints Chief of Staff, Unified Action Armed Forces, JCS Pub. 2 (Washington, D.C., 1959).

13. See the statement of General P. X. Kelley, Commander, RDJTF, before the Senate Armed Services Committee on the Indian Ocean and the Rapid Deployment Force, February 21, 1980.

14. See U.S. Joint Chiefs of Staff, Rescue Mission Report (Washington, D.C.: JCS, August 1980).

15. Borneman, op. cit., p. 115.

16. A greater elaboration of the commands and their responsibilities can be found in Collins, op. cit., p. 25, and Bauer and White, pp. 87-89. Although the Unified Command Plan is classified, the geographic distribution of responsibility appears accurately displayed by Collins in the map on the page 86.

17. Harry H. Ransom, "Department of Defense: Unity or Confederation," in Mark E. Smith and Claude Johns, eds., American Defense Policy, 2nd edition (Baltimore: Johns Hopkins, 1968), p. 376.

18. Staudenmaier, op. cit., p. 85.

19. Toward this end, the Blue Ribbon Panel recommended streamlining the military command structure with one command for the strategic forces and one for the general purpose forces. The Panel further proposed a unified logistics command for providing supply distribution, maintenance and transportation services to the combatant

commands through the integration of the existing separate component transportation organizations.

20.   Harold Brown, "Planning our Military Forces," Foreign Affairs, June, 1967, pp. 277-290.

21.   Willard Pearson, "Fit to Fight Where?" Army, Vol. 16, No. 6 (July 1966), pp. 54-59.

22.   Ibid.

23.   See the discussion of ROAD by General Hamlett, Deputy Chief of Staff for Military Operations, U.S.A. in U.S. Congress, House Committee on Armed Services, Hearings on Military Posture and HR 9751 (Washington, D.C.: USGPO, 1962), p. 3507 ff.

24.   Pearson, op. cit., p. 56.

25.   "We Give Military Advice Only," U.S. News and World Report, February 25, 1955, p. 43. Quoted in James R. Henslick, "The Role of CONUS-based, Rapid Reaction Joint Forces During the Mid-range Time Frame" (Carlisle Barracks, PA: U.S. Army War College, 1971), unpublished research report, p. 9.

26.   Stanford Research Institute, "Environmental Conditions in Selected Areas of Potential Limited Warfare" (August 1957), p. 15. Quoted in Henslick, op. cit., p. 10.

27.   "Limited War: Where do they Stand: Army, Navy, AF," Army, Navy, Air Force Register, LXXX (May 23, 1959), pp. 24-25.

28.   Martin Binkin and Jeffrey Record, Where Does the Marine Corps Go From Here? (Washington, D.C.: Brookings, 1976), p. 6.

29.   Ibid., p. 8.

30.   Those combat-ready forces in the United States were part of the Continental Army Command (CONARC) and dedicated to rapid reaction.

31.   See the testimony of General Maxwell Taylor before the House Committee on Government Operations, 86th Congress, 1st session, (Washington, D.C.: USGPO, 1960), p. 794. See also Taylor, The Uncertain Trumpet, pp. 97-105. Samuel Huntington has pointed out that the Army was unable to secure acceptance of the need for a limited war force during the Eisenhower administration because they lacked State Department support. See The Common Defense, p. 351 ff.

32.   "Limited War, Where Do They Stand?" op. cit. For the early views of the separate services on limited war, see for the Army, James M. Gavin, War and Peace in the Space Age (New York: Harper, 1958); for the Navy, W. V. Davis, "The Navy in Limited War," Ordnance, XLII (March/April 1958), pp. 812-815; and for the Air Force, Robert C. Richardson, "Do We Need Unlimited Forces for Limited War?" Air Force, XLII (March 1959), pp. 53-56.

33.   Henry P. Vicellio, "Composite Air Strike Force," Air University Quarterly Review, Vol. IX, No. 1 (Winter 1956-1957), pp. 27-38.

34.   Ibid.

35.   "19th Air Force," New York World Telegram, August 11, 1961.

36.   "Readiness for the Little War," Military Review, Vol. XXXVII (April 1957), pp. 14-27, and "A Strategic Security Force" (May 1957), pp. 14-21.

37.   "Readiness for the Little War," p. 14. See also H. P. Rand, "A United States Counter-aggression Force," Military Review, XXXIX (July 1959), pp. 50-55, an article that urged the creation of a joint local war command including 6 Army divisions and airlift for two divisions.

38. The Gaither Report stressed that the vulnerability of American strategic forces was the greatest military danger facing the country. See Halperin, "The Gaither Committee," p. 283.

39. "Pentagon Plans Joint Unit to Use In a Limited War," New York Times, March 27, 1961. The article noted that the Chairman of the Joint Chiefs, General Lemnitzer, had received orders from the Secretary of Defense to develop a plan for an "Air Force-Army merger" with a May deadline.

40. "Ideas, Concepts, Doctrine: A History of Basic Thinking in the U.S. Air Force" (Maxwell Air Force Base, AL: Aerospace Studies Institute, 1971), p. 717.

41. "Military Combat Groups Unified," Baltimore Sun, September 24, 1951.

42. Forrest K. J. Kleinmann, "This is STRIKE Command," Army (April 1962) p. 16.

43. U.S. STRIKE Command, CINCSTRIKE/USCINCMEAFSA OPLAN 7080 (15 Sep. 70), p. 2. See also Joe Wagner, "STRIKE Command-Paper Tiger or Peacemaker?" Armed Forces Management, October 1963.

44. Although this study concentrates on STRIKE's ability to meet its limited contingency mission, it should be noted that the Command carried out many evacuation and mercy missions in Africa and Central America from 1964 until 1970. See Henslick, op. cit., p. 18.

45. Kleinmann, op. cit.

46. "Joint Command for TAC and STRAC Significant," Washington Post, September 25, 1961.

47. U.S. STRIKE Command Manual 10-2: Operational Functions/ Joint Task Force Headquarters Standing Operating Procedures (1 Aug. 70), pp. 1-3. Quoted in Henslick, op. cit., p. 18.

48. Clyde Box, "U.S. STRIKE Command," Air University Review (September/October 1964), pp. 3-14.

49. Thayer, Frederick C., Air Transport Policy and National Security (Chapel Hill: University of North Carolina Press, 1965), p. 239.

50. Kleinmann, op. cit.

51. Ibid.

52. Standing Joint Task Force Headquarters were also formed within the force package concept to provide three basic staff sizes to match the size of the combat force deployed (brigade, division or corps).

53. Henslick, op. cit., p. 19.

54. Blue Ribbon Defense Panel, p. 48.

55. The Unified Command Plan has outlasted its critics and remained a key document in the division of labor in U.S. defense policy. However, it may have maintained its integrity at the expense of its utility. According to its charter, the fundamental issue to be decided by the UCP is the manner in which normal contingency planning and operations are to be conducted. A reluctance to open up old organizational wounds has resulted in the proliferation of ad hoc headquarters to meet global challenges but lacking channels of command and control or newly created or assigned forces. The RDJTF was the most significant representative of this trend. (Personal interviews, U.S. Readiness Command J-5), March 1981.

56. Letter from General William Momyer, USAF, to General John D. Ryan, Chief of Staff, USAF, 19 February 1970. Momyer Papers. (Washington, D.C.: Office of Air Force History).

57.   General Bruce K. Holloway, Oral History Interview, August 16-
18, 1977 (Washington, D.C.: Office of Air Force History), p. 300. The
state of the strategic reserves was further documented in the Senate
hearings on military posture in June of 1969. The issue being examined
was the readiness of the active Army strategic reserve force. The
military's annual requirement for 450,000 replacements for North and
Southeast Asia and the need to return careerists to Vietnam "for a second
tour sooner than we would like" had turned the strategic reserve into
training units and robbed STRIKE of its remaining combat-ready forces.
An immediate objective, but one that would not be attained prior to the
demise of STRIKE Command, was "correcting the manpower shortages
and imbalances in the Army outside Vietnam whch resulted from the
expedient manner in which the Vietnam build-up was accomplished."
U.S. Congress, 1st session (Washington, D.C.: USGPO, 1969), Part 2, pp.
57-83.   See also "Pentagon Plans to Trim U.S. Strategic Reserve," New
York Times, August 7, 1967.

58.   U.S. STRIKE Command History, MacDill Air Force Base,
Florida, 1966, pp. 14-20.

59.   Personal interview.

60.   "Military Combat Groups Unified," op. cit.

61.   "Army, Air Force Set Up Unified Striking Force," St. Louis Post
Dispatch, September 20, 1961.

62.   "Joint Command for TAC and STRAC Significant," op. cit.

63.   "New Air-Ground Force Slated to Start Operations in Florida,"
New York Times, October 13, 1961.

64.   "STRAC-TAC Team Poses Big Operations," Navy, November
1961.

65.   Ibid. The Navy article continued: "Many observers, however,
view the merger as a carefully planned step in an evolutionary process.
This process, first planned by the Air Force staff, is calculated to
eliminate the separate services." Because the Air Force struggled long
and hard to achieve its own autonomy, such an accusation holds little
validity. For a good description of that struggle, see Perry M. Smith, The
Air Force Plans for Peace (Baltimore: John Hopkins, 1970). See also
W. A. Lucas and Raymond H. Dawson, The Organizational Politics of
Defense, International Studies Association, Occasional Paper, No. 2, 1975,
p. 102.

66.   Personal interview with General Paul D. Adams, Tampa,
Florida, March 26, 1981.

67.   Momyer Papers, op. cit. This assessment of STRIKE's failure to
smooth doctrinal differences seems a bit harsh. There is strong evidence
to support the contention that, prior to STRIKE, joint Army and Air Force
initiatives were well underway to solve the close air support problems
that had surfaced during the Korean War. General Weyland, the TAC
Commander, had pursued a TAC-STRAC agreement to combine the XVIII
Army Corps and the CASF concept as early as 1958. During this same
period, Army Chief of Staff Decker and his Air Force counterpart General
White agreed to approach these doctrinal differences under the codeword,
"Project Resolve." This is evidenced in a letter from General Weyland to
General White, March 18, 1958, White Papers (Washington, D.C.: Office
of Air Force History).

68.   This concept, in its broadest sense, calls for the use of aircraft
(both fixed-wing and rotary), organic to the Army "to assure the balance
of mobility, firepower intelligence, support and command and control."

Secretary McNamara attempted to assist in the resolution of this dispute by establishing the Tactical Mobility Requirements Board. Better known as the Howze board, its charter was to conduct a reexamination of the role of Army aviation and aircraft requirements. Given that General Howze was the Commander of the XVIII Corps and a pioneer in Army air mobility, the conclusions reached by the Board were foregone: "Adoption by the Army of the airmobile concept--however improperly it may be described and justified in this report--is necessary and desirable." See John J. Tolson, Air Mobility (Washington, D.C.: Department of the Army, 1973), p. 24.

69. Robert S. McNamara, DoD Annual Report FY 1963, p. 94.

70. U.S. Congress, House, Committee on Armed Services, Hearings on Military Posture and H.R. 9637, 88th Congress, 2nd session (Washington, D.C.: USGPO, 1964), p. 7005.

71. U.S. Congress, House, Committee on Appropriations, Department of Defense Appropriations for FY 1965, 88th Congress, 2nd session (Washington, D.C.: USGPO, 1964), Part 4, p. 315.

72. Quoted in Alan R. Scholin, "STRIKE," Air Force Magazine, May 1962.

73. U.S. Congress, House, Committee on Appropriations, Hearings on H.R. 7851, 87th Congress, 1st session (Washington, D.C.: USGPO, 1961), p. 25.

74. According to the established airborne doctrine in the XVIII Airborne Corps, the Army operation was seen as primarily conventional. The inclusion of the CASF command, however, implied that STRIKE forces would have a nuclear option. General Holloway stated: "The choice of action open to STRIKE forces range from no weapons to nuclear weapons." General Adams added that a broad function of the general purpose forces in the CONUS under STRIKE was to "provide a strong mobile strategic reserve for immediate employment after a nuclear exchange." And again, General Holloway: "We (STRIKE) did a lot of exercise particularly in the development of the use of theater nuclear warfare." Quoted by Scholin in "STRIKE," op. cit., and the Holloway Oral History, p. 292.

75. Scholin, op. cit.

76. Robert S. McNamara, DoD Annual Report FY 1964, p. 133.

77. STRIKE had not been allocated a specific mission in the Caribbean other than that of its more general world-wide mission of reinforcement to another unified command. Although General Holloway and others within STRIKE argued that contingency planning and operations in that region should have been assigned to STRIKE, those regional responsibilities remained with CINCLANT. Holloway admits that STRIKE's location in Florida was one of fortune rather than forethought: a political decision to keep the base open and the need for a long runway--not a prepositioning of the Command for a Caribbean contingency. See Holloway Oral History, p. 284.

78. New York Times, November 30, 1962.

79. Holloway Oral History, p. 284.

80. Personal interview.

81. Lyndon B. Johnson, The Vantage Point (New York: Popular Library, 1971), p. 190.

82. Personal interview. There are other views. General Bruce Palmer, Commander of the Headquarters in Santo Domingo, contended in his post-crisis debriefings that there had not been much help emanating

from STRIKE Command. See "Unilateral Corps," Army (September 1979), p. 30.

83.   U.S. Congress   Senate   Committee   on   Armed   Services, Department of Defense Appropriations for FY 1973, 92nd Congress, 2nd session (Washington, D.C.: USGPO, 1972), p. 346.

84.   Blue Ribbon Defense Panel, quoted in Halperin, op. cit., p. 377.

85.   Blue Ribbon Defense Panel, p. 48.   See also "U.S. to Drop STRIKE Command in Revamping World Forces," Washington Post, July 9, 1971.

86.   Momyer Papers, op. cit.

87.   Ibid.

88.   Quoted in Martin Caidin, The Long Arm of America (New York: E. P. Dutton, 1963), p. 230.   General Adams explains (on p. 231): "We can tailor a force for any situation; and this force--whether it be a company or an entire corps--can fight in any terrain such as the Arctic wastelands, deserts, jungles or mountains."

89.   The attempt here is not to malign the conduct of U.S. ground forces in Vietnam.   On the contrary, the general evaluations of U.S. combat   performance   in   that   war,   under   difficult   conditions, uncertain guidance and inadequate training, is quite good.   For varying views and approaches to this topic, see Thompson and Frizzell, eds., The Lessons of Vietnam (New York: Crane Russak, 1977); Zeb B. Bradford and Frederic J. Brown, The United States Army in Transition (Beverly Hills: Sage, 1973); Sarkesian, ed., Combat Effectiveness (Beverly Hills: Sage, 1980); Guenter Lewy, America in Vietnam (New York: Oxford University Press, 1978); and Douglas Kinnard, The War Managers (Hanover, New Hampshire: University Press of New England, 1977).   The purpose here is to examine, on a strategic level, how the strategy and tactics of U.S. armed   forces   were   limited   in   their   applicability   to   a   minor contingency owing to their operational doctrine and training that focused on the major contingency and to suggest that an assumption of force versatility   possesses   hidden   and   needless   risks   for   the   combat effectiveness of a limited contingency force.

90.   See Lessons of Vietnam, p. 59.

91.   This is a summary of responses to NSSM 1, quoted in Lessons of Vietnam, p. 9, and taken from the Congressional Record, Vol. 117, No. 76 (May 10, 1972), p. E4978.

92.   Ibid., p. 267.   On page 67, General Westmoreland argues that there was a good deal of innovation and ingenuity during the conduct of the war, despite a general clinging to an attrition strategy. Westmoreland points to the use of B-52s against enemy base camps, the use of CS gas, chemical defoliants and "Rome plows"--bulldozers used for felling large trees and neutralizing jungle hideouts.

93.   Robert W. Komer, "Bureaucracy Does Its Thing: Institutional Constraints on US-GVN Performance in Vietnam" (Santa Monica: RAND, August 1972), p. 45.

94.   Ibid., p. 46.

95.   History   of   the   Directorate   of   Plans,   July-December   1969 (Washington: Office of Air Force History, 1969).

96.   Henslick, op. cit., p. 20.

97.   U.S. to Drop STRIKE Command," Washington Post, July 9, 1971.

98.   Senator J. W. Fulbright, quoted in "Meeting The Isolationist Challenge," Fortune, June 1975.

99. Robert W. Tucker, A New Isolationism: Threat or Promise (New York: Universe Books, 1972).

100. Adam Yarmolinsky, The Military Establishment (New York: Harper and Row, 1971).

101. Ibid., p. 413.

102. Richard Haass, "Congressional Power: Implications for American Security Policy" (London: International Institute for Strategic Studies, 1979), Adelphi Paper #153, p. 19. For background hearings on the War Powers Legislation, see Hearings before the Committee on Foreign Relations, United States Senate (Washington: USGPO, 1973). See also W. Taylor Reveling III, "The Power to Make War" in Commission on the Organization of the Government for the Conduct of Foreign Policy (Murphy Commission), Appendices, Vol. 5 (Washington: USGPO, 1975), pp. 80-98.

103. Haass, op. cit., p. 21. It is not yet clear how the Supreme Court's June 1983 decision against the Legislative Veto will affect the War Powers Act.

104. Personal interviews with General Paul Adams (USA-Ret) and personnel actively assigned to J5, U.S. Readiness Command, March 1981.

105. General John J. Hennessey, "Strategy and Readiness," Strategic Review (Fall 1976).

106. Fact Sheet, Public Affairs Office, Headquarters United States Readiness Command (MacDill AFB, Florida, 1981), p. 1.

107. To REDCOM's credit, it should be noted that the capability to reinforce overseas commands is no small task and required considerably more than the preparation of supporting plans. USREDCOM is required to alert the component forces, progressively increase the deployment posture levels and serve as coordinating authority for the intertheater deployment of assigned augmentation forces. Thus, REDCOM retained many of the functions that STRIKE Command had assumed in the major force deployments to Southeast Asia. See Hennessey, op. cit.

108. Hennessey, op. cit.

109. Bornemann, op. cit., p. 80.

110. Ibid., pp. 91-93.

111. United States Readiness Command History, 1972 (MacDill AFB Florida, 1973), pp. 1-5.

112. See Drew Middleton, "Readiness Command Keeping Low Profile," New York Times, March 27, 1977, p. 15, and "MacDill's Pentagon South," Tampa Tribune, March 8, 1980, p. 1.

113. Thus, the Tactical Air Command questioned the role that tactical air forces would play in a rapid deployment strategy without STRIKE Command and considered the revival of the CASF concept as an interim measure. History of the Tactical Air Command, July 1971-1972, (Langley AFB, Virginia, 1973), Vol. I, p. 8.

114. Secretary of State Kissinger gave the interview to Business Week on December 23, 1974. It was reported in the Washington Post on January 3, 1975, and published in the magazine one week later.

115. See Barry Blechman, "Force and Diplomacy," Washington Post, February 7, 1975.

116. Drew Middleton, "Persian Gulf Energy as a Military Focus," New York Times, January 22, 1975, p. 2.

117. Blechman, op. cit.

118. Robert W. Tucker, "Oil: The Issue of American Intervention," Commentary (January 1975), pp. 21-31.

119. Ibid., p. 22.

120. Ibid., p. 23.

121. Maxwell D. Taylor, "The Legitimate Claims of National Security," Foreign Affairs, Vol. 52, No. 3 (April 1974), p. 587.

122. John K. Cooley, "Oil Seizure Talk Irks Saudis," Christian Science Monitor, March 12, 1975. The article was penned by a pseudonymous "Miles Ignotus," rumored to be Edward Luttwak, then a professor at Johns Hopkins. Luttwak denied authorship but admitted he "conveyed" the article to Harper's. A combination of the Tucker-Ignotus plan advocated an airborne assault and eventual military control along a shallow coastal strip from Kuwait to Qatar. As Cooley points out, U.S.-Saudi relations were strained by the publication of such articles.

123. Drew Middleton, "Military Men Challenge Mideast 'Force' Strategy," New York Times, January 10, 1975, p. 3.

124. John Collins and Clyde Mark, "Oil Fields as Military Objectives," Library of Congress, Congressional Reference Service (Washington: USGPO, 1975).

125. Ibid.

126. Ibid.

127. Robert W. Tucker, "American Power in the Persian Gulf," Commentary, Vol. 79, No. 5 (November 1980), pp. 25-41.

128. Generally regarded to be the view of CINCRED in early 1981. Personal interviews, USREDCOM, March 1981.

129. George C. Wilson, "War Planners Note Soviet Grip on NATO's Oil," Washington Post, July 9, 1977, p. 3.

130. "Carter Orders Steps to Increase Ability to Meet War Threats," New York Times, August 26, 1977, p. 1.

131. Lawrence J. Korb, "The 1979-1983 Defense Program," AEI Defense Review, Vol. 2, No. 2 (April 1978), p. 24. See also the DoD Annual Report FY 1979, pp. 1-10.

132. Ibid., p. 25.

133. Harold Brown, DoD Annual Report FY 1979, p. 8.

134. Ibid.

135. "Again, U.S. is Gearing up for Brushfire Wars," U.S. News and World Report (February 27, 1978), p. 24.

136. "Speech by President Carter at Wake Forest University," March 17, 1978, Survival, Vol. XX, No. 4 (July-August 1978), pp. 176-179.

137. "Carter Orders Quick Strike Force," Philadelphia Inquirer, March 20, 1978, p. 1.

138. Korb, op. cit., p. 2.

139. See Korb, op. cit. and DoD Annual Report FY 1979. No separate funds other than those previously allocated to the general purpose forces were programmed for a limited contingency force in the FY 1979 budget.

140. U.S. Congress, Congressional Budget Office, "U.S. Projection Forces: Requirements, Scenarios and Options" (Washington: USGPO, April 1978).

141. Ibid., pp. 46-54. The largest force sized to meet these contingencies was estimated at six ground divisions, eight air wings and four aircraft carriers, a total of 135,000 military personnel at a five-year cost of $32.7 billion. A smaller force, sized to a non-Soviet threat, would consist of 3 and 2/3 divisions, six air wings, four carriers and 100,000 men. The five-year cost for this force was estimated at $22.9 billion. Finally, an option that included the reconstruction of U.S. ground forces,

to include the creation of a "heavy" Marine division, would cost $25.6 billion. These force packages were not meant to imply newly-created units, but merely a separate accounting of existing forces allocated to a rapid deployment mission.

142. The study concluded that the U.S. "simply does not have the capability at present to move more than two divisions to the Gulf by air and sea in much less than one month." Strategic mobility for rapid deployment forces will be discussed in the following chapter.

143. Zbigniew Brzezinski quoted in Jan Austin and Banning Garrett, "Quick Strike," Inquiry, July 24, 1978.

144. Drew Middleton, "U.S. Earmarks Force for Fast Deployment in Middle East," New York Times, April 20, 1979, p. 12.

145. Quoted in "Troops Episode Spurs Development of Mobile Forces for Third World Moves," Baltimore Sun, October 3, 1979, p. 1. It is of some interest that the Caribbean scenario of the lesser contingency which in the past had provided the model for the non-Soviet "brushfire" was now, with the presence of the Soviet brigade, being expanded into a Soviet-proxy or "firefight" version of the limited contingency.

146. Ibid.

147. "Carter Budget Envisions a Quick Reaction Force," Washington Post, November 27, 1979, p. 8.

148. Ibid.

149. Richard Burt, "Should U.S. Create a Quick-Strike Force?" New York Times, December 1, 1979, p. 4.

150. Ibid.

151. See Lawrence J. Korb, "The FY 1981-1985 Defense Program," AEI Foreign Policy and Defense Review, Vol. 2, No. 2 (July 1980), p. 53.

152. "U.S. Plans Rapid Deployment Force Costing $9 Billion," Baltimore Sun, December 6, 1979, p. 2. See also "U.S. to Speed Rapid Response Capability by Military at five-year cost of $9 Billion," Wall Street Journal, December 6, 1979, p. 5.

153. General Kelley has repeatedly referred to PRM-10 in testimony as a conceptual basis for the need for the RDJTF. See his remarks before the Committee on Armed Services, Military Posture and H.R. 6495, p. 148.

154. W. O. Staudenmaier, "Contemporary Problems of the Unified Command System," op. cit.

155. Ibid.

156. Personal interviews, March 1981.

157. See the tesimony of General Lawson, Hearings on U.S. Interests in and Policies Toward the Persian Gulf, 1980, p. 94.

158. Statement by General P. X. Kelley before the House Armed Services Committee on Military Personnel and Rapid Deployment Forces, February 8, 1980.

159. Statement of General Volney Warner, CINCRED, before the House Appropriations Subcommittee on Defense and the Readiness Command, March 6, 1980.

160. "The RDF: What's been Done, What should have been Done," Defense Week, (June 30, 1980), p. 6.

161. This not only posed bureaucratic problems of control, but also offered operational questions of a centralized (Air Force) system versus a decentralized (Marine) system of close air support communications. It will be recalled that one of the main arguments against Marine Corps participation in the STRIKE Command was a desire not to dilute their

already established air-ground support system and a reluctance to enter the Army-Air Force doctrinal dispute over the mission. Although the Army-Air Force relationship has come a long way, primarily through efforts at the major command level (TAC-TRADOC), the Air Force interface with the Marine Corps remains under review at JCS levels. See "Marines, Air Force Squabble over RDF's Air Mission," Defense Week, (September 15, 1980).

162. As initially planned, the force was to draw on the units from both the Army and the Marines, with a three division force sized against the Iraqi threat being raised to meet a Soviet threat with 6 and 1/3 divisions by mid-1980s. However, the responsibilities to select the composition of varying force packages, from units that were available rather than assigned to the RDF, created friction between the Marine Commander of the RDJTF and Army general commanding its organizational parent, the Readiness Command. There were reports that the Army, through REDCOM, was attempting to lower the priority of the Marine units being assigned to the RDJTF, thereby simultaneously lowering the visibility and influence of Marine command and control of the assigned units. Personal interviews, USREDCOM and HQRDJF, March 1981. See also Richard Burt, "Army and Marines in Battle over Control of RDF," New York Times, December 10, 1980.

163. This was the official position being advocated by REDCOM in early 1981. Personal interviews.

164. Nor had the service positions on this doctrinal dilemma grown closer together since the dissolution of STRIKE Command. The REDCOM Commander urged that he should be given operational control of the force regardless of where it might be deployed and that the forces should be assigned to him full-time. The Marines were still arguing for a service-specific force or, at least, a leading role for their service under the command of CINPAC. But the Chief of Naval Operations was reluctant to support that position because naval forces in the Pacific were already "streched thin." However, CINPAC was also reluctant to relinquish command and control over the forces in the Indian Ocean. See "New Base is Urged for Mobile Force," New York Times, February 8, 1981.

165. "Marines Face New Role, as a Reserve for Europe," New York Times, June 30, 1975, p. 1.

166. In an attempt to deal with these fundamental issues of roles and missions internally, the Marine Corps in 1975 established the Haynes Committee. These deliberations drew a distinction between the two basic missions of U.S. ground forces: 1) to be prepared to fight in forward areas, where troops were already deployed, and 2) to be prepared to insert forces into and fight in areas without deployed forces. The Marines, with certain Army units, had previously been dedicated to the second mission. But the Board noted that if the Marines were to remain a viable fighting force, it was likely that forces allocated this power projection mission would be "inevitably assigned the other duty of taking the initiative against the enemy main force units." See William S. Lind, "A Proposal for the Corps: Mission and Force Structure," Marine Corps Gazette, (December 1975).

167. Binkin and Record, Where Does the Marine Corps Go From Here? (Washington: Brookings, 1976).

168. See the precis of the authors' thesis and a rejoinder by F. J. West, Jr., in "From the Halls of Montezuma To . . .?" Baltimore Sun, January 24, 1976, p. 14. Also see "Marines to Invade Turkey," op. cit.

The Marines also conducted operations in Norway in 1976. See "A New Role for the U.S. Marines," Washington Star, November 8, 1976.

169. According to this concept, the first of three brigades would be ready for airlift to distant spots by 1983. Each brigade would be supported by supply ships positioned ahead of time near anticipated contingency areas, while the brigade could operate for thirty non-combat days on its own. See "Marines to Form Rapid Reaction Force," Washington Post, December 6, 1976. Dov Zakheim has called airlift and the Marine Corps an "unlikely combination" in "Airlifting the Marine Corps," a paper presented to the conference on "Projection of Power" at the Fletcher School of Law and Diplomacy, Tufts University, April 23, 1980.

170. Quoted in "Marines to Form Rapid Reaction Force."

171. Also, like the Marines, they had turned to the major contingency in Europe to meet the perceived threat as well as organizational interests. In October 1976, the 101st deployed its helicopter-intensive force to central Europe. See "101st Airborne Undergoes Critical Test in Europe," Washington Post, October 7, 1976, p. G7.

172. "New Contingency Force for U.S.," Christian Science Monitor, June 22, 1979, p. 3.

173. Quoted in "Army is Drafting Plans for a Quick-strike Force," Washington Post, July 22, 1979, p. 2. See also "Unilateral Corps," op. cit.

174. See "Army Force Planning near Completion, General Says," Washington Post, September 18, 1979, p. 2.

175. U.S. Congress, CBO, "U.S. Projection Forces."

176. Ibid., p. 53.

177. U.S. Congress, Congressional Budget Office, "The Marine Corps in the 1980s" (Washington: USGPO, May 1980).

178. Ibid., pp. 41-44.

179. Ibid., p. 57, "The sizable forcible-entry capability that the Marines would provide would ensure that the Marines reinforcements (amounting to an additional 50,000 men) would need to rely less on other states to ensure that their equipment could be landed. . . . This combination of forcible entry/follow-on capability would also reinforce the deterrent effect."

180. Jeffrey Record, The Rapid Deployment Force.

181. Ibid., p. viii.

182. Kemp, op. cit., p. 367.

183. The biggest tactical argument against the uni-service Rapid Deployment Force, raised by the other services against this proposal for giving the mission to the Marine Corps, was the fact that such an arrangement would limit the flexibility with which the U.S. could respond to any crisis. In a paper prepared to refute a single-service force, the U.S. Readiness Command noted that "the optimum force for one kind of tactical situation in Southwest Asia may well be absolutely the wrong kind of force for another. We need to use the unique capabilities each of the military services offers if we're to have a sufficient range of capabilities. . . . Stripping services and their unique capabilities away from the RDJTF might simplify the RDJTF organization, but it will significantly complicate our force projection problem and reduce the credibility of our forces." From "Protecting Western Interests in Southwest Asia," MacDill AFB, Florida: USREDCOM (unpublished paper).

184. "Carter orders Pentagon to Plan Persian Gulf Defense, Officials Say," Baltimore Sun, September 10, 1977, p. 4.
185. George C. Wilson, "New U.S. Military Plan: European, Persian Focus," op. cit.
186. Richard Burt, "U.S. Defense Debate Arises on Whether Focus on Europe Neglects Other Areas," op. cit.
187. "Carter Orders Quick-Strike Force," op. cit.
188. Richard Burt, "How U.S. Strategy on Toward Persian Gulf Evolved," New York Times, January 25, 1980, p. 6.
189. U.S. Congress, House of Representatives, Committee on Foreign Affairs, Hearings on U.S. Interests in and Policies Toward the Persian Gulf, 1980, 96th Congress, 2nd session (Washington: USGPO, 1980), p. 74.
190. See Theodore Geiger and Neil J. McMullen, "Soviet Options in the Persian Gulf and U.S. Responses," New International Realities, Vol. V, No. 1 (July 1980), pp. 7-17. Thus, there is some evidence that the "half war" planning contingency of the "brushfire" had not been completely forgotten. But these arguments called for the insertion of this model of the lesser contingency into Southwest Asia and were not offered as encouragement for separate force planning to meet low-intensity scenarios in other regions.
191. See F. J. West, Jr., "Limited US-Soviet Conflict and the RDF," Marine Corps Gazette (August 1980), pp. 39-46.
192. William P. Baxter, "Russian Nervous about U.S. RDF," Army (December 1979), p. 38.
193. Personal interviews, USREDCOM, March 1981. The purpose of the Terms of Reference is to define the mission, command relationships, tasks and responsibilities of the RDJTF. The guidance is "dynamic" and "subject to revision as required."
194. Richard D. Gross, "Rapid Deployment Force Focuses on Southwest Asia," UPI News release, March 21, 1981.
195. Harold Brown, DoD Annual Report FY 1982, p. 81.
196. Ibid., p. 189.
197. Maxwell D. Taylor, Precarious Security (New York: W. W. Norton, 1976).
198. Maxwell D. Taylor, "Changing National Priorities," AEI Foreign and Defense Policy Review, Vol. 1, No. 3 (April 1979).
199. "Continuity and Change in the Eighties and Beyond," Proceedings of the National Security Affairs Conference, July 1979. See pp. 53-93. Among the panel participants whose works are referenced in this study were Edward Luttwak, General Taylor, F. J. West, Paul Wolfowitz and Dov Zakheim.
200. Ibid., p. 56. This is an excerpt from the paper presented the panel by Geoffrey Kemp, summarized earlier in this study.
201. Ibid., p. 55.
202. Personal interviews in PA&E and with Robert W. Komer, March 1981.
203. During the conduct of interviews regarding the development of this view, the key players were generally regarded to be Paul Wolfowitz, Albert Wohlstetter and Russel Murray II.
204. See Richard Burt's account in the New York Times on February 14, 1980. See also Kenneth Waltz, "A Strategy for the RDF," International Security, Vol. 5, No. 4 (Spring 198), pp. 49-73.

205. Fact Sheet, Public Affairs Office, HQRDJTF (MacDill AFB, Florida, 1981), p. 1. See also U.S. Congress Senate Committee on Armed Services DoD Authorizations for Appropriations for FY 1981, Part 1, Hearings on S 2294, 96th Congress, 2nd session (Washington: USGPO, 1981), p. 441.

206. "New Base is Urged For Mobile Force," op. cit.

207. A good deal of time was spent in additional Congressional testimony, repeated arguments for a service-specific RDF and an additional Congressional role in the decision making requested by Secretary of Defense Weinberger. See the opening statement of Senator William S. Cohen, "Hearings on the RDF before the Senate Armed Services Sub-committee on Seapower and Force Projections," March 12, 1981, and the transcripts of those hearings.

208. Drew Middleton, "New Strategy: Command Review Now an Urgent Priority," New York Times, April 22, 1981.

209. "U.S. Command set for the Persian Gulf may lead to big American force in the Area," Wall Street Journal, April 27, 1981, p. 2. See also "U.S. gets separate Strike Force," Boston Globe, April 25, 1981, p. 3.

4
Supporting the Limited Contingency: Mobility Systems for Rapid Deployment, 1960-1980

Neither the formulation of a strategy that called for a limited contingency force nor the organization of that force in any form could ensure an ability to move those forces rapidly, in adequate numbers, to a distant locale. A strategic mobility capability was essential to the conduct of a rapid deployment strategy. To meet those requirements, mobility systems to support that strategy were designed in the early 1960s. However, owing to a variety of factors, those systems were never procured in sufficient numbers to support simultaneously a rapid deployment to a lesser contingency with a major force movement to Europe. This chapter develops these early concepts and methods of strategic mobility systems, explains why these systems were not acquired in numbers sufficient to accomplish the mission and draws parallels between these past efforts to support a rapid deployment capability and similar initiatives in support of the Rapid Deployment Joint Task Force.

Logistics, the process of supplying and supporting military forces, does not contain in its program elements the sophisticated and expensive weapons systems that attract Congressional budgetary support. In terms of budgetary priority, logistic systems, supply channels, spare parts and storage sites rank well below the hardware they are designed to support. The concept of prepositioning supplies appears dull and prosaic compared to the acquisition of weapons systems intended to match the mystique of "2-1/2 wars" or the elan of the STRIKE Command. In that psycho-social dimension of strategy, few of those guarding the Congressional pursestrings choose to look beyond the hardware to the required infrastructure. Perhaps, nuclear weapons continue to be an attractive acquisition simply because they do not require a complex line of supply and support.

As Martin van Crevald has claimed in Supplying War,[1] logistical factors have been ignored by 99 percent of the military historians, an omission, he contends, which has warped their judgments and led to erroneous conclusions. Michael Howard has also agreed that no military campaign can be fully understood without a thorough analysis of the logistics involved.[2] Historically, U.S. force planners have appreciated the importance of logistics. From the Civil War to the end of World War II, the capacity to deploy and sustain the largest and best equipped forces proved to be decisive in the outcome of major conflicts.

Yet, in the battle for budgetary priority and program support over the last twenty years, strategic mobility systems in support of a limited contingency force have not fared well. During most of this period, except for a momentary pause to swing the supply lines to Southeast Asia, the logistic support system has been geared to supply the major contingency in Europe. However, this was not always the plan. Early in the 1960s, under the formulation of the "2-1/2 war" strategic concept, adequate forces were programmed to support the rapid deployment of forces to a lesser and simultaneous contingency. This chapter traces the pursuit of those and similar systems.

First, as has been customary throughout this study, a framework for analysis is introduced to provide a reference for the material that follows. This framework suggests the major theories, strategies and methods of rapid deployment that provide the conceptual background for the systems advocated and acquired. The rest of the chapter describes the systems and their relationships to these concepts in greater detail. To accomplish this, both a chronological and a functional approach is used. Thus, the first section describes the efforts to enhance rapid deployment capability by focusing on sealift and the case study of the Fast Deployment Logistics Ship. The second section suggests that the period of retrenchment characterized by the "1-1/2 war" strategic concept emphasized airlift as a primary means to rapid deployment. The final section examines both air and sealift systems in support of the RDJTF. Again, a method of asking focused, iterative questions will be employed in each section.

Framework for Analysis

Theories of strategic mobility. In theoretical approaches to a strategic mobility capability, the choice lies essentially between the concept of rapid deployment of a central reserve of ground forces, the basing of these forces overseas or some mix of the two, such as prepositioning of forces or supplies. There are advantages and disadvantages to each of these broad approaches.[3]

The term "forward strategy" has been used frequently to denote the policy of stationing a large force close to or within the area of U.S. security commitment rather than holding the force within the CONUS to be deployed as a strategic reserve.[4] One of the strongest arguments in favor of a forward deployment strategy is the demonstrated resolve to defend the area that the presence of force implies. Perhaps, the classic modern historical case is Korea where the absence of U.S. troops, coupled with the failure of the American Secretary of State to include the area within the U.S. defense perimeter, may have led the North Koreans to assume that the United States would not come to the aid of the South.[5] Thirty years after that initial attack and despite repeated efforts by several U.S. presidents to withdraw U.S. forces from Korea, a strategy of rapid deployment has not been substituted for the deterrent and defense value gained from the presence of U.S. troops and the prepositioning of U.S. equipment in Korea.

If stationing forces abroad clearly implies a commitment to come to the military defense of that state or region, it is unclear just how big a force is required to make that commitment appear credible. The "tripwire" theory suggests that only a small presence is required to trigger such a response.[6] The size of the U.S. troop commitment to Europe has often been debated in such terms. However, this reasoning ignores a dynamic analysis of the opposing forces, a method required to determine the warfighting effectiveness of the deployed force and its impact on the outcome of the conflict.[7] In addition, such tripwire strategies tend to ignore the possibilities of a strong conventional defense and imply a rapid escalation of the conflict to the level of a "tactical" nuclear exchange.

There are several advantages to stationing forces abroad in areas deemed worthy of such military presence: added credibility and, therefore, enhanced deterrence, a capability to deal with surprise attacks and an in-place infrastructure to cope with a major assault and to support reinforcements.[8] The principal disadvantage is cost. In the "burden sharing" debate that surrounded the economics of the NATO alliance in the early seventies, the United States sought to secure a number of relief measures for what it saw as a disproportionate U.S. contribution when measured in balance of payments deficits and budgetary outlays, stemming from its European garrison force.[9] This U.S. effort to reduce the cost of its overseas forces was a serious and continuing initiative, but generally met with little success.[10]

Although the costs accrued in the adoption of a forward strategy appeared acceptable in support of forces allocated to a major contingency, none of these options appeared particularly suitable for a limited contingency force. The stationing of forces overseas necessarily lost the flexibility deemed necessary for a versatile force. Prepositioning on land, attractive economically, suffered strategic shortfalls in terms of mobility. Sea-based prepositioning, although more attractive, was, nevertheless, limited in application, rapid break-out and movement of supplies. Therefore, an effective rapid deployment strategy to a lesser contingency seemed to require the development of strategic mobility systems within the United States to deploy quickly a military force to any threatened area.

Strategies of rapid deployment. If forces stationed abroad were judged too costly and too inflexible and if foreign policy commitments were not to be reduced, then the idea of creating a central strategic reserve of forces to meet these commitments, thereby accruing a tremendous saving and taking advantage of an economy of scale, had an enormous appeal. Under this concept, a single force of highly trained and well-equipped troops, able to deploy rapidly to any trouble spot, could meet U.S. commitments without the costs of overseas basing.

However, the perceived need to make this rapid deployment capability a global one complicated force and support planning for the limited contingency force. The question became not what single rapid deployment strategy to select, but what mix of strategies appeared most appropriate given a particular scenario or contingency. Because of numerous logistical alternatives as well as conflicting political and military requirements, this mix would not be a constant.

An added problem in the determination of a proper rapid deployment strategy was that, although the questions being asked in the early 1960s regarding support for a limited contingency force were clearly interrelated, the functional areas were organizationally compartmentalized. As Enthoven and Smith explained:[11]

> In 1961, each of these elements--the airlift, the sealift, the bases, the prepositioned equipment, the planned deployments and the readiness--was the responsibility of a different group of people in the Defense Department. The elements were seen as separate and unrelated entities.

However, even with some acceptance of the agreed-upon task to support a U.S. limited contingency force and an increasing centralization of the systems acquisition process imposed by the new Secretary of Defense, it was not easy to achieve agreement within the Department on "how many forces we wanted to move, where we wanted to move them and how fast."[12] The choice facing the force planners was phrased in the following fashion: "Do we want to get there quickly and in large numbers and pay the extra cost, or do we want to take our time, save money and accept greater risks?"[13]

Robert A. Levine examined various options in response to this question in a 1965 RAND memo.[14] Levine looked at four categories of conventional response in his study, ranging from a "non-response" to "slow", "rapid" and finally to "escalation." He posited that the rapid response option appeared as the most attractive from a strategic viewpoint, but pointed out that obtaining a capability for this rapid deployment strategy would be more costly to support in day-to-day costs. Although some of the other alternatives could prove to be more costly if the United States elected to respond to a crisis with conventional force, maintaining a force capable of rapid response incurred greater continuing and constant peacetime costs. Having the capability for rapid response meant the creation of a limited-contingency force in-being. No matter what mix of rapid deployment strategies might ultimately be selected, these "pre-aggression" costs inherent in the rapid response option would be greater than those of any other option. Levine argued that it was this cost that would prevent the United States from supporting a world-wide rapid deployment strategy based on a quick conventional response.

Given these costs, it became important to determine the most efficient way to construct a rapid deployment strategy. Systematic studies were accomplished at the RAND corporation as early as 1958 on the use of land-based prepositioning as a complement to airlift in the rapid deployment of forces.[15] One of these studies examined the desirability of stocking overseas some of the consumables required to support the deployment of tactical air units presently stationed within the borders of the United States. In these studies and others, the principal cost tradeoffs were between the acquisition of additional materiel and equipment and the storage cost incurred as opposed to the cost of acquiring and operating military air or seaborne transport systems to deploy the materiel. Also important, but usually unstated in these cost calculations, was the degree of responsiveness and flexibility lost by the mobility mix as it moved away from air and sealift towards a greater reliance on some system of prepositioning.

The most significant early study that tried to consider the appropriate mix of the "value" of rapid response was accomplished during 1964 by the Special Studies Group of the Joint Chiefs of Staff. Entitled "Rapid Deployment of Forces for Limited War," this series of studies examined alternative strategies of rapid deployment to counter possible enemy assaults in Europe, Korea and Southeast Asia. It was assumed throughout the analysis that the enemy attack would come in full force. Therefore, a considerable deployment would be required immediately, or a substantial amount of territory might be lost.[16]

To meet this challenge, the study compared three strategies, each requiring alternative speeds and, therefore, methods of deployment:

- a "forward strategy," emphasizing a capability to put fully equipped fighting men into action in a few days (a strategy of rapid deployment);
- a "defensive" strategy, emphasizing only enough immediate capability to maintain a foothold;
- an "intermediate" strategy, calling for a capability somewhat between the first two.

As Enthoven and Smith have related, the conclusions of this study essentially confirmed U.S. experiences in World War II and Korea. Rapid U.S. reinforcement of allied armies would measurably improve the indigenous forces' capability to resist. Rapid deployments would also permit counterattacks, thereby preventing the enemy from consolidating his position. If the United States could reinforce rapidly and halt the enemy advance before a significant amount of territory was captured, the war could be ended quickly at a much lower total cost. Discussing the report's conclusions, Dr. Lawrence Lynn, Director of Strategic Mobility and Transportation Division, ASD/Systems Analysis, stated: "If we moved several divisions into the troubled area within 30 days, the war would be shorter, there would be less destruction, the casualties would be lighter, and this total force to do the job would be smaller."[17]

These studies also enabled a quantitative cost criterion to be applied to force planning. In comparing the costs to fight a major conventional war with those resulting from a limited deployment, it was estimated that a savings of more than $10 billion could be amassed. Therefore, the studies advocated, from an economic as well as a strategic perspective, the acquisition of a significant U.S. capability for the rapid deployment of conventional forces.[18]

With the combined efforts of the JCS and the Systems Analysis office in OSD, a mathematical model of this rapid deployment strategy was constructed. Through an iterative process, systematic comparisons of rapid deployment strategies were made, comparing cost with capability. The recommendations of this analysis called for a force mix:[19]

Several years of analysis of this kind suggested that a balanced mix of airlift, sealift and equipment prepositioning to meet the U.S. deployment objectives consisted of 6 C-5A squadrons, 14 C-141 squadrons and 30 Fast Deployment Logistic Ships, prepositioned equipment in Europe and the Pacific, a Civil Reserve Air Fleet and 460 commercial general cargo ships. Such a posture would provide the capability of simultaneously reinforcing allied forces in Europe and rapidly deploying U.S. general purpose forces to counter a major conventional attack in Asia as well as meeting a minor contingency in the Western Hemisphere.

This complex system was designed to support the "2-1/2 war" strategic concept and fashioned to be both cost and mission effective. Logistic planning was, therefore, not specifically dedicated to a lesser contingency, but was intended to provide a range of support systems capable of rapidly deploying forces of differing sizes to distant and disparate locales. However, because these different systems had unique properties and were, to some degree, scenario-specific (C-5As required air base support, FDLs needed docking facilities), it was necessary to have a mix of strategic mobility systems available to assure access to any contingency, major or lesser.[20]

Methods of rapid deployment. A network of overseas bases is perhaps the one method of approaching a strategy of rapid deployment that can obviate this force mix--providing the bases are in the area of the planned defense and the forces stationed there are adequate to meet the threat without additional reinforcement. This is not normally the case. Further, the word "base" in the rapid deployment context does not generally connote the oases of micro-American culture fabricated by U.S. Forces and their dependents in Europe and Northeast Asia. Rather, a "base" can more usefully describe "any geographical region mobilized to provide support for a nearby theater of operations."[21] Not surprisingly, U.S. policy regarding the maintenance and support of these facilities has fluctuated with the expansionist/isolationist turns of American foreign and defense policy.

During the 1950s, as the U.S. Air Force shifted its strategic force posture from the short-range B-47 to the intercontinental B-52 and ultimately, although not completely, to the ballistic missile, the Department of Defense began to yield the territory that had provided these global outposts. This process was accelerated in 1961 after President Kennedy discovered that the Defense Department still controlled 6,700 bases of various size, with 2,230 of them overseas.[22]

In 1969, the first major study of the U.S. overseas basing system since 1958[23] found that the United States still maintained 429 major bases and 2,972 minor installations world wide, staffed by approximately one million men. However, the study noted that no radical reduction in the requirement for these bases could be accomplished without a concomitant reduction in U.S. defense commitments to its allies. The structure of overseas bases, like the sizing of general purpose forces, was related directly to U.S. treaties and security commitments abroad.[24]

This secret study, prepared at the direction of the Johnson administration by General Robert J. Wood (USA-Ret) and Robert M. McClintock, a senior foreign service officer, suggested that U.S. bases, similar to the forces themselves, should be tailored to meet the U.S. strategy of deployment. The study concluded:[25]

-   there is little likelihood of early or substantial cutbacks in overeseas bases as long as the United States intends to honor its treaty commitments;
-   even such developments in military technology as the C-5A or the attainment of rapid sealift would not eliminate the need for substantial numbers of overseas bases and the deployment of skilled personnel to support those systems;
-   to relinquish distant bases and concentrate forces nearer or within the United States might cost more than keeping the forces deployed to bases that were already paid for, or whose upkeep was minimal.

Cost, again, appeared to be the dominant factor in the trade-off analysis among the rapid deployment strategies and methods. One of the most striking calculations to emerge from the Wood-McClintock study was the estimated costs of withdrawing from overseas bases while simultaneously maintaining the capability to employ an equivalent force through some alternate means of rapid deployment.[26]

In addition to these arguments for maintaining U.S. overseas bases to enhance rapid deployment capabilities, as advanced in the Wood-McClintock study, also prevalent at this time were arguments that an efficient rapid deployment capability was preferable to the stationing of large forces overseas. Enthoven and Smith, relying on the versatility of military forces, posited that the costs were less, the balance of payments deficit reduced, and, most important, a greater flexibility in the force was achieved:[27]

> The same division that can be ready to go to Korea in a week can also be ready to go to Europe in a week. Thus, . . . we realize better world-wide coverage by having the division here and deployable. If the division is stationed in an overseas theater, it is tied to that theater. The inability to use the two U.S. divisions stationed in Korea for the Vietnam war is the most recent example of this problem. Also, psychologically, it is better not to station large forces overseas, since U.S. presence contributes to the feeling on the part of our allies that their security is mainly our business. Finally . . . it is highly probable that if one of our allies were attacked we would go to its defense. If we had a good rapid deployment capability, we could do so much more effectively.

As Enthoven and Smith also point out, there is a necessity to tie together deployment capability and force readiness. This requires a "strategic" reserve force ready for immediate deployment to any contingency. One of the most ardent and continual advocates of this concept, and so previously cited, is General Maxwell Taylor. Writing in Foreign Affairs in 1974, following the October War and the U.S. supply effort to Israel, Taylor expressed a fairly common disillusionment, at that time, with the utility of U.S. overseas bases.[28] Taylor argued that the fixed commitment of strength to one region represented by those bases existed to the detriment of the central reserve that could be available for global purposes. In organizing this central reserve, readiness was the main ingredient:[29]

> As the primary response available to the many minor conflicts which may affect our interests, such a force should be designed for movement overseas without having to await the mobilization of suitably trained Reserve units. . . . Further, it must be able to sustain itself in combat for several months without significant reinforcement from outside the regular establishment.

Key to Taylor's conception of a rapid reaction force was a conventional force in-being. But also important to the rapid deployment of such a force was a network of overseas bases or the concept of prepositioning equipment and consumables in a forward area. This practice of placing war reserve stocks and materiel on land near the anticipated battle area has been principally limited to the major contingency in Europe. In 1961, the Army placed over 100,000 tons of stores and vehicles in Germany to facilitate the rapid reinforcement of units from the United States.[30] Over the course of twenty years, this practice has grown more sophisticated and the amount of supplies more abundant.

The Prepositioned Overseas Materiel Configured to Unit Sets (POMCUS) program is presently considered to be a critical element of the U.S. capability to reinforce NATO ground forces. This initiative has continued the methods of the early 1960s by placing sets of equipment dedicated to large mechanized and armor units in rear storage areas and planning on airlift to ferry the troops to the equipment. The men and materiel are then "married up," thereby saving considerable time and numerous sorties of dedicated airlift.[31]

POMCUS, however, does not solve the rapid deployment problem, even for the major contingency in Europe.[32] Certain items, such as air defense systems and helicopters, cannot be easily stored and quickly made ready for combat or rapidly shifted from the storage site to the battle area. Prepositioning equipment in only one area tends to limit flexibility, while distributing the equipment over a number of sites becomes more costly and time consuming. In addition, POMCUS storage sites offer a lucrative target for enemy interdiction.[33]

These limitations placed on a strategy of prepositioning also apply to force planning for a limited contingency, perhaps with even greater impact. It has not proven possible to preposition equipment on land to aid rapid deployment forces in a lesser contingency in a particular region. One solution to this problem has been to preposition supplies on "forward floating depots" that could move rapidly to the contingency area and supply the required equipment. This technique was first used by the U.S. Navy's 7th Fleet by creating a force consisting of three old Victory ships loaded with war reserve materiel and stationing them in the Pacific in the early 1960s. Secretary McNamara indicated in 1962 that this policy of prepositioning, for what was then conceived to be a major contingency in Asia, could be extended to other theaters as well.[34]

These limitations and liabilities of prepositioning strategies pointed to the need to increase air and sealift to deploy rapidly the strategic reserve. Unfortunately, the precise requirements for this lift in support of the general purpose forces were not easily calculated. As Secretary McNamara testified in 1964:[35]

> First, they are subject to the most of the same uncertainties which affect the general purpose forces--the wide variety of possible contingencies, the uncertainties concerning the military strength of our opponents. . . . Second, the quick reaction capability which these forces help to provide can be achieved in a number of ways. . . . Each of these alternatives, and variations of them, has certain advantages and disadvantages. Finally, while we have a vast background of experience in the sealift area, we are only now beginning to test realistically the potential of airlift; . . . it has long been recognized that a rapid deployment capability can, to a significant if imprecisely known extent, substitute for additional forces. Once having invested in this capability however, it may also become economical to shift even more of the logistical burden from other modes of transportation to airlift.

There are a number of factors to be considered in examining airlift as a method of supporting a strategy of rapid deployment. Perhaps, the most significant constraint on early attempts to use this mode was the lack of experience and lack of aircraft available.[36] Airlift had been assigned an overall low priority by the Air Force, resulting from that service's primary concern with the mission of strategic bombardment. Although the Army viewed this lack of airlift as a threat to its organizational essence,[37] Air Force priorities and Congressional appropriations had consistently placed first-line combat aircraft above support airlift.

Another reason that U.S. airlift capacity for rapid deployment lagged was the relative cost of this option. Although airlift is quite obviously the most rapid means of deployment for limited amounts of cargo and personnel, it is also the most expensive per delivered ton-mile. A 1960 Congressional report examining the reason why airlift requirements had tended to be neglected in the defense budget noted that the airlift requirements had to compete with other Air Force programs in order to be funded.[38] Thus, airlift was frequently portrayed as an expensive way to accomplish a non-essential mission.[39]

Another limitation tied to airlift as a principal method of rapid deployment was the infrastructure required within or near the contingency area. The advantages of rapid force movement offered by airlift could be negated if a considerable delay resulted in the transportation of the ground forces from the landing zone to the battlefield. Moreover, that required infrastructure of airfield and support facilities, like prepositioned equipment, could prove particularly vulnerable to enemy attack.[40] One effort to counter these shortcomings was to design an aircraft capable of moving personnel and their equipment and with the ability to operate into austere airfields close to the battle areas. A more expensive approach has been to respond to this requirement by constructing additional intratheater airlift to move the men and their equipment from the staging area to the battlefield.

The use of the civil air fleet as an additional rapid deployment airlift option is available at little incremental cost, but one that possesses few advantages in a limited contingency. Although the Civil Reserve Air Fleet (CRAF) can be effective in moving large numbers of personnel fairly rapidly, these aircraft are not designed to operate in remote areas or under combat conditions, nor are they structured to carry military cargo or to support airborne operations. Although the use of these aircraft to ferry personnel can release military transports for cargo missions (as they were used during Vietnam), any degree of mobilization of the fleet would result in a disruption of normal commercial air routes. The conflict and competition between military and civilian applications for both air and sea transportation systems have been a continuing and troublesome theme in the attempts by the Department of Defense to procure adequate and independent air and sealift systems.[41]

While the acquisition of airlift in support of a strategy of rapid deployment suffered from clashes of organizational interests of mission and budget priority, sealift was often disregarded for this purpose and generally perceived as a slow means of transportation suitable only for long-term resupply and reinforcement. Congressional testimony on sealift in the early 1960s supported the view that the existing mix of military and civil ships, such as those in the Merchant Marine and the National Defense Reserve Fleet, was adequate for the missions assigned. As Secretary McNamara testified:[42]

> Our most recent studies of sealift requirements indicate the current combined military/civilian capabilities are generally adequate to meet our requirements. Accordingly, no important

changes have been made to our sealift forces presented to the Committee last year. Our main concern with respect to cargo sealift is not so much with the number of ships as with the quantitative characteristics of the small MSTS fleet. . . . We did consider a new construction program, but the requirement for these ships is not urgent enough.

This lack of projected shipbuilding and a new emphasis on airborne troop and cargo transport, coupled with the expansion of the responsibilities of the U.S. STRIKE Command at the expense of the Navy, caused considerable concern within that service.[43] It was the contention of the Navy that airlifted troops could not equal in combat effectiveness or staying power units provided with heavy equipment and full support by amphibious forces. Thus, the Navy advocated several roles for sealift in support of limited contingency operations.

The first of these was the traditional technique of amphibious assault. By history and tradition, the United States Marine Corps has claimed this version of the rapid deployment mission since the end of the Second World War. However, the declining utility of the amphibious assault as well as the political and military constraints placed on it suggested that the Marines (and Navy) would have to seek other tactics to ensure a rapid deployment role. Although the post-Vietnam appraisal of the Marine mission has fomented a widespread debate, the growing obsolescence of amphibious landings was noted in the early 1960s.[44]

A second approach to a sealift-enhanced rapid deployment capability was the use of "forward floating depots" (FFD), combining the economic attractiveness of prepositioning with the flexibility of seaborne forces. This concept was less to the Navy's liking than a floating mobile reserve which might include a Marine battalion embarked on amphibious ships rather than the mere storage of supplies. However, these FFDs provided the Navy an entry to the rapid deployment mission without having to defend Marine amphibious tactics. The original Navy concept was to combine high speed sealift of personnel with the forward floating depots. Also included in this seaborne version of a rapid deployment force was the roll-on/roll-off ship. This ship design would allow the rapid loading and unloading of materiel and equipment, thereby avoiding a costly delay in breaking out of storage the equipment placed on the FFDs.[45]

However, further study of the possible naval contribution to a rapid deployment strategy, plus an "awareness that modern ship building technology could provide fast, highly efficient storage ships,"[46] led to the development of an entirely new concept, the Fast Deployment Logistics Ship (FDL). The Navy believed that a substantial number of these fast-moving ships could take the place of the floating depots by quickly aiming at the point of crisis with equipment tailored for the contingency. Airlifted troops could again be "married up" with the equipment. As in the case of the FFDs, however, this concept was also limited in that the join-up operation could be accomplished only in a secure environment.

This introduction has suggested the theories, strategies and methods of rapid deployment that affected force planning in support of limited contingency forces. The remainder of this chapter examines in greater detail the systems selected in their support. This examination completes the functional approach to answering the central question posed by this study--why the United States was unable to structure a coherent limited contingency force during this period. The failure to procure adequate lift for rapid deployment forces may, in the end, have been the most serious shortfall. Even if the strategic concept had provided an adequate base for raising the forces and if a capable and autonomous organization had developed to direct those forces, a limited contingency force could not have performed its mission effectively without sufficient mobility systems to deploy the force. Strategies and organizations can undergo rapid change or can be muddled through or around with ad hoc decisions; but, without adequate mobility support, any limited contingency force is unable to act.

The issues raised in this framework for analysis--organizational interests, budgetary priority and civil-military conflicts--will reappear throughout this chapter as elements of the explanation of why this rapid deployment capability was never achieved. In order to focus these issues more precisely, the following questions will be addressed in each section:

What mobility systems were proposed in support of a rapid deployment strategy? Were these systems dedicated to a lesser contingency?

To what extent were these strategic mobility systems supported and acquired?

What was the impact of these strategic mobility systems on the capability of U.S. forces to deploy rapidly to a limited contingency?

SEALIFT: Mobility Systems for "2-1/2 Wars," 1961-1968

The focus on sealift in this section is not meant to imply that the strategic mobility program advocated in support of the lesser contingency during the Kennedy/Johnson administrations was solely dedicated to sealift. On the contrary, in the early days of the Kennedy administration, strategic airlift was seen as the primary method through which to attain a rapid deployment capability. Sealift, as suggested earlier, was initially seen as being of little consequence in the support of a rapid deployment force. The expansion of U.S. airlift capacity was, therefore, one of the first three improvements called for by the administration in its new emphasis on the general purpose forces.[47] The language in the President's 1961 State of the Union address made it clear that the perceived increasing likelihood of a limited war also increased the need for airlift:[48]

> Obtaining additional air transport mobility--and obtaining it now--will better assure the ability of our conventional forces to respond, with discrimination and speed, to any problem at any spot on the globe at any moment's notice. In particular it will enable us to meet any deliberate effort to avoid or divert our forces by starting limited wars in widely scattered parts of the world.

In response to the President's direction, several initiatives were undertaken by the Department of Defense to improve U.S. airlift capability. By adjusting procurement and production schedules, the June 1961 airlift program provided a total of 129 new long-range modern airlift aircraft (C-130Es and C-135s) compared with the 50 previously programmed for FY 1961.[49] This emphasis on airlift grew from a perceived need to deploy rapidly ground forces to meet those "widely scattered" limited wars.[50]

The central importance of airlift was underscored in 1962 during the Cuban Missile Crisis. The Reserve squadrons called to active duty were equipped with older C-119 and C-123 aircraft that were severely limited in range, payload and speed. These aircraft were not seen as effective contributors to a rapid deployment strategy. Therefore, additional procurement of the C-130 and the C-141 (beyond that of the July 1961 proposal) was planned as a result of the mobilization of general purpose forces in October 1962.[51]

With this early concentration on airlift, other methods of supporting a rapid deployment capability tended to be ignored. Prepositioning did receive some attention, with the continuation of past programs of equipment storage near European bases. To meet the need for pre-stocking in Asia, the administration developed and put into practice the forward floating depot concept. Under this program, old Victory ships were converted into floating warehouses or armories, attached to the 7th Fleet and positioned in Subic Bay off the Philippines.[52] The concept called for the ships to move to the trouble spot with their stored equipment and join up there with airlifted troops.

A second attempt to add sealift to the rapid deployment strategies being considered was the development of the "roll-on/roll-off" vessel. Through a design concept that eased the process of loading and unloading heavy motorized equipment, these ships were to provide a capability to move and position an entire armored division considerably sooner than a combination of FFD prepositioning and airlift. Early plans called for the construction of a Comet roll-on/roll-off vessel each year for a number of years beginning in 1963.[53] However, with three ships authorized through 1963 and two already active in the fleet, Congress eliminated the funding for the 1964 ship pending the completion of an evaluation of the ship's effectiveness.[54] These Congressional objections to the program stemmed not so much from the strategic shortcomings of the concept, but from challenges to these federally-sponsored and constructed ships emanating from the offices of the American Merchant Marine Institute.[55] This civil-military conflict over government-funded sealift was a portent of the more damaging debate that was to surround the FDL proposal.

Added to this growing conflict over the means to improve U.S. seaborne lift capability was a general disdain on the part of the administration both for sealift as a supporting system for rapid deployment and the quality of the U.S. ship building industry. Although Secretary McNamara had called in July 1961 for the reactivation of 15 troop transport ships,[56] by the following year he declared that he did not need the military transports then in use. In testimony before the Merchant Marine and Fisheries Committee in April 1962, the Defense Secretary also turned down proposals for the government subsidy of two luxury liners that could be used as troop transports in time of war. In addition to the inefficiencies of the U.S. ship building industry that appeared to make such a proposal cost-ineffective, McNamara objected to extensive government support of sealift on strategic grounds. He contended that the importance of sealift in defense planning had been reduced and that ships would be used in the future only for logistical support after the ground forces had been delivered by airlift.[57] This position was to come back to haunt the Defense Secretary in his later proposals for the FDL.

The administration's position on sealift was soon revised. Although the rapid deployment of U.S. troops was to remain a function of airlift, the perceived importance of sealift as a contributor to this effort called for a mix of rapid deployment systems. This reappraisal resulted from a series of studies that examined the need for rapid deployment systems over the long term.

In July 1964, the Special Studies Group of the Joint Chiefs of Staff on rapid deployment concluded that the strategy was cost effective in terms of approximately 20 percent fewer forces needed over the duration of the conflict, a likelihood of a shorter war and fewer casualties. In calling for an optimum mix of airlift, sealift and prepositioning, the study formed the basic rationale for rapid deployment strategies and the attendant procurement of strategic mobility systems.[58] Consequently, the Secretary of Defense established a number of strategic mobility work projects oriented toward achieving an improved and balanced strategic deployment capability. These work projects were detailed studies, each of a specific subject, within the areas of plans and programs, force readiness, airlift and sealift, facilities, prepositioning, logistic need for a strategic movement command.[59]

In March 1965, Secretary McNamara requested that a thorough study be made of the changes required in the Defense Department's organization to improve mobility planning and operations. The results of the study, published in July 1965 and known as the Conroy Report, recommended the establishment of a new military organization within the office of the Joint Chiefs of Staff to provide a principal point of contact for all strategic mobility planning and operations. In addition, the report recommended improving contingency planning and strategic movement operating procedures.[60]

Following review of the Conroy Report by the Department of Defense, the Secretary directed the establishment within OJCS of an organizational element to provide the focus called for in the report. One of the first studies undertaken was the "Strategic Movement Capabilities Plan, 1966-1970." "Movecap" considered the forces and equipment to be moved, the existing capability to deploy them, and the readiness of the units.[61] In his testimony before the Special Subcommittee on Military Airlift in October 1965, General Earle Wheeler, the Chairman of the Joint Chiefs of Staff, reported that a Joint Transportation Board had been established within the JCS, charged with a continuing review of airlift and sealift requirements. General Wheeler added that the establishment of a "focal point to concentrate on strategic movement matters" had led to further studies of rapid deployment strategies and methods:[62]

> I am aware that much has been said about the many studies that have been made regarding strategic mobility. I can assure you much good has come out of the efforts put into these studies . . . .
> Some of the military factors that must be considered when evaluating strategic mobility are readiness of units, their reception capabilities, and the type and magnitude of the threat to be encountered.
> Our task is to identify the proper mix of airlift, sealift, and prepositioning that will provide the proper military response.

In March 1966, the Office of Special Assistant to the JCS for Strategic Mobility was established to "analyze, evaluate and monitor strategic movement planning and objectives." One of the first responsibilities of the new assistant, Major General James C. Sherrill, was to update the "Movecap" study annually.[63] It was also time, after all the studying of the problem that General Wheeler acknowledged, to turn planning into action.

What mobility systems were proposed in support of a rapid deployment strategy? Were these systems dedicated to a lesser contingency?

These systematic studies of rapid deployment strategy and increased attention given to agencies developing these concepts resulted in a major change in U.S. rapid deployment strategy and methods. By 1965, the decision had been made to proceed with the recommendation for a new class of Fast Deployment Logistic Ships (FDLs) to replace the forward floating depots and provide a new dimension to rapid deployment capability. Secretary McNamara later explained that, aside from the limited form of mobile prepositioning exhibited by the FFD, the potential contribution of sealift to a rapid deployment strategy had been overlooked, primarily due to its slowness of response.[64] However, certain factors served to change this viewpoint: a better understanding of the force size required to support a rapid response requirement, the cost implications of attempting to meet this requirement through airlift alone and the belief that technological improvements now permitted the construction of fast and efficient sealift. Further study of the FFD concept and the emerging prospect of more capable ships[65]

> . . . opened up the possibility of an entirely new rapid deployment strategy in which sealift would play a much more prominent role. The FDLs would be used either in the FFD role or be held in a ready status in U.S. ports where heavy equipment, tailored to the mission, could be quickly loaded when the need to deploy arose.

It is important to note here that the support systems being developed in these studies were in response to looming contingencies, but were not allocated or assigned to the existing limited contingency force, that is, the U.S. STRIKE Command. Although the strategic concept of the "half war" was getting a good deal of attention as a rationale for strategic mobility systems and the STRIKE Command was well underway in its training and exercise functions, the systems being planned and procured were seen as flexible, capable of meeting a variety of major and lesser contingencies and generally service-specific. In terms of planning and procuring strategic mobility systems, the U.S. did not appear to be following its declared policy of "2-1/2 wars."

As late as 1968, when STRIKE Command was on the wane, systems to support a rapid deployment strategy had been planned, but not procured. Secretary McNamara described the contingencies and the systems needed to support a rapid deployment strategy in his Posture Statement of that year.[66] The most demanding contingency for force planning was a deployment to Southeast Asia to counter a conventional attack while simultaneously reinforcing U.S. troops in Europe and maintaining the capability to meet "a more limited contingency elsewhere." After testing a wide range of various combinations of airlift, sealift and prepositioning, it was determined that the most cost-effective force to meet these requirements should consist of: 6 C-5A squadrons, 14 C-141 squadrons, 30 FDLs, equipment prepositioned in both Europe and Asia, plus a Civil Reserve Air Fleet and 460 commercial cargo ships. This force mix had been determined analytically to meet the demands of the rapid deployment strategy to support the major and lesser contingencies that might occur. The task now was to procure these strategic mobility systems.

To what extent were these strategic mobility systems supported and acquired?

The attention paid to sealift in the late 1960s as a method of rapid deployment was a relatively new initiative. Bernard Brodie, as early as 1958, had remarked on the necessity of "guaranteeing the quick transportation of large bodies of men with their heavy equipment and supplies" through sealift.[67] But, just as airlift was accorded a secondary mission in the Air Force, so was sealift assigned a low priority in Navy programs and budgets. The early concentration of the Kennedy administration on airlift for rapid deployment, along with the establishment of STRIKE Command without a Navy component, offered little encouragement to the Navy to pursue a separate mobility program for U.S. Army ground forces that might conflict with more traditional Navy roles, missions and budgets.[68]

However, the original Navy concept of high speed sealift to transport troops to their prepositioned equipment aboard FFDs was expanded in a Navy study completed in 1964. "Logistic Support of Land Forces," of LOGLAND, demonstrated that seaborne systems could play a vital role in the deploying of ground forces. The increasing amount of heavy, non-air-transportable equipment being assigned to Army divisions made sealift appear especially attractive. A series of studies conducted and included in this report showed that a fast deployment ship could be constructed to store, transport and put ashore the equipment in support of the Army and would enhance the rapid deployment concept.[69]

LOGLAND further developed the concept of operating ships loaded with this equipment in forward objective areas or in regions where a lesser contingency appeared likely. Additional ships would remain in continental ports in some degree of readiness and partially loaded. When the order came to deploy, the FDLs would be capable of arriving at the designated area within only a few days, contributing the prestocked materiel to the troops arriving by aircraft.[70]

This Navy recommendation for a seaborne system came at a time when the CJCS Special Study Group was studying rapid deployment strategies, and the services were seeking ways of implementing such strategies. The FDL proposal appeared to round out a list of available alternatives, adding a sealift element to the previous mix of airlift and prepositioning.[71] This proposal was enthusiastically welcomed by an Army that had long complained of the inadequacy of both air and sealift as well as the lack of motivation on the part of the Air Force and Navy to procure sufficient numbers of those systems. FDL operational concepts were formally agreed to by the Chief of Naval Operations and the Chief of Staff of the Army in 1966. The concepts were "purposely developed on a broad and flexible basis to anticipate the various rapid deployment needs that the changing demands of strategy might require."[72]

According to this position, agreed upon by the administration and the Army and the Navy, the FDL would[73]

- satisfy U.S. requirements for specialized military sealift for rapid force deployment or reinforcement,
- help deter aggression by increasing the U.S. capability to deploy forces rapidly,
- increase force effectiveness at less cost than a system involving only airlift and land prepositioning,
- modernize U.S. prepositioning afloat,
- reduce requirements for additional prepositioning and forward deployment and
- possess desirable ship design features, such as high speed, ample storage capacity, and roll-on/roll-off capability.

Despite this agreed-upon mission, there was considerable disagreement as to whether the FDLs would be dedicated only to reinforcing the major contingency or if they also could be used to support rapid deployment to a lesser case. The ships' mobility and the apparent adequacy of land prepositioning in Europe to meet the immediate needs of the major contingency there suggested that the FDLs might primarily be used to support a major contingency in Asia (under the "2-1/2 war" concept) or to support deployment to a lesser contingency. But Secretary McNamara, seeking to cast the FDL in a defensive role and, perhaps, hoping to tie budgetary support for the program to the major contingency, chose not to orient the FDL towards the "half war":[74]

What I am saying is the small actions don't require and wouldn't benefit significantly from the FDL program. The FDL program is a large program, and it would be used in connection with relatively large actions. . . . I am simply saying the FDL does not give us an increased small-operation capability.

However, the Defense Secretary's testimony appeared to be in a minority regarding the proposed use of the fleet of FDLs. The Army, the Navy and other agencies within DoD concluded that the FDL was well suited to support a limited and rapid deployment. The Army Chief of Staff, General Harold K. Johnson, testified in 1967:[75]

It (the FDL) would be used any place that our government requires forces to be deployed. It could be used in either of two ways. One, to reinforce forces that are currently deployed in forward areas, specifically Europe and Korea. And second, it could be used in places where we might want to introduce forces.

According to one official U.S. Navy position, the prime purpose of the FDL ships was to act as a "deterrent to hostile military adventures in any region of the globe by providing a flexible means for stationing combat equipment for land forces near any area of potential trouble."[76] In his testimony to the Senate Merchant Marine and Fisheries Subcommittee, Assistant Secretary of Defense Paul Ignatius stated that the FDLs were programmed to "deploy their loads into the relatively unprepared and undeveloped areas characteristic of many potential contingency areas."[77] Thus, despite Secretary McNamara's protests to the contrary, the FDL was widely perceived as a method of transportation and support for a limited contingency force. To a considerable extent, it was this perception within Congress, seen within the wider context of the U.S. involvement in Vietnam, that led to the ultimate rejection of the program.

In his 1965 Posture Statement, Secretary McNamara advanced the first program for the procurement of the FDLs to replace both the forward floating depots and the proposed Comet "ro-ro" ships that had encountered prior Congressional opposition. The original concept called for the FDLs to be used as "forward mobile depots" stationed close to potential trouble areas. According to the DoD position, the converted Victory class FFD ships stationed in the Pacific could carry only one-third as much and travel half as fast as the FDL, lacked an "over the beach" capability and took many times longer to load and unload.[78]

The new program called for the construction of four FDLs in FY 1966, to be part of a fleet ultimately comprising 30 such vessels. Each FDL would be capable of carrying 8000-10,000 short tons of supplies and equipment, including tanks, personnel carriers and consumables. The FDL design also included the use of "flying crane" helicopters to lift lightweight cargo directly onto the shore, while the heavier equipment would be ferried to the beach by smaller amphibious boats. By design, all of the cargo could be offloaded in 20 hours, and 12 FDLs could provide enough equipment and supplies to support a fully-equipped infantry division, arriving and unloading within a week's time.[79] The estimated cost for each FDL was $32 million.

For a number of reasons, the U.S. Congress chose not to appropriate funds to support the procurement of the Fast Deployment Logistics ships. This lack of budgetary support has considerable implication for the explanatory purposes of this study. In inquiring into the reasons why the United States has failed to construct a coherent limited contingency force over the last twenty years, only the effort to acquire the necessary strategic mobility systems described in this chapter met head-on the difficulty of achieving budgetary support for a rapid deployment capability. The fundamental questions of supporting a declared defense policy and accomplishing effective general purpose force planning raised here go well beyond the FDL debate.

What was the impact of these strategic mobility systems on the capability of U.S. forces to deploy rapidly to a limited contingency?

The failure of the U.S. Congress to support the acquisition of the Fast Deployment Logistics ships reduced significantly the planned strategy and methods of rapid deployment, both in reinforcement of forces deployed and in support of rapid deployment to a lesser contingency. There were essentially four reasons why the FDL failed to generate Congressional support during the years 1965-1970. The first of these, but perhaps the least significant, was objections raised by both the House and the Senate Armed Services Committees regarding the total cost of the program--originally estimated at one billion dollars. The second basis for opposition to the FDL was the belief on the part of the American maritime industry and the affected labor unions that the creation of this DoD fleet would usurp the peacetime mission of the Merchant Marine. These organizations lobbied hard against the FDL, contending that the funds would be better spent in support of a massive civilian ship building program, with the new ships dedicated to defense-related missions in time of war. Hidden in this issue of the opportunity cost of the FDL was a third, more fundamental Congressional objection to the program--a reluctance of Congress to appropriate funds for support of logistical systems in lieu of weapons systems. The final reason for the defeat of the FDL is the least concrete of the four, yet nevertheless served as a major torpedo in the sinking of the fleet. Key players in both the Senate and the House argued that a rapid deployment strategy in general and the FDL in particular presented an "opportunity for intervention" that would result in the expansion of U.S. political commitments and encourage the use of military force in support of those commitments. Cast in the lengthening shadow of Vietnam, this position attracted a sufficient number of proponents to defeat the FDL proposal. The contention that the mere existence of any weapons system may determine the selection of a certain national response is a questionable, but nevertheless relevant theory that was later applied to force planning debates surrounding the Rapid Deployment Force.

The cost-effectiveness of the FDL, as presented by the administration, was not sufficient in itself to gain Congressional support for the program. The Report of the Senate Armed Services Committee, dated March 20, 1967, disapproved the program partially in response to the "excessive cost of the program," such as the not included costs of providing the necessary protection for these ships.[80] The report noted that the FDLs, when deployed in forward areas, would require an additional investment in both anti-submarine and anti-aircraft escort vessels. Secretary McNamara, armed with his studies supporting the most cost-effective way to achieve a rapid deployment capability, disagreed:[81]

> The objection that this program is too costly does not recognize that a combination of the FDLs, the C-5As and land prepositioning gives us the desired capability for the lowest cost to the government. To replace the thirty FDLs with the equivalent C-5A capability would cost three times as much as the FDL program. To increase our land prepositioning would not only be more costly, it would introduce unacceptable degrees of rigidity into our mobility posture. Disapproval of the FDL program would, therefore, cause a serious imbalance in our general purpose forces which could be overcome only at considerable extra cost.

The second principal issue raised in the Congressional debate on the FDL was the possible use of the ships for point-to-point cargo transport in peacetime, thereby displacing the routes and service provided by the Merchant Marine. Although Secretary McNamara argued that the FDL, designed as a military transport and possessing required storage characteristics, would be inefficient for this mission, the FDL critics remained unconvinced. Congressman Garmatz of Maryland was representative of those who challenged the FDL based on its threat to American civil shipping:[82]

> DoD is attempting to supplant one of the basic functions of the Merchant Marine . . . that is to serve as an auxillary arm to the military in times of emergency. If our seriously declining Merchant Marine had been properly supported over the years, it would have the capabilities today to successfully meet the nation's military and

commercial needs. . . . If Congressional intent had been followed instead of circumvented, DoD would not now be in such a frenzied hurry to develop a dubious system to meet maritime inadequacies to which it has itself contributed--by both its hostility and indifference toward the maritime industry.

The Department of Defense was unable to argue successfully that the FDLs would not be ultimately used to replace Merchant Marine transport.[83] One of the main points that bothered the privately owned shipping lines, the maritime industry and the labor unions was the use of the FDLs in peacetime. However, as a conversation between Mr. Blanford, the counsel of the House Committee on Armed Services, and General Johnson revealed, the FDL concept was being questioned on strategic grounds as well:[84]

> Mr. Blanford: Once the world settles down to where we only have two trouble spots instead of 52 and we have got 30 of these ships . . . sitting in Norfolk or some place with equipment . . . and some future Secretary comes along who is very cost conscious . . . and they say: Now it is a crime not to use these ships. So we will put them into MSTS and use them to carry cargo to supply our overseas commitments.
> General Johnson: I think your premise is wrong, that is, that the time is coming when we are going to have just two trouble spots in the world. All the studies we have done indicate that in the years since 1945 the number of trouble spots has increased rather than decreased . . . .
> Mr. Blanford: Perhaps, we should be building more carriers, General, instead of the FDLs; we should be building more carriers and a firepower they understand?

Thus, the proposed fleet of FDLs was caught between the Scylla of the Merchant Marine and the Charybdis of the carrier. If the need for a rapid deployment capability did not remain as a long-term strategy, then there was a probability that the FDLs would be diverted to a peacetime mission of point-to-point transport. But, if the U.S. was to be involved in a series of limited conflicts, it would be better to procure weapons systems that would allow the projection of "firepower they understand" rather than a fleet of supply ships.

The thesis expressed on behalf of the Committee by their counsel-- that the Navy did not really wish to fund an FDL program that amounted to logistic support for the Army and would rather devote its budget share to combat systems--is continued in a dialogue that, although enlightening and entertaining, reflects Congressional and service confusion regarding rapid deployment strategies and methods:[85]

> The Chairman (Mendel Rivers): The reason Mr. Blanford asked that and the great exuberance about which the Army is carrying the ball on the FDL program, we just assumed you would be willing for the entire FDL cost to come out of the Army's money--you would support that wouldn't you?
> General Johnson: No. We believe . . . that the responsibility for providing sealift for all of the forces . . . is the responsibility of the Navy.

The Chairman: Did this idea come out of the Army, Navy, Air Force or Marine Corps?

Secretary Nitze: The concept, the rapid deployment concept, was evolved in discussion between the Secretary of Defense's office and the JCS. I think it really sprang from consideration by the JCS . . . .

Admiral McDonald: I think it started, Mr. Chairman, back when they organized the STRIKE Command. That is when they started this strategic mobility, this question of delivering large numbers of troops long distances and having them ready to fight . . . it went from the C-141 . . . to the prepositioning, and then when they went to the C-5A, since that would take more troops further but still couldn't take all of the heavy equipment. It then became a question of, are we going to preposition more heavy equipment, or would it be better to put that in some form of a more modern ship . . .

The Chairman: And then they finally arrived at the FDL concept? Which is this?

General Johnson: I think the concept goes back significantly before that. I can recall . . . between 1953 and 1956, that the Army staff sought some way to project power overseas more rapidly. The volume and weight of Army equipment was such that using normal shipping, or even the aircraft of that day, we could never get any significant level of force into a troubled area within a reasonable period of time.

The Chairman: Who finally arrived at the FDL? Whose decision was this?

Admiral McDonald: I guess the type of ship was the Navy's in order to meet a stated Army requirement.

Mr. Chairman: I am leading up to this question: Would you assign top priority (to the FDL)?

Admiral McDonald: I agree that the ships should be funded through the Navy.

The Chairman: Is this thing as important to you as a nuclear attack force?

Admiral McDonald: No sir.

According to Mendel Rivers' line of reasoning, the service that gained the most from the FDL (the Army) should fund the project, leaving the other services free to procure the weapons systems they really wanted. Thus, support continued to lack a high priority in the Congressional pattern of authorization and appropriation as well as within the services tasked to provide that support.

Opposition to the FDL in the Senate, led by Richard Russell, Chairman of the Armed Services Committee, was based on a different premise. The Committee recommended that the program be halted on the contention that the ships would create the impression abroad that the United States "has assumed the function of policing the world."[86] The FDL, because it would be "constantly deployed in forward areas throughout the world," suggested that the U.S. would be drawn into war in new places in a series of lesser contingencies. "Some nations would consider this (the FDL) facility for intervention anywhere, anytime as an intimidation."[87]

Secretary McNamara rebutted these arguments in a letter to the House Armed Services Committee on April 13, 1967:[88]

It is not now, nor has it ever been, my intention to propel the United States into a role as world policeman; . . . we now have treaty commitments which may well involve us in combat. . . . If we are going to continue these commitments, then the FDL is a major factor in improving our combat capability; without it we will lack the ability to take full advantage of rapid deployment to lessen the cost and duration of war and to reduce casualties. . . . We have not taken on any new commitments because of the FDL program nor do we contemplate doing so . . . The total FDL force will not be routinely deployed in areas distant from our shores . . . . Hence, none of the FDLs would be routinely cruising on the high seas looking for trouble. This is why I feel it is highly unlikely that the mobility afforded by the FDLs will lead to undesirable involvements.

But Senator Russell was destined to have the last word in the debate. He continued to lead the forces opposed to the FDL on the grounds that the creation of a ready, rapid reaction capability would make it more likely that in a crisis the U.S. government would decide to use military force. The question being raised here was: "Does the availability of ready military options have any significant effect on decisions regarding the possible use of force?" The position of Secretary McNamara and the Department of Defense was that it did not. But the formulation of "Russell's Alternative" carried the day and scuttled the FDL fleet: "If Americans find it easy to go anywhere and do anything, they will always be going somewhere and doing something."[89]

Mr. McNamara was willing to tackle this more fundamental issue as well--that the U.S. Congress should not ratify political commitments to other countries without accepting the responsibility of supporting those commitments through the procurement of adequate forces:[90]

> The basic objection of the Senate was not to the procurement policy, but to the primary strategic objective. The thrust of the debate implies that were the Congress to supply the executive branch with the FDL ships, it would increase our combat readiness and, thereby, make more likely the deployment abroad of U.S. forces and their participation in foreign conflicts. No, I submit to you, gentlemen, this is a fundamental issue.

Congress was not prepared, in 1967, to debate this issue. It did not choose to reduce foreign obligations, but neither did it intend to fund forces that, while strengthening U.S. capabilities for rapid deployment, might encourage wider U.S. foreign and defense policy commitments in the future. Thus, despite repeated attempted launches, the DoD-proposed fleet of FDLs continued to founder on Capitol Hill.

Meanwhile, the estimated cost of the entire fleet had grown from an original $1 billion to $2 billion. When Clark Clifford succeeded Robert McNamara as Secretary of Defense in February 1968, he reviewed the policy and initiated a new approach. In an attempt to gain more widespread support for the program, Clifford cut the proposed buy to 15 FDLs and tied the purchase to a plan under which the Navy's Military Sea Transportation Service (MSTS) would charter to shipping firms up to 30 new, privately built cargo ships. This proposal, carried over into the FY 1970 budget by Secretary Laird, was also defeated. In an atmosphere of reduced defense spending and increased opposition to any

U.S. "intervention" capability generated by public opinion against the war in Vietnam, no funds were requested for the FDL in the FY 1971 budget.[91] A case study of the FDL can illuminate several facets of the weapon systems acquisition process. Important here is an appreciation of the failure to procure mobility systems in support of a rapid deployment strategy, and an understanding of why those forces were not acquired. The strategic concept, the allocation of forces and the organization in support of a limited contingency force were necessary, but insufficient in themselves to forge a coherent strategy of rapid deployment. Without the FDL, the U.S. capability for rapid deployment was diminished significantly. Without adequate sealift for the limited contingency force, future efforts to create a "half war" mobility capability would be limited to half-steps.

AIRLIFT: Mobility Systems for "1-1/2 Wars," 1968-1976

Despite the loss of the FDL, the architects of the rapid deployment strategy continued to argue that strategic mobility systems were essential. Writing in 1970, Enthoven and Smith pointed out that a good rapid deployment capability was still preferable to keeping large U.S. forces stationed overseas. Moreover, they posited that a peaceful world order would continue to depend substantially on a highly flexible U.S. capability to meet a lesser contingency. Although they acknowledged that "our allies ought to do more and that we ought to persuade them to do more," the effectiveness of this process of persuasion would be derived from a concerted U.S. effort to construct and maintain systems that would enable the rapid deployment of conventional forces worldwide.[92] To meet these needs in the decade of the seventies, without the FDL, the general purpose force planners turned to airlift. But airlift as a method of rapid force deployment had also encountered difficulties in terms of adequate support in the years preceding this change in emphasis. Thus, an understanding of the role played by airlift in this period requires a brief description of the development of airlift as a method of rapid deployment.

The development of airlift doctrine in the post-World War II Air Force proceeded along four lines.[93] The first was the use of airlift to move personnel, equipment and supplies. Second was a specialized logistic function to airlift high value items, thereby reducing supply pipeline times, inventory and costs. Third was the tactical airborne operation; and fourth, the strategic movement of ground forces. While the Air Force saw the first two airlift functions as most important in support of its strategic bombardment mission, the Army understandably was more interested in missions three and four. This difference in viewpoint and mission between the services set the stage for early organizational battles over airlift priorities.

Following the Korean War, the Tactical Air Command (TAC) rather than the Military Air Transport Service (MATS, later the Military Air Command, MAC), was charged with providing support to the Army. This original relationship reflected the need to facilitate joint service cooperation in the close air support mission and an emphasis on tactical rather than strategic mobility. To meet Army needs, two squadrons of C-124 aircraft were assigned to TAC. But these aircraft were soon transferred to MATS as a result of a 1955 Hoover Commission recommendation that airlift command and control be centralized.[94] With this transfer of responsibility and forces, it appeared that the Army had been deprived of airlift adequate to support its rapid deployment mission:[95]

> Because MATS was an airlift organization that was available only upon JCS allocation to any of the armed services, the Army took the position that it could not depend on MATS airlift for deployment of Army divisions. Before the two TAC wings were transferred to MATS, the Army considered them the only aircraft available and, after the transfer, concluded that no airlift at all was available.

The Army-Air Force doctrinal dispute surrounding these issues has been suggested elsewhere in this study. Essentially, the Army in the late 1950s was fighting for an increased limited conventional war capability. To support this mission, they wanted "predesignated" airlift units-- aircraft that could not be diverted to missions of greater priority-- available for the rapid deployment of ground forces to a lesser contingency.[96]

Because these issues involving service roles and missions proved difficult to solve within the joint service forum, the airlift issue gradually moved under the scrutiny of Congress. However, a civil-military dispute, not unlike that which stymied the FDL acquisition, also plagued the Congressional debate on adequate airlift. Therefore, when a House Defense Appropriations Subcommittee chaired by Representative Flood began hearings based on the Army's complaint of inadequate airlift capacity in 1956, the Subcommittee also examined charges emanating from the Hoover Commission that MATS was competing with the civilian airlines.

In a series of hearings in both the House and the Senate, this civil-military conflict frequently arose. The solution most often presented was that the Air Force should place more emphasis in MATS on supporting the Army. The result of this dedication would be a reduction in total available airlift capacity and, therefore, a lowering of MATS' competitive profile against the civilian air carriers.[97] The Air Force, in clinging to the traditional MATS mission of supporting the Strategic Air Command, failed to strengthen its case. Rather than agreeing on the need for additional intertheater airlift in support of the Army, the Air Force argued for the concept of an autonomous transport fleet poised in readiness in the United States to support the strategic mission. This image strengthened the Congressional perception that any air transport mission outside the CONUS was nonessential and, therefore, in direct competition with the airlines.[98]

The partial resolution of this conflict began with the work of the Subcommittee on National Military Airlift of the House Armed Services Committee in 1960, again chaired by L. Mendel Rivers of South Carolina. The Rivers panel was charged to look into all aspects of national airlift, including MATS, the Civil Reserve Air Fleet (CRAF) and the effectiveness of the air transport system in terms of its contribution to national defense.[99] For the first time in the lengthy Congressional probing into military airlift, this Congressional committee examined the effectiveness of airlift in support of the mission of rapid deployment, not simply with regard to the domestic issue of conflict with the civilian carriers. In order to deal with the legitimacy of the Army laments regarding the adequacy of airlift, it was necessary for the Committee to study JCS war plans--which other committees had been reluctant to do-- in order to draw the proper relationships between policy commitments and force planning in their support.[100]

Until 1960, under the strategy of massive retaliation, airlift mobility plans were based on three assumed situations. The first case assumed a scenario of a six-months' mobilization followed by a sixty-day general war. A second option visualized a general war without adequate strategic warining. The third situation was seen as a renewal of limited war in Korea.[101] The Committee concentrated on the worst case. Panel members generally assumed that lengthy strategic warning would not be forthcoming and, therefore, looked only at the total number of military and civilian aircraft available under the second scenario. As for the case of limited war, the Committee felt that if there were enough airlift to handle a general war/no warning situation, there would be adequate airlift for a lesser contingency elsewhere.[102]

The Rivers subcommittee ended its hearings with the conclusion that total airlift was inadequate to meet the wartime mission. To overcome these limitations, the Committee made numerous recommendations, including the immediate development of a military jet cargo aircraft, the modernization of the current MATS fleet and the upgrading of CRAF capability.[103] Based on these recommendations, Representative Rivers initiated appropriation legislation for over $300 million in airlift development and procurement.[104] Thus, the Air Force was given both the direction and the authorization to build an airlift force capable of not only supporting the Strategic Air Command, but also of projecting U.S. ground forces overseas.[105]

What mobility systems were proposed in support of a rapid deployment strategy? Were these systems dedicated to a lesser contingency?

In response to Congressional and Army prodding and to attain increased mobility for the general purpose forces under the new strategy of flexible response, Secretary McNamara called in 1961 for a 100 percent increase in airlift capability by the end of 1964. This program requested a $172 million increase in FY 1962 for airlift, delayed the planned elimination of some C-118 and C-124 squadrons and increased the acquisition rate for the C-130 and C-135.[106] Development of the jet transport, the C-141, was also expedited.[107]

Again in response to the Rivers Committee, the Air Force in 1961 proposed a large jet aircraft, "designed to accept all large general purpose forces equipment which could operate in a combat environment and substantially increase our total rapid mobility capability."[108] This aircraft, which was to become the C-5A, evolved from a specific Army requirement and was based on previous operational airlift experience. Designed to carry all of the equipment which was outsize to the C-141, the C-5A promised to end the normal practice of "tailoring" combat forces for air movement, with a corresponding loss of firepower. This additional capacity, of course, implied that the C-5A would have great utility in reinforcing U.S. troops deployed to a major contingency as well as facilitating the movement of heavy forces to a lesser case.

In 1963, an OSD/ISA study further helped convince the Air Force that the inability to deploy ground force quickly was the chief weakness in the nation's capability to wage limited war, especially if more than one contingency were to occur simultaneously.[109] Plans were soon underway to exercise the airlift of an entire division to both Europe and the Pacific --albeit, not simultaneously.[110] However, General Adams, the STRIKE Commander, testified before the House Armed Services Committee on the need to plan and prepare for the airlift of troops to both contingencies at the same time. According to CINCSTRIKE, this inability to support simultaneous contingencies meant that he could not accomplish his mission and that the U.S. could not meet its commitments.[111]

As evidence of the American ability to airlift forces in support of a major contingency in Europe, "Operation Big Lift" in October 1963 moved the personnel of an augmented armored division to Europe from the United States in 63 hours. However, the exercise did not demonstrate a capability for rapid deployment to a lesser contingency, but rather a reinforcement capability. As Representative Chamberlin pointed out:[112]

> We were all impressed with Operation Big Lift and our ability to move a division of troops by military aircraft in a short period of time. But Operation Big Lift was made possible because we prepositioned heavy equipment weeks and months in advance ... because airfields were ready to receive American aircraft. But it does not take much imagination on anyone's part to visualize a situation where we would not have prepositioned equipment, we would not get overflight rights or airfields would not be accessible to us.

Thus, although airlift to project some U.S. military power was available by the mid-1960s,[113] the capability to support simultaneous contingencies or to airlift an effective fighting force without the benefit of extensive prepositioning did not exist. Secretary McNamara acknowledged this fact in his 1964 Posture Statement:[114]

> With respect to the planning of airlift, our critical requirements appear to be those occurring in the first 30 days of a large-scale war in a remote area. Up until now it has not been necessary to determine peak deployment requirements with any precision, since we were obviously far short of any reasonable goal. However, by 1968 our airlift capability will be about four times that of 1961 and a better measure of our ultimate needs and goals is now necessary.

In September 1964, a joint Army-Air Force study called AIRTRANS-70 compared two alternative airlift forces: a 20-squadron C-141 force and a mix of C-141 and C-5A aircraft. This study found in favor of the mixed force based on its outsized capability and operating cost reduction as well as the funding that such a force would[115]

> ... provide a capability to deploy large forces rapidly from one area to another, thereby reducing risks to the general war posture in committing major forces to contingency areas and be capable of airlifting up to eight Army divisions during the early deployment period, resulting in a potential for ultimate savings in dollar costs, casualties and time required to conduct a limited war.

The study concluded that no other system or combination of rapid deployment methods--prepositioning or sealift--would provide an effective alternative to the airlift capabilities of the C-5/C-141 mix.

As the war in Vietnam began to absorb the airlift resources dedicated to both the major and the lesser contingencies as well as other program elements within the general purpose forces, it appeared that a rapid deployment objective would not be achieved through airlift alone. Moreover, just as the war had caused the FDL to be viewed in a different strategic light, so did it affect the perceived need for rapid deployment by airlift. Operation "Eagle Thrust," the airlift of the 101st Airmobile Division with their equipment from the U.S. to Vietnam, was accomplished in a little over one month on an "accelerated, but not an emergency basis."[116] Although Vietnam was seen as a limited war, it was a war with staying power, one that did not require rapid deployment support. However, the amount of lift that the war was consuming was enormous, making it clear by 1968 that U.S. strategic airlift was incapable of supporting simultaneous contingencies envisioned under the "2-1/2 war" strategic concept. In 1970, another Congressional panel would determine that airlift to support even the reduced strategic guidance of "1-1/2 wars" remained questionable.

To what extent were these strategic mobility systems supported and acquired?

According to the Nixon Doctrine, the United States would maintain its commitments but would act on American interests. In terms of military support, this meant that increased emphasis would be placed on local defense with the allies' own ground forces doing the fighting, supplied and supported by U.S. air and naval units. This post-Vietnam policy of military retrenchment without political disengagement contained implications for the systems needed to support a rapid deployment strategy. Defense Secretary Laird noted that, although U.S. rapid deployment capabilities were substantial, "our goal is to minimize the need for such deployments in the future--by helping our allies to build their own capabilities against localized aggression."[117]

In fact, as has just been suggested, U.S. rapid deployment capabilities in both air and sealift were severely constrained. In this regard, as in other defense policy issues, the Nixon administration was forced to adjust U.S. rapid deployment strategies to the realities of the existing force posture. As Mr. Laird suggested, under the Nixon Doctrine the need for strategic mobility systems was considerably eased. The principal missions of U.S. strategic mobity now became the reinforcement of NATO/Europe in the case of a major contingency and the rapid resupply of allied armies fighting a limited conventional war with indigenous ground forces.

Airlift as a method of strategic mobility had some additional attractions under the Nixon Doctrine. Opposition to the war in Vietnam had been extended to other U.S. military commitments abroad, as the FDL debate had suggested. However, a substantial airlift capability could be presented as a force multiplier, as a substitute for forward deployments and bases. The ability to redeploy troops by airlift meant, in some interpretations of the Nixon Doctrine, that U.S. overseas garrisons could be reduced without a commensurate loss in the perceived ability or willingness of the U.S. to meet its treaty commitments. Thus, airlift became a rationale for retrenchment rather than rapid deployment. Additional, but limited employment concepts of air mobility--CRAF and a "bare base" capability--would be offered as assistance to the apparently neglected role of airlift in support of rapid deployment to a lesser contingency.

In his 1969 testimony to the Military Airlift Subcommittee, Lt. General George S. Boylan, USAF, linked the deterrent contribution of a rapid deployment strategy, retrenchment under the Nixon Doctrine, and a continuing need for increased airlift capability:[118]

> The basic concept underlying strategic deployment consideration since 1965 has been based on a minimal overseas presence coupled with the demonstrated ability to move appropriate ground or air forces rapidly to actual or potential contingency areas. The strategy is based on the premise that the capability for rapid deployment of combat forces is a part of our deterrent posture and can provide an effective response to aggression and that an early response in strength can minimize the intensity of the conflict . . . . It is a credible airlift capability that will reassure our allies of our continuing commitment to their cause as we reduce our overseas forces as announced by the President.

According to General Boylan, the Air Force was equal to the task. He testified to the Price Subcommittee that the airlift forces of the 1970s would be able to deliver troops and equipment to any point in the world as rapidly as required:[119]

> The Air Force is now improving its mobility and capability to fight anywhere in the world by using newly developed lightweight equipment and shelters to better utilize the rapid mobility potential offered by the combination of the C-5, C-141 and CRAF. The combination of quick reacting ground and air forces able to move into any area of the world by jet aircraft is a significant factor to be considered by potential aggressors.

The Price Committee, despite this glowing testimony, was far less sanguine regarding the ability of airlift to meet U.S. commitments abroad. The findings and recommendations of the Price Report on strategic airlift requirements versus capabilities revealed the following:[120]

- the revised strategy of '1-1/2 wars' required an airlift force of at least six squadrons of C-5 aircraft and 14 squadrons of C-141s;
- the JCS study known as 'MOVECAP 70-74' revealed that even with the six squadrons of C-5s, a deficit of C-141s would exist in the total U.S. capability to meet only the NATO mobility requirement. Airlift remaining to support 'other world-wide demands' would be severely reduced by the NATO reinforcement needs;
- CRAF was not a substitute for military airlift capability, but a complementary force and possessed no outsized cargo capability:

Without this outsize airlift capability, the rapid deployment of certain types of Army divisions will be severely restrained and the time required to close the necessary force in times of emergency will be dangerously extended . . . .

In the opinion of this Committee, extending the time required to close the necessary military force is a risky calculation and endangers the success of the NATO contingency operation and the contingency plans for Asia.

In assessing U.S. airlift capability to meet rapid deployment requirements, the Price Committee touched on a number of issues, including the acquisition of the C-5 aircraft, the ability of the Air Force to employ air power under austere conditions and the ability of the CRAF to contribute to a rapid deployment strategy. Each of these areas will be examined briefly in the remainder of this section.[121]

The proponents of the C-5 argued that it would provide the ability to deploy fully-equipped forces to any spot on the globe with only a day's notice and transport time. This capability for swift intervention was seen as a facilitator for the flexible response strategy being formulated in the early 1960s and would give the United States a "remote presence" in any limited contingency, anywhere.[122] In Congressional testimony as early as 1964, the C-5A was being touted as a suitable method of supporting a rapid deployment strategy. Secretary McNamara noted several advantages to such an airlift capability.[123] First, over one-third of the equipment of an infantry division was too large for the not-yet-operational C-141. Moreover, it was suspected that the new Army air assault division being created would pose additional outsize cargo problems due to its large complement of helicopters. Because this division, the 101st, was being designed for a rapid deployment mission, a requirement arose for an aircraft able to move oversize cargo to forward areas.

The Defense Secretary noted that this operational requirement for outsize cargo mobility was not sufficient to justify the cost of developing a new aircraft. Preliminary studies suggested, however, that not only could this large transport carry all of the outsize items in the heavier Army divisions, but also that it could do so economically. In pursuit of this capability, a number of in-house studies were conducted by the service and OSD staffs and by the Weapons System Evaluation Group. These studies concluded, by the following year, that such a design and operational capability were achievable. More important for the rapid deployment concept, the studies convinced the Defense Department decision makers that "unless troops and equipment can be routinely delivered well forward in the theater of operations, many of the advantages of airlift would be lost."[124] Thus, from its inception, the C-5A was closely wedded to the support of rapid deployment to a lesser contingency. The design concept[125] called for the C-5A to carry troops and their equipment, with little advance notice, to primitive airfields in remote areas under austere conditions.

To meet these requirements, the original specifications for the C-5A were exceptionally ambitious. The aircraft was to be large enough to carry outsize equipment and be able to deliver a heavy payload over long distances (5800 nautical miles) without refueling. It was also to have the capability of landing on short (4000 feet) unimproved airfields, able to "kneel" for fast unloading, able to airdrop materiel and paratroops and to conduct these operations in weather conditions of minimum visibility.[126] The attempts on the part of the contractors to meet these desirable characteristics, not all of them successful, were included in the factors that led to the C-5A's reputation as a system plagued by excessive cost overruns and, ultimately, to a buy of the aircraft considerably short of the force projected as necessary to support the declared strategy.[127]

The C-5A program became a cause celebre for critics of defense spending rather than, like the FDL, critics of a rapid deployment strategy. Not that the C-5A was immune to such anti-intervention complaints, but these strategic arguments were not nearly as strident nor as effective against the C-5A as they were against the FDL. The reduction in the total buy of what was originally intended to be six squadrons of C-5As (120 aircraft) to four squadrons (81 aircraft) was predominantly a reaction against the growth in the cost of the program and was not motivated by fears of extending U.S. defense commitments.

Given the manner in which the mission of the C-5A was first characterized, the simultaneous opposition to the FDL program and the growing disenchantment of the public with the Vietnam war, this lack of opposition on a strategic basis is somewhat surprising. When the first C-5A was rolled out of the Lockheed plant in Georgia in March 1968, President Johnson declared: "For the first time, our fighting men will be able to travel with their equipment to any spot on the globe where we might be forced to stand. . . ."[128] Then Secretary of the Air Force Harold Brown spoke in similar terms regarding the C-5A's role in supporting a strategy of rapid deployment:[129]

> For the first time we will be able to airlift a regular infantry division anywhere in the world using approximately 500 C-141 flights, primarily for troops, and 270 C-5A flights to lift the equipment. With our programmed airlift force, we could take the first brigade of such a division from the mid-United States to the Far East in less than five days, and the entire division in about ten days.

In the Senate debate of 1969 that led to the decision to reduce the FY 1970 C-5A buy from 33 to 23, thereby halting the program at a total of 81 aircraft, objections to these global strategies of rapid deployment remained muted. However, there was an ironic twist to Senate support for the C-5A. The C-5A, under the rationale of the Nixon Doctrine, was seen as a system that would allow the withdrawal of U.S. troops from overseas bases and substitute for those bases a method of rapid deployment. Thus, Senator Symington argued for the C-5A based on the concept of "remote presence" as a guideline for U.S. defense policy. He urged a reduction in the number of U.S. military bases abroad, to be replaced by a "massive airlift" capability, embodied in the C-5A, that could move U.S. forces quickly to wherever they were needed. Senator Talmadge agreed with this interpretation of the C-5A's utility, which seemed to guarantee the ability of the U.S. to intervene when required without the political and economic costs of stationing U.S. troops abroad:[130]

> If we can have an air capacity with the mobility to transport thousands of troops to any part of the world within a matter of hours, together with their equipment, it will give us a military

presence which will be just as adequate as having these troops stationed there all the time.

In this respect, Senator Russell's opposition to the FDL and his support for the C-5A appears more coherent. The C-5A was increasingly seen, in an era of defense retrenchment, as a means of redeploying U.S. troops from Europe as well as Southeast Asia. However, this ability and willingness to retreat from overseas garrisons should not mean or convey a reluctance to send them back when U.S. vital interests were threatened. Therefore, Russell argued that those who "really mean it" when they argued for troop reductions abroad were obliged to support appropriations for increased strategic airlift because "you are not going to bring them home until you have some means to send them back."[132]

Russell's "alternative" arguments against the FDL were wielded against the C-5A by Senator Fulbright. In earlier hearings of the Joint Economic Committee, Fulbright warned that the possession of a greater airlift capability might tempt the United States to project military power to areas in which armed force was likely to be ineffective, inappropriate and counter-productive.[132] On the Senate floor during the debate, Senator Fulbright was willing to recognize that the C-5A, by itself, did not represent a commitment to use force in any contingency. However, it represented to him "a significant new facility for the making of new commitments in the hands of the executive."[133]

Despite the application of these FDL-like arguments, implying the C-5A would increase the likelihood for foreign policy commitment and defense policy involvement, the significant opposition to the aircraft remained based on cost and contracting procedures issues. An underlying assumption regarding the need for enhanced airlift capacity was preserved throughout the debate:[134]

> Mr. Symington: I appreciate the dialogue with the Senator from Wisconsin about the C-5A because I know he is not against the C-5A as such; he is merely questioning the number of C-5As that should be built. Is that correct?
> Mr. Proxmire: That is correct.

Even with this prevailing presumption of the need for the C-5A, the opposition to the cost escalation of the program was strong enough to reduce the total fleet procured from the original six squadrons programmed in the first formulation of the combined mix of rapid deployment systems to four squadrons.[135] Thus, the C-5A was added to the growing list of strategic mobility systems the Congress was unwilling to support.

What was the impact of these strategic mobility systems on the capability of U.S. forces to deploy rapidly to a limited contingency?

The implications of this reduction were unclear owing to differing interpretations of the total force required and the tendency to concentrate on force planning in support of the major contingency in Europe or Asia at the expense of a lesser contingency. Secretary Laird told two Congressional committees in 1970 that the smaller authorized number of C-5As would still be "sufficient to meet our basic needs for intertheater airlift movement."[136] However, a divergence of views existed among interpretations of "basic" and "adequate" force levels to meet the requirement for rapid deployment.

The Air Force position, supported by Representative Price and his subcommittee, called for the acquisition of two additional squadrons of C-5As. Based on the assumption of the time required to close the force, the amount of surface lift readily available and the adequacy of strategic warning, calculations by the JCS and the Air Staff in 1970 reinforced the requirement for a 96 UE (unit equipped) force of C-5As. The driving factor behind this force generation was the need to close the outsize cargo in an objective area at the same pace as the bulk cargo and the troops carried by the C-141s and the CRAF. Regardless of destination, the outsize cargo for a mechanized division required 84 C-4As, while an armored division needed 97 C-5As. From the analysis it was concluded that the buy of only 81 aircraft was insufficient to support the strategy of "1-1/2 wars" or a policy of rapid deployment.[137]

In contrast, an OSD/Systems Analysis report issued in June 1969, "Major Program Memorandum for Strategic Mobility Forces," in a projection of support systems required over the next five years, challenged the Air Force position. This analysis concluded that a three-squadron force (58 aircraft) of C-5As, plus other air and sea transport, would prove sufficient to support both a major and a lesser contingency. This cost-efectiveness study concluded that the C-5A was so costly to build and operate, it could be justified only on the amount of time saved as its contribution to the rapid deployment of forces. Therefore, the C-5A should be used only for outsized cargo and only during the first ten days of the conflict. After that, the criterion of urgency would have diminished significantly, and the C-141s and sealift could accomplish the task in a more cost-effective manner. Moreover, the Army's ability to mobilize its manpower was so limited that it could not use more than 58 aircraft per day for the first ten days; hence, any greater acquisition of C-5As was unnecessary and uneconomic: it yielded diminishing returns.[138]

Although the Air Force appeared resigned to the reduced buy of 81 C-5As and refrained from further procurement requests for the system in the FY 1971 budget, General Boylan's testimony before the airlift panel made it clear that such a limited force would eliminate the capability to conduct rapid deployment airlift operations to a lesser contingency simultaneously with a major reinforcement effort to Europe.[139] "Air Force analyses indicate that in a contingency requiring a major reinforcement of NATO Europe, our entire military airlift force would be needed to meet the movement demands of the first 30 days." With 4-1/2 squadrons programmed to meet the demands arising from a NATO contingency, it appeared that the limited contingency, for which the C-5A was ostensibly designed, would be left without adequate airlift.

A number of factors coalesced to encourage the Air Force to seek alternative methods of deploying air power to meet a limited contingency. The lack of fast sealift, apparently made permanent by the Congressional failure to fund the FDL, had shifted the responsibility of supporting the rapid deployment mission to airlift. However, the C-5A fleet was limited in numbers due to the cost escalation of the program and had encountered technical barriers to its limited war specifications. In addition, the C-5A appeared to be justified primarily in its role of NATO reinforcement-- partially owing to the anticipated troop withdrawals--rather than the projection of U.S. military power to the third world. Finally, the demise of STRIKE Command, the priority of the tactical mission, and an organizational interest in assuring an Air Force combat mission in deploying to the lesser contingency encouraged an alternative approach. For all of these reasons, over a period of years, the Air Force began to devote a good deal of effort to a so-called bare base capability.

Under the bare base deployment concept, the Air Force would acquire the capability to convert quickly an unimproved or abandoned airstrip in a remote area to a fighter base capable of conducting combat operations and receiving resupply by air.[140] This concept was probably born in the early 1960s in response to tactical deployments during the Cuban Missile Crisis. However, subsequent planning and exercises confirmed that supporting sustained combat operations in remote areas would require a major logistics effort. By 1965, this limited experience in the bare base concept led to an authorization for TAC to prepare an air-transportable equipment package that contained essential items for air base operations.[141]

The development of a credible bare base concept began in 1966 with the awarding of a contract to the Boeing Corporation for a set of air transportable containers. It was this new capability that led General Boylan to testify on the new rapid deployment capability permitted by "lightweight equipment and shelters." By 1967, the first series of Air Force directives were issued defining reaction standards for U.S. Air Force units under STRIKE Command tasking. However, it remained unclear whether bare base support equipment would be organic to the deploying fighter squadrons or be prepositioned. This question stemmed from the continuing question of a scenario-specific lesser contingency as well as organizational interests. Like any method of rapid deployment, the bare base concept could be improved significantly in terms of cost and time through the prepositioning of supply kits in the region for deployment. But the prestocking of supplies in a particular area surrendered the flexibility that the bare base concept was to provide.[142]

The bare base concept began to take on increased importance in support of the lesser contingency as U.S. presence overseas was reduced, as the Middle East became an area of increased U.S. interest and responsibility and as STRIKE Command's rapid deployment capability continued to wane. A major exercise of the bare base concept called "Coronet Bare" was conducted in October 1969 to determine the viability of conducting combat operations under austere conditions similar to those that might be encountered in a limited contingency in the Middle East. Although the exercise revealed shortcomings in the ability of the tasked units to meet the time criteria levied by the STRIKE Command, the exercise was judged successful in terms of its ability to sustain combat operations at a bare base.[143] As a result of this exercise and a subsequent program evaluation, one tactical fighter squadron was directed to attain operational capability for mobilization and bare base operation by FY 1972. Thus, as the STRIKE Command withered away, the Air Force looked to this new method of rapid deployment of tactical forces as an attempt to combine the swiftness of the old CASF concept with the sustainability of an air-transportable support package.[144]

The original bargain between the U.S. government and the civilian air carriers to establish a Civil Reserve Air Fleet was struck in 1951. That agreement was updated in a CRAF-DoD memorandum in September 1963 that provided for the calling of the airlines into government service, under prescribed conditions and with the approval, depending on the seriousness of the contingency and the amount of support required, of the Secretary of Defense or the President.[145] Throughout the duration of that agreement, an official call-up of civilian aircraft has never been required, as the commercial airlines, particularly during the Vietnam war, have been responsive to DoD without the declaration of a state of airlift emergency.

CRAF is extremely valuable in the rapid movement of people, but lacks certain characteristics essential for the rapid deployment of forces to a lesser contingency. Testimony before the House Airlift Subcommittee indicated that no CRAF aircraft had the outsize cargo capability to assist in the deployment of an Army division. Moreover, despite the subcommittee's recommendation that DoD offer an incentive for the commercial carriers to invest in the type of aircraft that could meet mlitary transport requirements; without a commercial need for an outsize cargo capability, that suggestion appeared unlikely to meet with favorable response.

In addition, the Air Force pointed out the need to recognize the limitation of CRAF's application to the limited contingency environment: civilian aircrews could not be required to fly in a combat situation, and normal CRAF operations required secure, rear-area offload bases. Yet, DoD studies showed that the advantages of rapid deployment offered by airlift were offset if the troops and equipment could not be delivered to the forward areas. Thus, CRAF labored under endemic handicaps, particularly with regard to support for the lesser contingency.[146]

The strictest test of U.S. airlift capacity during this period came, fittingly, under the Nixon Doctrine, with a massive resupply effort to a friendly government. On October 12, 1973, President Nixon ordered the Secretary of Defense to begin an immediate airlift of supplies to Israel, using military aircraft. The airlift began a day after the order and ended one month later.[147] The rapid deployment lessons learned from this experience were drawn by Secretary Schlesinger in his Posture Statements of 1974 and 1975.

The first lesson concerned the Soviet willingness and capability to intervene in the Middle East. The expansion of Soviet airlift capacity and airborne forces resulted in a modest, yet previously unrecognized intervention capability. The reported movement of 13 Russian transport aircraft and the alerting of Soviet airborne forces during the brief superpower confrontation suggested the need to bolster U.S. counter-intervention capability.[148] Therefore, the Defense Secretary called in 1974 for the enhancement of U.S. airlift in order to "accelerate the deployment of our forces." One of these enhancement methods was to "stretch" the C-141 and modify it for refueling in-flight. A second proposal was to replace the C-5A tanker, the C-135, with a new wide-bodied jet modified to serve as either a cargo aircraft or a refueler, thereby allowing long-range operations without relying on foreign bases.[149] A third measure proposed a new tactical transport (AMST) capable of landing on very short and unimproved fields under combat conditions.

The implementation of these proposals was delayed considerably owing to Congressional questions of need and system effectiveness.[150] In addition, despite the Defense Secretary's requests for airlift enhancement, airlift specifically allocated to the lesser contingency continued to be de-emphasized. Schlesinger's theory was if the airlift forces were prepared to support the major contingency, they would also perform well in the "off-design" case--as they had in the resupply of Israel.[151]

In the Defense Secretary's 1975 Posture Statement the focus for strategic mobility through airlift was again on the need for the rapid reinforcement of U.S. troops in Europe, not on the rapid deployment of U.S. forces from the CONUS to a lesser contingency elsewhere:[152]

> Despite all the uncertainties, if we have the capability to move, on the average, 10,000 tons a day in wide-bodied aircraft over a distance of about 4,000 nautical miles, without dependence on intermediate bases, we should be able to meet most of the demands on our strategic airlift.

Although airlift with this capacity could adequately support the time-phased deployment schedule for resupply and reinforcement to NATO, it was unlikely that these criteria would provide for rapid and sustained airlift to a lesser contingency, whether the case existed simultaneously or if it occurred in a distant region, such as the Persian Gulf.[153]

Thus, by the end of the Nixon/Ford administration, the strategy of rapid deployment had not been measurably enhanced by a reliance on the method of strategic airlift. Like the other general purpose forces after Vietnam, the focus on strategic air mobility was on the major contingency in Europe, with little separate effort channeled to capabilities devoted to a limited contingency. Without rapid sealift the requirement for quick deployment of U.S. forces depended on airlift. But the reduced buy of the C-5A, operational constraints on that aircraft and inherent limitations in the bare base and CRAF concepts strained severely a realistic strategy of rapidly deploying U.S. ground forces to a limited contingency. When the Carter administration recognized the need for such a capability and searched for mobility systems in support of the Rapid Deployment Force, the U.S. strategic mobility capacity would be, once again, judged insufficient.

Mobility Systems for Rapid Deployment Forces, 1977-1980

The preceding chapter suggested that the need for rapid deployment forces and, therefore, for the strategic mobility systems in their support were not considered high priority items in the early defense budgets structured by the Carter administration. Airlift and sealift enhancement programs included in these budgets were normally NATO-oriented policies carried over from pervious administrations. Defense programs that did not contribute directly to the strengthening of U.S. forces earmarked to fight in Europe were generally regarded as being of secondary strategic interest and were funded accordingly. This NATO emphasis limited, to a considerable extent, support systems advocated to transport a limited contingency force from early 1977 until the events in Iran, Cuba and Afghanistan in 1979.

Strategic mobility programs considered during this period were marked by attitudes of fiscal austerity and a willingness to fund only those programs clearly in support of a major military effort. A RAND study completed in March 1977, "Strategic Mobility Alternatives for the 1980s" examined only the systems required to reinforce U.S. troops committed to NATO. In the process of projecting the airlift mix of C-5As, C-141s and the CRAF required to meet U.S. needs in the coming decade, the report concluded that meeting the requirements of NATO reinforcement would "provide a capability adequate to serve most other conceivable needs."[154]

A 1978 JCS study of the resources available for strategic mobility, "Strategic Mobility Requirements and Programs--1982" examined the capabilities of the existing systems and suggested that requirements for simultaneous deployments to contingencies in separate theaters could not be met. However, a Government Accounting Office evaluation of this study, while acknowledging that the JCS document represented a comprehensive examination of strategic mobility requirements and programs, questioned the budgetary justification for increased strategic mobility expenditures.[155]

In another respect, this concentration on the need for adequate strategic support systems for European deployment served to highlight the significant shortfalls in strategic lift and to urge continuation of air and sealift enhancement programs. Because mobility systems were, by their nature, considered flexible and fungible, these ongoing initiatives also improved, to some extent, capability to deploy rapidly a limited contingency force.

What strategic mobility systems were proposed in support of a rapid deployment strategy? To what extent were these systems dedicated to a lesser contingency?

One of the catalysts to this process of growing concern with the adequacy of strategic lift was a government-wide, war-mobilization command-post exercise code-named "Nifty Nugget." While not an actual mobilization, Nifty Nugget, conducted in October 1978, was the most comprehensive simulation of national mobilization ever attempted. The scenario for the exercise called for a thirty day period of preparation and mobilization for an all-out conventional war against the Warsaw Pact in Europe. Although NATO-oriented, the lessons learned from this exercise had implications for needed improvements in mobility support systems that extended beyond a U.S. capability to meet only the major contingency.

The chronology, events and results of Nifty Nugget, although both interesting and revealing, are best left to other studies and reports.[156] Most important here is the impetus provided by the exercise to several ongoing efforts to enhance U.S. lift capabilities and a heightened perception of the importance of these systems in conducting any conventional war. Although it is not possible to draw a direct cause and effect relationship between the outcome of Nifty Nugget and the support or proposal for certain mobility programs, it seems clear that a good deal of the emphasis placed on strategic mobility within the Carter administration first stemmed from an analysis of this exercise.

- A new agency, the Joint Deployment Agency (JDA) was established to revise and amend existing JCS mobility plans. The purpose of this agency is to forecast mobility requirements for possible contingencies and to make realistic estimates of scenario air and sealift needs. The JDA, according to its mission statement, is the centralized coordinator for land, sea and airlift, for the planning and movement of forces, equipment and supplies in support of contingency operations.[157]

- An interagency group was formed within the National Security Council to coordinate requests and correct flaws in the existing mobility plans of civilian government agencies while, at the Department of Defense, mobilization and deployment study groups processed budgetary changes and proposals in existing mobility programs.
- Prepositioning measures were given greater emphasis. The POMCUS program in Europe was extended, raising to six the number of division sets to be prepositioned for NATO reinforcement.[158] The need for prepositioning was also seen as necessary in preparation for a lesser contingency although land-based prepositioning appeared inappropriate. POMCUS, unlike other strategic mobility initiatives that could enhance non-NATO deployments, was judged counter-productive to a capability to deploy to a lesser contingency. Secretary Brown noted that DoD was "carefully monitoring the impact of establishing additional POMCUS on the availability of equipment for other purposes."[159] The requirement to preposition additional equipment in Europe was likely to exacerbate existing shortages and reduce the readiness of forces that might be deployed to a non-NATO contingency.
- A series of sealift enhancement measures were encouraged, including funds for increasing the size of the Ready Reserve Fleet from 14 to 34 ships, and the initiation of a search to acquire a fleet of modern cargo ships for rapid deployment by sea.
- Airlift enhancement programs were promoted, including the C-141B stretch/refueling modification, C-5A and C-141 utilization rate increases and CRAF enhancement. However, these measures continued to be characterized by a lack of urgency and a NATO orientation. The CRAF program in 1979 shifted emphasis from the modification of existing aircraft that increased military cargo capability to the incorporation of these outsize-cargo modifications during aircraft production. While cost-effective, this alteration in the approach to CRAF enhancement considerably delayed a rapid deployment capability that, for the lesser contingency particularly, was already seriously constrained.[160] The planned procurement of the Advanced Tanker Cargo Aircraft (ATCA, the KC-10) was one airlift program specifically offered to improve U.S. rapid deployment to a limited contingency, although Secretary Brown noted the tanker "would also improve our capability to reinforce Europe."[161]

Later, in announcing the formation of the Rapid Deployment Force in 1979, Secretary Brown stated that the mobility systems being proposed in support of this limited contingency force owed a good deal to the Nifty Nugget exercise. That simulated mobilization revealed that air and sealift required for a NATO war would rob those systems from forces designated to deploy to a lesser contingency. Thus, Nifty Nugget had demonstrated--on paper--that existing U.S. strategic mobility capability was not capable of supporting the "1-1/2 war" strategic concept.[162]

However true that post facto appraisal, the strategic mobility programs initiated and continued as a result of Nifty Nugget remained

NATO-specific. Motivation to construct the strategic mobility systems needed to support a limited contingency awaited the stimulus of external events.

To what extent were these systems supported and acquired?

The deepening crisis in Iran throughout 1979 shifted the U.S. strategic focus to the Persian Gulf and raised serious questions regarding the American ability to deploy effective armed forces to that region. As contingency planning progressed, the conviction also grew within the Department of Defense that long-distance intervention by tactical air or naval forces would not possess the persuasive power or the stabilizing effect produced by a quick intervention with ground forces. However, traditional methods of U.S. military intervention with light Marine forces or Army airborne units now seemed inappropriate. With the sophisticated weapons systems provided the Middle East and Gulf states by both the United States and the Soviet Union and the increasing likelihood of a limited US/USSR confrontation in the region, the need was to deploy a relatively heavy force in order to meet a technologically-advanced adversary.[163]

The obvious problem emerging from the strategic analysis was that the U.S. lacked the support systems to move a significant force to the threatened area rapidly enough to affect the outcome favorably. As this review process continued through the summer of 1979, it became apparent that, whatever final form the "rapid deployment forces" might assume, increased air and sealift were sure to be required.[164]

In testimony before the Subcommittee on Europe and the Middle East of the House Committee on Foreign Affairs, Under Secretary of Defense Robert Komer made it clear that "across-the-board" improvements in strategic lift were required if the RDF was to prove effective:[165]

> Mr. Hamilton: When you use that phrase, "rapid deployment forces," what are the elements of that? Obviously the manpower, but what about the prepositioned ships, the airlift capability?
> Mr. Komer: The RDF would include all that is necessary to give us the capability to respond to a contingency, particularly in the Indian Ocean. . . . It would include the strategic mobility or the intra-theater mobility which was required.
> Mr. Hamilton: We have that capability to some degree today, don't we?
> Mr. Komer: We are particularly deficent in several areas. First, we do not have the prepositioning ships, although we are leasing some in the interim. Second, we do not have the airlift which is why we are asking for the CX. Third, . . . we are not totally satisfied with command, control and communications. Fourth, we have not gotten all the facilities which we want . . . .

These laments were echoed by the armed services chiefs. Army General E. C. Meyer complained about the lack of airlift for the Army forces that would probably be assigned to the Rapid Deployment Force. Air Force leaders agreed. Only the C-5A was capable of a direct flight from the United States to the Persian Gulf, and that aircraft was plagued by wing structural problems that limited its performance in terms of range and payload.[166]

Like the Army Chief of Staff, the Marine Commandant, General Barrow, warned that his forces were also extremely short of lift. There was only enough amphibious lift available to land a Marine Amphibious Force in a single contingency rather than one each in the Atlantic and the Pacific, as envisioned in Marine doctrine and called for by the U.S. strategic concept. Navy leaders decried the shortages of cargo ships to transport and support troops to third world regions that lacked prepositioned supplies. Deputy Secretary of Defense Graham Claytor stated that the U.S. sealift capability, "essential to crisis action and mobilization, is in serious and growing jeopardy." Claytor warned that the continuing erosion of the U.S. merchant fleet, the ship building industry and its labor force would weaken the national defense.[167]

In testimony before the House Committee on the Merchant Marine and Fisheries, the Director of Logistics for the Joint Staff added his voice to the mounting complaints regarding the inadequacy of U.S. strategic mobility capability.[168] Vice Admiral Kent Carroll stated that the Navy could no longer support an earlier Army contingency plan to deploy four divisions to the Middle East and questioned whether the Navy could provide for the current plan to send two and one-third divisions to the Persian Gulf in a timely manner. The committee, called to explore the shortfalls in sealift exposed by Nifty Nugget, noted that the U.S. was ill-prepared to conduct sealift operations in a limited contingency and could meet European reinforcement schedules only with the aid of a 400-ship supplement provided by the NATO allies. Of the 150 ships in the National Defense Reserve Fleet (NDRF), only 13 could be made ready within 5 to 10 days, while only 11 ships from the Sealift Readiness Program (SRP) were suitable for military cargo.[169]

With U.S. strategic mobility inadequacies well documented, the deteriorating situation in Iran, the Soviet presence in Cuba and the threatened Soviet invasion of Afghanistan led President Carter in October 1979 to call for the enhancement of "the capability of our rapid deployment forces to protect our own interests and to act in response to requests for our allies and our friends."[170] Therefore, for the first time in the Carter administration, the defense budget for FY 1981 gave decided emphasis to strengthening the U.S. "ability to move forces rapidly to potential trouble spots." Although this budget was formulated prior to the Soviet action in Afghanistan, Secretary Brown noted the "clear picture of increasing Soviet pressure beyond their borders" that had emerged prior to December 1979.[171]

Included in the FY 1981 budget were a number of programs designed to improve U.S. rapid deployment capability to a contingency in the Persian Gulf. However, these programs appeared to concentrate solely on the Gulf as the region of the most likely limited contingency while ignoring the need for rapid deployment capabilities to other lesser contingencies. Nevertheless, the specific programs proposed ranged through the spectrum of rapid deployment strategies and methods, as Secretary Brown explained in his remarks to the Council on Foreign Relations in March 1980.[172]

In the area of prepositioning, the Defense Department was launching a program to provide a number of maritime prepositioning ships, similar in concept to the old FFDs, that would provide greater deployment felxibility and avoid the problems of large permanent U.S. bases overseas.

While these ships were being procured, constructed or modified, a near-term prepositioning option necessitated a fleet of commercial-type vessels to provide an interim storage and offload capability in the area. The plan called for the loaded ships to be prepositioned within a few days' transit time to the Persian Gulf.

Secretary Brown also pointed to major improvements being programmed in air and sealift capabilities. Procurement of the KC-10 tanker, initiated several years before, would be accelerated. The United States was also beginning a long distance deployment of outsize cargo. To bolster sealift capability, the U.S. was in the process of acquiring high-speed civilian ships to provide rapid deployment by sea, although this appeared as a supplement to airlift.

A third element of this strategy was access to facilities in the Persian Gulf/Indian Ocean regions, including a continued build-up of the U.S. facilities on Diego Garcia. Such access would improve the U.S. ability to sustain naval and air deployments and enable the U.S. to come to the assistance of states in the area without taking them to host or support permanent U.S. outposts.

These force programs had been derived from an analytical process similar to the JCS special study group work that had resulted in the rapid deployment mix of forces designed in the mid-1960s. Lt. General Richard Lawson, Deputy Director of Plans for the JCS in 1980, alluded to the current analysis and force planning process in his testimony to the House Committee on Foreign Affairs:[173]

> What we did, Mr. Chairman, was to tabulate up the kinds of forces that we have seen and used in the past in contingency efforts, and that we could opt to use in the future.
>
> Then we shredded out a whole series of scenarios, and we put together the package of the force that would be needed to accommodate that particular scenario that ranged all the way from very small organizations to a large rapid deployment force.
>
> Then having drawn that, we stood back and tried to see what things we needed . . . and that is when we came up with the ideas of prepositioning and on a fast sealift and this CX and really looked at a combination of those, trying to find the optimum mix of the three.
> . . .

It appeared that this new analytical look at rapid deployment support requirements in 1980 had resulted in a mix of the same rapid deployment strategies and forces that had emerged from similar studies undertaken in the 1960s. Although not generally collected together in a coherent fashion, the 1980 balanced mix of airlift, sealift and equipment prepositioning appeared to consist of:[174]

- 70 C-5As and 234 C-141 A/B (Active)
- 60-200 CX aircraft (IOC FY 1986)
- CRAF (231 passenger and 111 cargo)
- 7 near term prepositioning ships (NTPS)
- 15 T-AKR prepositioning ships (MPS)
- 8 SL-7 fast sealift ships
- 170 ships from the SRP
- 43 ships from the RRF by 1986

What was the impact of these strategic mobility systems on the capability to deploy forces to a limited contingency?

In contrast to the strategic mobility programs of the McNamara years in which the support systems had been generated by, but not dedicated to specific contingencies--the prepositioning, sealift, and airlift programs now being offered by the Carter administration seemed to focus exclusively on the Persian Gulf.

Prepositioning. In August 1979, the Secretary of Defense proposed a seaborne prepositioning scheme to increase the responsiveness of ground forces to react quickly to a limited contingency. Called the Maritime Prepositioning Ships (MPS), these floating warehouses appeared to be direct descendants of the FFDs placed in the Pacific two decades earlier. The concept called for the construction and equipping of 15 prepositioned ships, five of which would be stationed in the Persian Gulf/Indian Ocean region, with equipment and supplies sufficient to support a Marine Amphibious Brigade for 30 days. As with the FFD, the MPS plan called for the ground forces to be airlifted to the area and then married up with their equipment. With the originally requested funding placed at $3 billion, the first three ships were scheduled to be operational by 1983.[175]

The rationale for prepositioning at sea rather than on shore proved just as persuasive in the Indian Ocean as it had in the Pacific. Under Secretary of Defense Robert Komer explained the system's attractiveness during FY 1981 appropriations hearings: "The most cost-effective way to provide heavy equipment rapidly in the Indian Ocean is to preposition it on ships."[176] The Under Secretary noted that, in contrast with the situation in Europe, the axes of attack of a limited war in the Persian Gulf could not be predicted accurately. If the U.S. were to store equipment in Somalia, but the contingency occured in Saudi Arabia, the additional transport of supplies over 2000 miles would be required. Under these circumstances and given the enormous distances within the region, "it would be much more flexible for us to have the equipment on ships and, in an emergency, start the ships moving toward the area where we thought the contingency would arise."[177]

In his testimony to the House Armed Services Committee on appropriations for the MPS, General Kelley, the RDF commander, outlined the properties required of these ships in order for the effective support of a limited contingency force that could vary widely in size and capability.[178]

- First, the ships should be capable of 'spread-loading.' This meant that the types of equipment and supplies could be spread over a number of ships to allow redundancy and insurance against the loss of a single ship and the total loss of a necessary item.
- Secondly, the ships must be capable of supporting selective unloading. This allowed certain items to be reached and unloaded quickly without the unloading of the entire ship.
- Finally, the ships had to be capable of 'over the beach' capability, so that the timing of the arrival of the equipment would not be dependent on 'somebody else's port or port faciities.'

General Kelley also supported prepositioning as an important element of the rapid deployment strategy and explained the rationale for a fleet of ships large enough to store a month's worth of equipment and consumables:[179]

> If you focus on strategic sealift, one of the problems when you start flatfooted is time. The time to open up the sea line of communications from the east coast to ... the Middle East--when we talk 20-knot ships is roughly 30 days by the time you load and deploy the ships into the area.
> So what we are saying is that prepositioned equipment should save precious airlift and could be there much faster than by normal sealift.

As a final advantage of the prepositioning concept, General Kelley noted that the MPS fleet was a relatively innocuous, over-the-horizon force that would not be construed as a politically provocative move or a military threat. On the other hand, transporting a Marine Amphibious Brigade would require approximately 25 amphibious ships, plus additional support and escort ships. This "large signal" had the potential for lowering the threshold of confrontation.[180]

One of the main criticisms levied against this program is that the ships were extremely vulnerable and could operate only in a benign environment. However the biggest immediate drawback of the prepositioning plan was that the ships, even with a smooth progression of the procurement process, could not be operational before 1983. Therefore, consideration was given in January 1980 to the immediate purchase of some commercial roll-on/roll-off ships to implement a near-term fix and provide an immediate prepositioning capability in the Persian Gulf.[181] In March, Deputy Secretary Claytor announced that seven cargo and tanker ships would be acquired and used to prepare for the possible rapid deployment of U.S. air and ground forces during the period before the initial operating capability of the MPS. Mr. Claytor declared that recent events, "particularly those in Southwest Asia," had led to the conclusion that a deployable sealift capability was needed more quickly than would be available under the MPS acquisition plan.[182]

The seven-ship near term program (the NTPS) was necessarily smaller in scale than the MPS plan. Owing to the lack of commercial hulls that could be acquired quickly and refitted to military cargo and dehumidified, the force that deployed to Diego Garcia in July 1980 could support a Marine force of 10,000 troops as opposed to 15,000 and for 15 days rather than 30.[183] Because the NTPS program had not been funded in the FY 1981 budget, operations and maintenance funds from the 1980 budget were allocated to initiate the project.[184] In retrospect, that solution seemed the only alternative, for the Marine Corps opposed any transfer of funds from the MPS project to the near-term scheme, and as the members of the Armed Services Committee were willing to admit, the history of adequate funding for logistic support systems, as has been emphasized throughout this chapter, was neither long nor distinguished.[185]

Mr. Fazio: There is, I think, a great concern that we have . . . always ignored these programs in peacetime. And I think they're not at the point where most of us think they ought to be. And, of course, our focus has been recent too. Just as priorities are set at DoD that way--so are they in the Congress.

Admiral Cowhill: There is no question about it. Those logistic forces . . . these kinds of ships don't have much sex appeal when compared to an Aegis cruiser or an SSN and, therefore, are rarely funded. The Navy doesn't push them and this committee and others do not push them because in peace time there is no requirement.

This type of reasoning that shunted aside strategic mobility systems in order to make room in the budget for systems that supported more clearly the services' essential missions was also present in the RDF debate. Marine Commandant Barrow stressed repeatedly during the appropriations hearings that the MPS was simply a limited means of enhancing strategic mobility and not a substitute for the U.S. ability to project power into a hostile environment. The MPS, despite its support of the Marine mission and its assistance to the Corps in granting them a major role in the Rapid Deployment Joint Task Force, was still, for budgetary purposes, outside the mainstream of the Marine Corps mission. General Barrow pointed out the necessity of securing a suitable port before any prepositioning fleet could begin to unload its cargo. This, suggested the General, would be most likely accomplished by amphibious assault:[186]

We must not be lulled into the perception that commercially designed and crewed ships are substitutes for war ships. The level of the amphibious fleet is already below that considered necessary by the Joint Chiefs of Staff to carry out the national strategy with reasonable assurance of success.

General Barrow stated his impression of the NTPS as an "ad hoc arrangement to meet an immediate requirement" as opposed to awaiting the development of the new ships to provide long term prepositioning. He explicitly stated that he did not favor taking funds from the MPS to support this interim capability. More important, he stressed the need to support combat systems over any logistics system.[187]

Sealift. The acquisition of SL-7 container ships was another interim measure to provide rapid deployment capability to the Persian Gulf and in some respects was reminiscent of the FDL program of the 1960s. These ships were built in the late 1970s for commercial trade, had a top speed of over thirty knots and were seen as a means to meet the "high-speed surge requirement" by sea. In his testimony to the Committee on Armed Services, Vice Admiral Carroll stressed that the ships were available, suitable and, because of the high fuel costs involved in operating such a ship, unlikely to be built again in the future. The SL-7s also possessed good containership capability, but their optimal configuration would be found with a "ro-ro" conversion. The Admiral made it clear that the SL-7 approach "in no way replaces or substitutes for the Marine Prepositioning Program," but rather provided a "complementary early surge capability from great distances." In a passage most reminiscent of the FDL debate, the Navy emphasized that the fleet of SL-7s also would not compete with commercial shipping in any way:[188]

We would not at any time use such ships for the peacetime movement of Department of Defense cargo or in any other way that would compete with the commercial sector. Except for short-term annual operational testing, the ships would only be operated on an emergency basis or as a result of a deliberate decision to deploy forces.

The SL-7s displayed other similarities with the FDL. The eight ships would cost an estimated $341.5 million, would be capable of moving an Army mechanized division to the Persian Gulf in 20-26 days and would be stationed at "load-out" ports in the CONUS ready "at a moment's notice to begin loading up the equipment of RDF-earmarked units."[189] The fact that the ships were already built and the opportunity cost relatively small led to little opposition to this program: no FDL-like objections were raised against the SL-7s, either on commercial or strategic grounds. In an age of expanding U.S. vital interests and because the SL-7s apparently were to be dedicated to the Persian Gulf contingency alone, "Russell's Alternative" seemed not to apply.

Airlift. A number of airlift enhancement programs were already under way by the time the U.S. defense focus shifted to the Rapid Deployment Force and the Persian Gulf. However, NATO reinforcement had been the dominant theme of these improvements rather than the development of a specific airlift plan to support any lesser contingency deployment. Moreover, as a Congressional Budget Paper suggested, the two contingencies offered different goals for modification of the airlift force. If NATO reinforcement was the primary purpose, then the objective of the airlift improvement program should be to increase airlift capacity. If, however, an airlift enhancement program were to be oriented towards improving a rapid deployment capability to a lesser contingency, "wartime flexibility should be the primary goal."[190]

Prior to an emphasis on the need for airlift to support the RDF, those enhancement programs were oriented toward NATO. These included the C-141B stretch modification, CRAF enhancement, the Advanced Medium Short Takeoff and Landing Transport (AMST) and the C-5A wing modification. None of these programs addressed what was judged to be the most critical airlift shortfall with regard to the unimproved airfields in the third world.[191] Without effective and efficient intratheater airlift, programs to improve intertheater airlift seemed inappropriate. Therefore, the Secretary of Defense directed the Air Force to cancel the AMST and initiate a new long-range transport program known as the CX.[192]

The dominant factors in the design of the CX became the outsize cargo capability and the need to land under austere or combat conditions on short or interdicted runways. This capability, it was testified, would improve the flexibility of the deployed force, decrease ground line of communications requirements and close the combat force in the allocated time while complicating enemy interdiction efforts. There appeared to be no technical barriers to the CX such as those which plagued the C-5A. Air Force General Kelly Burke testified:[193]

We believe that it is now possible to build an airplane . . . that can carry outsize cargo to intercontingental ranges and still land on 3000 or 4000 foot strips and get 90% as much strategic airlift as if you built the same strategic aircraft that could only land at big airports.

The Air Force recommended that the CX should be significantly smaller than the C-5A, thereby maximizing taxi and parking capabilities at smaller airports. It should have a payload of approximately 135,000 pounds, sufficient to carry one M-1 tank or two M-2 armored fighting vehicles. The CX, in addition to its austere field capability, would also be air-refuelable.

Although the CX was no more closely linked to the C-5A than the SL-7 was to the FDL, the CX encountered stiff Congressional opposition, primarily on the grounds of cost and program uncertainty. Although the ultimate buy of the CX was expected to amount to between $6.6 and $12 billion for a fleet of 130-200 aircraft, initial funding for the project was disapproved. The House Armed Services Committee reduced the original proposal for $80 million to $50 million, but stipulated that the first $10 million be spent on mission and design studies, with a Congressional review required before the allocation of the remaining funding.[194]

One of the strongest arguments against the purchase of a new aircraft was the cost of the system compared to a major improvement in rapid deployment capability. A Congressional Budget Office study concluded that "a major new procurement of new organic planes would be required to reduce delivery time substantially."[195] As many as 400 of the then-planned AMSTs or 100 new C-5As would be required to reduce closure times for an Army division by only one week. In contrast to similar advantages offered by more extensive prepositioning or rapid sealift, the cost for airlift appeared excessive. With a significant opportunity cost involved, both for other airlift enhancement programs or for the substitution of fast sealift, the prospects for the CX seemed bleak.

In September 1980, the House Appropriations Committee settled on a reduced budget for the CX proposal, but continued to criticize Air Force planning for the aircraft:[196]

No one is able to say what a CX will look like, what its capability will be or what it will cost. No one is able to say how the CX fits with the other airlift, sealift or prepositioned assets already available or planned. Even the Secretary of the Air Force has failed to make a convincing case for the CX.

Facilities and Access. The original conception of the Rapid Deployment Force contained in PD-18 called for the deployment of "light, mobile and flexible U.S. forces" that could deploy and conduct operations in the Middle East or the Persian Gulf without relying on permanent bases in the area. The accent on U.S. land-based presence in support of the RDF has, therefore, been placed on "access to facilities" rather than on the permanent stationing of U.S. troops within the region.

In his testimony before the House Committee of Foreign Affairs, Under Secretary of Defense Robert Komer pointed out the reasons for a reliance on facilities rather than bases.[197]

- First, bases were seen as a political liability, 'given the national systems and the sensitivities of the nations in the area.'
- Second, as a result of rapid deployment studies, it became clear that the U.S. could surge forces into the area through other strategies and methods. Bases were not required for power projection or for the prepositioning of supplies.
- Third, overseas bases were expensive. It would be a more cost-effective approach if the Department of Defense helped the local countries to build up the facilities necessary to support a surge capability without constructing U.S. bases.

Thus, the United States faced political as well as logistical problems in improving its deployment capabilities to the Persian Gulf. As explained in testimony to Congress, no country is likely to grant a priori approval for access and overfight rights to conduct limited contingency missions. Rather, the U.S. will be forced to ask for these rights in each new situation. The reasons and willingness of host nations to grant this permission will similarly vary with the climate of Arab public opinion and the circumstances of the action. Thus, political support will be highly scenario-dependent.[198]

The only permanent base for U.S. operation in the region is on the American-operated, British-owned island of Diego Garcia, 2250 nautical miles from the Straits of Hormuz. In other initiatives, the Department of Defense expected to gain access to facilities on the island of Masira off the coast of Oman, at the formerly Soviet-occupied port of Berbera in Somalia and in Mombassa, Kenya. It was also apparent, at the close of 1980, that the U.S.-Egyptian connection would likely prove influential in the ability of the United States to project power in the region. U.S. AWACS aircraft began operating from Egypt in June 1980, and a U.S. tactical fighter squadron deployed for operations with the Egyptian Air Force in the fall of 1980. Perhaps of greater significance, the Rapid Deployment Joint Task Force, with 1400 troops of the 101st division, conducted exercise "Bright Star" in the Egyptian desert in November 1980.[199]

At the end of 1980, although some improvement in mobility support for the RDJTF was underway, problems still remained. Secretary Brown noted that existing U.S. strategic mobility forces could not meet all of the deployment objectives established. Citing a recent DoD study identifying significant shortfalls in the event of a NATO reinforcement effort and a simultaneous response to a crisis in the Persian Gulf, the Defense Secretary concluded: "Our early capabilities in either a NATO conflict or a smaller contingency elsewhere are too austere for us to be complacent."[200]

However, Secretary Brown, in acknowledging this shortfall, failed to point out another side of this dilemma. If the capability of the United States to deploy forces simultaneously to both NATO and Southwest Asia was inadequate, then a series of lesser contingencies could strain logistic lines to the breaking point. Thus, the growing emphasis on the need for a rapid deployment capability to the Persian Gulf, while clarifying U.S. strategic mobility shortcomings, also tended to obscure the realization that "the smaller contingency elsewhere" might occur as a series of conflicts, widely dispersed and distributed through a range of half war scenarios.

TABLE 4.1
Mobility Systems For Rapid Deployment

JANUARY 1968		JANUARY 1981
"2-1/2 Wars"	STRATEGIC CONCEPT	"1-1/2 Wars"
STRIKE COMMAND	ORGANIZATION	RDJTF
Reinforce allies in Europe	PURPOSE	To be able to support simultaneously deployments to Europe and to other potential trouble spots
Rapidly deploy general purpose forces to counter a major conventional attack in Asia		
Meet a minor contingency elsewhere		Meet inter-theater and intra-theater requirements of a dual contingency

FORCE MIX

Proposed	Acquired/Remaining	Proposed
Airlift:		
6 C-5A Squadrons (120 a/c)	81/70	--
14 C-141 Squadrons (224 a/c)	224/234	--
CRAF (465 B707/DC8)	(231 Passenger, 111 Cargo) wide-body	50-200 CX
Prepositioning:		
Europe (POMCUS)	2 Sets/4 Sets	6 sets by mid-1983
Asia	3 FFD/0	--
Middle East	0/0	7 NTPS in Persian Gulf 15 T-AKR MPS by 1987
Sealift:		
30 FDL	0/0	8 SL-7
460 General Cargo ships	460/385	--

This chapter has suggested the reasons why adequate strategic mobility systems were not available to support rapid deployment strategies emerging in the 1980s. This gap between strategy and force posture was not created because a new focus on the strategic importance of the Persian Gulf and the resulting establishment of the RDJTF represented a new rapid deployment concept. On the contrary, mobility systems in support of such a strategy, the C-5A and the FDL, had been advocated and programmed in the early 1960s. Yet, these systems were never brought to fruition. The C-5A program became oriented primarily towards the support and reinforcement of a NATO contingency, while the programmed buy was substantially reduced. The FDL fell victim to political rather than economic or management failures. However, mobility support for the RDJTF has borrowed in concept and design from these earlier systems. The CX, the MPS, and the SL-7 are spin-offs from systems of an earlier era, although the global role of these systems has been deemphasized considerably from the rapid deployment rhetoric of the 1960s. Although a geographic focus may enhance both the budgetary support and deployment capability of certain systems and services, such a concentration does little to justify the variety of systems needed to support deployments to a range of lesser contingencies.

The current problem is to provide a strategic mobility force that is capable of meeting these concurrent requirements. As in the past, the selection of a strategic mobility force mix in support of a limited contingency will depend on a number of factors, not the least of which is cost. Questions regarding the proper mix of airlift, sealift, and prepositioning continue to remain scenario-dependent. But, systems acquisitions decisions in support of a limited contingency force focused primarily on the Persian Gulf region become simplified in an important aspect. The RDJTF, as an independent unified command, assigned a specific area of responsibility and allowed to plan for a certain scenario enjoys many force planning advantages over previous versions of rapid deployment forces. Force planning for a specific contingency facilitates the elimination of a strategic mobility-force mismatch that has plagued efforts to construct a coherent limited contingency force during the last twenty years. The task in the 1980s is to extend strategic mobility planning to gain the capability to deploy forces rapidly to a range of lesser contingencies which remain imbedded in the strategic concept of the "half war."

NOTES

1. Martin van Crevald, Supplying War (Cambridge, England: Cambridge University Press, 1977).
2. Michael Howard, "The Forgotten Dimensions of Strategy," op. cit., p. 978.
3. Neville Brown has noted that "theater reserves" could be considered a third alternative to strategic mobility. Presumably, he is referring to those forces stationed in the CONUS, but specifically dedicated to the major contingency in Europe. A theater reserve could be dedicated to a lesser contingency as well. See Neville Brown, Strategic Mobility (New York: Praeger, 1963), p. 27.

4.   There are other uses of the term "forward strategy."   See Brown, op. cit., p. 9.   The most common contemporary usage of the term, or that of "forward defense," refers to the stationing of troops in the assumed contingency area.   That strategy has its own advantages and disadvantages that cannot be covered here.   For a background to those issues, see John Newhouse, U.S. Troops in Europe (Washington, D.C.: Brookings, 1972), Alvin Cottrell and Thomas Moorer, "U.S. Overseas Bases," The Washington Papers, Vol. 47 (Beverly Hills and London: Sage, 1975) and U.S. Congress, Congressional Budget Office, "Force Planning and Budgetary Implications of the U.S. Withdrawal from Korea" (Washington, D.C.: USGPO, May 1978).

5.   Secretary of State Acheson made his press-club luncheon speech in January 1950, indicating that South Korea would have to depend on the United Nations for its defense.   The North Korean attack occurred in June 1950.   See Paul Hammond, The Cold War Years, p. 45, and Dean Acheson, Present at the Creation (New York: Norton, 1969), pp. 355-357.

6.   Neville Brown has related that Marshall Foch, prior to 1914, stated that he needed only one British soldier in France, provided it could be guaranteed that the man would be killed in action on the first day of the war.   Few today would advocate such a singular deterrent to aggression, but the tripwire theories spring from this concept and offer equally low levels of confidence.

7.   See Newhouse, op. cit.   The question becomes how many divisions should the U.S. place in Europe to hedge against the likelihood of a Warsaw Pact attack under certain scenarios.   A dynamic analysis using firepower ratios will yield an average calculation that can serve to justify that permanent force deployment or a reinforcement after M-day.   Thus, the U.S. force size in NATO is not an arbitrary choice, nor is it based on tripwire reasoning.   Nor, with the annual cost of a deployed division approaching $3 billion, is it a trivial choice.

8.   An additional benefit is the acclimatization of the deployed force to the region and a familiarity with the terrain and the territory. These are also advantages that can accrue to a scenario-specific rapid deployment force. See Brown, op. cit., pp. 10-11.

9.   At the June 1973 meeting of the NATO Defense Planning Committee, Secretary of Defense Schlesinger asked NATO to undertake a multilateral program designed chiefly to relieve the United States of its balance of payments deficits and to assist the U.S. in playing the added budgetary costs of stationing troops in Europe. See the New York Times, June 8, 1973, p. 7, and July 28, 1973, p. 1.

10.   Although the Senate reversed itself later in the same day, it voted in September 1973 to reduce all U.S. forces abroad by 40%.   The Jackson-Nunn Amendment attempted a more persuasive approach by requiring the United States to reduce its NATO expenditures by the same percentage that the European allies failed to offset U.S. balance of payments deficits incurred by U.S. troops in Europe. See C. Gordon Bare, "Burden Sharing in NATO: The Economics of Alliance," Orbis, Vol. 20, No. 2 (Summer 1976), pp. 417-437.   The United States had not originally intended to keep troops in Europe following the post-war restoration of stability, and the attendant costs of maintaining the garrison force are a continuing problem within the Alliance.   In 1958, Eisenhower brought pressure on the Federal Republic of Germany to assume more of these costs and, in 1960, ordered U.S. dependents home from Europe to lessen the balance of payments deficit.   Kennedy, concerned that this act was

seen as an American abandonment of Europe, cancelled this directive in
1960. See Hammond, op. cit., p. 145.

11.   Enthoven and Smith, op. cit., p. 234.
12.   Ibid.
13.   Ibid., p. 235.
14.   Robert A. Levine, "The Choice of Strategy to Meet
Conventional Aggression: How Large a Conventional Capability?" (Santa
Monica: RAND, 1965), RM 4123-ISA.
15.   See Richard B. Rainey, Jr., "Mobility--Airlift, Sealift, and
Prepositioning" (Santa Monica: RAND, 1966), P33303.
16.   This argument had differing interpretations, such as the later
suggestion to trade territory for time in Lynn Davis' formulation of PRM
10. The alternative strategies are listed by Enthoven and Smith on p. 235.
17.   Quoted in Robert L. Robinson, "Military Strategy and Congress:
The Case of the FDL" (Newport RI: Naval War College, 1970),
unpublished thesis.
18.   Enthoven and Smith, p. 236.
19.   Ibid., p. 237.
20.   Rainey, op. cit., p. 24.
21.   As defined by Neville Brown, op. cit., p. 21.
22.   By 1965, Secretary McNamara had directed the closing of 59
foreign bases at a reported annual saving of $140 million a year.
"U.S. Bases Abroad Stir a New Debate," New York Times, April 9, 1969, p.
1. Although the U.S. build-up in Vietnam reversed this downward trend in
the number of U.S. bases overseas, the quantity began to decline again
with the U.S. withdrawal from Southeast Asia. By 1976, there were only
29 Air Force bases overseas, down from 107 in 1958. See John R. Pickett,
"Airlift and Military Intervention" in Ellen P. Stern, ed., The Limits of
Military Intervention, op. cit.
23.   The 1958 analysis of U.S. overseas bases was referred to as the
Nash Report.
24.   "U.S. Bases Abroad Stir a New Debate."
25.   Ibid.
26.   Thus, the study found that to surrender all U.S. bases in Japan
and Okinawa and to replace them with new bases on U.S. territory in the
Pacific would cost approximately $10 billion over ten years. Seven billion
of this amount would be required to substitute other methods of rapid
deployment in lieu of the abandoned bases. See "U.S. Bases Abroad Stir A
New Debate."
27.   Enthoven and Smith, p. 241.
28.   Maxwell D. Taylor, "The Legitimate Claims of National
Security," op. cit.
29.   Ibid., p. 590.
30.   Neville Brown, op. cit., p. 181.
31.   See Harold Brown, DoD Annual Report FY 1979, p. 227.
32.   See Harold Brown, DoD Annual Report FY 1980, p. 201.
33.   As pointed out by Secretary of Defense Harold Brown, they are
possibly no more vulnerable than other ports or airfields in the theater.
34.   Testimony of Robert S. McNamara before a subcommittee of
the House Committee on the Merchant Marine and Fisheries, April 18,
1962, quoted in Neville Brown, op. cit., p. 18. However, the equipment
placed on these ships was quickly absorbed by forces deployed to the
Pacific during the Vietnam build-up, and the concept was not revived
again--with the exception of the ill-fated FDL--until the need for a

similar system was perceived in the support of U.S. rapid deployment capability to the Persian Gulf in 1980.

35. Statement to the House Armed Service Committee on January 29, 1964. Quoted in James McBride and John Eales, Military Posture, (Washington, D.C.: Center for Strategic Studies, 1964), p. 105.

36. This shortfall stemmed partially from disagreement between the Army and the Air Force regarding airlift priority. As suggested earlier in this study, the service requirements for strategic airlift were judged from differing organizational interests and perspectives.

37. Without the capability for moving long distances rapidly, the Army would be deprived of its core mission of ground combat. This would mean that the Air Force, Navy and Marines would dominate the lesser contingency mission. This debate is related from the Army's perspective in The Uncertain Trumpet, pp. 102-105. See also the 1968 testimony of Army Brigadier General W. R. Desabry on his view of the inadequacy of both air and sealift support in past operations, U.S. Congress, House Subcommittee on Defense Appropriations for FY 1969 (Washington, D.C.: USGPO, 1968), Part 6, pp. 364-367. An Air Force acknowledgement of the doctrinal split and the resulting airlift shortfall is documented in Neil Sorensen, "The Development of the Air Mobility Strategy" (Maxwell AFB, Alabama: Air War College, 1980), unpublished research report, pp. 45-59.

38. As noted in Secretary McNamara's 1963 testimony on airlift to a House Armed Services subcommittee. See "SecDef Reports on National Military Airlift Plans," Army Navy Air Force Journal and Register, August 10, 1963.

39. Secretary McNamara later testified to the value of prepositioning by comparing the cost of the equipment with the value of the transportation systems required to deliver it. See "SecDef Reports."

40. One proposed solution to this problem was to airdrop troops directly on the battlefield from the C-141 aircraft, thereby bypassing the delays at an overseas assembly point. However, this ran into organization difficulties owing to a blurring of the distinction between the airlift and troop carrier mission.

41. See the discussion of the utility of Civil Air Fleets in Neville Brown, op. cit., pp. 167-172. Also see U.S. Congress, House Committee on Armed Services, Hearings on the Posture of U.S. Airlift, 95th Congress, 1st session (Washington, D.C.: USGPO, 1977). The conflict between the proposed FDL and civilian shipping interests will be discussed in the following section.

42. Testimony of Secretary McNamara, January 29, 1964. Quoted in McBride and Eales, op. cit., p. 108.

43. See Hanson W. Baldwin, "The Navy at Ebb Tide," The Reporter, January 30, 1964.

44. Neville Brown, op. cit., pp. 105-115. Secretary of Defense Schlesinger questioned the need for a Marine amphibious assault force in his February 1975 Posture Statement, pp. III-26. Binkin and Record published their study in 1976.

45. See Secretary McNamara's January 1964 Posture Statement. The testimony is quoted in McBride and Eales, op. cit.

46. Tom Klein, "The Capacity to Intervene" in Leonard Rodberg and Derek Shearer, eds., The Pentagon Watchers (New York: Doubleday, 1970), p. 193.

47. In addition to an expansion in airlift capability, Kennedy called for an increase in Army and Marine Corps manpower levels. See John F.

Kennedy, "Annual Message to Congress on the State of the Union, January 30, 1961," Public Papers (Washington, D.C.: GPO, 1962), Vol. I, pp. 19-28. See also his Special Message to Congress on the defense budget on May 25, 1961, op. cit., p. 401.

48.　Ibid.

49.　Testimony of Robert S. McNamara to the House Arms Service Subcommittee on Airlift. The full text of the testimony is published in "SecDef Reports on National Military Airlift Plans," Army Navy Air Force Journal and Register, August 10, 1963.

50.　Testimony of Robert S. McNamara, U.S. Congress, Senate Committee on Armed Services, Hearings on Military Procurement Authorizations for FY 1966, 89th Congress, 1st session (Washington, D.C.: GPO, 1965), p. 77.

51.　"SecDef Reports on National Military Airlift Plans."

52.　"U.S. Putting Supply Ships in Far East as Deterrent," New York Times, May 1, 1962. See also "U.S. 'Floating Armories' Stationed in Far East," Washington News, July 30, 1963. One of the factors that led to this concept of prepositioning at sea was the significant maintenance cost associated with storing equipment in hot and humid climates.　On temperature-controlled, dehumidified ships, that cost was considerably lowered.

53.　Testimony of Robert S. McNamara, U.S. Congress, House Committee of Armed Services, Department of Defense Appropriations for FY 1963, 87th Congress, 2nd session (Washington, D.C.: GPO, 1962), Part 2, p. 108. The opportunity to procure additional roll-on/roll-off ships had not been pursued by DoD. Congress in 1954 authorized the procurement of 6 such vessels, but only one Comet-type ship was in service and available during the 1958 Lebanon crisis.

54.　Statement of Secretary of Defense Robert S. McNamara before the House Armed Services Committee, January 27, 1964, p. 95.

55.　U.S. Library of Congress, Legislative Reference Service, "United States Defense Policy in 1963" (Washington, D.C.: GPO, 1964), p. 50.

56.　"SecDef Reports on National Military Airlift Plans."

57.　"McNamara Fights Liner Subsides," New York Times, April 19, 1962.

58.　See Enthoven and Smith, How Much is Enough, pp. 235-236.

59.　Personal Papers of Major General James C. Sherrill, 1969. (Washington, D.C.: Office of Air Force History).

60.　Ibid. The Conroy Report was officially titled "Report of the DoD Study Group on the Adequacy of Mobility Planning and Operations."

61.　See Tom Klein, "The Capacity to Intervene" in Rodberg and Shearer, op. cit., p. 195.

62.　General Earle D. Wheeler, U.S. Congress House Committee on Armed Services, Special Subcommittee on Military Airlift Hearings, 89th Congress, 1st session (Washington, D.C.: GPO, 1965), pp. 6790-6793.

63.　Sherrill Papers. The Office of Strategic Mobility is described publicly in "Why Defense's 'Mr. Tranportation' is a Key in Military Planning," Armed Forces Management (September 1966), pp. 57-61.

64.　Statement of Secretary of Defense Robert S. McNamara before the House Armed Services Committee, January 28, 1968, p. 140.

65.　Ibid., p. 141.

66.　Ibid. See also Enthoven and Smith, op. cit., p. 237.

67. Bernard Brodie, A Guide to Naval Strategy (Princeton: Princeton University Press, 1958), p. 252.

68. See Hanson W. Baldwin, "The Navy at Ebb Tide," The Reporter, op. cit.

69. See Robert L. Robinson, "The Case of the FDL," op. cit. and "Can Fast Deployment Ship Program Revitalize U.S. Shipbuilding Industry?" Armed Forces Management (January, 1966), p. 73.

70. Klein, op. cit., p. 193.

71. Alain Enthoven, "The Role of Systems Analysis in the FDL," included in testimony in U.S. Congress, House, Committee on Armed Services, Hearings on Military Posture for FY 1969, 90th Congress, 2nd session (Washington, D.C.: GPO, 1968), p. 8913.

72. R. L. Madhouse, "The FDL Surfaces Again," United States Naval Institute Proceedings (June 1968), pp. 54-66.

73. U.S. Congress, Senate, Committee on Armed Services, Hearings on Department of Defense Appropriations for FY 1969 and H.R. 18707, 90th Congress, 2nd session (Washington, D.C.: GPO, 1968), p. 538.

74. Testimony of Secretary McNamara, U.S. Congress, House, Committee on Armed Services, Hearings on Military Posture and H.R. 9240, 90th Congress, 1st session (Washington, D.C.: GPO, 1968), p. 538.

75. Ibid., p. 627.

76. "The Fast Deployment Logistics Ship Project" (Washington, D.C.: U.S. Navy, October 1966), quoted in Robinson, op. cit.

77. Testimony of Paul Ignatius to the Senate Merchant Marine and Fisheries Subcommittee, quoted in Klein, op. cit., p. 204.

78. Statement of Secretary of Defense Robert S. McNamara to the House Armed Services Committee, February 18, 1965, p. 118.

79. Hearings on H.R. 18707, p. 1097.

80. Reference to the Report of the Senate Armed Services Committee on the FDL is made in a letter from Secretary McNamara to Chairman Rivers of the House Armed Services Committee on April 13, 1967. The entire letter is printed in Hearings on Military Posture and H.R. 9240, pp. 575-576.

81. Ibid.

82. Ibid., p. 1080.

83. One of the reasons this proved difficult was the final disposition of the Victory FFDs in the Pacific. In 1964, an exercise called "Quick Release" tested the feasibility of storing the equipment and judged successful the concept of marrying up airlifted troops with the stored supplies. But the prepositioning afloat concept was one of the first casualties of the Vietnam war, based on both the need for the equipment stored on the ships and for the future tonnage those ships could deliver to Southeast Asia. General Johnson testified that the prepositioned supplies were merely part of the war reserve materiel that had been required for the war. But the fact that the ships were unloaded and then diverted to point-to-point cargo routes strengthened the arguments of those who suggested the same fate awaited the FDL. Hearings on Military Posture and H.R. 9240, p. 668. See also Hanson W. Baldwin, "FDL," Marine Corps Gazette (March 1967), pp. 18-26.

84. Hearings on Military Posture and H.R. 9240, pp. 609-610.

85. Ibid., pp. 636-637.

197

86. Ibid., p. 1098. The description of the Senate position is described in an article included in the testimony, "Defense--the LOGLAND Jam," Time (March 31, 1967).

87. Klein, op. cit., p. 210. For Senator Russell's comments on the FDL, see the Congressional Record for March 21, 1967, pp. 7511-7512.

88. Hearings on Military Posture and H.R. 9240, pp. 575-576.

89. Quoted in Graham Allison, "Military Capabilities and American Foreign Policy" (Cambridge: John F. Kennedy School of Government, October 1973), p. 1. Russell was known as a strong advocate of the military in general and the Georgia-built C-5A in particular. Therefore, his position on the FDL seems anomalous. Surely, both he and Rivers were influenced by the maritime lobby, but Tom Klein has suggested that Russell turned against the FDL "when he perceived a threat from the Pentagon to keep the C-5A contract out of Georgia if he did not go along with the FDL" (op. cit., p. 210). There are probably more coherent ways of explaining Russell's opposition (see p. 174 of this study). In any event the position formulated as "Russell's Alternative" has a good deal more Allison in it than Russell: "Capabilities created to increase the government's options by generating information and alternatives that would otherwise be unavailable also, and of necessity, create interests in and often lobbies for the use of these capabilities." See Allison, pp. 12-15.

90. Hearings on Military Posture and H.R. 9240, p. 933.

91. See "Controversy over the FDLs to Flare Anew," Baltimore Sun (April 21, 1969), p. C-8, and "FDL Ship Plans," San Diego Union (February 12, 1970), p. 5.

92. See Enthoven and Smith, op. cit., p. 241.

93. Neil Sorensen. "The Development of the Air Mobility Strategy."

94. Frederick Thayer, Jr., Air Transport Policy and National Security (Chapel Hill: Air University of North Carolina Press, 1965), p. 130.

95. Ibid., p. 135.

96. "Predesignation" was the term used by the Army to mean that certain airlift units would be dedicated solely in support of Army transportation requirements. See Taylor, The Uncertain Trumpet, pp. 102-105.

97. See Thayer, op. cit., p. 109.

98. Ibid. One attempt to resolve this airlift controversy was a plan presented by the Federal Aviation Administration in 1959 (the Quesada Plan) to create an air "merchant marine." This air fleet was to be a commercial venture, would reduce the military airlift mission to the support of war plans and would consequently result in a reduction of approximately 100 aircraft from the military airlift fleet. Not surprisingly, the proposal was opposed by the Secretary of the Air Force and MATS and rejected by the Senate.

99. U.S. Congress, House, Committee on Armed Services, Report of the Special Subcommittee on National Airlift (Washington, D.C.: USGPO, 1960), p. 4027.

100. Thayer, op. cit., p. 202.

101. Report of the Special Subcommittee on Airlift, p. 4030.

102. Thayer, op. cit., p. 203.

103. Report of the Special Subcommittee on Airlift, p. 4051.

104. Thayer, op. cit., p. 204.

105. Sorensen, op. cit., p. 66. These extraordinary measures of the Congress taking separate action (although encouraged by the Army) to appropriate funds to support force planning for a rapid deployment capability were necessary because, as the Rivers Committee noted, it was unlikely that sufficient funds would be obtained for airlift through the normal, service-requested, budgetary channels. With this Congressional prodding, the Air Force was willing to admit the need for a strategic airlift force in support of this mission. On March 4, 1960, Generals White and Lemnitzer signed an agreement which spelled out the number of Army units that airlift would be expected to deploy to various parts of the world within given periods of time. However, the actual capability to meet these goals was lacking. See U.S. Congress, House Committee on Armed Services, Hearings on Military Posture for FY 1962, 87th Congress, 1st session (Washington, D.C.: USGPO, 1961), p. 106.

106. "SecDef Reports on National Military Airlift Plans." See also "Limited War Forces Stressed by Kennedy," Washington Evening Star, January 30, 1961. In a news conference on February 2, 1961, Secretary McNamara noted that the acceleration of the C-135 program would result in a jet airlift capability four years ahead of the original schedule.

107. On March 17, 1961, Air Force Systems Command designated the aircraft the C-141. On April 5, a contract was let with Lockheed for five research, development, test and evaluation aircraft. In January 1962, the mockup of the aircraft was complete; in August 1963 the first C-141 was rolled out. The C-141 was in full operation by the fall of 1967. Sorensen, op. cit., p. 67.

108. Air Force Review of the C-5A Program, Department of the Air Force, July 1969, p. I-2.

109. U.S. Air Force, Historical Division Liaison Office, Strengthening USAF Airlift Forces, 1961-1964 (Washington, D.C.: Historical Division, February 1966).

110. "Overseas Airlift Studied for Entire Division," Washington Star, July 28, 1963.

111. "Airlift Need is Asserted by General," Baltimore Sun, August 8, 1963.

112. Quoted in McBride and Eales, op. cit., p. 116.

113. During this period the C-124 was the major airlift system available for "rapid" deployment. When coupled with the C-133 (an aircraft originally designed a missile transporter), the fleet could carry about 90% of Army equipment. But owing to their limited range and load restrictions, these and other propeller-driven aircraft failed to represent an adequate capability to deploy general purpose forces within desired time criteria. By 1964, before the advent of the C-141, the entire airlift force could provide only 494 million ton-miles of capacity in a 30-day period. The proposed fleet of C-141/C-5 aircraft was able to carry three times this amount, with half the number of aircraft. Air Force Review of the C-5A Program, p. 5-2.

114. Statement of Secretary McNamara to the House Armed Services Committee, January 29, 1964, quoted in McBride and Eales, op. cit., p. 106.

115. Air Force Review of the C-5A Program, p. 5-2.

116. Klein, op. cit., p. 197. "Operation Eagle Thrust" (November-December 1967) was the largest and longest single airlift in Air Force history. Over 10,000 troops and nearly 5,400 tons of equipment for two brigades and support elements of the 101st division were transported from

Fort Campbell, Kentucky, to Bien Hoa/TanSonNhut, Vietnam. Total sorties included 369 C-141 and 22 C-133.

117. Testimony of Secretary of Defense Melvin Laird, U.S. Congress, Senate, Department of Defense Appropriations for FY 1972, 92nd Congress, 1st session (Washington, D.C.: USGPO, 1971), Part 1, p. 136.

118. Testimony of Lt. General George S. Boylan, USAF, Deputy Chief of Staff, Programs and Resources, to the Military Airlift Subcommittee of the House Armed Services Committee (Price Committee), quoted in "America's Strategic Airlift Capability: A Risky Calculation," Armed Forces Journal, July 18, 1970.

119. Ibid.

120. The findings and recommendations of the Price Committee are recorded verbatim in "America's Strategic Airlift Capability."

121. The civil-military dispute over airlift remained, despite the ground broken by the Rivers Committee ten years earlier. The Price panel advocated limiting the use of the C-5A to outsize cargo only, thereby eliminating the C-5 from routine cargo missions that could then be contracted to commercial carriers.

122. See Berkley Rice, The C-5A Scandal (Boston: Houghton Mifflin, 1971).

123. U.S. Congress, House, Committee on Armed Services, Hearings on Military Posture and H.R. 9637, 88th Congress, 2nd session (Washington, D.C.: USGPO, 1964), pp. 7048, 7821.

124. Testimony of Robert S. McNamara, U.S. Congress, House, Committee on Armed Services, Hearings on Military Posture and H.R. 4016, 89th Congress, 1st session (Washington, D.C.: USGPO, 1965).

125. Size of the design was not a technical problem: Boeing had the 747 design by 1963. But to put such an aircraft into austere environments was extremely ambitious technically. See Robert Art, "Why We Overspend and Underaccomplish," op. cit.

126. Testimony of Robert S. McNamara, Hearings on Military Posture and H.R. 9240, p. 938. See also F. Theodore Helmer, "Management Innovations in System Acquisition," in Endicott and Stafford, eds., op. cit., pp. 276-285.

127. The C-5A was certainly the best documented cost overrun in systems acquisition history, owing to newly instituted costing procedures and techniques like "total package procurement." While not pretending to defend cost overruns, Enthoven and Smith pointed out that 1) a cost increase of 60% would be judged successful by pre-1961 standards, 2) cost increases of 60% are not unique to the Defense Department and 3) an excess of actual cost over contract cost does not equate to excess cost over "should cost" or the actual worth of the system. See How Much is Enough?, pp. 239-240.

128. Quoted in Klein, op. cit., p. 200.

129. Ibid., p. 201.

130. For the most part, the Senate debate on the C-5A was conducted from September 3 to September 9, 1969. See the Congressional Record for those dates, S10065 to S10329.

131. Ibid.

132. U.S. Congress, Hearings of the Joint Economic Committee (Washington, D.C.: USGPO, 1969), Part 1, p. 116.

133. Congressional Record, September 9, 1969. Also see Rice, p. 123, and Klein, p. 207.

134.   See Senator Proxmire's criticism of the procurement procedures for the C-5A in the Congressional Record, August 13, 1969, S-9972-81.
135.   New York Times, November 15, 1969, p. 1.
136.   Quoted in Donald W. Cable, "A Slower Rapid Response," Armed Forces Management, April 1970.
137.   Ibid.
138.   See Rice, op. cit., and Klein, pp. 207-208.
139.   Quoted in "America's Strategic Airlift Capability."
140.   For planning purposes, a "bare base" was defined as an airfield having one or more runways, taxiways, a parking ramp and potable water, but without any additional support faciities.
141.   Like their sea-based cousins, the FFDs, these supply packages were quickly absorbed during the initial stages of U.S. force deployments to Vietnam. History of the Tactical Air Command, 1965 (Washington, D.C.: Office of Air Force History, 1965), pp. 836-864.
142.   See "U.S. Developing Instant Air Bases," New York Times, November 1, 1970, p. 1.
143.   "Coronet Bare" Final Report, Bare Base Evaluation, 14-28 October 1969 (Eglin AFB, FL: USAF Tactical Weapons Center, 1969).
144.   Ibid.
145.   There are three stages of required civilian participation under the CRAF agreement. Stage I is approved by the Secretary of Defense to support counterinsurgency or local wars. Stage II is approved by the President for limited wars, while Stage III also calls for presidential approval and full mobilization under general war conditions. A declared airlift emergency need not be related to a national state of alert, but only defines a situation in which the airlift demand exceeds the existing military capability.
146.   Testimony to the Price Committee, quoted in "America's Strategic Airlift Capability."
147.   United States General Accounting Office, "Airlift Operations During the 1973 Mid-East War" (Washington, D.C.: USGPO, 1975), p. 1. During the resupply effort, MAC delivered 22,497 tons of cargo to Israel.
148.   See Drew Middleton, "Big Soviet Airlift Capability Altering the Power Balance," New York Times, October 26, 1973, p. 22, and Charles W. Corddry, "U.S. Alert Works," Baltimore Sun, October 26, 1973, p. 1.
149.   Drew Middleton, "U.S. Strategic Airlift has Growing Role," New York Times, November 15, 1975, p. 9.
150.   In 1976, the Senate Armed Service Committee, concerned with an apparent lack of coordination among these enhancement alternatives, directed the DoD to undertake a thorough review of these requirements. A summary of the JCS study is included in The Posture of Military Airlift, 95th Congress, 1st session (Washington, D.C.: USGPO, 1977), pp. 25-44.
151.   DoD Annual Report FY 1975, p. 95.
152.   DoD Annual Report FY 1976, p. III-33.
153.   Some of the factors which made the airlift equation to the Persian Gulf more difficult to solve included the extra distance, the lack of enroute bases, utilization and sortie rate calculations, problems with overflight rights and access to facilities in the region and the lack of refueling in-flight capability for the C-141 as well as the lack of proficiency for C-5A crews in in-flight refueling, as evidenced by the 1973 Israeli airlift.
154.   The study was RAND 1941/11-AF, March 1977, quoted in Westhoff and Stouffer, op. cit.

155. Ibid.

156. See Walter R. Shope, "The Lessons of Nifty Nugget," Defense 80 (December 1980), pp. 14-22, and John J. Fialka, "The Grim Lessons of Nifty Nugget," Army (April 1980), p. 40. Shope notes that one of the most significant discoveries in the course of the exercise was the separation between operational contingency planning and resource allocation. Fialka concentrates on the results, specifically the reforms and shortfalls. See also U.S. Department of Defense, "An Evaluation Report on Mobilization and Deployment Capability Based on Exercise Nifty Nugget-78" (Washington, D.C.: DoD, June 30, 1980).

157. Fact Sheet, "The Joint Deployment Agency" (MacDill AFB: Public Affairs Office, January 1981), p. 1.

158. The POMCUS program for divisions 5 and 6 was not funded by Congress in FY 1982, but was included again by the Reagan administration in the FY 1983 defense budget.

159. Harold Brown, DoD Annual Report FY 1980, p. 205.

160. Ibid., p. 204.

161. Ibid., p. 207.

162. John J. Fialka, "RDF to Cost $10 Billion," Washington Star, December 15, 1979, p. 2.

163. Drew Middleton, "U.S. Earmarks Force for Rapid Deployment in Mideast," New York Times, April 20, 1979, p. 12.

164. Jim Hoagland, "A Carter Doctrine for Mideast Oil?" Washington Post, January 3, 1979, p. D1.

165. Hearings on U.S. Interests In and Policies Toward the Persian Gulf, p. 94.

166. See George C. Wilson, "U.S. Military Lacks Rapid Deployment," Washington Post, October 3, 1979, p. 1. Also see "Plan to Replace Wings of C-5As is Questioned as Too Costly," Washington Post, August 26, 1980, p. 8.

167. Wilson, "U.S. Military Lacks Rapid Deployment."

168. John J. Fialka, "Defense Admits Problems in Ability to Sealift Troops," Washington Star, December 13, 1979, p. 18.

169. U.S. sealift capability is derived from five sources: the Military Sealift Command, the National Defense Reserve Fleet, the Sealift Readiness Program, the U.S. Merchant Marine and U.S.-controlled foreign flag shipping. As of January 1, 1980, the U.S. Merchant Marine included 170 dry cargo ships and 56 tankers that could be committed under the SRP and 560 active merchant ships, of which about 275 cargo ships and 100 tankers are considered useful for military sealift. Approximately 7 to 9 SRP ships would be required to deploy one mechanized Army division.

170. Quoted in Edgar Prina, "Pentagon Studying Plan for Rapid Deployment Fleet," San Diego Union, October 5, 1979, p. 1.

171. Quoted in Raymond Coffey, "Defense Spending Stresses Mobility," Chicago Tribune, January 29, 1980, p. 6.

172. Harold Brown, "Remarks to the Council on Foreign Relations, March 6, 1980," Selected Statements (Washington, D.C.: USGPO, May 1980), pp. 60-61.

173. Hearings on U.S. Interests In and Policies Toward the Persian Gulf 1980," p. 94.

174. Compiled from the DoD Annual Reports for FY 1980, 1981 and 1982.

175.   Lawrence J. Korb, "The FY 1981-1985 Defense Program," p. 54. See also "Defense Budget Preview: New Shipbuilding Plan Announced," Seapower (January 1980), p. 32.

176.   Testimony of Robert Komer, U.S. Congress, House, Committee on Armed Services, DoD Authorization for Appropriations for FY 1981, Hearings on Military Posture and H.R. 6495, 96th Congress, 2nd session (Washington, D.C.: USGPO, 1980), Part 1, p. 457.

177.   Hearings on Military Posture and H.R. 6495, Part 3, pp. 1248-1249.

178.   Testimony of Lt. General P. X. Kelley, Hearings on Military Posture and H.R. 6495, Part 3, p. 130.

179.   Ibid., p. 136.

180.   Ibid., p. 144.

181.   R. A. Sulik, "Near Term Fix-NTPS," Marine Corps Gazette, August 1980, pp. 52-56.

182.   "Rapid Deployment Supply Ships Will Go to Indian Ocean in June," Philadelphia Inquirer, March 6, 1980, p. 16. See also Charles W. Corddry, "U.S. to Place 7 Shiploads of Gear in Indian Ocean," Baltimore Sun, March 6, 1980, p. 2.

183.   Hearings on Military Posture and H.R. 6495, Part 3, p. 146.

184.   Ibid., p. 485.

185.   Ibid., p. 179.

186.   Ibid., Part 2, p. 857.

187.   Ibid., Part 3, p. 460 ff.

188.   Written statement of Vice Admiral Kent Carroll, Director for Logistics, JCS, Hearings on Military Posture and H.R. 6495, Part 3, p. 168.

189.   Jeffrey Record, The Rapid Deployment Force, p. 35. See also Hearings on Military Posture and H.R. 6495, Part 1, p. 441.

190.   U.S. Congress, Congressional Budget Office, "U.S. Airlift Forces: Enhancement   Alternatives   for   NATO   and   non-NATO Contingencies," p. 6.

191.   Ibid.

192.   This CX requirement was based on a representative set of missions reflecting possible future scenarios. Factors identified and included in the process of concept design included threat, onload bases, route structure and offload bases. See Thomas D. Pilsch, "The CX Requirement," Airlift Operations Review (January 1981), pp. 8-17.

193.   Hearings on Military Posture and H.R. 6495, Part 3, p. 382.

194.   George C. Wilson, "CX Cargo Plane Takes a Direct Hit," Washington Post, October 22, 1980, p. 8.

195.   "US airlift Forces," p. 56.

196.   "CX Cargo Plane Takes a Direct Hit." In a reaction to this proposal for the acquisition of an airlift aircraft without a specific mission, Congress directed the Defense Department to conduct a major analysis "to define the requirements and describe the parameters that validate the need for and the mix of additional prepositioning, sealift and airlift, including "outsize."   The project, called the Congressionally Mandated Mobility Study (CMMS), affirmed the need for increased oversized and outsized airlift (as well as a sealift and prepositioning program) and was, therefore, offered in justification of the CX. However, over apparent objections of the Air Force, Defense Secretary Weinberger cancelled the CX (the McDonnell Douglas C-17) and offered in its place a purchase of 44 new C-5s and 40 KC-10 tankers. This decision was made

despite Air Force arguments "that the C-5 will not be able to land or take off effectively from the austere airfields that will greet the RDF, especially on desert stretches near a Mideast battlefield." See "Lockheed's Galaxy is Chosen as Weinberger Tells Air Force to Abandon Plan for the C-17," Defense Week (January 20, 1982), p. 1, and "Strategic Mobility: Shortfalls and Solutions," Defense 82 (March 1982), pp. 11-15.

197. U.S. Interests In and Policies Toward the Persian Gulf, 1980, p. 76.

198. Ibid., p. 410.

199. Strategic Survey 1980-1981 (London: The International Institute for Strategic Studies, 1981), p. 18.

200. Harold Brown, DoD Annual Report FY 1981, p. 198.

5
Force Planning for the Half War: The RDJTF as a Limited Contingency Force

Introduction

A prognosis of the international situation in the next two decades argues for the planning of general purpose forces capable of rapid deployment to a series of separate and possible sequential limited contingencies in support of U.S. foreign and defense policy. In particular, it appears such a force is required to meet successfully an era of continued competition with the Soviet Union beyond the confines of Europe and focused, in the immediate future, on Southwest Asia. However, the recent effort to construct a Rapid Deployment Joint Task Force, although it made considerable strides in terms of force design and allocation, was only a half-step in this force planning process. By illuminating past attempts to construct such a limited contingency force, this study attempts to identify ways by which current force planning efforts in this sphere can be both effective and enduring.

A straight forward presentation of historical facts or trends does not guarantee the future selection of sound policies. Ernest R. May has argued that policymakers frequently use history badly.[1] The purpose of this book has not been to draw force planning "lessons" from the past, but rather to assist in the understanding of the underlying strategic, organizational and political dynamics which appear to be persistent. Policymakers can use history in a more discriminating fashion. By seeking alternative parallels to a current situation, past experience may be applied more critically and systematically in deliberations on policy choice. The purpose of this study has been to aid that process by presenting the major strategic variables in a framework for analysis in order to describe and explain why the United States has, up to now, failed to construct a coherent limited contingency force.

This chapter consolidates the analysis previously presented in a brief summary of how "half war" forces were inadequately planned in terms of strategy, organization and support. With the findings reviewed, an effort will then be made to present the requirements for an effective limited contingency force.

The force planners' task is to determine how many units of various systems should be procured and operated in order to carry out a given strategy under a wide set of circumstances. Force planners considering a lesser contingency over the last twenty years have faced great uncertainty. Vague references to U.S. global interests generally prove to be insufficient guidelines on which to base a purposeful military strategy or a cohesive force posture. Thus, military planners engaged in conventional contingency planning for non-specific scenarios were restricted to general objectives and capabilities. To hedge against uncertainty, the force planner attempted to construct a flexible force for operation in an unknown environment. These past efforts elevated concepts of organizational flexibility and force versatility to the sine qua non of a viable lesser contingency capability. Without specific objectives, a number of possible scenarios resulted in a range of military objectives that required a variety of armed forces. Under these ill-defined conditions, plans remained unclear, deployment schedules uncertain and the consequences of simultaneous contingencies unforeseen.

The historical evolution of general purpose force planning for a limited contingency presented here argues that the same strategic, organizational and logistic barriers that have operated in the past to prevent the construction of a coherent limited contingency force designed to achieve a global deployment and operational capability will continue to constrain such an ambitious force in the future. But the presence of these obstacles does not require a retreat from the requirement to support U.S. foreign policy commitments with a credible conventional deterrent. On the contrary, the thesis here is that the United States must conduct its general purpose force planning in a manner which will conceptually, organizationally and logistically support forces to meet separate, concurrent conventional contingencies that may threaten vital interests.

The "Half War" Strategic Concept

The strategic concept--the statement of how many and what kinds of wars the United States should be prepared to fight--is not a complete or precise basis for force planning. The second chapter of this study, in charting the rise and fall of the "half war" as an element of the strategic concept from 1960 to 1980, argued that the "half war" planning contingency took on a variety of meanings, locales and levels of intensity. Thus, over the score of years since 1960, the "half war" was envisioned as a minor contingency in the Western Hemisphere (early in the Kennedy administration), a counter-insurgency in Vietnam (early in the Johnson administration), a non-Asian "contingency elsewhere" (early in the Nixon administration) and a lesser contingency in the Persian Gulf or the Middle East (early in the Carter administration).

Regardless of the strategic concept in which it was imbedded, the "half war" as a basis for force planning has been rife with uncertainty and derived from both a complex and changing threat and the belief that the U.S., as a global power, must have flexible forces capable of meeting worldwide interests. But without a specific scenario, a particular theater or adversary and an assigned region of responsibility, a force planner looking at the lesser contingency was required to support operational plans that spanned the globe and design forces capable of responding to a range of conventional conflicts.

The thrust of this argument, as demonstrated by the study of three differing strategic concepts over the last twenty years, is that the "half war," as an approach to force planning for a lesser contingency, has been wrong-headed in its attempt to embrace a wide range of conventional conflict under a single convenient, but imprecise concept. This concept has led to an attempt to aggregate an array of disparate conventional scenarios into a single threat that could be countered successfully with a single general purpose force. This has resulted in two significant trends that have affected force planning over the last twenty years. First, rapid deployment forces designed to fight this "half war" were conceived of as flexible and sophisticated organizations composed of versatile forces that could meet any military challenge anywhere. Secondly, the requirement for the deployment of this force simultaneously with the reinforcement of U.S. forces dedicated to a major contingency required extensive strategic mobility systems dedicated to the lesser case. Although additional forces were allowed for and allocated to meet the "half war" in whatever form, these units were never provided the lift to guarantee rapid deployment.

These two trends require further elaboration. Although the perception of the "half war" as a "brushfire" initially involved the United States in Vietnam, the uncertainty of U.S. objectives and the attendant escalation of that conflict resulted in a military effort considerably greater than a "brushfire," but a political commitment far less than that which should have been dedicated to a major contingency. Although a reflection on the U.S., experience in Vietnam appears to demand that future lesser contingencies be more precisely enumerated in terms of locale, adversary, level of intensity and allocation of forces, any attempt to delineate the lesser contingency in more precise terms was blurred by a post-war retrenchment in both strategy and force posture. In attempting to steer a course between "overinvolvement and underinvolvement," the Nixon Doctrine was bound to avoid future "brushfire" conflicts. However, the doctrine was characterized by ambivalence in both its pronouncement and implementation.[2] While Melvin Laird's rhetoric called for a "0-war" strategy of deterrence rather than warfighting, the U.S. continued its military course of engagement and disengagement in the "field of fire" that was Vietnam.

The perception that the United States could not effectively wield the military instrument in support of its diplomacy in the Third World extended into the Carter administration.[3] Secretary of Defense Brown, in accepting the "1-1/2 war" strategic concept, acknowledged that while the flexibility inherent in a system of strategic mobility and a ready reserve force should be maintained, "we can probably make a larger proportion of our ground and tactical air forces more specifically equipped for operation in Europe than in the past."[4]

However, the threat suggested by the extension of Soviet interest and control to areas well beyond central European borders in December 1979 caused that emphasis on the NATO contingency to be reevaluated. While conventional wisdom pointed to an emerging power vacuum in Iran demanding U.S. presence, Afghanistan was interpreted as a completely new order of provocation. For the first time since World War II, Soviet rather than surrogate forces were used to maintain Russian control in a region generally regarded as lying outside the accepted sphere of Soviet influence. With the Soviet invasion, the focus of U.S. strategic concern shifted to the Persian Gulf, and a capability for meeting the "firefight" version of a lesser contingency was raised to a high priority. However, force planning for "half wars" at the lower end of the spectrum of conflict remained minimal.

An examination of the additional lesser contingencies the United States might be forced to meet reveals that these scenarios requiring limited U.S. support--repressed in a Eurocentric strategic concept-- remain credible threats to American interests. The possibility exists that in addition to a simultaneous conflict in the Persian Gulf and NATO Europe, the U.S. could also be required, in the event of a North Korean attack on the South, to deploy reinforcements to Northeast Asia. U.S. defense officials, in admitting that American capability to respond to the "1-1/2 war" was less than adequate, conceded that U.S. strategic mobility support and fighting forces would be stressed to failure by this "one and two half-wars" scenario.[5]

By 1980, the probability that the United States might have to face more than one lesser contingency simultaneously appeared to be increasing. Thus, one "half war" as an element of the strategic concept and as a basis for force planning no longer retained its relevance: the likelihood of sequential or simultaneous lesser contingencies required forces to meet each event. These forces would now have to be planned and allocated based on a priority system taking into account U.S. commitments and interests and programmed within realistic budgetary constraints. Therefore, effective and enduring force planning for lesser contingencies must reject past concepts of flexible organizations composed of versatile forces to meet any contingency through as-available strategic mobility systems. A revised strategic concept would suggest the need to be prepared for a series of specific, significant, sequential or possibly simultaneous contingencies.

"Half War" Organizations

The third chapter of this study examined three major attempts to create organizations purported to direct and control armed forces dedicated to meeting a lesser contingency. The uncertainty attending the strategic concept of rapid deployment to an undefined limited contingency made more difficult the organizational task of uniting available forces to accomplish this mission. From this uncertainty grew the requirement for a large and complex organization malleable enough to meet these ill-defined goals. But large organizations, particularly those imposed over already existing bureaucratic structures, are not inherently flexible. In each case examined, these organizations revealed fatal flaws in attempting to deploy and employ assigned forces, to meet all circumstances and contingencies. Moreover, the environment surrounding the organizational planning for a lesser contingency has been less than favorable. Torn by service cleavages, deprived of assigned forces and denied budgetary support, these organizations met with little mission accomplishment.

STRIKE Command was formed in 1961 in response to a perception of a global threat and as a means of placing greater emphasis on a conventional response to limited wars. From its inception, STRIKE was hampered by conflicting organizational interests, lack of a joint service doctrine for combined operations and a reluctance on the part of certain services to participate. However, even as a joint command restricted to ground and air forces, STRIKE was unable to resolve successfully the doctrinal dispute regarding Air Force close air support and Army air mobility.

Such disagreement hobbled the command. Because force employment was likely to occur in an area with little established infrastructure or command organization in place, it was imperative for the services to develop procedures of close cooperation and coordination.

However, without a specific area of responsibility or an assigned mission, joint doctrine succumbed to more powerful organizational interests.

It is possible that STRIKE Command could have accomplished a limited unification of the Army's STRAC and the Air Force's CASF. However, these forces, allocated to a strategic reserve rather than assigned to STRIKE, were soon absorbed by the Vietnam war. STRIKE Command, in General Adams' phrase, turned into a "deployment outfit" rather than a unified combatant command. Even the assignment of a geographical area of responsibility in the Middle East proved futile. Lacking organic naval forces and deprived of its ground and air forces by an unforeseen major contingency in Southeast Asia, STRIKE Command, by 1968, possessed few combat-ready forces to deploy in any mode to any lesser contingency.

In addition to stripping STRIKE Command of its operational capability, the Vietnam war also encouraged a widespread public aversion to any intervention-oriented force. Forces designed to deploy rapidly to global trouble spots were now seen as stepping stones to wider, and unwanted, U.S. commitments. In a time of retrenchment and reconsideration of U.S. global military involvement, STRIKE Command was at best anachronistic, at worst provocative. If, as the Nixon Doctrine implied,[6] the United States would no longer provide the manpower to fight limited wars, an organization designed to deploy such forces appeared as a nonessential luxury in a defense budget noted for its austerity.

The transformation from STRIKE Command into Readiness Command, therefore, also reflected a change in the perception of means available to conduct limited contingency operations as well as an alteration in the perception of the threat post-Vietnam. A growing isolationist sentiment, plus the passage of legislation limiting U.S. involvement in Southeast Asia (as well as the War Powers Act), suggested that budgetary support for rapid deployment forces would be curtailed. If U.S. vital interests were formed in the minds of men, as Bernard Brodie has asserted,[7] rather than in objective reality, the mindset prevailing within the U.S. government in the early 1970s appeared to limit the territory for which U.S. ground forces would fight to the plains of Central Europe.

At the turn of the administrations in 1977, the campaign promises of the new President and the limits set by the public mood continued to restrict U.S. military pledges of assistance solely to the major contingency.[8] An increased interest at senior decision-making levels within the Carter administration to extend U.S. intervention forces occurred at a time when U.S. capability to act was constrained by public opinion and the administration's reluctance to request additional funding in support of such a capability. Therefore, when a rapid deployment force for the Persian Gulf region was first designed, it suffered from considerable uncertainty. Although Secretary Brown alluded to the deployment of a strike force of highly mobile units that could be deployed to Southwest Asia, the makeup of these units, the adversary perceived and the organizational framework for the force remained unspecified.

The entry of the USSR into Afghanistan suggested that U.S. forces might encounter Soviet forces beyond the confines of a NATO scenario. But the Soviet action also brought with it old fears of a global communist challenge and the need for the United States, once again, to be able to respond with military force to any global contingency. This wider view of

US/USSR competition was a major departure from the post-Vietnam U.S. defense policy extended from the Nixon/Kissinger Doctrine in which there had been a tendency to "consider third world crises in their specific local and regional setting rather than to press them into the matrix of global East-West competition."[9] President Carter's personal reappraisal of the Soviet threat post-Afghanistan suggested the need to respond to this threat with conventional forces and strengthened the requirement for a counter-intervention capability.

This heightened perception of the threat, coupled with uncertainties relating to the utility of military force in the region of the Persian Gulf, resulted in the initial conception of the Rapid Deployment Force as one that carried with it the organizational baggage--and military impotence-- of past failed efforts. The first uncertainty regarded the adversary. Should the force be structured to cope with the most likely case of internal instability, or should it be aimed at deterring or defending against a Soviet invasion of the oil fields? This uncertainty led to a number of organizational struggles over the composition and mission of the Rapid Deployment Joint Task Force.[10]

The original chain of command called for the RDJTF to report directly to both the Commander of the Readiness Command and the JCS. Struggles over service doctrine, roles and missions added further barriers to the design of a coherent organization.[11] These organizational issues and interests were of such magnitude that they could not be resolved at the Unified Command or Joint Chiefs of Staff level. The ultimate organizational design of the RDJTF was debated by Congress and decided by the Secretary of Defense.

Thus, in an examination of three cases over two decades, combatant commands designed to manage conflict in a lesser contingency experienced consistent and similar failures: a lack of joint and unified service participation, a struggle over roles and missions and an inability to deploy and employ attached forces in regions of responsibility. What was ostensibly an economical and efficient organizational structure in peacetime, turned out to be a wasteful and cumbersome command in time of crisis.

"Half War" Support

The task of the logistician is to determine the availability of the resources, how best these resources can be concentrated at the time and place they are needed and, perhaps most important, how to transport and support the forces required. The acquisition of strategic mobility systems in adequate numbers to support rapid deployment forces over the last twenty years has proved unsatisfactory. Shortfalls in the design, acquisition and employment of these transport systems intended to support rapid deployment strategies have in turn plagued the efforts of "half war" forces and organizations. As developed in the previous chapter, Secretary McNamara was willing to point out the inherent uncertainties in constructing strategic mobility systems designed to support rapid deployment: there were a variety of contingencies requiring a mix of delivery systems; the identity and, therefore, the strength of the adversary was unknown; and a range of conventional capability was required. Because different contingencies would require differing forces, a mix of strategic mobility systems was a must.[12]

The perception of the threat that engendered this rapid deployment transportation force was identical to the one prompting the creation of STRIKE Command. The world was seen as an East-West battlefield; the prize was the allegiance of the third world. It was, therefore, necessary to have the capability to oppose aggression, prop up governments favorable to the United States or demonstrate U.S. interest across a wide spectrum of conflict and contingencies. The rapid deployment strategy was developed to meet these interests without stationing large forces overseas, thereby providing force flexibility and, ostensibly, reducing costs. The backbone of such a strategy would be adequate strategic mobility.

As attractive as this concept was on paper, it becomes clear from the examination conducted here of the program failures over the last two decades that the lift and the logistical systems to support such a strategy were never acquired. The major problem was not one of resource availability, but of resource allocation. The maintenance of a ready, in-being force and the procurement of a sophisticated mix of mobility systems incurred a continuing peacetime "preaggression" cost that proved difficult to defend on the grounds that certain contingencies might arise. In addition, questions were raised regarding the ultimate use of the military air and sea transport fleets in peacetime. Such capabilities appeared to infringe on the commercial territory and economic well-being of private carriers. A combination of FDL "anti-intervention" arguments during Vietnam and C-5A "cost-overrun" statistics served to diminish significantly the procurement of the optimum mix designed in support of the projected and planned-for contingencies. Moreover, the gradual escalation of the war in Southeast Asia and the lengthy, but secure lines of communication seemed to reduce the premium that had been placed on rapid deployment to a lesser contingency.

But, if rapid deployment support systems were seen as unnecessary during the Vietnam war, they were seen as superfluous after its termination. The lowered perception of the threat and the limits imposed on the defense budget in accordance with the Nixon Doctrine ensured that forces dedicated to the support of a lesser contingency would lose priority. Without the requirement to deploy troops to the Third World, there was no need for a capability to do so. Thus, budgetary support for the rapid deployment methods that had survived the war would have to be based, in the future, on their contribution to the support of a major contingency.

Therefore, the strategic mobility systems that did spill over from the McNamara formulation to the Rapid Deployment Force were the airlift and prepositioning methods dedicated to the support of a NATO contingency. However, these capabilities remained severely limited, both in sea and airlift. Without the FDL, the C-5A became the workhorse of strategic mobility. But that aircraft had been reduced, not only in total numbers acquired, but also in its specifications to meet requirements for operation in an austere or remote environment. Similarly, methods of utilizing CRAF, bare base techniques or land prepositioning all possessed inherent drawbacks when applied to a lesser contingency. In a time of reduced spending and a focus on Europe, these shortfalls were not regarded as particularly serious, especially given the fungibility of these systems that were expected to perform adequately, although perhaps not simultaneously with a major reinforcement effort, in an off-design scenario.

Again, a heightened perception of the threat changed the outlook and breathed new life into old systems and concepts. As the Persian Gulf received the increased attention of U.S. force planners and the enhanced awareness of Congress, the United States embarked upon a combination of airlift, sealift and prepositioning programs. However, a good deal of uncertainty remained to complicate this force planning process. Without adequate bases in the region, prepositioning had to be accomplished at sea. Airlift also required facilities on land, but the issue of overflight rights and access to landing bases remained clouded. Fast sealift, perhaps the most applicable system to the scenario envisioned, remained largely unavailable. The failure to procure an adequate strategic mobility force in the past now acted to constrain the limited contingency force of the future. Moreover, although the scenario-specific qualities of this new effort could be lauded from an operational standpoint, the logistic concentration on the Persian Gulf did little to extend U.S. strategic mobility capabilities to other lesser contingencies elsewhere.

The debate over U.S. rapid deployment forces and their support has underscored the contradictions between the uncertainties inherent in contingency planning for a wide range of possible scenarios and locales and the need to plan general purpose forces for rapid deployment to a specific area of vital interest. The traditional solution to this dichotomy has been to construct a flexible force to deal with all varieties of possible threat and conditions. This approach to force planning for a lesser contingency by aggregating the varied forms of low intensity conflict has never proven workable. Forces were not so versatile, organizations not so flexible and requisite mobility systems not so available. The need, therefore, is to disaggregate the cases and to plan forces and their support dedicated to the most salient of these contingencies. The argument being presented here suggests that the solution to the military defense of vital interests lies not in a call for a greater and unattainable flexibility of force, but in the planning and dedication of a specific force to a specific theater based on a specific scenario to assure the attainment of a specific objective. The requirements for such a force suitable for meeting a range of conventional contingencies, along with an examination of the current work of other students of these issues, are looked at in the following section.[13]

Requirements for a Limited Contingency Force: Contingency Specific

This functional analysis of force planning for a lesser contingency has suggested the need for a unified command possessing dedicated and multi-service forces, assigned a specific region of responsibility, oriented towards a specific scenario with forces sized to meet a certain threat and provided with organic or assigned lift adequate to meet rapid deployment criteria. A contingency-specific force would enjoy strategic, organizational and logistical advantages.

From the viewpoint of the strategic concept, the "half war" as a non-specific basis for force planning has proved impractical, if not counterproductive. While the "half war" remained an element of the strategic concept during the period under examination, it lacked the precision required to overcome resource constraints and, thereby, failed to gain the funding, assigned forces and adequate support required to meet the multitude of missions subsumed under the "half war." Moreover, as a lesser contingency without definition, the "half war" allowed anti-intervention arguments to be levied against valid requirements for strategic mobility systems.

The "half war" as a strategic concept has been overtaken by events. The strategic dilemma that now faces U.S. force planners is the need to prepare for and, thereby, deter multiple and various kinds of contingencies in different locations and at different levels of intensity that may occur simultaneously or sequentially with a NATO-Warsaw Pact conflict. Additionally, American decision makers must also be willing to face the hard choices of deciding which of these contingencies demand the extra effort and expenditure required to construct a coherent force in its defense. In their deliberations, these decision makers may find focusing on a single lesser contingency as inappropriate and atavistic as was the "half war" as a planning contingency. What appears most likely is a series of lesser contingencies which must be accorded a variable priority depending on the degree of U.S. interest and commitment as well as the extent of enemy capabilities and intentions.[14]

The attempt to structure organizations to unite a specific contingency force under a single command has also suffered from the perceived need to assign the force a global mission. This concept of flexible employment deprived rapid deployment forces of assigned units and replaced them with forces to be tailored to a specific contingency under a deployment headquarters. But this concept imposed barriers of command, control and communication between the deployment commander and the units assigned and allowed conflicting service allegiances and disputes to intrude upon the forces' cohesiveness. Without organic forces or support, STRIKE Command could neither deploy forces rapidly nor employ them within its own region of responsibility.

The unavailability of lift for the all-purpose force proved to be a significant liability in preventing the force from accomplishing a global mission. The mobility systems designed to support rapid deployment were never procured in adequate numbers. Because the systems were inherently flexible, it was assumed that strategic mobility requirements sized to support the major contingency could also provide for a lesser deployment. But this concentration on NATO reinforcement meant that the transportation needs of forces earmarked for a lesser contingency could not be met simultaneously.

These shortfalls in the strategy, the organization and the support for a non-specific "half war" force have led to the conclusion that a modern limited contingency force must be based and planned on a specific case. However, arguments for the global deployment capabilities of a STRIKE-like command can still be heard, although these views generally lack the comparative and historical perspective that has been developed here. Geoffrey Kemp, for example, recently advanced a strong argument for the sizing and configuration of an intervention force to be independent of specific scenarios and geographic areas.[15]

Kemp's first reason for opposing a contingency-specific force is that the United States is a global power with worldwide interests. The pursuit of these interests, in an environment of increasing global interdependence, creates a "strong possibility" that the use of force will be required. However, owing to the complexity of the international political system, "it is impossible to predict when or where such events may occur and what level of military force may be required."[16] Kemp's second point follows from his first. The establishment of an all-purpose force will demonstrate U.S. political resolve. He further claims that establishing forces for specific contingencies "reflects the very worst type of planning: reactive, scenario specific and often too late to be effective."[17]

This position is worthy of examination because it is representative of the thinking that formed the conceptual basis for STRIKE Command and is reminiscent of the early arguments in favor of a rapid deployment force. In the first place, Kemp downplays the importance of specific U.S. commitments as a guide to general purpose force planning. Given global interests, Kemp argues, no contingency-specific force can suffice. Because the U.S. finds itself increasingly involved with disparate conflicts, the fundamental requirement for a power-projection capability continues to grow.

However, such an approach appears to sacrifice the U.S. ability to respond effectively to a contingency involving vital interests to a capability to demonstrate U.S. resolve in much less serious events. In this regard, Kemp may have confused the discrete use of armed force for political objectives--a force without war--with the larger and more serious issue of a lesser contingency in the Persian Gulf or elsewhere. In a work cited previously, Blechman and Kaplan derived empirical evidence that suggested the demonstration of U.S. resolve through the movement and threat of military force may have a positive outcome in the short term. These kinds of force movements, the type that Kemp appears to favor, would not be precluded by the construction of a limited contingency force focused on a specific case. In addition, the same study warned that symbolic low-level uses of force may be disregarded by those intended to be influenced if the situation is one in which U.S. policy-makers "have not seriously contemplated the need for, or the consequences of, using large forces in a more manifest way."[18] Thus, a limited contingency force may be most effective if it is tied in commitment and matched in strategy to a specific contingency in which the U.S. has declared its vital interests.

Similar reasoning suggests that Kemp's second point may also rest on faulty assumptions. Given that the accepted manner and practice of sizing general purpose forces over the last twenty years has been to examine their ability to meet the deterrence and defense requirements of a specific contingency against a certain threat, it is difficult to see why that method should not be applied to a limited contingency force as well. Moreover, there seems to be little reason to suspect that a contingency-specific force would be "too late to be effective," while a more global force would be characterized by rapid response. Certainly, this presumption was not borne out by the STRIKE Command experience. On the contrary, it appears that forces assigned a specific mission, trained and exercised in that contingency and allocated adequate lift and appropriate prepositioning modes would be far more credible both in deterrence and defense than a force which either has failed to demonstrate such capability or is likely to lose its resources to another contingency of higher priority.

But the key point in the refutation of Kemp's argument is that a force for all contingencies simply cannot be effectively manned, organized or supported to meet the variety of conditions and cases that may face it. In postulating scenarios that may occur in the Persian Gulf, Kemp points out "that there is an enormous difference between dispatching a token force for purposes of presence and peace-keeping and dispatching a war-fighting force equipped, climatized and with enough logistical support to conduct major operations in desert warfare."[19] He is right. But that "enormous difference" should not be sufficient, in itself, to restrict U.S. military options only to that first alternative of a "token force" in an area of vital interest.

Kemp's argument that the United States may be required to respond with military power in the Persian Gulf region across a wide range of scenarios does not square with his opposition to a limited contingency force designed for operation in that region. The creation of such a contingency-specific force does not require that the total force be deployed or employed. But the credibility of an element of that force sent to "stabilize" internal unrest in a Gulf state will surely be enhanced and its deterrent value increased by the availability of a rapid deployment force that is highly capable and specifically trained for theater operations. Moreover, it is usually agreed that the most effective deterrent force is one stationed directly in the country of concern (such as U.S. forces in Germany and Korea). A force specifially charged with the defense of the Persian Gulf, although stationed over the horizon, should also profit from this enhanced deterrent effect.

In the final analysis, the limited contingency force that Kemp argues for, "capable of a wide range of missions in different theaters ... (having) the maximum flexibility to operate in a global context,"[20] has proved to be an unrealistic goal in terms of the required strategy, organization, and support. Kemp's justification for such a force is that the United States as a global power must be concerned with worldwide events and must be prepared to defend those widespread interests. It is not this reasoning, but his method in supporting it that is faulty. The same force planned and designed to meet a range of conventional conflicts in Southwest Asia should not be the same force tasked to defend U.S. interests in Northeast Asia or the Caribbean--or NATO for that matter--if only for the reason that such a force would be strained to the breaking point if called upon to respond simultaneously to multiple theaters or contingencies. From an operational perspective, the United States cannot afford to trust the protection of its vital interests to a force that, as history shows, is likely to be ill-conceived, poorly organized and inadequately supported.

Requirements for a Limited Contingency Force: Multi-Service

A second major requirement for a limited contingency force emerging from this analysis is that it be composed of all services under a unified command rather than limited to a single or joint service participation. This assessment can be supported by referring to the functional framework of strategy, organization and support.

One of the factors limiting the strategic concept of the "half war" was that it tended to blur the requirements of lesser contingency force planning. If the "half war" was merely a "brushfire" that required only a show of force, there was adequate room at this lowest level of conflict to envision a service-specific rapid deployment force. Indeed, the Army's Airborne Corps and the U.S. Marine Corps were long considered the most appropriate units for this type of mission and were fashioned in its support. However, as the level of intensity of the conflict increases, so does the requirement to utilize the unique capabilities of each of the armed services. A limited contingency force sized against a Soviet threat in the Persian Gulf is likely to require the land, sea and air forces of the

216

separate services. The multi-service composition of this force does not rule out a limited show of force, predominantly single-service, that could have taken place under the aegis of the Rapid Deployment Joint Task Force. However, deliberately limiting the U.S. response to a token show of force by a single service in a region which could confront light U.S. forces with heavy and sophisticated enemy forces would be irresponsible.

The organizational arguments for a single-service rapid deployment force are perhaps the strongest of the three. Problems of organizational interest, interservice rivalry and doctrinal divergence have plagued the STRIKE Command and the Readiness Command and the Rapid Deployment Joint Task Force. These problems could be lessened significantly, so the argument goes, by reducing the command organization to a single service. (There are, of course, intraservice disputes as well.) However, a meaningful loss in combat capability that would result from the extraction of several services from the command seems too great a price to pay for an organization that may function smoothly, but be overpowered militarily. A better approach would be not to reduce the number of services committed to the force, but to heighten the commitments of the services assigned. In light of past experience, this seems most attainable through the creation of a multi-service command that directs and controls its own assigned forces.

Because all services are short of lift,[21] it is difficult to argue convincingly that either a single- or a multi-service force would more effectively meet a rapid deployment strategy. What does seem clear is that multi-service participation in the limited contingency force will allow a greater number of strategic mobility options to meet various logistical demands. In the most serious case in the Persian Gulf, U.S. action to repel a Soviet invasion could easily require the rapid airlift of ground troops, an amphibious landing to secure ports or airfields, the rapid sealift of supplies and equipment, and the movement and offloading of stores prepositioned on ships.

The strongest argument for a single-service limited contingency force has been put forward by Jeffrey Record. His basic position is that the mission of rapid deployment should be granted in its entirety to the Marine Corps. Such an intervention force[22]

... would stress quality at the expense of size, immediate responsiveness at the expense of delayed augmentation from the United States, sea-based power projection capabilities at the expense of air-transported Army forces and land-based tactical air power and logistical self-sufficiency at the expense of dependence on facilities ashore.

In making this proposal, Record's arguments are not only tactical. He displays an awareness, if not a single-mindedness, of the inter-service contests that have debilitated the rapid deployment commands in the past. Record's emphasis on the need to overcome these service rivalries is understandable. But the assignment of the rapid deployment mission to a single service may be a self-destructive way of accomplishing an organizational goal while ruling out the attainment of essential military objectives. Although a limited contingency force composed solely of Marines would surely soften one side of the organizational debate and continue to perform well its traditional show of force and amphibious missions, there is serious doubt as to how effectively such a force could perform on a modern land battlefield against a sophisticated opponent. A rapid deployment of Marine forces may be appropriate to a lesser contingency in the Caribbean; but, given the possible escalation of the threat and level of intensity of the conflict in Southwest Asia, such a force could not act as an adequate or credible deterrent to major conventional operations in the Persian Gulf region.

Thus, the most powerful argument against a Marine-intensive limited contingency force focused on the Persian Gulf is simply that it would not be an adequate military force to meet the range of conceivable conflict in that region. While the development of a capable multi-service force with responsibility for that area would not preclude a limited deployment of certain elements of that force to restore order and stability in a "brushfire" version of the lesser contingency, limiting that command's capability to respond to a range of scenarios to the capabilities of a single service permits the possibility of reduced deterrent effect and the subsequent loss of defined territory and interests if the conflict were to escalate to a US-USSR "firefight."

Record's argument is not limited to organization. He identifies the general shortfalls that have plagued rapid deployment force planners: inadequate strategic and tactical mobility, a small forcible entry capability, the deficiencies of logistical support, a lack of access within the region and the hostility of local populations. In the face of these difficulties, Record sees the solution as a small agile tactical force, based and supplied at sea and dominated by the Marine Corps. Any attempt to combine U.S. forces in a multi-service effort, Record fears, will result in the creation of a "fatally flawed instrument" owing to its organizational ineptitude and basic inability to counter effectively the larger Soviet forces in the region.

This perception of the threat is the key area in which Record's proposal fails. In stressing the importance of command relationships, Record neglects to consider various scenarios within a lesser contingency that determine the ultimate force size required. Most damaging to his assessment, Record merely assumes away the Soviet threat based on a number of highly questionable propositions: caught in a quagmire in Afghanistan, the USSR will be self-deterred from further aggression in the region; U.S. forces are no match for Soviet forces in the area; and because a US-USSR conflict in the Gulf would probably spread to a major contingency in Europe, U.S. forces committed to NATO could not be diverted to Southwest Asia.[23]

Assuming away a serious threat is a poor basis for force planning, particularly when it was precisely the increased probability of Soviet intervention that caused President Carter to declare the region as one of vital interest to the United States and, ultimately, to establish the RDJTF. Mr. Record's concern, with some justification, is that the existing force would take on the worst characteristics of the STRIKE Command—an organizationally divided command without assigned forces or logistical support. But, by incorporating the strong capabilities of each of the services into the RDJTF—an advantage not enjoyed by STRIKE Command—a multi-service limited contingency force appears to offer greater tactical flexibility and lower risks than a single-service force.

Thus, the economic attractiveness and organizational singularity of Record's proposal are outweighed by military realities. However, it would be improper to suppose that the forces in-being are sufficient to meet the more complex mission and that more force and lift will not be required if a rapid deployment force is to assume the characteristics and capabilities of the limited contingency force outined here. As Geoffrey Kemp has admitted, such a force will necessitate an overall increase in the defense budget. As well as counteracting low levels of violence, the limited contingency force[24]

> ... must be capable of conducting high-intensity operations which will require the use of maritime forces, including amphibious forces, heavy ground forces and tactical fighter forces capable of air defense and deep interdiction. This, in turn, will require that great emphasis be given to support requirements for such forces, including local infrasturcture and logistics.

Requirements for a Limited Contingency Force: Adequate Logistics

The main arguments structured against additional lift for a limited contingency force are not that such a force does not require the lift, but rather that adequate systems already exist or that new systems are too expensive to procure. In the first case, adequate strategic mobility systems appear to exist only within the framework of an outdated strategic concept. While it is possible that U.S. forces could adequately meet a major contingency in Europe and a lesser one in Asia simultaneously, it is equally likely that the current mobility and logistics chains would prove inadequate to that task.[25] Clearly, if the multiple-contingency scenario were extended to include the Persian Gulf as a concurrent third contingency, the U.S. would suffer a severe deficit in forces and support systems.[26]

The cost of increasing strategic lift dedicated to a limited contingency force is not trivial, but there are options available to enhance U.S. strategic mobility at affordable costs. While airlift remains the fastest way to move men and materiel to a possible war zone, sealift and prepositioning provide volume at a much lower price. Thus, some analysts have suggested that the deployment problem can be solved more rapidly and inexpensively through the acquisition of fast sealift rather than through the development of the CX or similar aircraft.[27]

This is not to suggest that the logistics equation in support of a limited contingency force is easy to solve. Despite modest, yet significant steps initiated by the Carter administration to improve the U.S. capability to move military cargo by sea and air, a classified study conducted in early 1981 was reported to reveal "an alarming gap between the amount of equipment and supplies the Pentagon says U.S. troops would need in 1986 to fight a war in Europe and 'half a war' in the Middle East and the amount of such cargo that can be delivered to them."[28] But the study went on to suggest that given existing political and economic constraints, a number of proposals and programs could significantly limit these differences through additional airlift, sealift and prepositioning. What is required is not only a choice among these systems based on the contingency, but a long term commitment to them as well.

Closely related to the need for adequate logistics support for conventional forces dedicated to a limited contingency is a network of support bases or facilities in the area to encourage allied cooperation, enhance host nation support and facilitate realistic training and exercises. Such a network exists in Europe, Northeast Asia and, to some extent, in the Caribbean, but is sorely lacking in Southwest Asia. In that regard, U.S. initiatives to gain access to facilities in Egypt, Kenya, Somalia and Oman appear as an important step, as does the series of "Bright Star" military exercises in the region. Others have pointed out that in order to serve as a credible deterrent against Soviet action, U.S. presence or "facilities" will also be required in the northern reaches of the territory designated as Southwest Asia.[29]

Requirements for a Limited Contingency Force: Deterrence and Defense

Glenn Snyder once defined the central theoretical problem in the field of national security policy as distinguishing between the concepts of deterrence and defense. Snyder noted that it was commonplace to say that the primary objectives of American defense policy were to deter enemy attackers and defend successfully if deterrence failed, but that it was "less widely recognized that different types of military force contribute in different proportions to these two objectives."[30] This dichotomy exists in force planning for a limited contingency. There may be a significant difference in sizing forces to meet the mission of presence, or a "trip-wire" force, which some believe provide an adequate deterrent, and in preparing to deploy a force equipped and supported to defend in high-level conventional operations. The difference is one of both confidence levels and the danger of escalation. When the objective is conventional deterrence and defense, the danger is that a low-confidence trip-wire deterrent implies a possibility of rapid escalation to nuclear conflict.

The study of conventional deterrence lacks precision; therefore, the application of the functional framework employed here to the deterrence/defense debate is somewhat inconclusive. Certainly, the strategic concept of the "half war," in subsuming a variety of forms of limited conflict under its domain, served as a poor guide to the deterrent requirements of a limited contingency force. As George and Smoke have argued, deterrence in the case of limited conflict is largely a context-dependent problem.[31] Thus, an attempt to extend conventional deterrence across a wide range of contingencies with a force that could not be tailored to a specific case or region resulted in a force of questionable deterrent and defense value. Without a clear relationship between the force posture and its declared deterrent and defense objectives, the force may easily devolve into a low-confidence trip-wire with nuclear weapons required to bolster its deterrent value.

Kenneth Waltz has raised the deterrence/defense question with regard to the strategy for the rapid deployment force.[32] In inquiring into the best strategy to be adopted, Waltz points out that varied approaches to the purpose and functions of the RDJTF have confused the conceptual planning. Waltz describes two basic forces that could meet U.S. objectives of deterrence and defense in the Persian Gulf. The first would be a warfighting defensive force, similar to a capable conventional limited contingency force described in this chapter. The second, which he prefers, would be an asset-seizing deterrent force.

To meet delicate problems of Middle East diplomacy while simultaneously deterring the Soviet Union, Waltz advocates an asset-seizing deterrent force that can meet both internal and external threats. The key to the construction of this force, which he does not design in detail, is "linking a minimal defense to America's strategic deterrent."[33]

If the flow of Persian Gulf oil is vital to U.S. interests, then the invocation of nuclear retaliation should prevail. Given an imbalance of interests in the region, the attacker has to believe that the defender will retaliate. That, for Waltz, is enough to deter.[34]

But Waltz questions his own formulation of a nuclear-emphasis rapid deployment force. How can we expect nuclear deterrence to operate in the Persian Gulf when it is being questioned in Europe? How can the deterrent be extended in an era of strategic and tactical parity in nuclear arms? How can we expect nations to build up their conventional defenses or reject an indigenous nuclear weapons capability if the United States holds to the nuclear umbrella as a solution to regional conflicts? These questions deserve better answers than Waltz provides. "Nuclear weapons," he admits, "demand that their use be carefully planned, limited and controlled."[35] Most would agree. The problem is that no one has yet figured out how those plans, limits and controls will be adhered to once a nuclear exchange is initiated. A reliance on a nuclear deterrent in any lesser contingency fails to provide a high level of confidence regarding the probability of avoiding future conflict. Nor does it obviate the hard choices inherent in the construction of a limited contingency force designed to defend U.S. interests in the region.[36]

Requirements for a Limited Contingency Force: Summary

Through historical description of U.S. limited contingency force proposals, examination of those programs' failures and consideration of alternative approaches, this study has reached the following conclusions regarding the requirements for the construction of a coherent limited contingency force capable of supporting vital U.S. interests.

1. Contingency-specific. If the region is vital to U.S. interests, planning must be devoted to a force capable of defending those interests in that area. A focus on a particular region and threat encourages efforts to secure access to facilities and promotes initiatives for land and sea prepositioning. A contingency-specific orientation allows forces to be sized against a specific threat, to be trained in the tactics and environment and permits the exercising of the force within the region.

2. Assigned multi-service forces under a unified command. Any force denied the unique capabilities of a single service will lack that much in capability. The inclusion of each component in the limited contingency force does not require that all units from each service be employed in every situation. However, the force must have the capability of operating flexibly in the region and sequentially employing its own forces under centralized command and control and with organic communications support.

3. Sized against the major threat. While "worst case" planning is often maligned, the result of failing to plan for the greatest threat can end in disaster. The concerns of scholars that a force sized to meet the most serious scenario must then be employed in that form are without foundation. Similarly, escape mechanisms--such as a counterattack strategy to take actions in areas apart from the region in conflict to those where the United States happens to enjoy a military superiority

TABLE 5.1
A Strategic Concept Envisioning Multiple Contingencies, 1981

1 War	+	1/2 War (Gulf)	+	1/2 War (NEA)	+	1/2 War (Caribbean Basin)
Warsaw Pact attack in Europe		Soviet/proxy attack in Southwest Asia		Non-Chinese attack in Northeast Asia		Insurgency/revolution in Caribbean
Allied Support		Limited allied support		Limited support		No support
Vital to U.S.		Vital to U.S.		Vital to U.S.		Not vital

FORCES
(Army and Marine Divisions)

	1 War	1/2 War (Gulf)	1/2 War (NEA)	1/2 War (Caribbean Basin)
CONUS	5	4	1	--
DEPLOYED	6	--	2	--
STRATEGIC RESERVES	--	--	--	1
RESERVES	4 + 4	--	--	1

STRATEGIC CONCEPT

Assumes that multiple, simultaneous contingencies are likely and could be linked with a major contingency in Europe. Forces must be allocated and strengthened in order of priority, depending on the threat and the contingencies that can best be estimated. Four Reserve divisions are fully equipped and prepared for rapid mobilization and deployment in support of the NATO contingency.

Sources: William W. Kaufmann, "The Defense Budget," op. cit., p. 175. Walter S. Mossberg, "US in Defense Strategy Switch Plans Power to Fight 2 Big Wars Simultaneously," Wall Street Journal, June 15, 1983, p. 12. George C. Wilson, "US May Hit Soviet Outposts in event of Oil Cutoffs," Washington Post, July 17, 1981, p. 1. Drew Middleton, "US and Distant Conflicts: Europe Fears Military Shift," New York Times, June 11, 1981.

or the invocation of nuclear threats--can only escalate the conflict needlessly. A strong credible conventional force capable of halting the advance of the perceived adversary can best meet the requirements of deterrence and defense.

4. Adequately supported. A limited contingency force must possess organic or dedicated air and sealift, a program of appropriate prepositioning, a capability to gain access to needed facilities and a power projection capability. The limited contingency, in terms of logistic support, must be considered as a lesser excluded case: forces assigned to the command must be guaranteed adequate mobility systems, even during a major reinforcement or resupply effort.

5. Based on a revised strategic concept. The United States must accept the prospect of meeting multiple crises simultaneously. In the event of a Persian Gulf contingency that threatens a US-USSR confrontation, the United States will not have the luxury of borrowing units dedicated to NATO for deployment to Southwest Asia. It is also possible that a contingency in Northeast Asia or in the Caribbean could erupt at the same time. But a strategic concept that calls for a preparation to fight multiple contingencies should not be construed as a renewal of the global "half war." Just as the British did in the past, the United States must now decide which regions really do involve vital interests and pledge to defend those places. In the forseeable force planning future, those areas appear to number only four: Central Europe, Southwest Asia, Northeast Asia, and the Caribbean.

This chapter, in consolidating the analysis presented previously, has reemphasized that the attempts to plan rapid deployment forces during 1960-1980 were not successful. Strategic concepts containing the "half war" were only partially formed, organizations were fractionated, support was neglected. These shortcomings have made evident the requirements for a coherent limited contingency force in the next decade. How these requirements are being addressed in the planning of rapid deployment forces for the 1980s is the subject of the final chapter.

NOTES

1. Ernest R. May, Lessons of the Past (New York: Oxford University Press, 1978), pp. xi-xiii.

2. On one level, the Nixon Doctrine ruled out intervention in internal struggles in foreign countries while suggesting that a "nuclear shield" would defend an ally threatened by a power possessing atomic weapons. What remained unclear was what the U.S. would do in the event of aggression that was conventional and external. Nixon's suggestion--one that has since been revived--was that this sort of problem might be dealt with through a collective security system. See Kissinger, White House Years, pp. 223-226.

3. However, concern was being expressed by the defense cognoscenti that the lesser contingency was being ignored as a planning factor as a result of the increased emphasis within the Carter

administration on the European case. In 1977, Geoffrey Kemp and Harlan Ullman expressed concern that "both the public debate and the institutional process are becoming more and more concerned with the strategic nuclear and the NATO-Warsaw Pact Central Front balance; . . . other contingencies should be examined in order to reach some conclusions about the relative dangers of this apparent over concentration." Op. cit., p. 71.

4.   DoD Annual Report FY 1980, p. 99.

5.   Offered in the testimony of Under Secretary Robert Komer, previously cited. Despite these realizations, the Carter administration "took the position that the capabilities already incorporated in the force structure for a minor contingency (approximately three divisions and five tactical fighter wings) were sufficient to cope with an emergency in the Gulf." See William W. Kaufmann, "The Defense Budget" in Joseph A. Pechman, ed., Setting National Priorities: The 1982 Budget (Washington, D.C.: Brookings, 1981), p. 153 ff.

6.   The Nixon Doctrine stated: "In cases involving other types of aggression (local wars) we shall furnish military and economic assistance when requested and as appropriate. But we shall look to the nation directly threatened to assume the primary responsibility of providing the manpower for its defense." See Kissinger, White House Years, p. 225.

7.   Brodie, War and Politics, p. 364.

8.   An opinion survey published at the time of the election noted a new desire to put an end to the perceived decline in the military status of the United States, expressed in terms of an increased willingness to come to the aid of Europe and Japan. But, although a more activist foreign policy role was acceptable to most Americans, the study noted that the "next President must understand that this desire does not translate into support for indiscriminate intervention." Not that it ever did. See Wiliam Watts and Lloyd A. Free, "Nationalism, not Isolationism," Foreign Policy, 24 (Fall 1976), pp. 3-26.

9.   Strategic Survey 1979 (London: International Institute for Strategic Studies, 1980), p. 1.

10.   If the purpose of the force was to lend American assistance to stabilize the political situation in the Western-oriented Gulf states, the composition of the RDJTF might be limited to the traditional light deployment units, particularly the Marine Corps. If the purpose of the force was to defend against Soviet intervention, a multi-service force of significant capability was required. In either case, too visible a link with the United States might weaken the regimes in question in a domino-like extension of the Iranian revolution. Thus, military "presence" remained an inadequate solution in the immediate area, and the requirement for an "over the horizon" force demanded a rapid deployment capability. The debate has been addressed in the Hearings on the RDF before the Senate Armed Services Subcommittee on Seapower and Force Projection, March 12, 1981. More recently, W. Scott Thompson has argued that U.S. forces may be required to halt an imperial Soviet march to the Indian Ocean. See "The Persian Gulf and the Correlation of Forces," International Security, Vol. 17, No. 1 (Summer 1982).

11.   These conflicts included a quarrel between the Air Force and the Marines over the control of airspace in the objective area, questions regarding responsibilities of the Navy-directed Pacific Command in the Indian Ocean area and doubts expressed about the future of the Marine

Corps amphibious and rapid deployment missions, if not the future of the Corps itself.

12. Enthoven and Smith, op. cit., p. 237.

13. This argument is directed toward the planning of forces to meet a non-NATO contingency in a vital area opposing Soviet/proxy forces and is not meant to preclude a flexible special operations force capable of responding to low-intensity conflict or Iran-like rescue missions. Indeed, recent moves to bolster U.S. capability in this area are also needed-- although clearly less vital. See Richard Halloran, "Military is Quickly Rebuilding its Special Operations Forces," New York Times, July 19, 1982, p. 1, and "Army Plans New Command to Curb Leftist Insurgencies," New York Times, September 17, 1982, p. B-6.

14. For a list of these possible contingencies and potential U.S. combat deployments required at "M + 40," see William W. Kaufmann, "The Defense Budget," p. 175, and the table on page 219.

15. Geoffrey Kemp, "Contingency Planning and Persian Gulf Options" in Continuity and Change in the Eighties and Beyond, pp. 61-76.

16. Ibid., p. 61.

17. Kemp does not make it clear why he believes a force established specifically to respond to a certain contingency would be slower to respond than non-specific forces. On the contrary, the assumption here is that specific forces with dedicated lift should be able to respond more quickly than present alternatives.

18. Blechman and Kaplan, Force Without War, p. 532.

19. Kemp, op. cit., p. 75.

20. Ibid., p. 76.

21. See Zakheim, "Airlifting the Marine Corps," for an argument for increasing and relying upon a combination of airlift and amphibious operations.

22. Jeffrey Record, The Rapid Deployment Force, p. vii.

23. For a good discussion on the dangers of assuming away a Soviet threat in the region and also for a reasonable assessment of the contributions that a well-planned U.S. limited contingency force could provide in Southwest Asia, see Joshua M. Epstein, "Soviet Vulnerabilities in Iran and the RDF Deterrent," and Dennis Ross, "Considering Soviet Threats to the Persian Gulf," International Security, Vol. 6, No. 2 (Fall 1981), pp. 126-180. See also Francis Fukuyama, "The Soviet Threat to the Persian Gulf" (Santa Monica: RAND P-6596, January 1980) and Thompson, "The Persian Gulf and the Correlation of Forces," op. cit.

24. Kemp, op. cit., p. 76. Thompson suggests a five-year cost of $82.5 billion (1980 dollars) above current expenditures. For other cost projections, see Congressional Budget Office, "U.S. Projection Forces: Requirements, Scenarios, and Options" (Washington: USGPO, April 1978), pp. 41-54.

25. See the discussion of airlift assets adequate to meet the "1-1/2 war" strategic concept in Congressional Budget Office, "U.S. Airlift Forces: Enhancement Alternatives for NATO and non-NATO Contingencies," pp. xi-xvii.

26. See the discussion of multiple contingencies in Kaufmann, The Defense Budget, p. 161.

27. Ibid., p. 173. The cost of the CX or C-17 in the McDonnell Douglas version of the design encountered considerable Congressional opposition. Both the House and Senate Appropriations Committees cut funds for the CX in the FY 1982 budget, with the Senate providing $15

million for research and development and both the House and Senate appropriating $50 million for the acquisition of existing widebodied aircraft. See "Military to consider offers from Boeing, Lockheed, before choosing transport jet," The Wall Street Journal, December 2, 1981, p. 48. The choice to cancel the C-17 and procure 50 Lockheed C5Bs and 44 McDonnell Douglas KC-10 aircraft has been characterized by F. Clifton Berry as an "airlift tragedy." See Air Force Magazine, August, 1982.

28.   Patrick Oster, "U.S. Ability to Move War Gear Lags," Chicago Sunday Times, July 28, 1981, p. 4.

29.   See Ross, op. cit., p. 178.   For an implication that the Gulf states' fears for their own security from a more local threat may also work in favor of American interests in gaining access to the region see David Ottaway, "Fear of Iran Edges Wary Persian Gulf States to Closer U.S. Ties," Washington Post, February 24, 1982, p. 20. See also George Wilson, "U.S. Plans Maneuvers with Oman," Washington Post, August 25, 1982, p. 1.

30.   Glenn H. Snyder, "The Theory of Deterrence" in John F. Reichart and Steven R. Sturm, eds., American Defense Policy (Baltimore: Johns Hopkins Press, 1982), pp. 154-160.

31.   George and Smoke, op. cit., p. 54. See also John Mearsheimer, Conventional Deterrence (Ithaca: Cornell University Press, 1983).

32.   Kenneth N. Waltz, "A Strategy for the Rapid Deployment Force," International Security, Vol. 5, No. 4 (Spring 1981), pp. 49-73.

33.   Ibid., p. 63.

34.   Albert Wohlstetter has noted that a trip-wire in the Persian Gulf, where there is little Western conventional force, would be more likely to frighten our allies in the region than to deter the Soviet Union. In general, Wohlstetter argues that "to declare a bare trip-wire policy does not register a determination to use nuclear weapons in a time of crisis; rather, it registers a lack of will to prepare before the crisis to meet a non-nuclear threat on its own terms." See "Meeting the Threat in the Persian Gulf," p. 50.

35.   Waltz, p. 68.

36.   William W. Kaufmann discusses this point in a NATO context in "Defense Policy," Agenda for the 1980s (Washington, D.C.: Brookings, 1980), pp. 298-299.

6
Planning for Rapidly Deployable Forces in the 1980s

Introduction

The planning of general purpose forces to meet a limited contingency in the 1980s, despite lessons learned in the past, is not likely to vary greatly from previous attempts. Thus, the strategic concept--the image of how many and what kinds of wars the United States should be prepared to fight--will remain a guide to this force planning process. That strategic concept, in turn, will spring from a perception of the threat. The forces designed and deployed in support of that strategic concept will be responsive to a net assessment of U.S. military strength vis-a-vis its principal adversaries. Finally, the priority assigned to forces planned to meet a lesser contingency (one outside NATO Europe) in the 1980s will again confront constraints of budgetary restrictions and face trade-offs with competing programs. Thus, the strategic concept adopted in the 1980s, to be examined first in this chapter, is likely to have a major impact on U.S. efforts to deploy forces rapidly to "half war" contingencies. However, this chapter differs from the previous historical development of strategic concepts in that the strategic concept guiding future force planning is not yet fully formed. To make use of previous chapters, the framework for analysis here will remain the same.

The second section of this chapter will also use a framework developed earlier. In an examination of organizations likely to influence U.S. force planning for limited contingencies in this decade and beyond, the same critical issues emerging from an historical study of "half war" organizations will be used to consider the structural requirements of a coherent limited contingency force of the future. The most important factors in this regard, as suggested earlier, were:

- the degree to which the command is unified;
- the degree to which units from each armed service component are dedicated to the organization;
- if a specific scenario, contingency or adversary is assigned to the organization for planning purposes;
- if forces assigned to the organization are either trained or exercised for combat operations in a specific theater.

The 1980s have already seen a new command dedicated to the purpose of rapidly deploying forces to a limited contingency. In January

1983, the United States Central Command (USCENTCOM) was formed—a unified command reporting directly to the Secretary of Defense.[1] This second section will focus on the new organization and evaluate it in light of the above criteria.

To keep faith with the methodology employed thus far, the third section of this concluding chapter will examine logistical support for limited contingency forces in the 1980s. Here, the prospects for prediction are complex. Strategic concepts can easily be altered, while organizations rise and fall; but strategic mobility systems are not easily modified once designed and deployed. However, these systems, as documented in Chapter 4, repeatedly fall victim to organizational interests, budgetary priorities and civil-military conflicts. There is no guarantee that logistical systems planned in the beginning of the decade will be in place at the end. The extent to which these latest programs will be acquired and, therefore, the effect they will have on the ability of U.S. forces to move quickly to lesser contingencies of the future, is problematical.

This conclusion, then, reiterates the requirements for a coherent limited contingency force and projects those desiderata into the future. If the conclusions of this study are valid, then rapidly deployable forces in the 1980s must be contingency-specific, assigned to a unified command, sized against a major threat in an area of responsibility and adequately supported. How do current U.S. planning efforts meet these criteria?

Planning for Rapid Deployment in the 1980s

Before 1969, American force planners were faced with the possibility of a simultaneous war against the Soviet Union and the People's Republic of China and a lesser contingency that varied in locale, adversary and intensity. Since that time, and until 1981, this "2-1/2 war" strategic concept was reduced to a "1-1/2 war" planning factor, owing ostensibly to the low probability of the United States' having to face militarily the USSR and the PRC at the same time.[2] The thrust of the argument here has been that the non-European contingency can no longer be afforded such a low priority in the planning of general purpose forces and that U.S. defense policy has suffered from a failure to disaggregate the "half war" from other planning contingencies.

The analysis presented here did not call for an abandonment of a contingency basis for conventional force planning, but argued to make those contingencies both explicit and related to U.S. vital interests. However, the Reagan administration, in apparently rejecting the force planning guidance of preparing for "1-1/2 wars," has moved early in the 1980s to establish a new strategic concept.[3] In his FY 1983 Posture Statement, Secretary of Defense Weinberger posited that not only should the previous strategic concept be rejected, but also that the United States should prepare to cope with Soviet aggression, or Soviet-backed aggression on several fronts simultaneously.[4]

The most complete statement of the Reagan administration's strategic concept has been offered by the Under Secretary of Defense for Policy, Dr. Fred Ikle. Writing in early 1982, Ikle argued that U.S. conventional forces must be capable of responding to a wide range of possible contingencies and of possessing a capacity to wage counteroffensive operations in areas not of the adversary's choosing—the so-

called "horizontal escalation" concept.[5]   This strategy, particularly as
applied to a non-European contingency, has two dimensions:[6]

First, it calls for a U.S. capability rapidly to deploy enough
force to hold important positions and to interdict and blunt a Soviet
attack: this capability must convince enemy planners that they
cannot count on seizing control of a vital area before U.S. forces
are in place. . . . Second, the strategy recognizes that we have
options for fighting on other fronts and for building up allied
strength that would lead to consequences unacceptable to the Soviet
Union.

Ikle goes on to reject the planning factors inherent in a strategic
concept, calling for the United States to prepare to fight some mixed
number of wars. For Ikle, "such mechanistic assumptions neglect both the
risks and the opportunities that might be confronted."[7] The U.S. cannot
decide in advance on its force planning by defining the risk occasioned by
a certain contingency. Rather, the size of the forces must be "steeped in
much broader and more fundamental judgments than some arbitrary and
facile assumption about the number of 'wars', or fronts, that must be
prepared for."[8]
While such a flexible approach seems attractive, it counters
traditional methods of force planning that examine plausible campaigns in
specific regions, determine the force level required to meet that threat
and then select force structures based on prudent risk and resource
constraints. This matching of defined objectives and available resources
is a good definition of strategy.[9] Clearly, the number of contingencies
foreseen and the forces planned in their behalf are directly related to a
perception of the threat. A major change in threat perception, one that
began to emerge in the late 1970s, has led to a new formulation of the
strategic concept for the 1980s.

**What was the perception of the threat?   How did this threat
perception affect the formulation of the strategic concept?**

In attempting to undo the "artificial rigidities" that past strategic
concepts had allegedly imposed upon U.S. capabilities to cope with a
variety of lesser contingencies, the U.S. was also faced with an additional
complicating factor: the growth of Soviet military power. According to
another architect of the Reagan administration's strategic concept, it was
gains in Soviet conventional war fighting capability (in addition to the
perceived vulnerability of U.S. land-based strategic forces) that placed an
added strain on U.S. ability to deter conventional conflict. The United
States, in formulating a new strategic concept, was responding to a sense
of threat: "Indeed, a prime reason for the greater requirements for
U.S. capabilities in regions such as Southwest Asia (SWA) was that
increase in the quality and quantity of Soviet weaponry capable of being
employed in those areas."[10]
Thus, in the early 1980s, the U.S. perception of the Soviet threat to
its vital interests was a grave one. Secretary Weinberger pointed out that
the U.S. defense effort had not "taken sufficient account of the
continuing increase in the military capabilities of the Soviet Union" and
that "Soviet power threatens us directly."[11] So serious was this vision of
the threat that a document entitled <u>Soviet Military Power</u> was appended

to the FY 1983 Annual Defense Report. Yet, the Defense Secretary claimed that the 1983 document was already outdated by the FY 1984 Report, owing to the "rapid pace of Soviet force improvements."[12] The failure of the United States to equal this pace had "not only enabled the Soviet Union to turn to a more offensive posture," but also had resulted in "a shift in the military balance."[13]

This reevaluation of military strategy reached by comparing U.S. military capabilities with those of its Soviet adversary has yielded a number of corollaries to the revised strategic concept that appears to dominate American defense policy in the early 1980s.[14] First, and perhaps existing separately from the strategic rationale, it is evident that the United States must build up its military forces. Secondly, unlike the alteration of the strategic concept in the late 1960s, this strategic switch promises increased defense spending.[15] Third, the new strategic concept suggests a move away from traditional military strategies that were reactive and defensive in nature. While Secretary Weinberger notes that U.S. peacetime strategy is one based on deterrence and defense, Dr. Ikle cautions us not to confuse the defensive orientation of peacetime U.S. strategy with the offensive tactics of war. Thus, the United States will no longer telegraph its wartime strategy to Soviet planners. A genuine U.S. counter-offensive threat, one that could affect the outcome of the war, will inject an element of uncertainty and, therefore, of deterrence into the adversary's risk calculus.

The application of this strategic concept to generate a build-up of U.S. forces capable of carrying an offensive to the Soviet Union suggests a fourth element of the strategy: "The United States must become more flexible in its ability to cope with threats world wide."[16] Therefore, a limited contingency in the Persian Gulf or elsewhere, to put the strategic concept into language used in this book, cannot be thought of as a "half war." Rather, given Soviet capabilities of power projection, a "brushfire" engagement in the Gulf could rapidly escalate into a US/USSR "firefight." Nor was there a guarantee that the decision to escalate such a conflict horizontally would remain solely an American one.

A final element of this emerging strategic concept in the early 1980s is an emphasis on U.S. maritime superiority. Like other concerns that have generated this concept, this component also appears to react to a sense of threat. The statement of Thomas Hayward, Chief of Naval Operations, that the U.S. had "lost its margin of maritime superiority over the Soviet Union"[17] ensured that a substantial naval force build-up--often referred to as a 600-ship Navy--would be planned and programmed. This naval role has also been interpreted not only as a defensive one of protecting sea lanes, but also one of conducting "offensive operations against naval forces and facilities, should that be required after attacks are launched by them."[18] In order to regain this required maritime dominance, both numbers and capabilities of ships are necessary.[19]

Thus, the change in the U.S. strategic concept being proposed in the early 1980s was based to a significant extent on a changed perception of the threat. While it can be argued that containment of the Soviet Union guided actions taken by the Carter administration as much as it did other post-war administrations, the choice between confrontation or cooperation during most of the Carter presidency was left to the Soviets. The Reagan administration, however, appeared to lean more toward a confrontational stance with the Russians and emphasized the central role the USSR played in the formulation of American foreign and defense policy. "The Soviet Union underlies all the unrest that is going on," stated the President-elect. He continued: "If they weren't engaged in this game of dominoes, there wouldn't be any hot spots in the world."[20] Thus, the primary task the United States faced in the early 1980s was to revitalize containment by building and brandishing America's military might.[21]

How were forces designed and deployed in support of the strategic concept? What priority was allocated to forces planned to meet a lesser contingency?

In his first report to Congress, Secretary Weinberger emphasized the importance of planning conventional forces for many different contingencies and the need to cope with a wide range of threats.[22] In structuring U.S. land forces, the attempt was to strike a balance between "heavy" and "light" forces in order to improve their capabilities and responsiveness. The dilemma attending the rapid deployment of such forces was admitted in the FY 1983 Posture Statement:[23]

> Those forces that are most rapidly deployable are least suited for large-scale combat against heavily armored forces. The more capable mechanized and armored divisions place a severe strain on our strategic airlift resources. . . .

Despite the acknowledgment of this constraint, the Reagan administration did not shrink from the task of planning forces in support of the new strategic concept nor from allocating those forces to meet a range of contingencies. The long-term goal was "to be able to meet the demands of a worldwide war, including concurrent reinforcement of Europe, deployment to Southwest Asia (SWA) and support in other potential areas of conflict."[24]

Focusing particularly on a contingency in the Persian Gulf, Secretary Weinberger devoted a section of his FY 1983 annual report to "Rapid Deployment Forces for Southwest Asia." In that section he noted that "although no new combat forces were created for the RDJTF," its commander has been given operational control over several Army and Air Force units.[25] In addition, the RDJTF Commander had access to a "reservoir of forces" which were described "in generic terms" by the table on page 233.

Yet, this impressive listing of forces available for deployment to a SWA contingency was not greatly expanded over the baseline force of the Carter years. By the end of FY 1984, the total U.S. planned force structure would continue to consist of 19 active divisions (16 Army and 3 Marine) and 10 Reserve divisions. While naval and air forces were expected to grow at a greater rate over the five-year plan, these numbers did not appear adequate to support the ambitious strategy being formulated, nor were they allocated specifically to a non-European contingency. Thus, the modification of the strategic concept and the apparent elevation of non-European contingencies to a priority equal to that of a NATO-Warsaw Pact scenario had not affected significantly U.S. general purpose force planning in the near term.[26] Therefore, while the issue of priority among lesser contingencies appeared to be resolved in favor of a desired capability to conduct concurrent combat operations in all theaters of concern, owing to a "collective failure to preserve an adequate balance of military strength during the past decade or two,"[27]

U.S. forces appeared unable to deter or defend on such a scale. Thus, the architects of the Reagan defense policy were forced from the top to adopt a bottom line: increase defense spending.

What was the impact of budgetary or public opinion constraints on the process of force planning for a lesser contingency?

In stark contrast to the early Carter years, neither budgetary constraints nor perceptions of limits imposed by public opinion affected the Reagan administration's initial formulations of defense policy. Secretary Weinberger's first Posture Statement made clear the assumption that Ronald Reagan had been granted a mandate that permitted, even demanded, the rearming of America.

But more defense spending is not a military strategy, and the strategic concept being formulated by defense planners within the Reagan administration appeared as one particularly difficult to implement. While initial defense budgets essentially mirrored the programs of their predecessors, albeit with fuller funding, the Reagan/Weinberger team was determined to make up for what they regarded as underfunding in the past. The continued efforts on the part of the administration to advocate increases in defense spending of approximately 10 per cent per year in real dollars contributed to a gathering public debate on the defense budget; and, if public opinion polls are to be believed, an apparent decline in public support for such spending sooner than might have been imagined:[28]

> Thus, they (public opinion polls) have shown a drop from 71 per cent in February 1980 to 14 per cent in 1983 of those who said they favored an increase in defense spending. At the same time, those favoring a decrease rose from 6 per cent to 45 per cent, while the share of respondents who were for maintaining current defense levels rose from 21 to 33 per cent.

Objections to the size of the defense budget came from three principal quarters: fiscal, industrial and strategic. In the first case many of the Pentagon's traditional Congressional allies were, by early 1983, expressing concerns echoing those of its long-time opponents: real increases in defense spending, coupled with significant tax cuts, were resulting in large federal deficits, higher interest rates and uncertain and imbalanced economic growth.[29]

Those concerned with the ability of the defense industrial base to respond to the defense initiatives of the Reagan administration argued that throwing money at a sluggish industrial base through inadequate and inefficient weapons acquisition procedures might be counterproductive. Increasing defense budgets without concern for how these weapons systems were to be procured was likely to result in "reduced force readiness and sustainability, declining industrial productivity and responsiveness, and greatly reduced quantities of military equipment."[30]

From the perspective of this study, the strategic critique of the revised concept and the attendant defense spending was most telling. Writing in the annual Brookings volume of Setting National Priorities,[31] William Kaufmann argued persuasively that the size and allocation of the forces planned were, in some cases, unrelated to both national and regional security. While the administration's force planners rejected the

TABLE 6.1
Combat Forces Available to the RDJTF, 1982

Army

1   Airborne Division
1   Airmobile/Air Assault Division
1   Cavalry Brigade Air Combat (CBAC)
1   Mechanized Infantry Division
Rangers and Unconventional Warfare Units

Marines

1-2   Marine Amphibious Forces (MAF)*

Air Force

4-11   Air Force Tactical Fighter Wings (with support air forces)
2   Squadrons of Strategic Bombers (the Strategic Projection Force)

Navy

3   Carrier Battle Groups (CVBGs)
1   Surface Action Group
5   Air-ASW Patrol Squadrons (VP)

Headquarters

1   Army Corps Headquarters
1   Naval Forces Headquarters
1   Air Force Forces Headquarters

*A MAF typically consists of a reinforced Marine division and a Marine aircraft wing (roughly twice the size of an Air Force tactical fighter wing).

Source: Casper W. Weinberger, Secretary of Defense Annual Report to the Congress, Fiscal Year 1983, p. III-103.

concept of contingency planning, the pursued objectives remained basically unchanged from previous defense regimes, with a focus on Europe and the Persian Gulf. But Kaufmann warned this administration was attempting to do too much too fast. Incomplete programs were likely to impose "severe limits on the number of units that could be deployed quickly in a worldwide emergency."[32]

Irrespective of these criticisms, the Reagan administration refused to retreat from its budget in support of the revised strategic concept. Because of the perceived likelihood of a direct Soviet challenge to U.S. interests in a range of contingencies, all of these "firefight" scenarios required ample and adequate support. Although the "half war" had been raised to a priority almost equal to a European contingency, it was becoming difficult to disaggregate or differentiate among competing contingencies. The strategic concept being formulated demonstrated once again the difficulty of reconciling declaratory policy, force planning and budgetary programs into coherent form. Organizationally, however, that process was aided by the evolution of the RDJTF into a new joint-service unit, the Central Command.

Organizing for Rapid Deployment in the 1980s

In Chapter 3 the suggestion was made that organizations fashioned to lead limited contingency forces were to some extent a function of the prevailing strategic concept. In the days of the ambitious "2-1/2 war" strategy, the STRIKE Command was created, at least initially, to fight the "half war" on a global basis. At a time when the United States was contracting its global reach and reducing its strategic concept, rapidly deployable forces were subsumed under Readiness Command, a non-combatant command. Only when U.S. vital interests were perceived to be threatened in the Persian Gulf was a new Rapid Deployment Joint Task Force formed, and that approach, as documented here, relied first on "brushfire" forces to meet a possible "firefight" contingency.

Therefore, it might have been expected, based on the escalatory and global strategic concept just described, that a Rapid Deployment Force for the eighties would be modeled in the image of STRIKE Command--in a general purpose forces' version of a policy of massive retaliation--rather than fashioned as a mirror-image of USREDCOM. Such is not the case. The new Central Command, established in January 1983, has much in common with the traditional structure and mission of a unified command and displays few characteristics of a rapid deployment force designed to extinguish global brushfires. This section of the chapter examines the organization of USCENTCOM in order to describe its role, explain its function, and predict its contribution to organizing for rapid deployment in this decade.

Is the organization a unified command with direct control over its assigned forces?

To answer the first part of the question, USCENTCOM bears most of the trademarks of a unified command. USCENTCOM is composed of all four services with a single unified commander.[33] The creation of the Central Command required a change in the Unified Command Plan and the assignment to USCENTCOM of an area of responsibility previously shared by the U.S. European Command and the Pacific Command as well as some areas previously unassigned. One of the principal advantages of having a single command in the region is that the countries affected are able to deal with only one organization on most security issues.[34]

While the allocation of this vital region to a single unified command appeared as a rational choice, there was a bureaucratic rationale as well. The RDJTF had been plagued by conflicting and controversial command arrangements--some more apparent than real. But it became clear that the separate military services were somewhat reluctant to surrender to a contingency task force units earmarked for other areas of responsibility. Nor were they willing to cede operational control or grant geographic sovereignty to the task force commander--particularly one of another service.[35] The Army, for example, was unwilling to commit a majority of its strategic reserve planned to reinforce NATO to a Persian Gulf contingency, while the Navy's reluctance to "chop" to the RDJTF Commander stemmed from its traditional view of the global mission of naval forces in the event of war.

It appears that the creation of a unified command has overcome many of the difficulties that surrounded the initial force planning of the RDJTF. Personnel billets previously left vacant by services reluctant to participate have been filled with highly qualified people. The Headquarters itself is now considerably larger than it was as the RDJTF, having grown from 258 personnel in March 1980 to 846 three years later. Further, these spaces now appear allotted in a balanced ratio among the four services, and the initial impression of the RDJTF as a Marine/Air Force-intensive force has been lessened.[36]

USCENTCOM's control over its forces can be characterized as somewhat looser than that possessed by the RDJTF. Although no new combat forces were created for the RDJTF (nor have they been for USCENTCOM), the RDJTF Commander was given operational control over "several Army units and Air Force tactical fighter squadrons."[37] Whether or not this administrative change was made to facilitate the organization of forces tasked for rapid deployment or if it responded primarily to charges in the press and academe that the RDJTF was only a "paper" force, is not clear. At any rate, the placing of these forces under the operational control of a limited contingency force was short lived. With the transition from the RDJTF to USCENTCOM, the same forces "formerly available to the RDJTF are available on a priority basis for USCINCCENT planning, exercises and operations as necessary,"[38] but are not assigned to the operational command. However, USCENTCOM does have access to a "reservoir of additional forces" that would be assigned depending on the size and nature of the contingency. This force packaging concept is reminiscent of STRIKE Command, except that now the U.S. Readiness Command, STRIKE's replacement, in conjunction with the Joint Deployment Agency, would assemble the forces for deployment.[39] Although USCENTCOM's loose control over its to-be-assigned forces is not that different from other unified commands that depend on CONUS-based reinforcements, USCENTCOM is unique in that its headquarters and its component commands are not located within the area of responsibility. Further, while USCENTCOM is tasked with developing and implementing contingency plans for that region, it has limited assigned forces in peacetime.

What USCENTCOM does possess as a unified command, which the RDJTF did not, are subordinate Service Component commands. The Commander, U.S. Army Forces, Central Command (COMUSARCENT), is the Commander of the Third U.S. Army at Fort McPherson, Georgia. The Commander of the naval forces assigned to USCENTCOM is located at Pearl Harbor, and the Commander of USCENTCOM's air forces also commands, on a day-to-day basis, the Ninth Air Force at Shaw Air Force Base, South Carolina. In addition, USCENTCOM has available to it a joint unconventional warfare task force composed of special operations forces from the three services.[40] Like other unified commands, USCENTCOM has to live with the fact that the daily operations and training allegiances of the component commands lie with their separate services rather than with the Unified Commander. But the presence of these components clearly strengthens USCENTCOM's role and mission and enhances service cooperation to a greater extent than did the weaker organization of the joint task force.[41]

Are units dedicated to the command from each armed service component?

Combat units from each of the armed services are available rather than assigned to USCENTCOM, yet the component commands just described and the joint headquarters staff give USCENTCOM a truly multi-service flavor. Thus, the move to a unified command seems to have terminated the debate--conducted more in the press and on Capitol Hill than in the Pentagon--on whether a U.S. limited contingency force in the 1980s should be service specific, maritime-intensive or a truly unified command.

It is again somewhat surprising that an administration favoring the mobility and maneuver of a "maritime" as opposed to a "coalition" strategy would move in the direction of a unified command with an assigned area of responsibility, but those steps now appear irreversible. It is perhaps not so surprising that those advocating a primary role for the Marine Corps in a limited contingency force have not yet given up hope. Writing in the Summer 1983 edition of Policy Review, Jeffrey Record argues that the current force posture of USCENTCOM will be "slow on the draw" if required to deploy to the Persian Gulf because of the distance and the lack of available forward bases. Instead of a multi-service force based in the CONUS, Record calls, again, for a Navy/Marine RDF based at sea.[42]

While Secretary Weinberger has admitted the shortcomings of a unified command without forces or headquarters in the theater and has stated that "the feasibility of locating the headquarters in the SWA region is presently under study,"[43] Record's voice now sounds like a gratuitious rebuttal in a debate already decided. Part of that judgment may have been rendered based on a revitalization of the Marine Corps that occurred without its having to play a dominant role in the RDJTF. Although it may have been a "staggering blow," as some have contended,[44] when the Marine Corps was not designated as the rapid deployment force, the contributions of the Marine Corps in the early stages of the RDJTF, along with the presence of a Marine Amphibious Brigade earmarked for rapid deployment to the Persian Gulf, seem to have allayed the concerns of those most worried about the future of the Corps.[45]

More than a bureaucratic or organizational rationale, it was probably the perception of the threat in the region that led to the multi-service composition of the force. Robert Komer has pointed out that deterrence and defense against a Soviet military threat in the Persian

TABLE 6.2
U.S. Force Commitments to Rapidly Deployable Forces, By Service,
August 1982

Combat Forces	Numbers of Personnel
ARMY	
82nd Airborne Division	100,000
101st Airborne Division (Air Assault)	
24th Infantry Division (Mechanized)	
6th Combat Brigade (Air Cavalry)	
Various ranger and special forces units	
AIR FORCE	
1st Tactical Fighter Wing (F-15)	30,000
27th Tactical Fighter Wing (F-111)	
347th Tactical Fighter Wing (F-4)	
354th Tactical Fighter Wing (A-10)	
366th Tactical Fighter Wing (F-111)	
552nd Airborne Warning and Control Wing (E-3A)	
150th Tactical Fighter Group, Air National Guard (A-7)	
121st Tactical Fighter Wing, Air National Guard	
Reconnaissance squadrons	
Tactical airlift squadrons	
Conventional Strategic Projection Force	
Various other units	
NAVY	
3 Aircraft carrier battle groups	42,000
1 Amphibious Ready Group	
5 Squadrons of antisubmarine warfare patrol aircraft	
18 Near-term prepositioning ships	
MARINE CORPS	
Marine amphibious force (division + wing)	50,000
7th Marine Amphibious Brigade	
Total--All Services	222,000

Source: Congressional Budget Office from data contained in Fact Sheet, Public Affairs Office, HQ Rapid Deployment Joint Task Force, August 1982.

Gulf is a "tricky proposition." Contrary to Record's plan to withdraw U.S. ground forces from Europe and concentrate instead on maritime forces in the Indian and other oceans, Komer argues that neither local maritime superiority nor putting the Marines ashore in Oman could prevent a Soviet land grab of the Persian Gulf oil fields. Moreover, although there exist significant obstacles to both Soviet and American rapid deployment to the region, even a limited presence of U.S. forces could prove temporarily adequate as a trip-wire deterrent.[46] A focus on the Soviet threat in Southwest Asia or in other regions of concern is, therefore, likely to continue to stress the importance of a multi-service rapid deployment force under a unified command structure.[47]

Is a specific scenario or geographic area of responsibility assigned the command for contingency planning?

On October 1, 1981, the Rapid Deployment Joint Task Force was chartered as a separate force and was assigned operational planning responsibility for Southwest Asia. This narrowed scope, according to Secretary Weinberger, allowed the commander to "develop detailed plans for the wide range of possible contingencies in that region."[48] Now, with the establishment of the first new unified command in 35 years, this geographic area--to include Jordan and the Sinai--is assigned to USCENTCOM and documented in the Unified Command Plan. (See map on the following page.)

Further, as just suggested, the scenario envisioned to guide force and operational planning was becoming increasingly Soviet intensive. In the language of the FY 1984 Posture Statement, the primary mission of USCENTCOM "is to deter Soviet aggression and to protect U.S. interests in Southwest Asia."[49] However, it has been questioned if this is the most likely scenario that a U.S. force planner will face in the region, giving ammunition to those who argue that USCENTCOM should prepare for the most probable case, not the worst.

These arguments against worst-case planning appear to have history as well as significant budgetary savings on their side. But conjecture on the scale of Soviet capabilities and intentions in SWA or any other region is well beyond the scope of this study. Suffice it to say, that a Soviet invasion of Iran would appear to be for them an exceptionally risky and low-confidence affair.[50] Yet, as Thomas McNaugher has suggested, even a limited series of Soviet moves into a region would pose problems for the United States. "To the extent that a limited Soviet attack would yield greater leverage over the key regions where choices affect the flow of oil," Soviet leverage over Western interests would increase.[51]

A related problem remarked on by McNaugher is that although the Carter Doctrine implied the Soviet Union as the "outside force" threatening U.S. interests in the region, it did not define geographically those interests around the Gulf. In one sense, the creation of the Central Command, including the Gulf in its area of responsibility, has accomplished that. On the other hand, it is important to understand the nature of the Soviet threat in the region and to decide on what is both likely and inimical to U.S. interests in the region.[52] This focused planning process, now being undertaken by a well-staffed joint headquarters, may be one of the most significant contributions that Central Command can make to the organization of a coherent limited contingency force in the region.

Area of Concern for U.S. Rapid Deployment Forces in Southwest Asia

SOURCE: Adapted by Congressional Budget Office from U.S. Department of Defense Annual Report FY82.

Are forces assigned to the command trained and exercised for combat in a specific region or contingency?

Yes and no. The problem is forces that could be assigned to USCENTCOM and deployed to Southwest Asia are also assigned to USEUCOM or USPACOM or both and are, therefore, also trained and exercised in other regions for other contingencies. Barring the creation of new and separate forces for each region or contingency, an event that given the current budget debate and a commitment to the all volunteer force appears unpromising in the near term, steps to free these allocated forces for concurrent Southwest Asia duty become more complex and incremental. A few steps in that direction are mentioned at the conclusion of this chapter. More important here is that the establishment of a planning and implementing headquarters capable of deploying and commanding forces in a specific theater (and exercising them as well) appears as a major improvement over the STRIKE concept of a global responsibility with less than regional capabilities.

The creation of Central Command, therefore, moves away from the organizational image characterizing U.S. conventional force planning in the past--a strong, central reserve under a versatile command structure that could respond quickly to any global contingency. But, in tasking the same units to do double or triple duty, the issue of force versatility and concurrent availability has not been resolved.[53]

Nor is it likely to be. The "strategy-force mismatch," if that is how the baseline force structure compared with an ambitious strategic concept can best be described, is not a dichotomy easily fused. William Kaufmann suggested that only a "median" hedge against a greater than expected threat to vital U.S. interests could require 361,000 additional members of the armed forces.[54] In a world of constrained defense budgets, the luxury of singularly dedicated forces, trained and exercised for a specific contingency, appears unaffordable--particularly, if that number of contingencies is large. As in the past, hard choices will have to be made regarding U.S. and allied contributions to areas of vital interest. From an organizational perspective however, deploying and employing these heavily tasked forces under commands assigned to and familiar with a specific area of responsibility is a marked improvement over the old "go anywhere, do anything" limited contingency force.

Additionally, it should be pointed out here that this focus on USCENTCOM and Southwest Asia should not be interpreted as the final resting place of U.S. rapidly deployable forces, although that combination does appear as a key to creating coherent limited forces for other areas of vital interest. Rapid deployment forces--in small letters--still exist, as does the need for them, and USCENTCOM at its best still solves only part of the problem. Thus, the Congressional Budget Office has argued that rapid deployment forces could be used in areas other than Southwest Asia and in a recent study opts for the old terminology of RDF rather than focusing budgetary issues on CENTCOM.[55] Secretary Weinberger's statement may make the point more clearly:[56]

In general terms, we need a 'rapid deployment capability' primarily for those areas of the world in which the U.S. has little or no nearby military infrastructure or, in some cases, maintains no presence at all. There are many locations where we might need to project force, not only in Southwest Asia and the Middle East, but also in Africa, Central America, South America, the Caribbean and elsewhere.

And:

The primary focus on our rapid deployment programs is on enhancing the readiness of our existing forces for distant deployment and providing additional training, mobility and support for them.

Thus, the Central Command probably will never be directed to deploy its forces to regions outside its area of responsibility, but the forces themselves are clearly vulnerable to out-of-area tasking. In this regard, USCENTCOM can be seen as a case study for the organization and management of limited contingency forces, but not as a panacea for rapid deployment requirements.

As a final comment on USCENTCOM's contributions to a coherent limited contingency force for Southwest Asia, it is important to note that U.S. capability to conduct offensive operations in the region is enhanced through the frequent and realistic exercises conducted under USCENTCOM's supervision. The exercise of assigned forces plays several constructive roles: increasing operational readiness and familiarizing assigned forces with their area of responsibility as well as demonstrating U.S. resolve and capability through a show of military force. Thus, the series of "Bright Star" exercises in the region should reap more benefits than their cost.[57]

According to the FY 1984 Posture Statement, USCENTCOM will, by 1988, "have access to a combat-ready force capable of rapidly deploying and sustaining a substantial number of ground divisions with appropriate air and naval support."[58] But, despite this significant promised increase in the capability of USCENTCOM, particularly when compared with the RDJTF of the late 1970s, the formation of new strategic concepts and organizations is far easier to accomplish than the actual movement of limited contingency forces. The following section examines the prospects for strategic mobility in the 1980s.

Supporting Rapid Deployment in the 1980s

It has been said that amateurs speak of operations, while professionals talk logistics. As in the past, neither the formulation of a strategy that requires a rapid deployment capability nor the organization of a command dedicated to that purpose can assure the ability to move those forces in the time required for them to prove effective. Although a strategic mobility capability remains fundamental to rapid deployment requirements--indeed, all that separates them is warning time--major improvements in logistics have generally not accompanied accelerated changes in strategic concept and organization. Moreover, it appears at first glance that factors constraining the acquisition of improved strategic lift in the past will continue to act as barriers in the future. This portion of the chapter documents recent efforts to enhance U.S. strategic mobility programs and suggests the impact these initiatives may have in the decade ahead. As has been the custom throughout this study, the method of asking focused, iterative questions will again be employed.

What mobility systems have been proposed in support of a rapid deployment strategy? **Are these systems dedicated to a lesser contingency?**

Unfortunately for those pondering new systems of mobility to match strategy and organization in the 1980s, no new systems have been invented. The classic forms of projecting power overseas remain airlift, sealift, prepositioning and access to facilities.[59] During the first weeks of mobilization, airlift and prepositioning make their major contributions to a rapid deployment strategy. In the subsequent weeks, sealift and continued access to regional bases and facilities will provide the dominant means of transporting material for the reinforcement and sustainability of the in-place force. Therefore, all elements are important in maintaining a rapid deployment capability. Accordingly, improvements have been advocated and pursued by the Department of Defense in each area.[60]

- Airlift: Procurement of 50 C-5 aircraft and 44 KC-10 tanker/cargo aircraft, continued C-5 and C-141 modifications, a restructured CRAF enhancement program and continued research and development on the C-17.
- Sealift: Conversion of the 8 SL-7 ships to roll-on/roll-off capability and the funding of on-load/off-load programs to enable easy transfer from one lift mode to another.
- Prepositioning: The phasing out by 1986 of the Near Term Prepositioning Ships in favor of the Maritime Prepositioning Ships, capable of storing equipment and supplies for three Marine Amphibious Brigades, plus additional POMCUS in Europe.
- Access to facilities: Accomplishment of agreements with regional nations to preposition material and to use facilities during conflict or exercises.

Earlier, this study suggested the perceived fungibility of strategic mobility systems. The global utility of these systems continues to guarantee they will not be allocated solely to support a limited contingency in a certain region. The rationale is bureaucratic as well as strategic and economic. Such forces will not receive Congressional funding if they are seen, like the FDL, as an invitation to intervention. Conversely, they will more readily receive legislative support if, like the C-5, they display the capability for supporting a variety of U.S. commitments, particularly a major contingency in Europe. The Defense Department is not unaware of this phenomenon and, although it may well see newly proposed strategic mobility systems as enhancing rapid deployment to a range of scenarios, prefers to propose and discuss these systems under the heading of strategic mobility.[61]

Under that heading in the FY 1984 Posture Statement, the U.S. long term strategic mobility goal is "to be able to meet the demands of a worldwide war, including concurrent reinforcement of Europe, deployment to Southwest Asia and the Pacific and support for other areas." In the near term, the program is more modest than this logistical interpretation of a "3-1/2 war" strategy: "to reinforce NATO . . . in 10 days or to deploy a joint task force with required support forces to Southwest Asia within six weeks"--a more realistic "1-1/2 war" formulation.

To what extent have these systems been supported and acquired?

Airlift: Improvements have occurred in the existing airlift fleet. The C-141B "stretch" program was completed in 1982, increasing the carrying capacity of the C-141 and adding in-flight refueling capability as well. The service life extension program to remedy structural deficiencies in the wings of the C-5A is also on schedule and due to be completed by FY 1987.[62]

In a major procurement decision in January 1982, the Department of Defense, over alleged Air Force objections, proposed to increase airlift funding over the next five years by $5 billion in order to expedite the delivery of 50 C-5 aircraft. This option was defended over the competing C-17 program in that, given the immediate need for rapid deployment capability to Southwest Asia, this was the quickest way to increase airlift capacity. It was also judged doubtful that Congressional support for the development and acquisition of a new strategic mobility system would be forthcoming when the need for the C-17 had not been made clear.[63]

The C-17, however, may yet prove to be the airlift version of the B-1 bomber, although its reincarnated form is uncertain. The FY 1984 defense budget "includes a request for funds to continue research and development related to the C-17."[64] As before, the new airlifter is designed to carry outsized cargo (including the M-1 tank) and to operate from austere airfields, "thus greatly improving our ability to respond to global contingencies."[65]

Concurrently with the C-5 and C-17 programs, the Air Force and DoD have also sought to improve the quality and quantity of the Civil Reserve Air Fleet (CRAF). However, the first attempts to implement a CRAF improvement program--modifying wide-bodied aircraft during the production phase to be easily convertible from passenger to cargo-carrying capability--met with considerable resistance in Congress. Initial opposition appeared to be derived from old fears that the government would be subsidizing the airlines and appropriating them for public purposes. When a limited program was finally approved, the costs proved so exorbitant that CRAF enhancement funds were deleted from the FY 1983 budget.[66] Since then, $147.4 million has been placed in the 1984 budget, and with the program described as "the least expensive means of adding cargo capability," a renewed request is being forwarded by DoD to the aircraft industry.[67]

Sealift: In FY 1981-1982, the Department of Defense acquired eight high-speed SL-7 container ships, now being converted to roll-on/roll-off configuration.[68] These ships are purported to be capable of moving a mechanized division to the Persian Gulf in three weeks; although even with "ro-ro" capability, loading and unloading will add days to that mobilization forecast.[69] In addition, the Navy has programmed funds to expand the size of Ready Reserve Fleet from 29 cargo ships to 61 ships and 16 tankers by FY 1988. These ships, part of the National Defense Reserve Fleet, should be available for use within 10 days of notification, thus "reducing the time required to begin sealift operations."[70]

Prepositioning: The third major area in which additional strategic mobility can be acquired for the 1980s is prepositioning. While the POMCUS program in Europe has been the primary focus of this program thus far, it appears that maritime prepositioning has more to offer force planners preparing for a lesser contingency. In the Persian Gulf, the Maritime Prepositioning Ship (MPS) for the first Marine Amphibious

Brigade will be on station in 1984, with the three Brigade program completed by 1986. By that time the six-ship NTPS force will be replaced, with the depot ships remaining on station in Diego Garcia.[71]

Access to facilities: In any region in which the United States does not enjoy basing rights, access to enroute support, overflight rights and facilities for conducting combat operations become extremely important. Toward that end, the United States has reached formal agreement with a number of nations for permission to "preposition materiel, to use regional facilities during crises or to conduct routine training exercises during peacetime."[72] The emphasis here is not on constructing new U.S. bases or raising the visibility of the United States in the region, but on improving the capabilities for host nation support and guaranteeing that support will be available when needed.

In Southwest Asia, such an approach fits nicely with the USCENTCOM mission: to arrive on invitation only and to depart as soon as possible after the job is done.[73] In seeking facilities in SWA, U.S. efforts cover a wide geographic region. Egypt has offered access at Ras Banas on the Red Sea, a strategically located facility that will be upgraded by a substantial U.S.-funded construction program. Diego Garcia, far from the Straits of Hormuz, still remains a key maritime prepositioning base. Relatively small, but also significant construction projects have been negotiated for access rights in Oman, Kenya, and Somalia.[74]

These access rights not only enhance U.S. plans for rapid deployment to the region, they also further prepositioning initiatives. Thus, in addition to Diego Garcia, there are plans to store spare parts at Ras Banas in Egypt as well.[75]

What is likely to be the impact of these strategic mobility systems on the capability to deploy forces to a limited contingency?

Airlift: The combination of airlifting personnel to "marry-up" with prepositioned equipment has often appeared as the most effective rapid deployment method to a region that can be pre-designated. One of the inherent problems in this synergism is that the equipment must have been prepositioned properly and close to the conflict and remain in good working order. Time to break out the equipment, outfit the troops and then transport them to the battlefield will reduce the effectiveness of the method. Further, the process itself is a difficult one to rehearse on a large scale, yet its importance is too great to allow low confidence in its operation.[76]

There are other drawbacks. Airlift is expensive, requires long lead times to develop the regional infrastructure required and can deliver only small amounts of supplies and equipment when compared with sealift. Finally, current aiflift posture, owing to reasons already documented here, bears little resemblance to a force poised to deliver forces to austere environments or capable of moving forces simultaneously to distant and distinct regions. As long as airlift lacks the versatility required and the C-17 or any new airlifter remains politically vulnerable, the airlift contribution to rapid deployment to non-European contingencies in the 1980s is ikely to remain limited.[77]

Sealift: With airlift playing a limited role, sealift may offer the best alternative to enhance U.S. rapid deployment capabilities in this decade. Although sealift has generally not been characterized as a rapid deployment force multiplier, when combined with prepositioning and airlift already in place and when cost-benefit analyses are accomplished, sealift comes out looking surprisingly good.

However, a major program to construct fast military sealift is also likely to encounter political and bureaucratic objections. The first of these may be a rehash of counter-FDL, counter-intervention arguments. At a time of public debate regarding the proper role of the use of force in Central America as well as Southwest Asia, the ability to deploy rapidly significant force levels with their equipment to a wide range of contingencies may remain politically suspect and unpopular with the Congress.

If vestiges of the "Vietnam syndrome" can be overcome, a more likely obstacle to enhanced sealift is civil-military arguments over government interference in private shipping. Most recently, the Navy has been accused of failing to follow through on one of President Reagan's campaign promises to help the merchant marine by shifting more supply operations to private firms. The shipping industry has long contended that it is cheaper to have supply vessels within the Military Sealift Command manned by civilian crews, but the Navy has not concurred. A new fleet of ships under government control is likely to raise once again the issue of government interference in private shipping by using such vessels for point-to-point cargo missions.[78]

A growing concern with the expansion of the Soviet merchant fleet may tip the scales in favor of sealift and the building of new fast ships. Now the world's fifth largest fleet (the U.S. is eighth), the Soviet merchant fleet poses a military as well as an economic threat. Although few regard this "gap" as threatening, the point that the USSR fleet is now better equipped to support Soviet power projection is uncontested. Retired Admiral Thomas H. Moorer has called the USSR merchant marine the "greatest disparity" between U.S. and USSR combat capability based on its capacity to conduct significant deliveries of cargo during wartime and missions of electronic surveillance during peace.[79] If a perception of a threat can foment strategic and organizational change, perhaps it can also motivate improvements in strategic mobility.

Prepositioning: Land-based prepositioning requires the support of the host nation in terms of land and maintenance of the stored equipment. Although that may prove to be a relatively small budgetary expenditure, the political cost can be high. Highly visible stockpiles of U.S. equipment--valuable as a deterrent and a coupling mechanism in Europe--negate an "over-the-horizon" U.S. role in other regions. Further, such prepositioning may cause regional states to question the providing nation's non-aligned status or to accuse it of hosting an American "intervention" force. In Southwest Asia only a few countries are willing to offer sites for U.S. prepositioning. Moreover, prepositioning is essentially untried in battle and depends critically on the proper location of the equipment. In Southwest Asia or in other regions where the axis of expected attack is not as evident as in Western Europe, land-based prepositioning will continue to play a limited role.

Access to facilities: Prepositioning also depends on U.S. bases in the region of the contingency or agreed upon access to facilities where U.S. presence is minimal. Given the lack of available bases in Southwest Asia, for example, the negotiation of "contingency access rights" in some nations may be the best the U.S. can do in the near term. Efforts to gain access to air bases to the north in the USCENTCOM region of responsibility are also politically complicated. In Egypt, U.S. efforts to improve the installation at Ras Banas have run into a number of difficulties. One dispute, over whether Egyptian or American contractors would be used, nearly resulted in breaking off the negotiations. Although a compromise was reached, it appears that most of the $93 million authorized by Congress in FY 1983 will not be spent. Adding to Congressional concern was the stipulation by former President Sadat that the U.S. would have access to the base only if requested by a friendly Arab country to help repel an armed attack.[80]

In Turkey, the United States has signed an agreement to build one new air base and modernize two others, putting "NATO fighter bombers within easy striking distance of Soviet forces nearest to the Persian Gulf."[81] But the operative word here is "NATO," for Turkey has in quiet and diplomatic tones refused to grant permission for U.S. use of these bases in a unilateral U.S. deployment to the Persian Gulf while assuring the use of the bases in the event of a NATO contingency. It may be, of course, that the contingencies are not divisible and that a major initiative on the part of the United States to strengthen the southern flank of NATO through increased aid and the deployment of U.S. forces to Turkey could also deter Soviet actions in the Persian Gulf.

Base development and construction is a discipline unto itself, one that has come a long way since the first experiment in bare-base operations. In mid-1980, the U.S. Air Force updated its bare-base capability by deploying twelve F-4 aircraft to Egypt. Although the overall performance was judged successful, the most severe shortcoming was the "lack of large quantities of bare-base equipment." Also, such operations are still limited by the requirement for a long, modern runway and access to water. A final weakness in the system is the large amount of airlift required to deploy and sustain a relatively minimum force.[82] While the RDJTF was clearly not adequately staffed to do the kinds of base development planning required for similar operations, one of the major benefits of the presence of a unified command, such as USCENTCOM, is the additional logistic expertise to allow for such planning.[83]

Another major window of opportunity that the creation of USCENTCOM may allow the United States to exploit in gaining access and influence in the Southwest Asia region or other likely limited contingency areas is the coordinated use of security assistance programs. Such programs, embodying military aid and foreign military sales, can shore up host nation support and infrastructure and tie the target countries more closely to the United States. As the single manager for military activities in its area of responsibility, USCENTCOM, in October 1983, assumed primary responsibility for military assistance and arms sales in the region. This gives the command an opportunity to fit these programs with U.S. strategy in the region while enhancing regional stability and maintaining a relatively low profile.[84]

It appears in the early 1980s that security related aid and military sales have become important elements of American foreign and defense policy in regions of growing interest. Under current proposals, FMS financing for Egypt will be $1.3 billion in 1986, an increase of 136% over the 1981 amount. Significant percentage increases are also indicated for Morocco, Sudan, and Turkey. If security assistance is not a direct opening to military basing rights abroad, it is certainly a key to the door of facilities use.[85]

A robust policy of military aid or sales to any region must be selective.[86] Warnings of increasing economic dependency and difficulties in debt financing should not be lightly regarded. But in this decade of requirements for U.S. rapid deployment capability, it appears that much of the groundwork can be established through coordinated programs of security assistance. Most attractive here is a multilateral strategy oriented toward regional cooperation that could reinforce host nation support and domestic infrastructure while matching U.S. objectives in the region. A unified command with area responsibility is surely the most effective organization to pursue such a policy.[87]

Conclusion

The intent of this study was to argue that the United States in its past planning of general purpose forces has tended to concentrate on two, and then one, primary or major contingencies at the expense of other, lesser contingencies. In the halcyon days of U.S. nuclear supremacy, such a policy was both politically and economically attractive, if strategically unwise. The "half wars" inbedded in those past strategic concepts, owing to a number of factors including extended U.S. interests and Soviet power projection capability, can no longer be adequately planned for by subsuming them under a major European conflict. Contingency and force planning for these "half wars" of prior decades are likely to dominate U.S. efforts in this decade and the next.

Certainly, the major U.S. defense effort in terms of forces and budgets must continue for the immediate future to be allocated to NATO-Europe. But the same criteria used to determine appropriate levels of European defense must now be applied to measure U.S. readiness for deployment and contingency operations in other areas. In an historical development of U.S. force planning for limited contingencies, this study focused on three elements of U.S. military strategy.

- The strategic concept: The United States must determine where its vital and regional interests lie and construct strategies and forces to defend those interests. Key to this principle is the matching of the force structure with the strategy in size, character and readiness. The simple aggregation of the various "half wars" into a single strategic concept not only prevented adequate force planning to meet a range of contingencies, but also contributed to confusion as to which of these peripheral interests demanded and deserved U.S. military commitment. While a strategic concept too narrowly drawn may invite aggression, too grand a concept must depend on the shadow rather than on the substance of power. In the end, there appears to be no substitute for making difficult decisions regarding the number and the location of contingencies that affect U.S. vital interests and planning general purpose and rapidly deployable forces to meet those contingencies.

- The organizational role: When the limited contingency has been disaggregated to focus on a specific region and a particular adversary in the Persian Gulf, Northeast Asia or the Caribbean, forces can then respond to the threat, be tailored to the region and exercised within it. The command structure that has proved over time to be the most effective in leading multi-service forces in such a region against a given threat is the unified command. In that regard, the creation of USCENTCOM, with its area of responsibility as one of defined national interest, appears as a step in the right organizational direction. Prescient force planners might extend this concept and anticipate the need for a similar command in other, as yet unassigned geographic regions. If the alarm bells begin to ring in southern Africa later in this decade, a command and control mechanism already in place, modeled along the lines of USCENTCOM, may significantly enhance the rapid deployment of U.S. forces and the attainment of U.S. policy objectives in that region.

- The mobility equation: Regardless of the number of in-place forces or amounts of prepositioned equipment, strategic mobility systems are required to reinforce or deploy forces to the contingency area. Along with the need for greater strategic lift capability in a combination of forms dependent on the contingency are requirements for political, logistical and military support from the states in the region. The most promising system to enable U.S. forces to deploy rapidly with sustainability in the future appears to be fast sealift. Accompanying that acquisition of added deployment capability should be the formulation of a multilateral strategy that weaves together programs of host nation support, foreign military sales and security assistance.

While the original purpose of this study, in focusing on the above elements of a rapid deployment strategy, was to explain why the United States has enjoyed little success in constructing a coherent limited contingency force over the last two decades, this final chapter has speculated on the prospects for such a force in the next. A completion of this effort demands at least a suggestion as to how this force might be constructed. Larger force levels and increased strategic lift will be required. A coherent limited contingency force cannot be constructed, as the Carter administration had hoped, from solely existing capabilities. But neither must it be fabricated from whole cloth. The following approaches are offered from the perspective that the creation of a military capability to support U.S. interests in contingency areas outside NATO Europe is both necessary and attainable within reasonable budgetary constraints.

1. Structure U.S. forces in support of a limited contingency force for the region of responsibility. Current estimates for an effective ground component of a limited contingency force to meet an enemy above the "brushfire" level range from 4 to 6 divisions. Although limited initiatives are underway to increase the manpower of the armed services, a force of this size, barring conscription and the declaration of a national emergency, is not likely to be raised in the near term. Therefore, units to meet a lesser contingency must be extracted from the ten active-duty CONUS divisions.[88] However, the majority of these forces are already earmarked for NATO reinforcement. The most obvious, immediate, and

low-cost option to meet this need is to dedicate the required active forces to the "half war" (for example, to USCENTCOM and the Persian Gulf contingency) and replace those NATO-pledged units with equivalent and strengthened divisions and air wings from the National Guard and Reserve. For a number of reasons, this option seems prudent: the calling of Reserves has been generally decoupled from a lesser contingency; Reserve and Guard units, particularly tactical air, train for and in the European environment, and rapid deployment is not as essential in NATO Europe because there is no need for a preemptive strategy, a show of force or the rapid insertion of military force to enhance deterrence.[89]

A restructuring of the active forces committed to a limited contingency is also important. One of the most common complaints regarding the RDJTF as a fighting force was that it appeared as a composite of traditional force structures, tending to emphasize large unit tactics and long supply lines. However, if multi-service units assigned to a limited contingency force were restructured to emphasize scenario-specific flexibility and mobility, it is possible that a more cost effective and combat effective force could be employed. Among these improvements could be tactics and weapons oriented specifically to mountain or desert warfare, the use of light weight infantry fighting vehicles and adequate strategic and tactical lift capable of inserting the force at the right time and place.[90]

2.   Allied burden sharing. If the United States is to extend its vital interests--and those of its industrialized allies--to non-European contingencies, it may be helpful to seek additional allied contributions to ease the American defense burden in regions of current commitment. The need for NATO support of U.S. initiatives in the Persian Gulf, for example, has been officially acknowledged. In somewhat of a watershed decision, the Final Communique issued at the meeting of the Defense Planning Committee of NATO in May 1980 recognized that the "altered strategic situation in Southwest Asia warrants full solidarity and the strengthening of allied cohesion as a response to new challenges."[91] Although the communique noted that the burden of defense of the region had fallen largely on the United States, the Ministers "agreed on the need for ensuring that at the same time as the U.S. carries out the efforts to strengthen defense capabilities for Southwest Asia ... Allied capabilities to deter aggression and defend NATO Europe are also maintained and strengthened."[92] Ministers pledged themselves to increase their efforts to improve the capabilities of the full spectrum of forces committed to the alliance and agreed to do their utmost to meet additional burdens for NATO security resulting from increased U.S. activity and responsibilities in the Persian Gulf.

With regard to NATO support of U.S. military action in Southwest Asia, the communique of the December 1980 Ministerial meeting also clarified the European commitment. The Ministers agreed that it would be essential to "prepare against the eventuality of a diversion of NATO-allocated forces" that might occur as a result of a U.S. deployment to Southwest Asia. To assist the United States in that event, the NATO Ministers "affirmed the intention of their countries to provide host nation support to facilitate the reception and employment of reinforcement forces."[93] This commitment has been interpreted to mean additional support within Europe to release U.S. mobility systems from their European tasking (for example, a European CRAF), support for U.S. forces being deployed through Europe to the Persian Gulf (as was not always available in 1973)[94] and access to enroute facilities in and around the Gulf.[95]

While these burden sharing issues are frequently captured by the current interests centered on Southwest Asia, the principle should not be restricted to this or European theaters. Similar initiatives should be continued to elicit a greater sharing of the defense burden by Japan and the combining of multi-national, economic, military and political efforts among the states in the Caribbean basin.

3. Improving linkages with the countries in the region. Close ties between the United States and regional states will increase mutual confidence in the U.S. commitment to regional security and will facilitate U.S. entry into the area if a threat so dictates. Most important is maintaining a capability for access that allows for rapid deployment and tactical flexibility.[96] An additional goal is to gain increased participation of the regional states in security planning and providing host nation support. As Geoffrey Kemp has suggested, a united military effort in Southwest Asia including the U.S., Turkey, Egypt, Saudi Arabia and Oman, could pose a formidable alliance considering the forward bases, logistical support, infrastructure and additional armed forces that would result from such a coalition.[97]

Major U.S. initiatives on a bilateral basis to expand host nation support and provide military assistance are also likely to prove productive. In the Persian Gulf region, despite growing U.S. arms transfers to the region, most "pro-Western" states have little to offer, except their strategically-placed territory, in the way of military capability. Saudi Arabia, North Yemen, Oman and the United Arab Emirates all face severe manpower shortages and lack necessary technical skills. The key assistance these nations may be able to provide, in addition to facilities access, is the logistical support required for U.S. force deployment. One way to enhance this support is through coordinated programs of security assistance. Indeed, the proffering of host nation support by the regional states may well be the most important element in the long term ability of the United States to deploy forces rapidly to a limited contingency.

In the end, it will not be an abstract strategic concept, a single organization or a new mobility system that alters, directs or transports U.S. rapid deployment strategy in the 1980s, but the willingness of the American government and people to support the force structure required to meet U.S. security interests. Those forces, those interests and those contingencies are subject to change. Until the end of this century, however, the planning of U.S. general purpose forces to meet a range of limited contingencies will play an important role in guaranteeing U.S. security and supporting U.S. commitments. The strategic, organizational and logistic experiences of the past two decades have shown us how not to go about it. The challenge in the 1980s is to learn from these experiences and to construct a coherent limited contingency force by matching rapid deployment strategies, organizations and support.

NOTES

1. The Organization of the Joint Chiefs of Staff, United States Military Posture for FY 1984, p. 56. USCENTCOM is charged with U.S. security interests in Southwest Asia, the Persian Gulf and the Horn of Africa, a region collectively referred to as the "central area." The terminology has created some confusion, particularly for Europeanists fond of referring to the "central region."

2. Some analysts might argue that the "half war" mission was excepted from the strategy of containment in that it did not seek to defend vital U.S. interests from Soviet encroachment. See Barry R. Posen and Stephen Van Evera, "Defense Policy and the Reagan Administration: Departure from Containment," International Security, Vol. 8, No. 1 (Summer 1983), p. 10.

3. See the discussion in Posen and Van Evera, pp. 28-34, and the speech by Thomas C. Reed reported by the New York Times, "U.S. Policy said to focus on prevailing over Russians," June 17, 1982, p. B17. However, one should also note Secretary Weinberger's FY 1984 report which stresses, in an overview of U.S. defense strategy, that "our strategy is defensive." Annual Report to the Congress FY 1984, p. 32.

4. Weinberger, Annual Report FY 1983, p. I-15.

5. For an analysis of the horizontal escalation concept, see Kevin Lewis and Mark Lorell, "Out of Area Escalation: Concepts, Historical Lessons and Applications" (Santa Monica: RAND, forthcoming).

6. Fred Charles Ikle, "The Reagan Defense Program: A Focus on the Strategic Imperatives," Strategic Review (Spring 1982), pp. 11-34. Much of this article is included verbatim in Secretary Weinberger's FY 1983 Posture Statement. See also Ikle, "Strategic Principles of the Reagan Administration," Strategic Review (Fall, 1983) pp. 13-18.

7. Ibid.

8. Ibid.

9. See Gaddis, Strategies of Containment, p. 23-24.

10. Dov S. Zakheim, "The Unforeseen Contingency: Reflections on Strategy," Washington Quarterly (Autumn 1982), pp. 158-166.

11. Weinberger, Annual Report FY 1984, p. 19.

12. Ibid., p. 25. Some find this continual stress on the Soviet threat as unhelpful both to domestic resolve and to alliance solidarity. See Posen and Van Evera, op. cit. and Michael Howard, "Deterrence and Reassurance," Foreign Affairs (Winter 1982/1983), pp. 309-343.

13. Ibid., p. 27. For other interpretations of the military balance in the early 1980s, see Strategic Survey, 1982-1983 (London: IISS, 1983) and The Military Balance, 1982-1984 (London: IISS, 1983).

252

14. The following presentation relies heavily on the arguments presented by the Special Assistant to the Assistant Secretary of Defense (International Security Policy), Dov Zakheim, in the article cited earlier.
15. For the foreign policy implications of this approach, see Charles W. Kegley, Jr. and Eugene R. Wittkopf, "The Reagan Administration's World View," Orbis, Vol. 26, No. 1 (Spring 1982), pp. 223-244.
16. Zakheim, op. cit.
17. Cited in Zakheim, op. cit. See the written statement of Admiral Thomas B. Hayward in Military Posture and H.R. 2970 and H.R. 2614, Hearings before the House Committee on Armed Services (February, March, April 1981), Part 3, p. 592.
18. Weinberger, Annual Report FY 1984, p. 41.
19. Force planning for a 600 ship Navy, based on a 15-strong aircraft carrier force, receives criticism from at least two perspectives. First, the plan to take the battle to the Soviet homeland is an exceptionally risky one and may require even larger forces if such an operation is to be undertaken with any degree of confidence. Second, such a counteroffensive risks vertical (nuclear) as well as horizontal escalation. See Posen and Van Evera, op. cit., pp. 29-30. This emphasis on maritime superiority contained in the strategic concept of the Reagan administration has given rise to new discussions on an old strategic debate. For a supporting view, see Jeffrey Record and Robert J. Hanks, U.S. Strategy at the Crossroads: Two Views (Cambridge: Institute for Foreign Policy Analysis, 1982) and for a rebuttal, Robert W. Komer, "Maritime Strategy vs. Coalition Defense," Foreign Affairs (Summer 1982), pp. 1124-1144.
20. Quoted in Kegley and Wittkopf, op. cit., p. 230. See also President Reagan's 1983 Orlando speech in which he referred to the USSR as an "evil empire," Weekly Compilation of Presidential Documents, Vol. 19, March 14, 1983, Washington: GPO, 1983, pp. 367-369.
21. See Robert Osgood's characterization of the Reagan administration's defense policy in "The Revitalization of Containment," Foreign Affairs, Vol. 60, No. 3, pp. 465-502.
22. Weinberger, Annual Report FY 1983, p. I-14.
23. Ibid., p. III-3.
24. Ibid., p. III-91.
25. Ibid., p. III-103.
26. In 1981, U.S. deployable battle ships numbered 479. The FY 1984-1988 program "projects that the deployable battle force will grow to about 610 ships . . . by the early 1990s." Weinberger, Annual Report FY 1984, p. 140. The Air Force fighter force consists of 25 wings, projected to reach 28 wings by FY 1988. Weinberger, Annual Report FY 1984, p. 162. Also see "Army reported ready to seek a new division," Philadelphia Inquirer, December 24, 1983, p. 8. This report states that Army Chief of Staff J.A. Wickham favors reorganizing an existing division of 16,000 into a force of 10,000 for the rapid deployment mission.
27. Weinberger, Annual Report FY 1983, p. I-4.
28. Herschel Kanter, "The 1984-1988 Defense Program: The Debate Continues," Strategic Review, Vol. XI, No. 2 (Spring 1983), p. 38.
29. See "Weinberger defies fund-cutters to act," Chicago Tribune, February 1, 1983, p. 4; "Five year arms plan reaffirms growth," New York Times, February 1, 1983, p. 1; and Hedrick Smith, "Impasse reported in battle on funds for military," New York Times, September 16, 1982, p. 1.

30. Jacques S. Gansler, "Can the Defense Industry Respond to the Reagan Initiatives?" International Security, Vol. 6, No. 4 (Spring 1982).

31. William W. Kaufmann, "The Defense Budget" in Joseph A. Pechman, Setting National Priorities: The 1984 Budget, pp. 39-79. See also his critique of the Reagan program in the 1983 issue.

32. Ibid., p. 56. This critique is also heard within the Pentagon. See Richard Halloran "Military Forces Stretched Thin, Army Chief Says," New York Times, August 10, 1983, p. 1.

33. Because the CINCs of unified commands normally hold four-star rank, a move might be expected to elevate the USCENTCOM commander to that level. See Thomas L. McNaugher, "Balancing Soviet Power in the Persian Gulf," The Brookings Review (Summer 1983), pp. 20-24, and Strategic Survey, 1982-1983, p. 135.

34. "United States Central Command," information booklet.

35. Strategic Survey 1982-1983, p. 135. Now that the issue of a unified command in Southwest Asia has been resolved, there are few global disputes left. The new arena for such a bureaucratic struggle appears to be outer space. A dispute over space policy has also erupted within DoD with the Navy resisting an Air Force proposal that all military operations in space be unified under one command. See Richard Halloran, "Military Divided over Space Policy," New York Times, July 5, 1983, p. 11, and Fred Hiatt, "Military Considers Unified Space Command," Washington Post, August 27, 1983, p. 5.

36. Interviews, USCENTCOM, July 1983. One who visited the RDJTF in 1981 is also impressed with a change in style of operation. While the RDJTF was based in a distant bunker at MacDill Air Force Base, surrounded by barbed wire and guarded by fatigue-clad security police, the new USCENTCOM now occupies a modern building near the main gate. Combat dress is now worn only occasionally, the multi-service role is more apparent, and the sense of urgency has been replaced by one of long-term concern and planning for the area of responsibility.

37. Weinberger, Annual Report FY 1983, p. III-103.

38. Weinberger, Annual Report FY 1984, p. 194.

39. The functions of the Readiness Command and the Joint Deployment Agency have remained relatively unchanged by the formation of USCENTCOM. REDCOM remains a unified command that oversees U.S.-based Army and Air Force general purpose forces and provides these forces to unified commands abroad. The JDA, co-located with REDCOM and USCENTCOM at MacDill, is not a command, but a transportation management agency that provides centralized control and coordination for the deployment of U.S. forces.

40. Remarks prepared for delivery by Lt. General Robert C. Kingston, USA, CINCUSCENTCOM, San Antonio, Texas, April 7, 1983.

41. Interviews, USCENTCOM, July 1983.

42. "RDF too slow, Analyst Claims," Washington Times, June 20, 1983. In his latest prescription for a U.S. maritime strategy, Record's view of USCENTCOM is little changed from his attack on the RDJTF: it lacks sufficient forces and secure access to military facilities. These flaws should impel the Defense Department either to withdraw forces from Europe to bolster the Persian Gulf force or alter the force to be composed of naval and amphibious assault units. See Record and Hanks, op. cit., p. 28.

254

43. Weinberger, Annual Report FY 1984, p. 194. See also "Pentagon to open HQ in Persian Gulf," Chicago Tribune, December 1, 1983, p. 5.

44. See Michael Wright, "The Marine Corps faces the Future," The New York Times Magazine, June 20, 1982, pp. 16-19.

45. Even Jeffrey Record is more content: "Now the Corps is back in business of thinking about and doing things in that part of the world in which it was designed to fight--outside Europe." Ibid.

46. Komer, "Maritime Strategy vs. Coalition Defense," op. cit. Although a trip-wire deterrent is not the best alternative, it might serve a short-term purpose if one admits that the Soviet Union also faces severe barriers in deploying its forces to the Persian Gulf. See Epstin, "Soviet Vulnerabilities in Iran and the RDF Deterrent," op. cit. and Kevin Lewis, "Reorganizing U.S. Defense Planning to deal with new Contingencies: US-Soviet Conflict in the Third World" (Santa Monica: RAND, August 1982).

47. However, not all analysts are convinced that U.S. forces deploying to SWA should be sized against the Soviet threat. A recent CBO study suggests that an appropriately sized force limited to more modest police-like responsibilities would fit better current budget constraints and would pose less of a threat to forces already earmarked for NATO contingencies. Congressional Budget Office, "Rapid Deployment Forces: Policy and Budgetary Implications" (Washington: CBO, February 1983).

48. Weinberger, Annual Report FY 1984, p. 194.

49. Ibid.

50. See Epstein and Posen, op. cit.

51. McNaugher, op. cit.

52. Ibid. Thus, this debate over "likely" or "worst case" planning in the region mirrors the "half war" issue on a smaller scale. Can U.S. forces planned for a "firefight" against the USSR also deploy effectively to meet an internal, "brushfire" conflict? The simple answer of the "lesser included case" should not be allowed to forego force planning for a more limited contingency, nor should it be forgotten that many of the forces allocated to a "worst case" may, in the event of other contingencies, be unavailable for rapid deployment.

53. One promising effort in regard to meeting issues of force versatility and coherence is the experiment with regimental-style personnel systems, such as Project Cohort, now being introduced in the U.S. Army. Although the major purpose of these programs is to reduce personnel turbulence, a spin-off may be the creation of forces, tasked and trained for specific contingencies, which accrue a great deal of experience in those regions. For an examination of the issues involved in modifying the current individual replacement system in the Army, see Jeremy J. J. Phipps, "Unit Cohesion: A Prerequisite for Combat Effectiveness" (Washington: National Defense University, 1982).

54. William Kaufmann "U.S. Defense Needs in the 1980s" in Brent Scowcroft, ed., Military Service in the United States (Englewood Cliffs: Prentice Hall, 1982), pp. 31-37.

55. See CBO, "Rapid Deployment Forces: Policy and Budgetary Implications," op. cit.

56. Weinberger, Annual Report FY 1984, p. 191. Because the phrase "rapid deployment forces" implies specific units may be designated as an RDF, the current JCS/OSD preferred terminology is "rapidly deployable forces."

57. During "Jade Tiger 83," U.S. forces that could be tasked by USCENTCOM performed air defense exercises in Oman, Sudan and Somalia. "Bright Star 83" employed 5,500 U.S. troops in a summer desert exercise in Egypt, Sudan and Somalia. While there are considerable advantages in employing assigned forces in their region of responsibility, there are also disadvantages. For example, the deployment of ground combat forces to Honduras in the fall of 1983 was delayed "because of prior troop commitments, costs and lack of transport." Some "off the record" comments suggested that the large exercise in Central America "would underline the worldwide commitments that overextended the armed forces instead of demonstrating military power." See Richard Halloran, "U.S. Held Unready for Show of Force," New York Times, July 31, 1983, p. 11. Political sensitivities pose other problems. See "Egypt is Silent About Maneuvers With U.S.," New York Times, August 7, 1983, p. 6.

58. Weinberger, Annual Report FY 1984, p. 205.

59. A recent RAND study has concluded that a combination of traditional strategic mobility methods will still be required to support rapidly deployable forces in the future. While the study argues that only prepositioning allows for really quick deployment, it also concludes that no single system supplies all desirable attributes without significant risks and drawbacks. See "Improving U.S. Capability to Deploy Ground Forces to Southwest in Asia in the 1990s" (Santa Monica: RAND N-1943-AF, February 1983).

60. Weinberger, Annual Report FY 1984, p. 200.

61. These strategic mobility systems are discussed in greater detail in the FY 1984 report beginning on page 207.

62. Weinberger, Annual Report FY 1984, p. 212.

63. Vincent C. Hughes, "The Airlift Enigma and a Plan for the Future," Armed Forces Journal International (October 1982), pp. 25-32. See also Donald Lambro, "Air Force didn't want the C-5 in the first place," St. Louis Globe-Democrat, September 27, 1982, p. 16. Lambro argues that the Air Force wanted the C-17 capability to land on austere airfields--a capability the original C-5 was supposed to have. While the official explanation for the C-5 decision was one of urgency, that the C-5 would be delivered three years before the C-17, "internal Air Force documents" argued that the delivery dates would differ by "about a year." Lambro, writing from St. Louis, the home of McDonnell Douglas, claims the choice was based on Lockheed's misfortunes, not on the need for rapid deployment support.

64. Weinberger, Annual Report FY 1984, p. 212.

65. Ibid. Five C-5s have planned funding for FY 1984, with an added ten aircraft proposed for authorization in FY 1985. The procurement of these aircraft will raise the C-5 inventory to 127 by 1989. While the proposed acquisition of 60 new KC-10 tanker/cargo aircraft could be used in certain rapid deployment scenarios, their primary role is to support tactical fighter deployment, not lift combat cargo. See Hughes, op. cit.

66. Hughes, op. cit.

67. Weinberger, Annual Report FY 1984, p. 212.

68. Funds for this conversion were approved in FY 1982, and FY 1984 requested funds should complete the conversion of the remaining four ships. Weinberger, Annual Report FY 1984, p. 213.

69. Strategic Survey 1982-1983, p. 136.

256

70. Weinberger, Annual Report FY 1984, p. 214. An important partner to sealift and to rapid deployment capability in the 1980s is a capability to conduct "logistics over the shore," or LOTS. For a critique of present U.S. capability to conduct these operations as well as for recommendations to correct these deficiencies in reasonable cost and time, see Dan J. Beakey, "Logistics over the Shore" (Washington: National Defense University Monograph 82-6, 1982).

71. Ibid. While the NTPS program allows a Marine brigade to be put ashore at well equipped ports within 48 hours, the MPS system can move a division's worth of equipment ashore during that time in unimproved areas using its own offloading capability. These operations also have to occur in a relatively benign environment. See Strategic Survey 1982-1983, p. 136.

72. Weinberger, Annual Report FY 1984, p. 202.

73. Interviews, USCENTCOM, July 1983.

74. Weinberger, Annual Report FY 1984, pp. 204-205.

75. Strategic Survey, 1982-1983, p. 136. A plan to increase fuel storage capacity at Lajes Air Base in the Azores supports rapid deployment to Europe and Southwest Asia and suggests that similar facilities would be required for large-scale deployments to other regions.

76. William W. Kaufmann, Planning Conventional Forces, p. 24.

77. Although funds have been requested for C-17 R&D, its future is unclear. In 1983, Congress directed that all but $1 million of an appropriated $60 million be taken from other, lower priority Air Force programs. Congress to date has remained ambivalent in its support of the C-17, and the administration has not formulated a detailed program or proposed a total buy of the aircraft. See CBO, "Rapid Deployment Forces," pp. 34-35. Also see "Congress Dispute Stalls Buildup of Military Airlift," New York Times, July 20, 1982, p. 18, and "New Potshots at the C-17," St. Louis Globe Democrat, July 11, 1983.

78. See Robert F. Morrison, "Navy Accused of Hedging on Reagan Pledge," Journal of Commerce, July 15, 1983, p. B-1.

79. "Huge Expansion of the Russian Merchant Fleet Poses Economic and Military Problems for West," Wall Street Journal, July 22, 1983, p. 38.

80. The five-year improvement program at Ras Banas is now expected to cost about $400 million. See Richard Halloran, "Talks are Cut off on a base in Egypt," New York Times, May 20, 1983, p. 8, and "Both Sides say Egypt will build U.S. Base," Washington Times, May 25, 1983, p. 2.

81. George C. Wilson, "U.S.-Turkey Pact sets air forces nearer to USSR," Washington Post, November 7, 1982, p. 1. See also "Turkey plans to build NATO Military Air Base," New York Times, November 28, 1983, p. 7.

82. Lewis C. Sowell, "Base Development and the Rapid Deployment Force" (Washington: National Defense University No. 82-5, 1982).

83. Interviews, USCENTCOM, July 1983.

84. There are those who do not favor expansive U.S. security assistance programs. Harry J. Shaw has argued that military aid may add more to the economic peril of the recipients than it does to their military security and advocates development aid in its place. He also contends that the economic viability and political stability of countries buying large quantities of U.S. arms may be undermined owing to the large debts created. See "Debts and Dependency," Foreign Policy, No. 50 (Spring

1983), pp. 105-123. Others would argue that security assistance programs directed under USEUCOM were meeting these goals, were seen as less threatening by the recipients and could be better managed from Stuttgart than from MacDill.

85. Shaw, p. 106. See President Reagan's policy letter of July 8, 1981, approving a new conventional arms sale policy that described arms transfers as an "indispensable component" of U.S. foreign policy and rescinded many of the security assistance restrictions imposed by the Carter administration. Some, however, have pointed out that the arms transfer policies of the two administrations did not differ that much, despite the rhetoric. See Andrew K. Semmel, "Evolving Patterns of U.S. Security Assistance, 1950-1980," in Charles W. Kegley, Jr. and Eugene L. Wittkopf, Perspectives on American Foreign Policy (New York: Sr. Martin's Press, 1983), pp. 79-96.

86. In some cases, U.S. arms transfer policy can act as, what Thomas McNaugher has called, a "surrogate for prepositioning." An example is in Saudi Arabia where AWACS aircraft dedicated to Saudi air defense allow a U.S. presence. Continued Saudi purchases of sophisticated U.S. aircraft, munitions and spare parts, including the sale of 100 M-60 tanks (and rumors of a significant M-1 sale), can bolster Saudi military capabilities while easing the projection of U.S. power into the region. See McNaugher, op. cit.; Strategic Survey 1982-1983; and "U.S. Plans to Sell 100 M-60 tanks to Saudi Arabia," Baltimore Sun, August 2, 1983, p. 2.

87. Inteviews, USCENTCOM, July 1983 and "USCENTCOM Security Assistance Policy Paper," dated July 20, 1983.

88. William W. Kaufmann, "Defense Policy" in Agenda for the 1980s (Washington: Brookings, 1980) pp. 309-310.

89. USINCEUR would probably disagree with such a proposal. However he would also find it more agreeable than Jeffrey Record's plan to meet limited contingencies by withdrawing U.S. non-nuclear forces from Germany with the attendant alterations in the U.S. Army's size and force structure. See Record and Hanks, op. cit., p. 29. Moreover costs to enhance Reserve force improvements are not prohibitive. The FY 1984 budget for 16 divisions and 15 air wings of Guard and Reserve forces amounts to $11.6 billion. For an additional $28.2 billion, stretched over the five-year program, these forces could gain the equipment and training required to make them comparable with active duty forces. See William W. Kaufmann, "The Defense Budget" in Setting National Priorities: The 1984 Budget, p. 67.

90. See Steven Canby, "General Purpose Forces," International Security Review (Fall 1980), and "Pentagon Studies Fund Shift for Light Divisions for Army," Washington Post, August 9, 1983, p. 1.

91. U.S. Department of State incoming telegram subject: "Final Communique issued at the end of the meeting of the Defense Planning Committee of NATO in Ministerial Session held in Brussels on 13 and 14 May 1980," p. 1.

92. Ibid.

93. U.S. Department of State incoming telegram, subject: "DPC Ministerial Communique for 9-10 December Meeting," p. 3.

94. The fact that U.S. military action in the Persian Gulf in the 1980s rests on a far different set of assumptions than did the U.S. resupply effort to Israel in 1973 implies that European support is far more likely to be forthcoming. Obviously, European states are under

pressure from their Arab oil suppliers as well as that from the United States.

95.   The answer to continued U.S. and European defense of vital NATO interests, to include those "out of area" concerns, is not, as some advocate, a major withdrawal of U.S. forces from Europe, but rather a concerted effort to share the defense burden. The prospect for a stalwart conventional defense of the central region in Europe, and therefore for a strong conventional deterrent, is considered by many to be good and achievable without major budgetary sacrifices in competing economic sectors.   One simple measure that would allow both additional warning time to NATO and the reduction of manpower requirements during peacetime is a system of obstacles or field fortifications along the inner-German border, concentrated along the major axes of expected attack. Such fortifications, already in place in South Korea, need not present a "Maginot line" mentality nor preclude counter-offensive actions by NATO forces. See Kaufmann, Setting National Priorities: The 1984 Budget, pp. 65-66.

96.   As stressed by General David C. Jones, "Testimony before the Senate Armed Services Subcommittee on Seapower and Force Projection," March 12, 1981. Author's transcript.

97.   Geoffrey Kemp, "Military Force and Middle East Oil" in David Deese and Joseph S. Nye, eds., Energy and Security (Cambridge: Ballinger, 1981), p. 371. See the discussions regarding the concept of a "cooperative security framework" in U.S. Congress, Hearings on U.S. Interests and Policies toward the Persian Gulf, 1980, p. 69. Obviously these are severe political constraints acting against the construction of such a coalition.

Bibliography

Books

Acheson, Dean. Present at the Creation. New York: Norton, 1969.
Aliano, Richard A. American Defense Policy From Eisenhower to Kennedy. Athens: Ohio University Press, 1975.
Ball, Desmond. Politics and Force Levels. Berkeley: University of California Press, 1980.
Bauer, Theodore W. and White, Eston T. Defense Organization and Management. Washington, D.C.: National Defense University, 1975.
Beauffre, Andre. Strategy for Tomorrow. New York: Crane Russak, 1974.
Binkin, Martin and Record, Jeffrey. Where Does the Marine Corps Go From Here? Washington, D.C.: Brookings, 1976.
Blaufarb, Douglas S. The Counterinsurgency Era. New York: The Free Press, 1977.
Blechman, Barry M. and Kaplan, Stephen. Force Without War. Washington, D.C.: Brookings, 1978.
Bradford, Zeb and Brown, Frederic J. The U.S. Army in Transition. Beverly Hills: Sage, 1973.
Brennan, Donald G., ed. Arms Control, Disarmament and National Security. New York: Braziller, 1961.
Brodie, Bernard. A Guide to Naval Strategy. Princeton: Princeton University Press, 1958.
_____. War and Politics. New York: Mac Millan, 1973.
Brown, Neville. Strategic Mobility. New York: Praeger, 1964.
Caidin, Martin. The Long Arm of America. New York: E.P. Dutton, 1963.
Campbell, John C. Defense of the Middle East. New York: Harper and Row, 1958.
Clausewitz, Karl von. On War. Middlesex, England: Penguin, 1968.
Collins, John M. American and Soviet Military Trends Since the Cuban Missile Crisis. Washington, D.C.: Center for International and Strategic Studies, 1978.
_____. Grand Strategy. Annapolis: Naval Institute Press, 1973.
_____. U.S.-Soviet Military Balance: Concepts and Capabilities. New York: McGraw Hill, 1980.

Cordier, Sherwood S. U.S. Military Power and Rapid Deployment Requirements in the 1980s. Boulder: Westview, 1983.

Cottrell, Alvin J. and Hahn, Walter F. Naval Race or Arms Control in the Indian Ocean? New York: National Strategy Information Center, Inc., 1978.

Cyert, Richard and March, James. A Behavioral Theory of the Firm. Englewood Cliffs, NJ: Prentice Hall, 1963.

Deese, David A. and Nye, Joseph H., eds. Energy and Security. Cambridge, MA: Ballinger, 1981.

Deitchman, Seymour J. Limited War and American Defense Policy. Cambridge, MA: MIT Press, 1969.

_____. New Technology and Military Power. Boulder, Colorado: Westview Press, 1979.

Donovan, James A. Militarism, USA. New York: Charles Scribner's Sons, 1970.

Dulles, John Foster. War or Peace. New York: MacMillan, 1970.

Eccles, Henry E. Logistics in the National Defense. Harrisburg, PA: Telegraph Press, 1959.

Eisenhower, Dwight David. Waging Peace. New York: Doubleday, 1963.

Endicott, John and Stafford, Roy, eds. American Defense Policy. Baltimore: Johns Hopkins, 1977.

Enthoven, Alain C. and Smith, K. Wayne. How Much is Enough? New York: Harper and Row, 1971.

Etzold, Thomas H. and Gaddis, John L., eds. Containment. New York: Columbia University Press, 1978.

Gaddis, John Lewis. Strategies of Containment. New York: Oxford, 1982.

Gavin, James M. War and Peace in the Space Age. New York: Harper, 1958.

Gelb, Leslie H. and Betts, Richard. The Irony of Vietnam. Washington, D.C.: Brookings, 1979.

George, Alexander; Hall, David; and Simons, William. The Limits of Coercive Diplomacy. Boston: Little Brown, 1971.

George, Alexander and Smoke, Richard. Deterrence in American Foreign Polcy. New York: Columbia University Press, 1974.

Gordon, Kermit, ed. Agenda for the Nation. Washington, D.C.: Brookings, 1968.

Graber, Doris A. Crisis Diplomacy. Washington, D.C.: Public Affairs Press, 1959.

Greenwood, Ted. Making the MIRV. Cambridge: Ballinger, 1975.

Halperin, Morton, and Kanter, Arnold. Readings in American Foreign Policy. Boston: Little Brown, 1973.

Halperin, Morton. Limited War in the Nuclear Age. New York: John Wiley, 1963.

_____. Contemporary Military Strategy. New York: Little Brown, 1967.

_____. Bureaucratic Politics and Foreign Policy. Washington, D.C.: Brookings, 1974.

Head, Richard and Rokke, Ervin, eds. American Defense Policy. Baltimore: Johns Hopkins, 1973.

Hilsman, Roger. To Move A Nation. Garden City, NY: Doubleday, 1967.

Hoeber, Francis; Schneider, William; Polmar, Norman and Bessette, Ray. Arms, Men and Military Budgets. New York: National Strategy Information Center, Inc., 1980.

Hoopes, Townsend. The Devil and John Foster Dulles. Boston: Little Brown, 1973.

Horelick, Arnold and Rush, Myron. Strategic Power and Soviet Foreign Policy. Chicago: University of Chicago Press, 1966.

Horton, Barry; Rogerson, Anthony and Warner, Edward, eds. Comparative Defense Policy. Baltimore: Johns Hopkins, 1975.

Huntingon, Samuel P. The Common Defense. New York: Columbia University Press, 1961.

Hurewitz, J.C., ed. Soviet-American rivalry in the Middle East. New York: Praeger, 1969.

Hammond, Paul Y. The Cold War Years: American Foreign Policy Since 1945. New York: Harcourt Brace and World, 1969.

International Security: The Military Aspect. Special Studies Report of the Rockefeller Brothers Fund. New York: Doubleday, 1958.

Johnson, Lyndon Baines. The Vantage Point. New York: Popular Library, 1971.

Kahan, Jerome H. Security in the Nuclear Age. Washington, D.C.: Brookings, 1975.

Kalb, Marvin and Kalb, Bernard. Kissinger. Boston: Little Brown, 1974.

Kaufmann, William W. The McNamara Strategy. New York: Harper and Row, 1964.

_____, ed. Military Policy and National Security. Princeton: Princeton University Press, 1956.

Luttwak, Edward N. The Political Uses of Seapower. Baltimore: Johns Hopkins, 1974.

Kegley, Charles W. and Wittkopf, Eugene L., eds. Perspectives on American Foreign Policy. New York: St. Martin's Press, 1983.

Kinnard, Douglas. The War Managers. Hanover, NH: University Press of New England, 1977.

Kissinger, Henry. White House Years. Boston: Little Brown, 1979.

_____. Nuclear Weapons and Foreign Policy. New York: Harper and Brothers, 1957.

_____. Years of Upheaval. Boston: Little, Brown, 1982.

Klare, Michael T. War Without End. New York: Vantage, 1972.

Korb, Lawrence J. The Joint Chiefs of Staff. Bloomington: Indiana University Press, 1976.

Lauren, Paul Gorden, ed. Diplomacy. New York: The Free Press, 1979.

Lawrence, Richard and Record, Jeffrey. U.S. Force Structure in NATO: An Alternative. Washington, D.C.: Brookings, 1974.

Lewy, Guenter. America in Vietnam. New York: Oxford University Press, 1978.

Martin, Laurence, ed. Strategic Thought in the Nuclear Age. London: Heinemann, 1979.

May, Ernest R. "Lessons" of the Past. New York: Oxford University Press, 1978.

McBride, James and Eales, John, eds. Military Posture. Washington, D.C.: Center for Strategic Studies, 1964.

Nash, Henry T. American Foreign Policy. Homewood, Illinois: The Dorsey Press, 1973.

Newhouse, John. U.S. Troops in Europe. Washington, D.C.: Brookings, 1972.

Osgood, Robert E. Limited War. Chicago: University of Chicago Press, 1957.

_____. Limited War Revisited. Boulder: Westview, 1979.

_____, ed. Retreat From Empire. Baltimore: Johns Hopkins, 1973.

Owen, Henry, ed. The Next Phase in Foreign Policy. Washington, D.C.: Brookings, 1973.

Pechman, Joseph A., ed. Setting National Priorities: Agenda for the 1980s. Washington, D.C.: Brookings, 1980.

_____. Setting National Priorities: The 1978 Budget. Washington, D.C.: Brookings, 1977.

_____. Setting National Priorities: The 1982 Budget. Washington, D.C.: Brookings, 1981.

_____. Setting National Priorities: The 1984 Budget. Washington, D.C.: Brookings, 1983.

Peck, Merton J. and Scherer, Frederic M. The Weapons Acquisition Process. Boston: Harvard Graduate School of Business Administration, 1962.

Quandt, William B. Decade of Decisions. Berkeley: University of California Press, 1971.

Quester, George. Nuclear Diplomay. New York: Dunellen, 1970.

Record, Jeffrey. The Rapid Deployment Force. Cambridge: Institute for Foreign Policy Analysis, 1981.

Record, Jeffrey and Hanks, Robert J. U.S. Strategy at the Crossroads. Cambridge, MA: Institute for Foreign Policy Analysis, 1982.

Rice, Berkely. The C-5A Scandal. Boston: Houghton Mifflin, 1971.

Rodberg, Leonard S. and Sherer, Derek, eds. The Pentagon Watchers. New York: Doubleday, 1970.

Sarkesian, Sam C., ed. Defense Policy and the Presidency. Boulder: Westview, 1979.

_____, ed. Combat Efectiveness. Beverly Hills: Sage, 1980.

_____, ed. Nonnuclear Conflicts in the Nuclear Age. New York: Praeger, 1980.

Schilling, Warner R.; Hammond, Paul Y.; and Snyder, Glenn H. Strategy, Politics and Defense Budgets. New York: Columbia University Press, 1962.

Schlesinger, Arthur J. A Thousand Days. Boston: Houghton Mifflin, 1967.

Schneider, William and Hoeber, Francis, eds. Arms, Men and Military Budgets, FY 1977. New York: Crane Russak, 1976.

Schwarz, Urs. American Strategy: A New Perspective. New York: Doubleday, 1966.

Scowcroft, Brent, ed. Military Service in the United States. Englewood Cliffs: Prentice Hall, 1982.

Smith, Mark E. and Johns, Claude J., eds. American Defense Policy. Baltimore: Johns Hopkins, 1970.

Smith, Perry M. The Air Force Plans for Peace. Baltimore: Johns Hopkins, 1970.

Sorenson, Theodore. Kennedy. New York: Harper and Row, 1965.

Stern, Ellen P., ed. The Limits of Military Intervention. Beverly Hills: Sage, 1977.

Strategic Survey, 1976-1983. London: The International Institute for Strategic Studies.

Taylor, Maxwell D. Precarious Security. New York: W.W. Norton, 1976.

_____. The Uncertain Trumpet. New York: Harper and Row, 1959.

Thayer, Frederick C. Air Transport Policy and National Security. Chapel Hill: University of North Carolina Press, 1965.

The Military Balance. London: The International Institute of Strategic Studies, 1976-1983.

The Pentagon Papers. New York: Bantam, 1971.

Thompson, W. Scott. Power Projection. New York: National Strategy Information Center, Inc., 1978.

_____, ed. National Security in the 1980s. San Francisco: Institute for Contemporary Studies, 1980.

Thompson, W. Scott and Frizzel, Donald D., eds. The Lessons of Vietnam. New York: Crane Russak, 1977.

Tillema, Herbert K. Appeal to Force. New York: Thomas Y. Crowell, 1973.

Tucker, Robert W. A New Isolationism. New York: Universe Books, 1972.

van Crevald, Martin. Supplying War. Cambridge, England: Cambridge University Press, 1977.

Yarmolinsky, Adam. The Military Establishment. New York: Harper and Row, 1971.

Published Articles and Papers

"A Discussion of the Rapid Deployment Force with Lt. General P.X. Kelley." Washington, D.C.: American Enterprise Institute, 1980.

Adams, Paul D. "STRIKE Command," Military Review, Vol. 42, No. 5 (May 1962), pp. 2-10.

"Airlift/Sealift Capability Grows, but Problems Remain in Some Areas," Armed Forces Management, April 1967, p. 93.

Allison, Graham T., May, Ernest R., and Yarmolinsky, Adam. "Limits to Intervention," Foreign Affairs, Vol. 48, No. 2 (January 1970), pp. 245-261.

Allison, Graham T., and Morris, Frederic A. "What Determines Military Force Posture," Cambridge: Kennedy School of Government Discussion Paper, August 1975.

Allison, Graham T. "Conceptual Models and the Cuban Missile Crisis," American Political Science Review, 63, No. 3 (September 1969), pp. 689-718.

Art, Robert. "Why We Overspend and Underaccomplish," Foreign Policy (Spring 1972), pp. 95-99.

"Atomic Weapons and the Korean War," Bulletin of Atomic Scientists, VI (July 1950), p. 194.

Baldwin, Hanson W. "FDL," Marine Corps Gazette, March 1967, pp. 18-26.

_____. "The Navy at Ebb Tide," The Reporter.

Ball, George W. "Reflections on a Heavy Year," Foreign Affairs, Vol. 59, No. 3, pp. 474-499.

Bare, Gordon C. "Burden Sharing in NATO: The Economics of Alliance," Orbis, Vol. 20, No. 2 (Summer 1976), pp. 417-437.

Bell, Raymond E., Jr. "The RDF--How Much, How Soon," Army (July 1980), pp. 8-24.

Box, Clyde W. "U.S. STRIKE Command," Air University Review, September-October, 1964, pp. 4-14.

Brodie, Bernard. "Unlimited Weapons and Limited War," The Reporter XI (November 18, 1954), pp. 16-21.

Brown, Harold. "Planning our Military Forces," Foreign Affairs, June 1967, 177-190.

Bruen, John D. "Repercussions from the Vietnam Mobilization Decision," Parameters, Vol. II, No. 1 (Spring/Summer 1972), pp. 30-39.

Bull, Hedley. "Sea Power and Political Influence." London: IISS, Adelphi Paper 122, 1977.

Cable, Donald W. "A Slower Rapid Response," Armed Forces Management, April 1970.

Cameron, Juan. "What If?--U.S. Military Strategy for the Middle East," Military Review, Vol. 49, No. 11 (November 1979), pp. 8-17.

_____. "The Armed Forces Reluctant Retrenchment," Fortune, November 1970.

_____. "Our 'What If' Strategy for Middle East Trouble Spots," Fortune, May 7, 1979, pp. 154-158.

"Can Fast Deployment Ship Program Revitalize U.S. Shipbuilding Industry?" Armed Forces Management, January 1966, p. 73.

Canby, Steven. "General Purpose Forces," International Security Review, Fall 1980.

Cockle, Paul. "Analyzing Soviet Defense Spending: The Debate in Perspective," Survival, Vol. XX, No. 5 (September/October 1978), pp. 209-219.

Cottrell, Alvin J. and Moorer, Thomas H. "U.S. Overseas Bases," The Washington Papers, V:47 (Beverly Hills and London: Sage, 1975).

Current News, 1960-1983.

Davis, Paul. "Observations in the Rapid Deployment Joint Task Force: Origins, Direction, and Mission." Santa Monica: RAND, June, 1982.

Davis, W.V. "The Navy and Limited War," Ordnance, XLII (March/April 1958). pp. 802-805.

Deweerd, H.A. "Historian's Perspective," Army, January 1963, pp. 44-47.

Digby, James. "New Technologies and Superpower Actions in Remote Contingencies," Survival, March/April 1979, pp. 61-67.

_____. "The Emerging American Strategy: Applications to Southwest Asia." Santa Monica: RAND, May 1981.

Dulles, John F. "A Policy for Boldness," Life, May 19, 1952, p. 146.

_____. "The Evolution of Foreign Policy," U.S. Department of State Bulletin, 30 (January 25, 1954), pp. 107-110.

_____. "Challenge and Response in United States Policy," Foreign Affairs, 36 (October 1957), pp. 25-43.

Epstein, Joshua M. "Soviet Vulnerabilities in Iran and the RDF Deterrent," International Security, Vol. 6, No. 2 (Fall 1981), pp. 126-158.

Erikson, John. "Soviet Military Capabilities in Europe," RUSI Journal, Vol. 120, No. 1 (March 1975), pp. 65-69.

Feidman, Shai. "Peacemaking in the Middle East: The Next Step," Foreign Affairs, Vol. 59, No. 4 (Spring 1981), pp. 756-780.

Fialka, John J. "The Grim Lessons of Nifty Nugget," Army, April 1980.

Frisbee, John L. "Command Lines for Combat Forces," Defense/81 (August 1981), pp. 8-17.

Fukuyama, Francis. "The Soviet Threat to the Persian Gulf." Santa Monica: RAND P-6546 (January 1980).

Gaddis, John Lewis, and Nitze, Paul. "NSC-68 and the Soviet Threat Reconsidered," International Security (Spring 1980), pp. 164-176.

Gansler, Jacques. "Can the Defense Industry Respond to the Reagan Initiatives?" International Security, Vol. 6, No. 4 (Spring 1982).

Garique, Phillipe. "Strategic Studies as Theory," Journal of Strategic Studies, Vol. 2, No. 3 (December 1979), pp. 251-281.

Geiger, Theodore and McMullen, Neil J. "Soviet Options in the Persian Gulf and U.S. Responses," New International Realities, Vol. V, No. 1 (July 1980), pp. 7-17.

Gibney, Frank. "The Ripple Effect in Korea," Foreign Affairs, Vol. 56, No. 1 (October 1977), pp. 161-174.

Gilpatric, Roswell. "Our Defense Needs: The Long View," Foreign Affairs, Vol. 42, No. 3 (April 1964), pp. 366-378.

Gray, Robert C. "Learning from History: Case Studies of the Weapons Acquisition Process," World Politics, Vol. 31, No. 3 (April 1979), pp. 457-470.

Haass, Richard. "Congressional Power: Implications for American Security Policy." London: IISS, Adelphi Paper 153, 1979.

Halperin, Morton. "Limited War Bibliography." Harvard University: Center for International Affairs, 1962.

_____. "The Gaither Committee and the Policy Process," World Politics, Vol. XIII, No. 2 (April 1961), pp. 360-384.

Hassner, Pierre. "Superpower Rivalries, Conflicts and Cooperation." London: IISS, Adelphi Paper 134, 1976.

Hennessey, John J. "Strategy and Readiness," Strategic Review, Fall 1976, pp. 44-48.

Hoffman, Stanley; Huntingon, May, Neustadt and Schelling. "Vietnam Reappraised," International Security (Summer 1981), pp. 3-26.

Holzbauer, Joseph R. "RDF," Marine Corps Gazette, August 8, 1980.

Howard, Michael. "The Forgotten Dimensions of Strategy," Foreign Affairs, Vol. 57, (Summer 1979), pp. 975-986.

_____. "Deterrence and Reassurance," Foreign Affairs (Winter 1982/1983), pp. 309-343.

Huntington, Samuel P. "Trade, Technology and Leverage," Foreign Policy 32 (Fall 1978), pp. 63-80.

Ignotis, Miles (pseudonym). "Seizing Arab Oil," Harper's, March 1975, pp. 45-62.

Ikle, Fred C. "The Reagan Defense Program," Strategic Review (Spring 1982), pp. 11-34.

_____. "Strategic Principles of the Reagan Administration," Strategic Review (Fall 1983), pp. 13-18.

"Is the FDL Capability Essential in Supporting U.S. Commitments?" Armed Forces Management, September 1968, p. 66.

Janowitz, Morris and Stern, Ellen. "The Limits of Military Intervention," Military Review, Vol. 58, No. 3 (March 1978), pp. 11-22.

Jenkins, Brian M. "The Unchangeable War." Santa Monica: RAND RM-6278-2-ARPA (November 1970).

Kaiser, Robert G. "U.S.-Soviet Relationships: Good-Bye to Detente," Foreign Affairs, Vol. 59, No. 3, pp. 500-521.

Kanter, Arnold. "Congress and the Defense Budget, 1960-1970," American Political Science Review. Vol. 66, No. 1 (March 1972), pp. 129-143.

Kanter, Herschel. "The 1984-1988 Defense Program," Strategic Review, Vol. XI, No. 2 (Spring 1983).

Kaufmann, William W. Planning Conventional Forces, 1950-1980. Washington, D.C.: Brookings, 1982.

Kegley, Charles W. and Wittkopf, Eugene R. "The Reagan Administration's World View," Orbis, Vol. 26, No. 1 (Spring 1982), pp. 223-244.

Kemp, Geoffrey. "Contingency Planning and Persian Gulf Options," Proceedings of the National Security Affairs Conference. Washington, D.C.: National Defense University, November 1979, pp. 61-76.

Kemp, Geoffrey and Ullman, Harlan K. "U.S. Global Strategy: The Future of the Half War Planning Contingency," Proceedings of the National Security Affairs Conference. Washington, D.C.: National Defense University, July 1977, pp. 69-79.

Komer, Robert W. "Bureaucracy Does its Thing: Institutional Constraints on U.S.-GVN Performance in Vietnam." Santa Monica: RAND (August 1972).

_____. "Maritime Strategy vs. Coalition Defense," Foreign Affairs (Summer 1982), pp. 1124-1144.

Korb, Lawrence J. "The FY 1979-1983 Defense Program," AEI Defense Review, Vol. 2, No. 2, April 1978.

_____. "The FY 1981-1985 Defense Program," AEI Foreign Policy and Defense Review, Vol. 2, No. 2, July 1980.

Krulak, Victor H. "The RDF: Criteria and Imperatives," Strategic Review, Spring 1980, pp. 39-43.

Kuzmack, Arnold M. "Foreign Policy and Military Force Planning," Military Review, August 1972, pp. 13-22.

Levine, Robert A. "The Choice of Strategy to Meet Conventional Aggression." Santa Monica: RAND Memo RM-4123-ISA, July 1965.

Levy, Walter J. "Oil and the Decline of the West," Foreign Affairs, Summer 1980.

Lloyd, Norman. "Mr. Laird and the '0-War' Strategy for the 1970s," Army, February 1971.

Lloyd, Richmond M. and Lorenzini, Dino A. "A Framework for Choosing Defense Forces," Naval War College Review, Vol. XXXIII, No. 1 (January/February 1981), pp. 46-58.

Lucas, William A. and Dawson, Raymond H. "The Organizational Politics of Defense." International Studies Association, Occasional Paper No. 2, 1975.

"Limited War: Where Do They Stand: Army, Navy, Air Force," Army Navy Air Force Register, Vol. LXXX, May 23, 1959, pp. 24-25.

Lind, William S. "A Proposal for the Corps: Mission and Structure," Marine Corps Gazette, December 1975.

Madhouse, Richard L. "The FDL Surfaces Again," U.S. Naval Institute Proceedings, June 1968, pp. 54-66.

"Marines, Air Force Squabble Over RDF's Air Mission," Defense Week, June 30, 1980, p. 6.

Maynes, Charles and Ullman, Richard. "Ten Years of Foreign Policy," Foreign Policy, 40 (Summer 1980), pp. 3-17.

McNaugher, Thomas L. "Balancing Soviet Power in the Persian Gulf," The Brookings Review (Summer 1983), pp. 20-24.

Moorer, Thomas H. and Cottrell, Alvin J. "The Search for U.S. Bases in the Indian Ocean," Strategic Review, Spring 1980, pp. 30-38.

Nacht, Michael. "Toward an American Concept of Regional Security," Daedelus, Vol. 110, No. 1 (March 1981), pp. 1-22.

"Meeting the Isolationist Challenge," Fortune, June 1975, pp. 79-80.

Nathan, James A., and Oliver, James K. "Bureaucratic Politics: Academic Windfalls and Intellectual Pitfalls," Journal of Political and Military Sociology, Vol. 6 (Spring 1978), pp. 81-91.
_____. "The Evolution of International Order and the Future of the American Naval Presence Mission," Naval War College Review, Fall 1977 pp. 37-59.
New York Times, 1960-1983.
O'Neill, Bard E. "Petroleum and Security: The Limitations of Military Power in the Persian Gulf." Washington, D.C.: National Defense University, National Security Affairs Monograph 77-4, October 1977.
Osgood, Robert. "The Revitalization of Containment," Foreign Affairs, Vol. 60, No. 3, pp. 465-502.
Paulker, Guy J. "Military Implications of a Possible World Order Crisis in the 1980s." Santa Monica: RAND, R-2003-AF, November 1977.
Pearson, Willard. "Fit to Fight Where?" Army, Vol. 16, No. 6 (July 1966), pp. 54-59.
Pilsch, Thomas D. "The CX Requirement," Airlift Operations Review, January 1981, pp. 8-17.
Posen, Barry R. and Van Evera, Stephen. "Defense Policy and the Reagan Administration," International Security, Vol. 8, No. 1 (Summer 1983), pp. 2-34.
Powers, Bruce F. "Is the United States Prepared for its Most Likely Conflicts?" Santa Monica: RAND P-6592 (February 1981).
Pranger, Robert J. and Tahtinen, Dale R. "American Policy Options in Iran and the Persian Gulf," AEI Foreign Policy and Defense Review, Vol. 1, No. 2, 1979.
Quinlan, David A. "The Marine Corps as a Rapid Deployment Force," Marine Corps Gazette, March 1980, pp. 32-46.
Rainey, Richard B. "Mobility--Airlift, Sealift and Prepositioning." Santa Monica: RAND, P3303, 1966.
Rand, H.P. "A United States Counter-Aggression Force," Military Review, Vol. XXXIX (July 1959), pp. 50-55.
Ravanal, Earl C. "The Nixon Doctrine and our Asian Commitments," Foreign Affairs, Vol. 49, No. 2 (January 1971), pp. 201-217.
"Readiness for the Little War," Military Review, Vol. XXXVii, April and May 1957, pp. 14-128.
Richardson, Robert C. "Do We Need Unlimited Forces for Limited War?" Air Force, XLII (March 1959), pp. 53-56.
Rosenau, James N. "The Concept of Intervention," Journal of International Affairs, Vol. 22 (Summer 1968), pp. 165-176.
Ross, Dennis. "Considering Soviet Threats to the Persian Gulf," International Security, Vol. 6, No. 2 (Fall 1981), pp. 159-180.
Russell, Bruce and Nincic, Miroslav. "American Opinion on the Use of Military Force Abroad," Political Science Quarterly, Fall 1976, pp. 411-431.
Sagan, Scott D. "Lessons of the Yom Kippur Alert," Foreign Policy 36 (Fall 1979), pp. 160-177.
Scholin, Alan R. "STRIKE," Air Force, May 1962.
"SecDef Reports on National Military Airlift Plans," Army Navy and Air Force Journal and Register, August 10, 1963.
Selected Statements, 1970-1983.
Shaw, Harry J. "Debts and Dependency," Foreign Policy, No. 50 (Spring 1983), pp. 105-123.

Shope, Walter R. "The Lessons of Nifty Nugget," Defense '80, December 1980, pp. 14-22.

Simon, Herbert. "Theories of Decision Making in Economics and Behavioral Science," American Economic Review, Vol. 49, No. 3 (June 1959), pp. 253-283.

Sowell, Lewis C. "Base Development and the Rapid Deployment Force," Washington, D.C.: National Defense University, 1982.

"Speech by President Carter at Wake Forest University," Survival, Vol. XX, No. 4 (July/August 1978), pp. 176-179.

Staudemaier, W.O. "Contemporary Problems of the Unified Command System," Parameters, Voi. 9 (March 1979), pp. 84-94.

Sulik, R.A. "Near Term Fix--NTPS," Marine Corps Gazette, August 1980, pp. 52-56.

Taylor, Maxwell D. "Changing Military Priorities," AEI Foreign Policy and Defense Review, Vol. 1, No. 3, April 1979.

_____. "The Legitimate Claims of National Security," Foreign Affairs, Vol. 52, No. 3 (April 1974).

"The Rapid Deployment Force: What's Been Done, What Should Have Been Done," Defense Week, June 30, 1980, p. 6.

"Third World Conflict and International Security." London: International Institute for Strategic Studies, Adelphi Paper No. 166, Part I, 1981.

Trotman, J.T. "NATO in Theory and Practice," Survival, Vol. 13, No. 6 (November/December 1971), pp. 406-411.

Tucker, Robert W. "The Purposes of American Power," Foreign Affairs, Vol. 59, No. 2 (Winter 1980/1981), pp. 241-274.

_____. "Oil: The Issue of American Intervention," Commentary, January 1975, pp. 21-31.

Tucker, Robert W. "Oil and American Power--3 Years Later," Commentary, January 1977, pp. 29-36.

_____. "American Power and the Persian Gulf," Commentary, Vol. 70, No. 5 (November 1980), pp. 25-41.

"Unified Command for TAC and STRAC," Military Review, Vol. 41, No. 12 (December 1961), p. 97.

"Unilateral Corps: Is the U.S. Turning a New Strategic Corner?" Army, September 1979, p. 30.

Valenta, Juri and Butler, Shannon R. "Soviet Interests, Objectives and Policy Options in Southwest Asia." Carlisle Barracks, PA: U.S. Army War College, December 30, 1981.

Vicellio, Henry P. "Composite Air Strike Force." Air University Quarterly Review, Vol. 9, No. 1 (Winter 1956-1957), pp. 27-38.

Vigor, P.H. and Donnelly, C.N. "The Soviet Threat to Europe," RUSI Journal, Vol. 120, No. 4 (March 1975), pp. 69-74.

Waltz, Kenneth N. "A Strategy for the Rapid Deployment Force," International Security, Vol. 5, No. 4 (Spring 1981), pp. 49-73.

Watts, William and Free, Lloyd A. "Nationalism, Not Isolationism," Foreign Policy, 24, Fall 1976, pp. 3-26.

Wells, Samuel F., Jr. "Sounding the Tocsin: NSC-68 and the Soviet Threat," International Security (Fall 1979), pp. 116-158.

_____. "The Origins of Massive Retaliation," Political Science Quarterly, Vol. 96, No. 1 (Spring 1981), pp. 31-52.

West, Francis J., Jr. "Limited U.S.-Soviet Conflict and the RDF," Marine Corps Gazette, August 1980, pp. 39-46.

Whetten, Lawrence L. "The Arab-Israeli Dispute: Great Power Behavior." London: IISS, Adelphi Paper 128, 1977.

Wohlstetter, Albert. "Illusion of Distance," Foreign Affairs, June 1968, pp. 242-255.
_____. "Meeting the Threat in the Persian Gulf," Survey, Vol. 25, No. 11 (Spring 1980), pp. 128-188.
_____. "The Delicate Balance of Terror," Foreign Affairs, Vol. 37 (January 1959), pp. 211-213, 234.
Woolsey, R. James. "Planning a Navy: The Risks of Conventional Wisdom," International Security, Summer 1978, pp. 17-29.
Yankelovitch, Daniel. "Cautious Interventionism," Public Opinion, Vol. 1, March/April 1978, pp. 13-14.
Zakheim, Dov S. "Maritime Presence, Projection and the Constraints of Parity," Proceedings of the National Security Affairs Conference, Washington, D.C.: National Defense University, 1978, pp. 101-118.
_____. "The Unforeseen Contingency," Washington Quarterly (Autumn 1982), pp. 158-166.

Published Government Documents

U.S. Congress

U.S. Congress, Senate, Committee on Appropriations, Subcommittee on Department of Defense Appropriations, Hearings, 1960-1983.
U.S. Congress, Senate, Armed Services Committee, Hearings on Major Defense Matters, Part 1, 86th Congress, 1st session, 1959.
U.S. Congress, Senate, Committee on Armed Services. "Authorizing the President to order units and members of the Ready Reserve to Active Duty for not more than 12 months." 87th Congress, 2nd session, 1962.
U.S. Congress, House, Committe on Appropriations, Subcommittee on Department of Defense Appropriations, Hearings, 1960-1983.
U.S. Congress, House, Committee on Armed Services, Hearings on Military Posture, 1960-1983.
U.S. Congress, House, Committee on Armed Services, Hearings before the Special Subcommittee on National Military Airlift, 86th Congress, 1st session, 1960.
U.S. Congress, House, Committee on Armed Services, Subcommittee on Research and Development, Hearings on the Posture of Military Airlift, 94th Congress, 1st session, 1975.
U.S. Congress, House, Committee on Foreign Affairs, Hearings before the Subcommittee on National Security Policy and Scientific Developments, 93rd Congress, 1st session, 1973.
U.S. Congress, House, Committee on Government Operations, Hearings, 86th Congress, 1st session, 1960.
U.S. Congress, House, Committee on Foreign Affairs, Subcommittee on Europe and the Middle East, Hearings on U.S. Interests in and Policies Toward the Persian Gulf, 1980, 96th Congress, 2nd session, 1980.
U.S. Congress, Joint Economic Committee, Hearings before the Subcommittee on Economy in Government, Part 1, 91st Congress, 1st session, 1969.

270

Congressional Budget Office

"Force Planning and Budgetary Implications of U.S. Withdrawal from Korea." Washington, D.C.: USGPO, May 1978.
"Planning U.S. General Purpose Forces: Force Related to Asia." Washington, D.C.: USGPO, June 1977.
"Planning U.S. General Purpose Forces: Overview." Washington, D.C.: USGPO, January 1977.
"Rapid Deployment Forces: Policy and Budgetary Implications." Washington, D.C.: USGPO, February 1983.
"The Marine Corps in the 1980s: Prestocking, the Rapid Deployment Force and Other Issues." Washington, D.C.: USGPO, May 1980.
"U.S. Airlift Forces: Enhancement Alternatives for NATO and non-NATO Contingencies." Washington, D.C.: USGPO.
"U.S. Army Force Design: Alternatives for Fiscal Years 1977-1981." Washington, D.C.: USGPO, July 1976.
"U.S. Ground Forces: Design and Cost Alternatives for NATO and non-NATO Contingencies." Washington, D.C.: USGPO, December 1980.
"U.S. Naval Forces: The Peacetime Presence Mission." Washington, D.C.: USGPO, December 1978.
"U.S. Projection Forces: Requirements, Scenarios, Options." Washington, D.C.: USGPO, 1982.

Congressional Record

Congressional Reference Service

Collins, John M. and Mark, Clyde R. "Oil Fields as Military Objectives." Washington, D.C.: USGPO, 1975.
_____. "Petroleum Imports from the Persian Gulf." Washington, D.C.: USGPO, 1979.

Congressional Quarterly Alamanac

Legislative Reference Service: "United States Defense Policies in 1961, 1962 and 1963: Washington, D.C.: USGPO, 1961-1963.
Senate Committee on Armed Services: "NATO and the New Soviet Threat." Report of Senators Sam Nunn and Dewey Bartlett, 95th Congress, 1st session, Washington, D.C.: USGPO, 1977.
U.S. Government Accounting Office, "Airlift Operations in the 1973 Mid-East War." Washington, D.C.: USGPO, 1975.

Department of Defense
"An Evaluation Report on Mobilization and Deployment Capability based on Exercise Nifty Nugget-78." Washington, D.C.: Department of Defense, June 30, 1980.
Department of Defense Annual Reports, FY 1962-1984.
"Organization and Functions of the Joint Chiefs of Staff." (JCS Pub. 4) Washington, D.C.: 1959.
Proceedings of the 1977 Worldwide Strategic Mobility Conference. Fort McNair: National Defense University, May 1977.
"Report to the President and the Secretary of Defense by the Blue Ribbon Defense Panel." July 1, 1970.

"Report to the Secretary of Defense on the National Military Command Structure." (Steadman Report) July 1978.

Rescue Mission Report. Washington, D.C.: Joint Chiefs of Staff, August 1980.

Tolson, John J. Air Mobility. Washington, D.C.: Department of the Army, 1973.

Unified Action Armed Forces. (JCS Pub. 2) Washington, D.C., 1959.

United States Military Posture, FY 1965-1984.

United States Central Command, Information booklet, 1983.

Executive Department

Kennedy, John F. Public Papers of the President 1961-1963. Washington, D.C.: USGPO, 1964.

_____. A Compilation of Statements and Speeches. Washington, D.C.: USGPO, 1964.

Nixon, Richard M. U.S. Foreign Policy for the 1970s.
"A New Strategy for Peace," February 18, 1970.
"Building for Peace," February 25, 1971.
"The Emerging Structure of Peace," February 9, 1972.
"Shaping a Durable Peace," May 3, 1973.

Weekly Compilation of Presidential Documents, 1970-1983.

Office of Air Force History

Air Force Review of the C-5A Program. Washington, D.C.: Department of the Air Force, July 1969.

"Coronet Bare Final Report, Bare Base Evaluation." 14-28 October 1969. Eglin Air Force Base, Florida: USAF Tactical Weapons Center, 1969.

Ideas, Concepts, Doctrine: A History of Basic Thinking in the USAF, 1947-1961. Aerospace Studies Institute, Maxwell Air Force Base, Alabama: Air University, 1971.

Personal Papers of General William W. Momyer.

Personal Papers of Major General James C. Sherrill.

Personal Papers of General Thomas W. White.

Strengthening USAF Airlift Forces, 1961-1964. Washington, D.C.: U.S. Air Force Historical Division Liaison Office, February 1966.

USAF Oral History Interview with General Bruce K. Holloway, USAF. 16-18 April, 1977.

Unpublished Material

Bendell, Lee R. "The Nixon Doctrine and Military Strategy." Maxwell Air Force Base: Air University, October 1971.

Borneman, Frederick H., et al. "The Development, Promulgation and Implementation of Doctrine for Joint Operations." Carlisle Barracks, PA: U.S. Army War College, May 1975.

Cottrell, Alvin J. "The Employment of Sea Power as an Instrument of National Policy." Paper presented to the Conference on "Projection of Power," Fletcher School of Law and Diplomacy, Tufts University, April 23, 1980.

Fabyanic, Thomas A. "Conceptual Planning and the Rapid Deployment Joint Task Force." Paper prepared for the 20th annual conference of the Inter-University Seminar on Armed Forces and Society, 23-25 October 1980.

Fontaine, Roger W. "The Regional Projection of Military Power--The Caribbean." Paper prepared for the Conference on "Projection of Power."

Gibson, Cristann Lea. "Patterns of Demobilization: The U.S. and USSR After World War II." Denver: University of Denver Ph.D. dissertation, 1982.

Haffa, Robert P., Jr. "Superpower Confrontation in the Middle East: A Case Study of the Use of Coercive Diplomacy During the October War." Cambridge: MIT, May 1980.

Henslick, James R. "The Role of CONUS-based, Rapid Reaction Joint Force During the Mid-range Time Frame." Carlisle, PA: Army War College, 1971.

Mead, Dana. "U.S. Peacetime Strategic Planning, 1920-1941: The Color Plans to the Victory Program:" Cambridge: MIT, Ph.D. dissertation, 1967.

Miller, George D. "Power Projection--An Air Strategist's View." Paper prepared for the Conference on "Projection of Power."

Robinson, Robert L. "Military Strategy and Congress: The Case of the FDL." Newport: Naval War College, April 1970.

Sorenson, Neil. "The Development of the Air Mobiity Strategy." Maxwell Air Force Base, Alabama: Air War College, 1980.

Thayer, Frederic, Jr. "National Airlift Policy: A Study in Political Conflict, Economic Theory and Military Strategy." Denver: University of Denver, Ph.D. dissertation, 1963.

U.S. Department of State. Incoming telegrams, subject: NATO Ministerial Meetings.

Westhoff, H.H. and Stouffer, T.D. "Strategic Mobility Enhancement and Responsiveness of Marine Forces." Newport: Naval War College, 1980.

Zakheim, Dov S. "Airlifting the Marine Corps." Paper presented to the Conference on "Projection of Power."

Defense Documentation Reference Service (DDRS), 1960-1980.

Interviews

General Paul D. Adams, former Commander U.S. STRIKE Command, March 1981.

Robert W. Komer, Former Under Secretary of Defense for Policy, March 1981.

Office of the Secretary of Defense, Program Analysis and Evaluation, March 1981.

Headquarters, U.S. Air Force, Air Staff, January 1981.

Headquarters, U.S. Readiness Command, J-5, March 1981.

Headquarters, Rapid Deployment Joint Task Force, March 1981.

Headquarters, U.S. Central Command, July 1983.

Index

"Access" to facilities, 188, 244, 246
Adams, Paul D., 93, 97, 99, 101, 169, 209
Afghanistan, 1, 2, 60
Airlift
    method of rapid deployment, 152
    mobility for "1-1/2 wars," 166-178
    Air Force doctrine, 166
    in 1980s, 187, 243-244
Alvarez, Luis W., 27

"Bare base" concept, 176, 246
Bay of Pigs, 28
Berlin Crisis, 28, 30
Binkin, Martin, 91, 122
Blechman, Barry, 110, 214
Blue Ribbon Defense Panel, 95, 102
Brodie, Bernard, 159, 209
Brown, Harold, 10, 27, 52-55, 59-64, 88, 114, 180-183, 189, 207, 209
"Brushfire", 6, 12, 14, 20-23, 33-38, 50-59, 66, 67, 85, 90, 103, 207, 215,
    230
Brzezinski, Zbigniew, 52, 115, 124
Bundy, McGeorge, 39
Burke, Kelley, 187

C-X transport, 187-188, 202
C-5 transport, 168-176, 242
C-17 transport, 243-244
Carter, Jimmy
    administration of, 12, 50, 52, 59, 114
    defense budget of, 59
    doctrine of, 6, 60-64, 238
    speech at Wake Forest, 58, 115
Central Command (USCENTCOM), 234-241
Civil Reserve Air Fleet (CRAF), 167, 176-177, 243
Clifford, Clark, 165
Collins, John, 112
Composite Air Strike Force (CASF), 84, 91-92
Connally, John, 27

Cuba, 60, 100-101, 156

Davis, Lynn, 52
Defense Reorganization Act (1958), 83, 91
Diego Garcia, 185, 189, 244
Dominican Republic, 6, 101
Donovan, James, 84

Egypt, 189, 244, 246
Eisenhower, Dwight D.
    administration of, 10-24, 44
Enthoven, Alain C., 147, 149, 151, 166
Everest, Frank, 96

Fast Deployment Logistics Ships (FDL), 154, 159-166
"Field of fire", 6, 50, 55, 67, 86, 207
"Firefight," 6, 63, 66-67, 85, 126, 230
Ford, Gerald R.
    administration of, 55, 117
Force planning
    framework for, 9-11
    premises in 1960s, 32
    see "one and one-half" and "two and one-half" wars
Fullbright, J. william, 106, 174

Gaither Report, 24, 92
George, Alexander, 7, 12, 219
Gilpatric, Roswell, 30
Guam Doctrine, see Nixon Doctrine

"Half war," 6, 14
    defined, 4-5
    force planning for, 47-50
    strategic concept of, 206
    future of, 21
Hammond, Paul, 24
Hayward, Thomas, 230
Hennessey, John, 107
Hilsman, Roger, 26
Holloway, Bruce K., 96, 102
Howard, Michael, 145
Howze Board, 97, 135
Huntington, Samuel, 19, 52-53

Ikle, Fred C., 228-230
Iran, 1, 2, 60-62
Iraq, 48
Israel, 48-49

Jackson, Henry, 35-36
Japan, 59
Johnson, Harold K., 160, 163
Johnson, Lyndon B.
    administration of, 4, 24, 35-36

Joint Deployment Agency (JDA), 179, 235
Jordan, 48-49, 238

Kaufmann, William W., 23, 232-233, 240
Kaysen, Carl, 39, 41, 43
Kennedy, John F.
    administration of, 4, 9, 12, 25-29, 31, 155
Key West Agreement, 84
Khrushchev, Nikita, 28
Kissinger, Henry, 23-25, 40-41, 110
Kelley, Paul X., 122, 184-185
Kemp, Geoffrey, 58, 213-215, 218, 250
Kenya, 65, 189
Komer, Robert W., 64-65, 104, 118, 125, 181, 184, 188, 236, 238
Korb, Lawrence, 9, 58, 66, 115
Korea, 6, 7, 20-24, 57

Laird, Melvin R., 42-44, 47, 170, 174
Laos, 26, 28, 48
LeMay, Curtis E., 97
Levine, Robert A., 148
Limited contingency
    defined, 3-5
Lynn, Lawrence, 149

McNamara, Robert S., 7, 9
    strategic concept of, 26-27, 30-36, 42, 46
    and STRIKE Command, 96-99
    and sealift, 152-164
    and airlift, 168-172
McNaugher, Thomas, 238
Maritime Prepositioning Ships (MPS), 184-185, 244
May, Ernest R., 208
Momyer, William W., 95-97
Moorer, Thomas, 101, 245

Nacht, Michael, 50, 52
National Security Act (1947), 82, 84
"New Look," 19-26
"Nifty Nugget," 179-180
Nitze, Paul, 27
Nixon, Richard
    administration of, 42-44
    doctrine of, 6, 41-43, 47-51, 170, 210, 232
Nunn, Sam, 65
Nutter, G. Warren, 43
NSC-68, 19, 23, 53
NSC 162/2, 19, 20

Oman, 65, 189
"One and one-half war"
    strategic concept of, 38, 40-42
    forces for (table), 51
    in Carter administration, 54, 63

Osgood, Robert, 23, 41
Overseas bases, 150

Persian (Arabian) Gulf, 6, 7
    contingency in, 54-55, 111-113
    U.S. presence in, 61-62
Prepositioned Overseas Materiel Configured to Unit Sets (POMCUS), 152,
    180
Prepositioning, 152, 156, 184, 243-245
Presidential directive 18 (PD-18), 53, 60, 114, 121, 124
Presidential Review Memorandum 10 (PRM-10), 52-53, 118
Price Committee on strategic airlift, 171, 175

"Rainbow Plans," 18
Rapid deployment, defined, 5
Rapid Deployment Force, 61, 66
Rapid Deployment Joint Task Force, 64, 117-131
Readiness Command (USREDCOM), 13, 87, 107-117, 209
Reagan, Ronald
    administration of, 12, 228-232
Record, Jeffrey, 91, 122-123, 216-217, 236-238
Reserve forces, 9, 29-30, 45-49, 249
Rio Pact, 9
Rivers, Mendel, 163, 167-168
Rogers, Bernard, 122
Rostow, Eugene V., 58
Rumsfeld, Donald R., 49-50
Rusk, Dean, 27
Russell, Richard, 38, 160-164, 174

Saudi Arabia, 62
Schlander, Herbert, 38
Schlesinger, Arthur, 26, 28
Schlesinger, James, 49, 61, 110, 177
Schultze, Charles, 38, 44
Sealift
    method of rapid deployment, 153
    mobility for "2-1/2 wars," 155-166
    in 1980s, 243, 245
Sherrill, James C., 158
Smith, K. Wayne, 147, 149, 151, 166
SL-7 fast sealift, 186-187, 242
Smoke, Richard, 7, 219
Snyder, Glenn, 21, 219
Somalia, 65, 189
Southeast Asia, 19, 35
Southwest Asia, 1, 2, 3, 9, 13
    rapid deployment forces for, 65
    forces in 1980s for, 231
Soviet Union (USSR), 18, 19, 22
    and Middle East War, 48
    and combat brigade in Cuba, 60, 116
    invasion of Afghanistan, 60
Steadman Report, 118

Strategic Army Command (STRAC), 30-31 91
STRIKE Command (USSTRIKECOM), 13, 84, 93-107, 208
Syria, 48

Taylor, Maxwell, 25-28, 46, 111-112, 127, 151
"Tripwire" theory, 146, 192
Tucker, Robert W., 106, 111, 113
Turkey, 246
"Two and one half war"
    strategic concept of, 33
    assumptions of, 40-42
    forces for (table), 51
    logistic support for, 149

Ullman, Harlan, 58
Unified Command Plan (UCP), 83-84
    and STRIKECOM, 105
    and REDCOM, 109
    and RDJTF, 120
    and CENTCOM, 234, 238
U.S. Middle East Force, 99

Vandenberg, Hoyt S., 18
Vietnam, 6-7, 31-32
    troop deployments to, 35-36
    as a limited contingency, 103
Vietnamization, 40, 45, 47

Waltz, Kenneth, 219-220
War Powers Act, 106-107, 209
Warner, Volney, 119, 129
Warsaw Pact, 10, 20, 32
Weinberger, Caspar, 228-232, 236-240
Wheeler, Earle, 46, 157
Wilson, Charles, 27
Wolfowitz Report, 128

van Crevald, Martin, 145

Yarmolinsky, Adam, 106